Decision Analysis for Management Judgment

Fourth Edition

Paul Goodwin
The Management School, University of Bath

George Wright
Durham Business School, Durham University

WILEY

A John Wiley and Sons, Ltd., Publication

Library of Congress Cataloging-in-Publication Data

Goodwin, Paul.
    Decision analysis for management judgment / Paul Goodwin, George Wright. – 4th ed.
       p. cm.
    Include bibliographical references and index.
    ISBN 978-0-470-71439-3 (pbk.)
1. Decision making.   2. Management.   I. Wright, George, 1952-   II. Title.
HD30.23.G66 2010
658.4'03–dc22   2009018570

A catalogue record for this book is available from the British Library.

Typeset in 11/13pt Palatino by Aptara Inc., New Delhi, India.
Printed in Great Britain by TJ International, Padstow, Cornwall.

To
Chris
and
Josephine, Jamie, Jerome and Eilidh

Contents

Foreword by Lawrence D. Phillips

It is a curious fact that although the ability to take decisions is at the top of most senior executives' list of attributes for success in management, those same people are usually unwilling to spend any time developing this quality. Perhaps decision-making is considered to be as fundamental as breathing: essential for life, a natural and automatic process. So, why study it?

In this book, Paul Goodwin and George Wright show why: because research over the past 45 years has revealed numerous ways in which the process of making decisions goes wrong, usually without our knowing it. But the main thrust of this book is to show how decision analysis can be applied so that decisions are more effective. The beauty of the book is in providing numerous decision-analysis approaches in a form that makes them usable by busy managers and administrators.

Ever since decision theory was introduced in 1961 by Howard Raiffa and Robert Schlaifer of Harvard University's Business School, a succession of textbooks has chronicled the development of this abstract mathematical discipline to a potentially useful technology known as decision analysis, through to numerous successful applications in commerce, industry, government, the military and medicine. But all these books have been either inaccessible to managers and administrators or restricted to only a narrow conception of decision analysis, such as decision trees.

Unusually, this book does not even start with decision trees. My experience as a practicing decision analyst shows that problems with multiple objectives are a frequent source of difficulty in both public and private sectors: one course of action is better in some respects, but another is better according to other criteria. Which to choose? The authors begin, in Chapter 3, with such a problem, and present a straightforward technology, called SMART, to handle it.

My advice to the reader is to stop after Chapter 3 and apply SMART on a problem actually bothering you. Decision analysis works best on real problems, and it is most useful when you get a result you did not expect. Sleep on it, then go back and work it through again, discuss it with trusted friends and colleagues, altering and changing your representation of the problem, or your views of it, as necessary. After several tries, you will almost certainly have deepened your understanding of the issues, and now feel comfortable with taking a decision. The model doesn't decide; you do!

If you are then willing to invest some time and effort trying out the various approaches covered in this book, the rewards should be worth it. This fourth edition widens the scope of decision analysis as a result of experiences in applying it. No mathematical skills are needed beyond an ability to use a calculator to add, multiply and occasionally divide. But a willingness to express your judgments in numerical form is required (even if you are not convinced at the start), and patience in following a step-by-step process will help.

Whether your current problem is to evaluate options when objectives conflict, to make a choice as you face considerable uncertainty about the future, to assess the uncertainty associated with some future event, to decide on seeking new information before making a choice, to consult with colleagues before taking a decision, to reallocate limited resources for more effectiveness or to negotiate with another party, you will find sound, practical help in these pages. Even if you do not overtly apply any of the procedures in this book, the decision making framework provided in these chapters should help you to deal with complex issues more effectively and sharpen your everyday decision-making skills.

Lawrence D. Phillips
Department of Management
London School of Economics and Political Science

Preface

In an increasingly complex world, decision analysis has a major role to play in helping decision-makers to gain a greater understanding of the problems they face. The main aim of this book is to make decision analysis accessible to its largest group of potential users: managers and administrators in business and public sector organizations, most of whom, although expert at their work, are not mathematicians or statisticians. We have therefore endeavored to write a book that makes the methodology of decision analysis as 'transparent' as possible so that little has to be 'taken on trust', while at the same time making the minimum use of mathematical symbols and concepts. A chapter introducing the ideas of probability has also been included for those who have little or no background knowledge in this area.

The main focus of the book is on practical management problems, but we have also considered theoretical issues where we feel that they are needed for readers to understand the scope and applicability of a particular technique. Many decision problems today are complicated by the need to consider a range of issues, such as those relating to the environment, and by the participation of divergent interest groups. To reflect this, we have included extensive coverage of problems involving multiple objectives and methods that are designed to assist groups of decision-makers to tackle decision problems. An important feature of the book is the way in which it integrates the quantitative and psychological aspects of decision-making. Rather than dealing solely with the manipulation of numbers, we have also attempted to address in detail the behavioral issues that are associated with the implementation of decision analysis. Besides being of interest to managers in general, the book is also intended for use as a main text on a wide range of courses. It is particularly suitable for people following courses in management and administration, such as an MBA, or final-year undergraduate programs in business studies, quantitative methods and business decision analysis. Those studying for professional qualifications in areas such as accountancy, where recent changes in syllabuses have placed greater emphasis on decision-making techniques, should also find the book useful. Almost all the chapters are followed by discussion questions or exercises, and we have included suggested answers to many of these exercises at the end of the book.

Readers familiar with earlier editions of this book will note a number of changes in this new edition, which are designed to reflect the latest developments in the field. There is a new chapter (Chapter 4) which brings together enhancements of the simple multi-attribute rating method (SMART) and alternatives to this method. This chapter covers SMARTER, Even Swaps, the analytic hierarchy process and MACBETH, and reflects the convergence of some of these techniques. It also allows the reader to compare the merits of these different approaches to multi-attribute decision-making.

The chapter on how *unaided* decision-makers make decisions involving multiple objectives (Chapter 2) has been expanded to include topics such as decoy effects, choosing by unique attributes and the effect of emotions on decisions. We have improved the coverage of utility in Chapter 6, so that the shapes of utility functions are easier to interpret, and updated the 'test your judgment' quiz in Chapter 10. In Chapter 11 we have provided a new quiz to demonstrate the problem of providing coherent probability assessments, and have also included a section on how to evaluate probability estimates using calibration and Brier scores. This chapter now also considers the problems associated with communicating probability estimates to others.

A revised chapter on group decision-making (Chapter 13) includes a section on prediction markets to reflect the increased popularity of these markets for obtaining probability estimates and other forecasts from groups of people. This chapter also includes practical advice, based on the latest research, of how to apply the Delphi method. In addition, the coverage of scenario planning (Chapter 15) and expert systems and linear models (Chapter 17) has been extended and updated. In Chapter 17 we now also contrast the merits of making decisions based on careful analysis with those of snap decisions based on intuition, and we outline the idea of designing decisions so that people are encouraged to make the 'best' choices.

Inevitably, a large number of people provided support during the writing of the original version of this book and subsequent editions. We would particularly like to thank Larry Phillips (for his advice, encouragement and the invaluable comments he made on a draft manuscript of the first edition), Scott Barclay and Stephen Watson (for their advice during the planning of the book), Kees van der Heijden, Alan Pearman and John Maule (for their advice during the writing of the second edition) and the staff at John Wiley for their help and advice during the writing of this fourth edition. The design of this edition has also benefited from the comments of our students and from the reports of a number of referees who reviewed our proposals.

Accompanying website at
www.wileyeurope.com/college/goodwin

You will find valuable additional learning and teaching material at the *Decision Analysis for Management Judgment* website. Resources on the site include:

(1) Downloadable Microsoft Excel spreadsheets that are designed to demonstrate the implementation of:
   (i) SMART
   (ii) Bayesian revision of prior probabilities
   (iii) Negotiation problems.
(2) Additional exercises.
(3) A specimen examination paper with answers.
(4) Links to decision analysis resources on the Internet.

In addition, lecturers adopting the text are able to access:

(1) Detailed answers to end-of-chapter questions.
(2) Model teaching schemes for courses in decision analysis designed around the use of this textbook.
(3) Specimen coursework questions with suggested answers.
(4) Specimen examination papers with suggested answers.
(5) Downloadable PowerPoint slides to support the teaching of material appearing in the book's chapters.

Paul Goodwin
George Wright

Introduction 1

Complex decisions

Imagine that you are facing the following problem. For several years you have been employed as a manager by a major industrial company, but recently you have become dissatisfied with the job. You are still interested in the nature of the work, and most of your colleagues have a high regard for you, but company politics are getting you down, and there appears to be little prospect of promotion within the foreseeable future. Moreover, the amount of work you are being asked to carry out seems to be increasing relentlessly, and you often find that you have to work late in the evenings and at weekends.

One day you mention this to an old friend at a dinner party. 'There's an obvious solution', he says. 'Why don't you set up on your own as a consultant? There must be hundreds of companies that could use your experience and skills, and they would pay well. I'm certain that you'd experience a significant increase in your income, and there would be other advantages as well. You'd be your own boss, you could choose to work or take vacations at a time that suited you rather than the company and you'd gain an enormous amount of satisfaction from solving a variety of challenging problems.'

Initially, you reject the friend's advice as being out of the question, but, as the days go by, the idea seems to become more attractive. Over the years you have made a large number of contacts through your existing job, and you feel reasonably confident that you could use these to build a client base. Moreover, in addition to your specialist knowledge and analytical ability, you have a good feel for the way organizations tick, you are a good communicator and colleagues have often complimented you on your selling skills. Surely you would succeed.

However, when you mention all this to your spouse, he or she expresses concern and points out the virtues of your current job. It pays well – enough for you to live in a large house in a pleasant neighborhood and to send the children to a good private school – and there are lots of other benefits such as health insurance and a company car. Above all, the job is secure. Setting up your own consultancy would be risky. Your contacts might indicate now that they could offer you plenty of work, but, when it came to paying you good money, would they really be interested? Even if you were to succeed eventually, it might take a while to build up a reputation, so would you be able to maintain your current lifestyle, or would short-term sacrifices have to be made for long-term gains? Indeed, have you thought the idea through? Would you work from home or rent an office? After all, an office might give a more professional image to your business and increase your chances of success, but what would it cost? Would you employ secretarial staff or attempt to carry out this sort of work yourself? You are no typist, and clerical work would leave less time for marketing your services and carrying out the consultancy itself. Of course, if you failed as a consultant, you might still get another job, but it is unlikely that it would be as well paid as your current post, and the loss of self-esteem would be hard to take.

You are further discouraged by a colleague when you mention the idea during a coffee break. 'To be honest', he says, 'I would think that you have less than a fifty–fifty chance of being successful. In our department I know of two people who have done what you're suggesting and given up after a year. If you're fed up here, why don't you simply apply for a job elsewhere? In a new job you might even find time to do a bit of consultancy on the side, if that's what you want. Who knows? If you built up a big enough list of clients, you might, in a few years' time, be in a position to become a full-time consultant, but I would certainly counsel you against doing it now.'

By now you are finding it difficult to think clearly about the decision; there seem to be so many different aspects to consider. You feel tempted to make a choice purely on emotional grounds – why not simply 'jump in' and take the risk? – but you realize that this would be unfair to your family. What you need is a method that will enable you to address the complexities of the problem so that you can approach the decision in a considered and dispassionate manner.

This is a personal decision problem, but it highlights many of the interrelated features of decision problems in general. Ideally, you would like to maximize your income, maximize your job security, maximize your job satisfaction, maximize your freedom, and so on, so that the problem involves *multiple objectives*. Clearly, no course of action achieves all of these objectives, so you need to consider the trade-offs between the benefits offered by the various alternatives. For example, would the increased freedom of being your own boss be worth more to you than the possible short-term loss of income?

Second, the problem involves *uncertainty*. You are uncertain about the income that your consultancy business might generate, about the sort of work that you could get (would it be as satisfying as your friend suggests?), about the prospects you would face if the business failed, and so on. Associated with this will be your *attitude to risk*. Are you a person who naturally prefers to select the least risky alternative in a decision, or are you prepared to tolerate some level of risk?

Much of your frustration in attempting to understand your decision problem arises from its *complex structure*. This reflects, in part, the number of alternative courses of action from which you can choose (should you stay with your present job, change jobs, change jobs and become a part-time consultant, become a full-time consultant, etc.?), and the fact that some of the decisions are *sequential* in nature. For example, if you did decide to set up your own business, should you then open an office, and, if you open an office, should you employ a secretary? Equally important, have you considered all the possible options, or is it possible to create new alternatives that may be more attractive than the ones you are currently considering? Perhaps your company might allow you to work for them on a part-time basis, allowing you to use your remaining time to develop your consultancy practice.

Finally, this problem is not yours alone; it also concerns your spouse, so the decision involves *multiple stakeholders*. Your spouse may view the problem in a very different way. For example, he or she may have an alternative set of objectives to yours. Moreover, he or she may have different views of the chances that you will make a success of the business, and be more or less willing than you to take a risk.

The role of decision analysis

In the face of this complexity, how can decision analysis be of assistance? The key word is *analysis*, which refers to the process of breaking something down into its constituent parts. Decision analysis therefore involves the decomposition of a decision problem into a set of smaller (and, hopefully, easier to handle) problems. After each smaller problem has been dealt with separately, decision analysis provides a formal mechanism for integrating the results so that a course of action can be provisionally selected. This has been referred to as the 'divide-and-conquer orientation' of decision analysis.[1]

Because decision analysis requires the decision-maker to be clear and explicit about his or her judgments, it is possible to trace back through the analysis to discover why a particular course of action was preferred. This ability of decision analysis to provide an 'audit trail' means that it is possible to use the analysis to produce a defensible rationale for choosing a particular option. Clearly, this can be important when decisions have to be justified to senior staff, colleagues, outside agencies, the general public or even oneself.

When there are disagreements between a group of decision-makers, decision analysis can lead to a greater understanding of each person's position so that there is a *raised consciousness* about the issues involved and about the root of any conflict. This enhanced communication and understanding can be particularly valuable when a group of specialists from different fields have to meet to make a decision. Sometimes the analysis can reveal that a disputed issue is not worth debating because a given course of action should still be chosen, whatever stance is taken in relation to that particular issue. Moreover, because decision analysis allows the different stakeholders to participate in the decision process and develop a shared perception of the problem, it is more likely that there will be a *commitment* to the course of action that is eventually chosen.

The insights that are engendered by the decision analysis approach can lead to other benefits. Creative thinking may result, so that new, and possibly superior, courses of action can be generated. The analysis can also provide guidance on what new information should be gathered before a decision is made. For example, is it worth undertaking more market research if this would cost $100 000? Should more extensive geological testing be carried out in a potential mineral field?

It should be stressed, however, that, over the years, the role of decision analysis has changed. No longer is it seen as a method for producing optimal solutions to decision problems. As Keeney[1] points out:

> Decision analysis will not solve a decision problem, nor is it intended to. Its purpose is to produce insight and promote creativity to help decision-makers make better decisions.

This changing perception of decision analysis is also emphasized by Phillips:[2]

> ... decision theory has now evolved from a somewhat abstract mathematical discipline, which when applied was used to help individual decision-makers arrive at optimal decisions, to a framework for thinking that enables different perspectives on a problem to be brought together with the result that new intuitions and higher-level perspectives are generated.

Indeed, in many applications, decision analysis may be deliberately used to address only part of the problem. This *partial decision analysis* can concentrate on those elements of the problem where insight will be most valuable.

While we should not expect decision analysis to produce an optimal solution to a problem, the results of an analysis can be regarded as being 'conditionally prescriptive'. By this we mean that the analysis will show the decision-maker what he or she should do, *given* the judgments that have been elicited from him or her during the course of the analysis. The basic assumption is that of *rationality*. If the decision-maker is prepared to accept a set of rules (or axioms) that most people would regard as sensible, then, to be rational, he or she should prefer the indicated course of action to its alternatives. Of course, the course of action prescribed by the analysis may well conflict with the decision-maker's intuitive feelings. This conflict between the analysis and intuition can then be explored. Perhaps the judgments put forward by the decision-maker represented only partially formed or inconsistent preferences, or perhaps the analysis failed to capture some aspect of the problem.

Alternatively, the analysis may enable the decision-maker to develop a greater comprehension of the problem so that his or her preference changes towards that prescribed by the analysis. These attempts to explain why the rational option prescribed by the analysis differs from the decision-maker's intuitive choice can therefore lead to the insight and understanding that, as we emphasized earlier, are the main motivation behind carrying out decision analysis.

Applications of decision analysis

The following examples illustrate some of the areas where decision analysis has been applied.[3]

Improved strategic decision-making at Du Pont[4]

The Du Pont chemical company has used influence diagrams (see Chapter 7) and risk analysis (Chapter 8) throughout the organization to create and evaluate strategies. The analysis has allowed them to take into account the effect on the value of the business of uncertainties such as competitors' strategies, market share and market size. Among the many benefits of the approach, managers reported that it enhanced team building by providing a common language for sharing information and debate. It also led to a commitment to action, so that the implementation of the selected strategy was likely to be successful. One application alone led to the development of a strategy that was expected to enhance the value of the business by $175 million.

Structuring decision problems in the International Chernobyl Project[5,6]

Four years after the accident at the Chernobyl nuclear power plant in 1986, the International Chernobyl Project was undertaken at the request of the Soviet authorities. Decision analysis was used in the project to evaluate countermeasure strategies (for example, relocation of some of the population, changes in agricultural practice and decontamination of buildings). The use of SMART (Chapter 3) in decision conferences (Chapter 13) enabled groups of people from a wide variety of backgrounds – such as ministers, scientists and regional officials – to meet to structure the decision problem. They were thus able to clarify and elucidate the key issues associated with the strategies, such as the number of fatal cancers that they would avert, their monetary costs, the extent to which they could reduce stress in the population and their public acceptability. By using decision analysis, it was possible to evaluate the strategies by taking into account all these issues, regardless of whether they were easily quantified or capable of being measured on a monetary scale.

Selecting research projects at a large international pharmaceutical company[7]

Managers at a pharmaceutical company could not reach agreement on which of three large research and development (R&D) projects they should undertake in order to create value for the company. R&D projects in the pharmaceutical industry are characterized by great uncertainty arising from both threats and opportunities. Sometimes, future opportunities may have no relation to the original purpose of the R&D project. For example, new and unexpected drugs are often developed from a particular molecule that has been screened. These opportunities can substantially add to a project's value. Decision trees (Chapter 7) were used to create transparent representations of the options that would be open to the company if each project were undertaken and the risk that would be associated with it. The trees enabled the managers to assess where decisions should be delayed until new information was available, where new opportunities might arise and be pursued and the conditions where it would be appropriate to abandon a project. The approach drew attention to the key aspects of the problem and, most importantly, allowed the flexibility of the projects to be taken into account when they were evaluated, enabling a more informed decision to be made.

Petroleum exploration decisions at the Phillips Petroleum Company[8]

Petroleum exploration is notoriously risky. Scarce resources are allocated to drilling opportunities, with no guarantee that significant quantities of oil will be found. In the late 1980s and early 1990s, the Phillips Petroleum Company was involved in oil and gas exploration along the eastern and southern coasts of the United States. In deciding how to allocate the annual exploration budget between drilling projects, the company's managers faced two issues. First, they wanted a consistent measure of risk across projects. For example, they needed to compare projects offering a high chance of low returns with those offering a low chance of high returns. Second, they needed to decide their level of participation in joint drilling projects with other companies. For example, the company could adopt a strategy of having a relatively small involvement in a wide range of projects. The use of decision trees (Chapter 7) and utility functions (Chapter 6) allowed managers to rank investment opportunities consistently and to identify participation levels that conformed with the company's willingness to take on risk. Managers also gained insights into the financial risks associated with investment opportunities, and their awareness of these risks was increased.

Prioritizing infrastructure renewal projects at MIT[9]

The buildings and ground of the Massachusetts Institute of Technology (MIT) need to be constantly maintained and renewed, but resources for carrying out this work were limited. The department responsible for the work therefore needed a systematic method for prioritizing projects, such as the maintenance of heating, ventilating, air conditioning, plumbing and electrical systems and the refurbishment and replacement of roofs. This prioritization needed to reflect the risk of not carrying out a project. A series of workshops involving members of the infrastructure renewal team took place. At these workshops, a value tree (Chapter 3) was used to identify and agree the objectives against which the projects would be assessed. Typical objectives were to minimize the impact on the environment, to minimize the disruption of academic activities and to minimize the impact on the public image of the Institute. The analytic hierarchy process (Chapter 4) was then used to assess the relative weights that should be attached to these objectives, while utility functions (Chapter 6) were used to obtain a score for the consequences, in relation to each objective, of not carrying out a given project. By combining the weights and scores, an overall 'performance index' was obtained for the projects so that they could be prioritized. The application of these decision analysis tools led to a number of benefits. It allowed people from different professional backgrounds to apply their expertise to the process and reach a consensus. It also provided a consistent and defensible rationale for the prioritization. Most notably, the fact that discussions took place in the workshops about risks, objectives and priorities led to a change of culture in the department so that people were more willing to address these issues in an explicit and structured way.

Supporting the systems acquisition process for the US military[10]

In the past, the acquisition process for major military systems in the United States has been subject to much criticism because it has not produced defensible decisions underpinned by sound analyses and a clear rationale. As a result, decision analysis techniques such as SMART (Chapter 3) have been increasingly widely used to structure decision-making at the various stages of the process. For example, when the US Army air defense community needed to establish the most cost-effective mix of low-altitude air defense weapons, decision analysis was used to help a group consisting of both technical experts and senior officers to rank alternative weapon mixes. The process enabled a large number of criteria to be identified (e.g. flexibility at night, refuel capability, capability of defeating enemy fixed-wing aircraft) and allowed options to be explicitly evaluated by taking into account all of these criteria. Where decisions involved several organizations, the decision model was found have a valuable role in depoliticizing issues.

Prioritizing projects in a busy UK social services department[11]

Kent Social Services Department is responsible for the provision of services to the elderly, mentally handicapped, mentally ill, physically handicapped and children and families in south-eastern England. In the late 1980s, managers in the Department were facing an increasing workload with insufficient resources to handle it. The result was 'resource log-jams, random-seeming displacement of previously understood priorities, foreshortened deadlines and an overall sense of overload and chaos'. Decision analysis, based on SMART (Chapter 3) and the V·I·S·A package, was used by key personnel to develop and refine a consistent and structured approach to project prioritization. It enabled the many attributes associated with a project, such as benefits to the service, monetary costs, workload involved and political pressures, to be assessed and taken into account. However, the key benefits were seen to emanate from the process itself. It allowed a problem that had been 'a fermenting source of unrest [to be] brought to the surface, openly accepted to be a problem and shared'. As a result, 'the undercurrent of discontent' was replaced by 'enthusiasm for action'.

Selecting a wide area network (WAN) solution at EXEL Logistics [12]

EXEL Logistics, a division of one of the top 100 British companies that specializes in distribution solutions, has applied decision analysis to a number of problems. One problem involved the selection of a wide area network (WAN) for interconnecting around 150 sites in Britain. Seven alternative proposals needed to be considered. The decision was complicated by the need to involve a range of people in the decision process (e.g. professional information systems staff, depot managers and IT directors), and by the variety of attributes that applied to the WANs, such as costs, flexibility, performance, safety and supplier stability. By using decision conferencing (Chapter 13) together with SMART (Chapter 3), the team was able to agree a choice and recommend it with confidence to the company's board.

Planning under a range of futures in a financial services firm

ATM Ltd (a pseudonym) provides the electromechanical machines that dispense cash outside many of the banks and building societies in the UK. Autoteller machines, as they are called, are ATM's main products. However, several of the executives at ATM were concerned that the use of cash might be in swift decline in the European Union, as 'smart cards' – cards similar to debit cards but that store electronic cash – were being promoted by a competitor in the financial services sector. The executives did not feel able to predict the year in which cash transactions would cease to be significant, nor did they feel able to assess the potential rate of decline. By using scenario planning (Chapter 16), they felt able to identify critical driving forces that would accelerate or decelerate the move away from cash. As a result, they felt better placed to anticipate and cope with an unfavorable future – if such a future did begin to unfold.

Supporting top-level political decision-making in Finland[13]

Decision analysis based on the analytic hierarchy process (Chapter 4) has been used by groups of members (MPs) of the Finnish parliament to structure discussion and clarify their positions on decisions such as whether Finland should join the European Union (EU) or not. Such decisions are difficult because they involve many issues that are likely to have differing levels of importance. For example, in the EU decision, issues such as effects on industry, agriculture, national security, the environment and national culture needed to be addressed. The MPs found that the approach enabled them to generate ideas and structure the problems so that irrelevant or insignificant arguments were avoided in their decision-making.

Automating advice-giving in a building society front office

The Home Counties Building Society (a pseudonym) took advantage of deregulation in the UK financial services sector and investigated the possibility of offering tailored financial products – such as pension plans – at point-of-sale in their high street branches. They found that tailoring financial products to client characteristics, although theoretically straightforward, would not be practicable given the limited expertise of counter staff. One solution was to capture the expertise of the senior pensions adviser and deliver it via an expert system (Chapter 17) on a front-office desk. A clerk could type in client details and chat while the system matched the best pension plan, printed a hard copy of the details and explained – in plain English – the specific advantages of the recommended plan for the particular client.

Allocating funds between competing aims in a shampoo manufacturing company[14]

The managing director of a company that manufactures and markets a well-known brand of shampoo in a particular country had been asked by head office to justify his very large advertising budget. The managers responsible for distribution, advertising and promotion met with support staff and advertising agency representatives in a decision conference (Chapter 13). However, the insights revealed by a SMART model transformed their thinking, and the problem was then seen as one of improving the allocation of funds between distribution, advertising and promotion in order to achieve the objectives of growth, leadership and profit. An EQUITY resource allocation model (Chapter 14) enabled the participants to evaluate the costs and benefits of combinations of strategies from each expenditure area. This led to agreement on an action plan that was implemented within a month.

Overview of the book

The book is organized as follows. Chapter 2 discusses the biases that can arise when *unaided* decision-makers face decision problems involving multiple objectives. Chapter 3 then shows how decision analysis can be used to help with these sorts of problem. The focus of this chapter is on problems where there is little or no uncertainty about the outcomes of the different courses of action. Chapter 4 presents some alternative methods for handling decisions where there are multiple objectives. Uncertainty is addressed in Chapter 5, where we show how probability theory can be used to measure uncertainty, and in Chapter 6, where we apply probability to decision problems and show how the decision-maker's attitude to risk can be incorporated into the analysis.

As we saw at the start of this chapter, many decisions are difficult to handle because of their size and complex structure. In Chapters 7 and 8 we illustrate methods that can help to clarify this complexity, namely decision trees, influence diagrams and simulation models.

Of course, all decisions depend primarily on judgment. Decision analysis is not designed to replace these judgments but to provide a framework that will help decision-makers to clarify and articulate them. In Chapter 9 we look at how a decision-maker should revise judgments in the light of new information, while Chapter 10 reviews psychological evidence on how good people are at using judgment to estimate probabilities. The implications of this research are considered in Chapter 11, where we demonstrate techniques that have been developed to elicit probabilities from decision-makers. There is evidence that most managers see their role as one of trying to reduce and manage risks, where this is possible. In Chapter 12 we show how decision analysis models can provide a structure for risk and uncertainty management so that the aspects of the decision that have the greatest potential for reducing risks or exploiting opportunities can be identified.

Although, in general, decisions made in organizations are ultimately the responsibility of an individual, often a group of people will participate in the decision-making process. Chapters 13 and 14 describe problems that can occur in group decision-making and discuss the role of decision analysis in this context. Special emphasis is placed on decision conferencing and problems involving the allocation of resources between competing areas of an organization.

Major errors in decision-making can arise because the original decision problem has been incorrectly framed. In particular, in strategic decision-making the decision can be formulated in a way that fails to take into account fundamental changes that have occurred in the organization's environment. The result can be overconfident decisions that are made on the basis of outdated assumptions. Framing problems and the cognitive inertia that can be associated with them are discussed in Chapter 15, while Chapter 16 shows how scenario planning, an alternative way of dealing with uncertainty, can help to alert decision-makers to possible environmental changes. In Chapter 17, alternative forms of decision support, such as expert systems and bootstrapping, are contrasted with the decision-aiding methods we have covered in the book. We also ask whether snap decisions, based on intuitive judgments, should have any role in management decision-making and discuss how decisions might be designed so that people can be encouraged to choose the 'best' option. This last chapter also looks at the key questions that a decision-maker should consider in order to maximize the effectiveness of decision-aiding methods, and concludes with a summary of the types of problem that the different methods are designed to address.

References

1. Keeney, R.L. (1982) Decision analysis: an overview, *Operations Research*, **30**, 803–838.
2. Phillips, L.D. (1989) Decision analysis in the 1990s, in *Tutorial Papers in Operational Research (1989)*, ed. by Shahini, A. and Stainton, R., Operational Research Society, Birmingham, UK.
3. For wide-ranging discussions of decision analysis applications, see Keefer, D.L., Kirkwood, C.W. and Corner, J.L. (2004) Perspective on decision analysis applications, 1990–2001, *Decision Analysis*, **1**, 4–22; Kiker, G.A., Bridges, T.S, Varghese, A. et al. (2005) Application of multicriteria decision analysis in environmental decision making, *Integrated Environmental Assessment and Management*, **1**, 95–108; and applications reported in Figueira, J., Greco, S. and Ehrgott, M. (eds) (2005) *Multiple Criteria Decision Analysis: State of the Art Surveys*, Springer, New York, NY.
4. Krumm, F.V. and Rolle, C.F. (1992) Management and application of decision and risk analysis in Du Pont, *Interfaces*, **22**, 84–93.
5. French, S., Kelly, N. and Morrey, M. (1992) Towards a shared understanding. How decision analysis helped structure decision problems in the International Chernobyl Project, *OR Insight*, **5**, 23–27.
6. French, S. (1996) Multi-attribute decision support in the event of a nuclear accident, *Journal of Multi-Criteria Decision Analysis*, **5**, 39–57.
7. Loch, C.H. and Bode-Greuel, K. (2001) Evaluating growth options as sources of value for pharmaceutical research projects, *R&D Management*, **31**, 231–248.
8. Walls, M.R., Morahan, G.T. and Dyer, J.S. (1995) Decision analysis of exploration opportunities in the onshore US at Phillips Petroleum Company, *Interfaces*, **25**, 39–56.
9. Karydas, D.M. and Gifun, J.F. (2006) A method for the efficient prioritization of infrastructure renewal projects, *Reliability Engineering and System Safety*, **91**, 84–99.
10. Buede, D.M. and Bresnick, T.A. (1992) Applications of decision analysis to the military systems acquisition process, *Interfaces*, **22**, 110–125.
11. Belton, V. (1993) Project planning and prioritization in the Social Services – an OR contribution, *Journal of the Operational Research Society*, **44**, 115–124.
12. Marples, C. and Robertson, G. (1993) Option review with HIVIEW, *OR Insight*, **6**, 13–18.
13. Hämäläinen, R. and Leikola, O. (1996) Spontaneous decision conferencing with top-level politicians, *OR Insight*, **9**, 24–28.
14. Phillips, L.D. (1989) People-centred group decision support, in *Knowledge Based Management Support Systems*, ed. by Doukidis, G., Land, F. and Miller, G., Ellis Horwood, Chichester, UK.

How people make decisions involving multiple objectives 2

Introduction

This chapter looks at how decision-makers make intuitive decisions involving multiple objectives. Many decisions involve multiple objectives. For example, when choosing a holiday destination, you may want the resort with the liveliest nightlife, the least crowded beaches, the lowest costs, the most sunshine and the most modern hotels. As a manager purchasing goods from a supplier, you may be seeking the supplier who has the best after-sales service, the fastest delivery time, the lowest prices and the best reputation for reliability. Such intuitive decision-making is usually 'unaided' – by which we mean people face decisions like this *without* the support and structure provided by the decision analysis methods that we will introduce in the subsequent chapters.

Suppose we asked you to multiply 8 by 7 by 6 by 5 by 4 by 3 by 2 by 1 in your head. You could probably make a good guess at the correct answer but may, or may not, be surprised that the 'correct' calculator-derived answer is 40 320. Which do you believe produced the most valid answer? Your intuition? Or the calculator? Most of us would tend to trust the calculator, although we might run through the keystrokes a second or third time to check that we had not wrongly entered or omitted a number. The conclusion from this 'thought experiment' is that the human mind has a 'limited capacity' for complex calculations, and that technological devices, such as calculators, complement our consciously admitted cognitive limitations. This assumption underpins all of the decision analysis methods that are covered later in this book, but what happens if decision-makers are not aware of their cognitive limitations and make decisions without using these methods?

According to research by psychologists, decision-makers have a mental toolbox of available strategies, and they are adaptive in that they choose the strategy that they think is most appropriate for a particular decision. Simon[1] used the term *bounded rationality* to refer to the fact that the limitations of the human mind mean that people have to use 'approximate methods' to deal with most decision problems, and, as a result, they seek to identify satisfactory, rather than optimal, courses of action. These approximate methods, or rules of thumb, are often referred to as 'heuristics'. Simon, and later Gigerenzer *et al.*,[2] has also emphasized that people's heuristics are often well adapted to the structure of their knowledge about the environment. For example, suppose a decision-maker knows that the best guide to the quality of a university is its research income. Suppose also that this is a far better guide than any other attribute of the university such as quality of sports facilities or teaching quality (or any combination of these other attributes). In this environment, a prospective student who chooses a university simply on the basis of its research income is likely to choose well – the simple heuristic would be well matched to the decision-making environment. Quick ways of making decisions like this that people use, especially when time is limited, have been referred to as '*fast and frugal heuristics*' by Gigerenzer and his colleagues. We will first look at the heuristics that can be found in most decision-makers' mental 'toolboxes', and then we will consider how people choose heuristics for particular decision problems.

Heuristics used for decisions involving multiple objectives

When a decision-maker has multiple objectives, the heuristic used will either be compensatory or non-compensatory. In a compensatory strategy, an option's poor performance on one attribute is compensated for by good performance on others. For example, a computer's reliability and fast processor speed may be judged to compensate for its unattractive price. This would not be the case in a non-compensatory strategy. Compensatory strategies involve more cognitive effort because the decision-maker has the difficult task of making trade-offs between improved performance on some attributes and reduced performance on others.

The recognition heuristic

The recognition heuristic[2] is used where people have to choose between two options. If one is recognized and the other is not, the recognized option is chosen. For example, suppose that a manager has to choose between two competing products, but she has not got the time or motivation to search for all the details relating to the products. If she recognizes the name of the manufacturer of one of them, but not the other, she may simply choose the product whose manufacturer she recognizes. This simple heuristic is likely to work well in environments where quality is associated with ease of recognition. It may be that a more easily recognized manufacturer is likely to have been trading for longer and be larger. Its long-term survival and size may be evidence of its ability to produce quality products and to maintain its reputation. Interestingly, the recognition heuristic can reward ignorance. A more knowledgeable person might recognize both manufacturers and therefore be unable to employ the heuristic. If ease of recognition is an excellent predictor of quality, then a less knowledgeable person who recognizes only one manufacturer will have the advantage. Of course, the heuristic will not work well when ease of recognition is not associated with how good an option is. There is evidence that recognition has a strong effect on choice. For example, one study[3] found that 94% of people favored a familiar (although never tasted) brand of peanut butter over less recognized brands.

The recognition heuristic can be useful when choices have to be made on how to rank objects according to some criterion. If you are asked, for example, which of a list of cities has the largest population, then those city names that you recognize are likely, in fact, to have the larger populations. This is because greater population size will be generally linked to greater economic and commercial activity, which will, in turn, result in more news coverage of events in a city and, hence, greater recognition of that city's name. Thus, recognition can be a valid cue to population size. In fact, there is a high positive association between the number of times particular German cities are mentioned in the American newspapers and the probability of those cities being recognized by the American public.[4] A recent study[5] tested the performance of the recognition heuristic in predictions of the outcomes of tennis matches at Wimbledon. This study asked members of the general public how familiar they were with each of the tournament's contestants – deriving 'recognition rankings'. These rankings correlated well with the official rankings of the players and were just as good at predicting the final outcomes of the Wimbledon tournament. The results showed that, even in this dynamic environment, where the winning prospects of both new entrants and more established players vary over time, recognition is a good predictive cue.

People are also sensitive to the usefulness of the recognition cue in different tasks. For example, when asked to estimate the distance of a named Swiss city from a particular lake, the degree of recognition of a particular city's name was, quite sensibly, not used in estimations.[6]

The minimalist strategy[2]

In this heuristic, the decision-makers first apply the recognition heuristic, but, if neither option is recognized, they will simply guess which option is the best. In the event of both options being recognized, the decision-makers will pick at random one of the attributes of the two options. If this attribute enables them to discriminate between the two options, they will make the decision at this point. If not, then they will pick a second attribute at random, and so on. For example, in choosing between two digital cameras, both of which have manufacturers that are recognized by the decision-makers, the attribute 'possession of movie-shooting modes' may be selected randomly. If only one camera has this facility, then it will be selected, otherwise a second randomly selected attribute will be considered.

Take the last[2]

This is the same as the minimalist heuristic, except that, rather than picking a random attribute, people recall the attribute that enabled them to reach a decision last time they had a similar choice to make. For example, the last time a manager had to fly to a business meeting, he chose the airline that had the best reputation for in-flight catering, so he uses this attribute to make his choice for a forthcoming flight. If this attribute does not allow him to discriminate between the options this time, then he will choose the attribute that worked the time before, and so on. If none of the previously used attributes works, then a random attribute will be tried.

The lexicographic strategy[7]

In the last two heuristics, the decision-maker either selects attributes at random or uses attributes that have been used to make the decision in the past. However, in some circumstances, the decision-maker may be able to rank the attributes in order of importance. For example, in choosing a car, price may be more important than size, which in turn is more important than top speed. In this case, the decision-maker can employ the lexicographic heuristic. This simply involves identifying the most important attribute and selecting the alternative that is considered to be best on that attribute. Thus, the cheapest car will be purchased. In the event of a 'tie' on the most important attribute, the decision-maker will choose the option that performs best on the second most important attribute (size), and so on. This ordering of preferences is analogous to the way in which words are ordered in a dictionary – hence the name 'lexicographic'. For example, consider the words bat and ball. They both 'tie' on the first letter and also tie on the second letter, but on the third letter ball has precedence.

   Like the earlier heuristics, the lexicographic strategy involves little information processing (i.e. it is cognitively simple) *if* there are few ties. In spite of this, like the recognition heuristic, it can work well in certain environments – for example, when one attribute is considerably more important than any of the others or where information is scarce. However, when more information is available, the decision will be based on only a small part of the available data. In addition, the strategy is *non-compensatory*. With deeper reflection, a decision-maker might have preferred an option that performed less well on the most important attribute because of its good performance on other attributes.[8]

The semi-lexicographic strategy[7]

This differs slightly from the lexicographic strategy in that, if the performance of alternatives on an attribute is similar, the decision-maker considers them to be tied and moves on to the next attribute. For example, when you go shopping, you might adopt the following semi-lexicographic decision strategy: 'If the price difference between brands is less than 50 cents, choose the higher-quality product, otherwise choose the cheaper brand'. Consider the alternatives below:

Brand	Price	Quality
A	$3.00	Low
B	$3.60	High
C	$3.40	Medium

If you were to employ this strategy, then you would prefer A to B and B to C. This implies that you will prefer A to C, but a direct comparison of A and C using the strategy reveals that C is preferred. This set of choices is therefore contradictory. More formally, it violates a fundamental axiom of decision analysis, known as *transitivity*, which states that, if you prefer A to B and B to C, then you should also prefer A to C.[9]

Elimination by aspects (EBA)[10]

In this heuristic, the most important attribute is identified and a cut-off point, which defines the boundary of acceptable performance on this attribute, is then established. Any alternative that has a performance falling outside this boundary is eliminated. The process continues with the second most important attribute, and so on. For example, suppose that you want to buy a car and have a list of hundreds of cars that are for sale in the local paper. You could apply EBA to the list as follows:

(1) Price is the most important attribute – eliminate all cars costing more than $15 000 and any costing less than $6000.
(2) Number of seats is the next most important consideration – eliminate two-seater sports cars.
(3) Engine size is the third most important attribute – eliminate any of the remaining cars that have an engine less than 1600cc.

(4) You want a car with a relatively low mileage – eliminate any remaining cars that have more than 30 000 miles on the clock.
(5) Service history is next in importance – eliminate any car that does not have a full service history.

By continuing in this way, you eventually narrow your list to one car, and this is the one you choose.

Clearly, EBA is easy to apply, involves no complicated numerical computations and is easy to explain and justify to others. In short, the choice process is well suited to our limited information processing capacity. However, the major flaw in EBA is its failure to ensure that the alternatives retained are, in fact, superior to those that are eliminated. This arises because the strategy is *non-compensatory*. In our example, one of the cars might have been rejected because it was slightly below the 1600cc cut-off value. Yet its price, service history and mileage were all preferable to the car you purchased. These strengths would have more than compensated for this one weakness. The decision-maker's focus is thus on a *single* attribute at a time rather than on possible trade-offs between attributes.

Sequential decision-making: satisficing

The strategies we have outlined so far are theories intended to describe how people make a decision when they are faced with a *simultaneous* choice between alternatives. Thus, all the cars in the earlier example were available at the same time. In some situations, however, alternatives become available sequentially. For example, if you are looking for a new house, you might, over a period of weeks, view houses successively as they become available on the market. Herbert Simon[11] has argued that, in these circumstances, decision-makers use an approach called satisficing. In satificing, decision-makers stop searching as soon as they find an alternative that is satisfactory. Of course, this satisfactory option may not be the best available.

The key aspect of satisficing is the *aspiration level* of the decision-maker, which characterizes whether an alternative is acceptable. Imagine that your aspiration level is a job in a particular geographical location with a salary above a particular level and at least 3 weeks' paid holiday per year. Simon argues that you will search for jobs until you find one that meets your aspiration levels on *all* these attributes. Once you have found such a job, you will take it and, at least for the time being, conclude your job search. It is possible that you *might* have found a better job if you had been willing to make further job applications and go for further interviews.

Another important characteristic of satisficing is that the aspiration levels of decision-makers may change during the search process as they develop a better idea of what they can reasonably achieve. When you started the job search process, your expectations may have been unreasonably high. Earlier job offers that you turned down may now look highly acceptable.

Note also that satisficing is yet another example of a non-compensatory strategy. In the job search example, there were no considerations of how much holiday you would be prepared to give up for a given increase in salary. The final choice also depends on the order in which the alternatives present themselves. If you are searching for a car to buy, the car you choose will probably be different if you decide to change the order in which you visit the showrooms.

Simon's satisficing theory is most usefully applied to describe sequential choice between alternatives that become available (and indeed may become unavailable) as time passes. However, it may also be adopted in situations where, although all the alternatives are in theory available simultaneously, they are so numerous that it would be impossible to consider them all in detail at the same time.

Reason-based choice

Reason-based choice offers an alternative perspective on the way people make decisions. According to Shafir *et al.*,[12] 'when faced with the need to choose, decision-makers often seek and construct reasons in order to resolve the conflict and justify their choice to themselves and to others'. Reason-based choice can lead to some unexpected violations of the principles of rational decision-making.

First, it can make the decision-maker highly sensitive to the way a decision is framed. For example, consider the following two candidates, A and B, who have applied for a job as a personal assistant. Their characteristics are described below:

Candidate A	Candidate B
Average written communication skills	Excellent written communication skills
Satisfactory absenteeism record	Very good absenteeism record
Average computer skills	Excellent computer skills
Reasonable interpersonal skills	Awkward when dealing with others
Average level of numeracy	Poor level of numeracy
Average telephone skills	Poor telephone skills

Note that candidate A is average or satisfactory on all characteristics, whereas candidate B performs very well on some characteristics but very poorly on others. Research by Shafir[13] suggests that, if the decision is framed as 'which candidate should be *selected*?', then most people would select B. A selection decision will cause people to search for reasons for choosing a particular candidate, and B's excellent communication skills, very good absenteeism record and excellent computer skills will provide the required rationale. If, instead, the decision is framed as 'which candidate should be *rejected*?' then, again, most people would choose B – this candidate's poor interpersonal, numeracy and telephone skills will provide the necessary justification. Hence, positive features are weighted more highly when selecting, and negative features more highly when rejecting. This violates a basic principle of rational decision-making – that choice should be invariant to the way the decision is framed.

Other research has investigated how choice sets are narrowed.[14] Imagine that you are involved in the human resource function of a firm. Would the task of selecting only those job applicants to take forward for further consideration result in a different set of applicants to choosing those applicants to exclude from any further consideration? Research has shown that following the latter strategy of exclusion leaves more of the initial alternatives under consideration than the former strategy of inclusion. Also, the strategy of inclusion leads to a more extensive search to see how well a candidate performs on the multiple attributes that are important in the selector's evaluation process. By contrast, a strategy of exclusion results in a more cursory evaluation of those candidates that are rejected. The explanation for this effect is that including an alternative often requires more justification, and therefore more thought, than exclusion.

Another principle of rational decision-making is that of *'independence of irrelevant alternatives'*. If you prefer a holiday in Mexico to a holiday in France, you should still prefer the Mexican to the French holiday, even if a third holiday in Canada becomes available. Reason-based decision-making can lead to a violation of this principle. For example, suppose that you see a popular Canon digital camera for sale at a bargain price of $200 in a store that is having a 1 day sale. You have the choice between: (a) buying the camera now or (b) waiting until you can learn more about the cameras that are available. You have no problem in deciding to buy the camera – you can find a compelling reason to justify this in the camera's remarkably low price. Option (a) is clearly preferable to option (b). However, once inside the store you discover that a Nikon camera, with more features than the Canon, is also available at a one-off bargain price of $350. You now have conflict between the cheaper Canon and the more expensive, but sophisticated, Nikon. According to research by Tversky and Shafir,[15] many people would now change their mind and opt to wait in order to find out more about available cameras. This is because it is difficult to find a clear reason to justify one camera's purchase over the other. The availability of the Nikon camera has caused you to reverse your original preference of buying the Canon rather than waiting.

A final interesting consequence of reason-based decision-making is that, if an option has some features that are only weakly in its favor, or irrelevant, this can actually deter people from selecting that option. For example, in one study,[16] people were asked to choose between two brands of cake mix that were very similar in all features, except that the first carried an offer to purchase a collector's plate that most people did not want. The offer significantly lowered the tendency to choose the first brand. Apparently, this was because it was difficult to find reasons to justify this worthless bonus, and people felt that they might be exposed to criticism if they chose the option that was associated with it.

Factors affecting which strategies people employ

Many of the heuristics that we have described will tend to be applied to our choice process without our conscious control. Other heuristics can be consciously selected to simplify our choices. Overall, we tend to make choices without weighing the advantages and disadvantages of the various options in a comprehensive, detailed way. Factors that affect our choices include:

(i) the *time available* to make the decision;
(ii) the *effort* that a given strategy will involve;
(iii) the decision-maker's *knowledge about the environment*;
(iv) the *importance of making an accurate decision*;
(v) whether the decision-maker has to *justify his or her choice* to others;
(vi) a desire to *minimize conflict* (for example, the conflict between the advantages and disadvantages of moving to another job).

Payne *et al.*[17] argue that decision-makers choose their strategies to balance the effort involved in making the decision against the accuracy that they wish to achieve (the '*effort–accuracy framework*'). When a given level of accuracy is desired, they attempt to achieve this with the minimum of effort and use one of the simpler heuristics. Where greater weight is placed on making an accurate decision, more effort will be expended. There is also evidence that people often use a combination of strategies. When faced with a long list of alternatives, they use quick, relatively easy methods, such as elimination by aspects, to remove options to obtain a 'short list'. Then they apply more effortful strategies to select the preferred option from the short list. In addition, a requirement to justify a decision to others is likely to increase the likelihood that reason-based choice will be used. For whatever reasons, conscious or unconscious, deliberate or accidental, our intuitive decisions are likely to use only a proportion of the information that is available for, what could have been, a more comprehensive evaluation of alternatives.

Other characteristics of decision-making involving multiple objectives

Decoy effects[18]

Imagine that you are buying a new car from a dealer, but cannot choose between a relatively small, but sporty car that will be exciting to drive and that you think will enhance your image and a staid, reliable saloon that has plenty of space for your family and luggage. Both cars come with free insurance for a year. Suddenly, you discover that another branch of the dealership is offering the stately saloon at the same price, but *without* the free insurance. The attraction of the saloon at your branch of the dealers suddenly soars and you do not give a second thought to the smaller car. This is known as the decoy (or asymmetric dominance) effect. By creating a situation where one option (the staid car with the insurance) is clearly better than the other (the staid car without the insurance), the decision-maker is presented with an easy comparison. As a result, the attraction of the first option is enhanced. In fact, it now looks so attractive that it is perceived to be better than its original competitor.

Note that the staid car with the insurance is clearly superior to the same car without the insurance, and it is therefore said to exhibit dominance. However, when comparing the sporty car and the staid car without the insurance, it is not clear which should be preferred. Hence, the choice situation is said to exhibit asymmetric dominance – one of the deals clearly dominates the decoy, but the other does not. It is the offer that clearly dominates the decoy that becomes substantially more attractive in these situations. Of course, the car without the insurance (the decoy) would never be chosen, and it is therefore an irrelevant alternative. However, its presence changes the decision-maker's relative preference for the original options. As such, the decoy effect causes people to violate the principle of irrelevant alternatives that we referred to earlier. In spite of this, the effect has been found to apply in a wide range of situations, including purchasing decisions,[19] the selection of candidates for jobs[20] and, apparently, even partner selection.[21]

A similar phenomenon results from what are referred to as *phantom decoys*.[22] Unlike the decoys we have just discussed, these are options that asymmetrically *dominate* a particular option, but then turn out to be unavailable. For example, suppose you have difficulty choosing between two makes of laptop computer: a cheap brand that will be heavy to carry around and a more expensive, but much lighter model. You then see that a retailer is advertising a 20% price discount on the cheap, heavy model to the first 50 purchasers who arrive at its store. Unfortunately, when you get to the store, all of the deals have gone. In spite of this, the phantom decoy has been found to enhance the attraction of the original option relative to other options in many situations. As a result, you still choose the cheap model, in spite of the absence of the discount, because the phantom decoy has made it appear to be much better than the other laptop. Several explanations for this effect have been put forward. For example,[23] the discounted price has created a reference point for what we hoped to pay. We all hate losses – in fact, we hate losses more than we enjoy gains – and larger losses are regarded as being disproportionately more unpleasant. The loss of the discount is unwelcome, but, compared with the reference point, the sense of loss we would have in paying out for the expensive computer is much greater, and this computer now looks very unattractive.

Choosing by unique attributes

Research has shown that the degree to which attributes are shared across alternatives influences which alternatives are preferred. For example, if a decision-maker knows the legroom of a range of airlines' economy-class seating, then information on this attribute is shared. Conversely, if the legroom for only one airline's seating is known, then the attribute information is unique. Decision-makers tend to place more importance on attributes that possess unique rather than shared information.[24] Consider the following choice of vacation destinations:[25]

Destination A	Destination B	Destination C1	Destination C2
Good restaurants	Plenty of good nightspots	Plenty of good nightspots	Good restaurants
Attractive beaches	Beautiful scenery	Beautiful scenery	Attractive beaches
Good theaters	Good museums	Good museums	Good theaters
Pollution problem	Overcrowded	Pollution problem	Overcrowded
Expensive	Poor transportation	Expensive	Poor transportation
Long travel time	Possible bad weather	Long travel time	Possible bad weather

When alternatives A, B and C1 were presented, people's intuitive preferences were those in row 2 of the table below. When alternatives A, B and C2 were presented, people's preferences were those in row 3.

Destination A	Destination B	Destination C1	Destination C2
42%	30%	28%	—
20%	48%	—	32%

Note that the characteristics of alternatives A and B remain unchanged between the two sets of choices. However, the proportion of people choosing A over B changes between the two choice sets. When people choose between A, B and C1, the inclusion of C1 makes alternative A's unfavorable attributes shared and its favorable attributes unique (for example, both A and C1 have a pollution problem, but only A has good restaurants). When people choose between A, B and C2, the inclusion of alternative C2 makes alternative B's unfavorable attributes shared and its favorable attributes unique. An explanation for this change in preferences is that common features are cancelled out in our decision-making – because they cannot be used as a basis for making a choice – and greater attention is given to unique favorable attributes that are used to help make a choice. In short, we tend to focus on unique features of alternatives when making choices. This is the so-called 'attribute salience' effect.

Emotion and choice

Emotion can also influence how information is processed. Sad moods tend to prompt detailed analytic thinking, while happy moods tend to result in less detailed analysis. One study[26] investigated the relationship between the cloudiness of the sky and the importance that academic selectors placed on the academic attributes (e.g. school grades) and the non-academic attributes (e.g. leadership roles undertaken and athletic prowess) of candidates who had applied for admission to university. Perhaps surprisingly, candidates' academic attributes were weighted more heavily on cloudy days, and non-academic attributes were weighted more heavily on sunnier days. In fact, cloud cover was found to increase an academically focused candidate's probability of admission by 12%! In one unusual study,[27] on the influence of mood on decision-making, a person's sexual arousal (induced by the reading of sexually explicit material) was found to magnify the attractiveness of varied sexual activities while decreasing the importance of health and ethically related criteria. Another study[28] found that that those contestants who saw and smelt the prize of chocolate cookies felt more likely to win a competition than those contestants who were simply told what the winner's prize would be.

Apart from the effect of ambient mood on choice, the emotional or affective impressions attached to particular choice alternatives have also been shown to influence choice.[29, 30] Affective impressions can be both easier and, perhaps, more efficient than thinking through the advantages and disadvantages of alternatives. For example, people who have *positive* feelings about, say, either solar power or nuclear power tend to rate that power source as *higher* on benefits and *lower* on risk than people who have less positive feelings about the source of power supply. These associations become even stronger when the judgments of benefits and risks have to be made quickly – here, the influence of the 'affect heuristic' in guiding preference is more pronounced.

Justifying already made choices

When asked to make a choice, decision-makers may be unsure what their preferences are, and their preferences can change over time. One study[31] identified 'coherence shifts' in decision-makers' preferences for alternatives. In the first part of the study, individuals were asked to rate the importance of a range of job-offer attributes such as salary, commuting time, holiday entitlement, etc. Next, the participants were given the details of particular jobs that contained a mix of scores on the attributes that had been previously rated, and then the decision-maker was asked to choose the most preferred job. Finally, the participants were asked to rerate the importance of the attributes that they had already rated earlier on before making their choice These revisited ratings were found to have 'shifted' to provide stronger support for the favored job offer – the attributes where the favored job scored most highly were found to have increased in importance. This meant that the favored job was clearly separated out as superior to the non-favored jobs. Interestingly, when participants were asked 1 week later about their ratings of the various attributes of the jobs, these importance weightings were found to have returned to their initial, prechoice levels. As such, these 'coherence shifts' – where attribute evaluations change to provide support for the choices that we have made – dissipate over time. One implication from this research is that decision-makers may initially overvalue the choices that they have resolved to make. For example, if they have already decided to buy a product, they may overpay at the time of purchase. Consider bidding on eBay for a particularly desired item. If your maximum bid is beaten by another person, then there is a tendency to increase your maximum from the previously set limit. Only later does the expense of a successful bid become salient.

Partitioning the total cost of an item changes preferences

A total payment for a product or service can be presented in either partitioned or aggregated form. For example, the cost of a small television might be presented as

(i) $199 plus $30 shipping or (ii) $229 including shipping. Does display of the aggregated cost result in a higher perceived payment than display of the partitioned costs? Studies[32] have found that, when purchase intentions and product interest were measured, the smaller shipping charge was underweighted in the partitioned evaluation. Additionally, presenting the partitioned price led to lower recollections of the total price than did presenting the combined price. Adding the product cost to the shipping cost takes mental effort, and so the smaller shipping cost plays less of a role than it should in determining our preferences. The implication of this finding for vendors of products is clear-cut – display the product cost and the shipping cost separately.

Summary

This chapter has reported studies of how unaided decision-makers make choices when they want to achieve several objectives. In these circumstances, people tend not to make trade-offs by accepting poorer performance on some attributes in exchange for better performance on others. However, recent research has suggested that people's decision-making skills are not as poor as was once believed. In particular, the work of Gigerenzer *et al.*[2] indicates that humans have developed simple heuristics that can lead to quick decisions, involving little mental effort, and that these heuristics can be well adapted to particular tasks.

Does decision analysis have a role as an aid to management decision-making? We believe it does. The fast and frugal heuristics identified by Gigerenzer *et al.* enable us to make smart choices when 'time is pressing and deep thought is unaffordable luxury'. Major decisions, such as a decision on whether to launch a new product or where to site a new factory, do merit time and deep thought. Decision analysis allows managers to use this time effectively and enables them to structure and clarify their thinking. It encourages decision-makers to explore trade-offs between attributes and both clarifies and challenges their perceptions of risk and uncertainty. As the previous chapter indicated, use of decision analysis also provides a documented and defensible rationale for a given decision and enhances communication within decision-making teams.

The rest of this book is devoted to showing how decision analysis methods can provide these important benefits and hence overcome the limitations of unaided decision-making. The next chapter introduces a method designed to support decision-makers faced with decisions involving multiple objectives of the type that we have described in this chapter. As we shall see, in contrast to heuristics such as the lexicographic strategy or elimination by aspects, this method is designed to allow decision-makers to make use of all relevant information that is available and to make compensatory choices.

Discussion questions

(1) In what circumstances is the recognition heuristic likely to work well?
(2) A manager is ordering 40 inkjet printers for staff working in the company's main office. Details of the available models are given below. The print quality score has been produced by an independent magazine. The score ranges from $1 = $ very poor to $5 = $ excellent.

Mode	Price	Mono printing speed (ppm)	Print quality score	Noise level (dBA)
Solar	$200	12.0	5	45
Symbol	$159	7.8	4	46
Real	$169	5.4	3	38
CCC	$250	6.0	5	40
Tiger	$80	4.1	4	48
Linwood	$110	5.6	4	43
GA	$185	5.4	4	40
Superb	$210	7.2	4	45
Multitask	$170	6.1	5	36
AR52	$237	14.0	5	48
Zeta	$105	7.0	2	45
Multitask 2	$118	9.1	3	43

Use the above information to demonstrate how the manager could apply each of the following strategies to choose the computer, and discuss the advantages and disadvantages of using these strategies:
(a) Lexicographic
(b) Semi-lexicographic
(c) Elimination by aspects
(d) Satisficing.
(3) After her examinations, a student decides that she needs a holiday. A travel agent supplies the following list of last-minute holidays that are available. The student works down the list, considering the holidays in the order that they appear, until she comes across one that is satisfactory, which she books. Her minimal requirements are:
  (i) The holiday must last at least 10 days.
  (ii) It must cost no more than $1500.
  (iii) It must not be self-catering.

(iv) It must be located in accommodation that is no more than 5 minutes' walk from the beach.

Determine which holiday she will choose from the list below, and discuss the limitations of the strategy that she has adopted.

Location	Duration	Cost	Self-catering?	Walking time to beach
Canada	7 days	$750	No	2 minutes
Barbados	10 days	$1200	No	4 minutes
Canary Isles	14 days	$2000	No	10 minutes
Greece	10 days	$1100	Yes	2 minutes
Spain	10 days	$1000	Yes	5 minutes
Turkey	14 days	$1000	No	1 minutes
California	14 days	$975	No	0 minutes
Florida	10 days	$1800	No	30 minutes
Mexico	14 days	$1500	No	8 minutes

References

1. Simon, H.A. (1982) *Models of Bounded Rationality*, MIT Press, Cambridge, MA.
2. Gigerenzer, G., Todd, P.M. and the ABC Research Group (1999) *Simple Heuristics that Make Us Smart*, Oxford University Press, Oxford, UK.
3. Hoyer, W.D. and Brown, S.P. (1990) Effects of brand awareness on choice for a common, repeat purchase product, *Journal of Consumer Research*, **17**, 141–148.
4. Goldstein, D.G. and Gigerenzer, G. (2002) Models of ecological rationality: the recognition heuristic, *Psychological Review*, **109**, 75–90.
5. Serwe, S. and Frings, C. (2006) Who will win Wimbledon? The recognition heuristic in prediction of sports events, *Journal of Behavioral Decision Making*, **19**, 321–332.
6. Pohl, R.F. (2006) Empirical tests of the recognition heuristic, *Journal of Behavioral Decision Making*, **19**, 251–271.
7. Tversky, A. (1969) Intransitivity of preferences, *Psychological Review*, **76**, 31–48.
8. Note that, when the lexicographic strategy is only employed after the recognition heuristic has failed to discriminate between options, because they are both recognized, it is referred to as the 'Take the best' heuristic.
9. Fishburn, P. (1991) Nontransitive preferences in decision theory, *Journal of Risk and Uncertainty*, **4**, 113–124.
10. Tversky, A. (1972) Elimination by aspects: a theory of choice, *Psychological Review*, **79**, 281–299.

11. Simon, H.A. (1955) A behavioral model of rational choice, *Quarterly Journal of Economics*, **69**, 99–118.
12. Shafir, E., Simonson, I. and Tversky, A. (1993) Reason-based choice, *Cognition*, **49**, 11–36.
13. Shafir, E. (1993) Choosing versus rejecting: why some options are both better and worse than others, *Memory and Cognition*, **21**, 546–556.
14. Levin, I.P., Prosansky, C.M., Heller, D. and Brunick, B.M. (2001) Prescreening of choice options in positive and negative decision making, *Journal of Behavioral Decision Making*, **14**, 279–293.
15. Tversky, A. and Shafir, E. (1992) The disjunction effect in choice under uncertainty, *Psychological Science*, **3**, 305–309.
16. Simonson, I., Carmon, Z. and O'Curry, S. (1994) Experimental evidence on the negative effect of product features and sales promotions on brand choice, *Marketing Science*, **13**, 23–40.
17. Payne, J.W., Bettman, J.R. and Johnson, E.J. (1993) *The Adaptive Decision Maker*, Cambridge University Press, Cambridge, UK.
18. Huber, J., Payne J.W. and Puto C. (1982) Adding asymmetrically dominated alternatives – violations of regularity and the similarity hypothesis, *Journal of Consumer Research*, **9**, 90–98.
19. Kivetz, R., Netzer, O. and Srinivasan, V. (2004) Extending compromise effect models to complex buying situations and other context effects, *Journal of Marketing Research*, **41**, 262–268.
20. Slaughter, J.E. (2007) Effects of two selection batteries on decoy effects in job-finalist choice, *Journal of Applied Social Psychology*, **37**, 76–90.
21. Sedikides, C., Ariely, D. and Olsen, N. (1999) Contextual and procedural determinants of partner selection: of asymmetric dominance and prominence, *Social Cognition*, **17**, 118–139.
22. Pratkanis, A.R. and Farquhar, P.H. (1992) A brief history of research on phantom alternatives – evidence for 7 empirical generalizations about phantoms, *Basic and Applied Social Psychology*, **13**, 103–122.
23. Pettibone, J.C. and Wedell, D.H. (2007) Testing alternative explanations of phantom decoy effects, *Journal of Behavioral Decision Making*, **20**, 323–341.
24. Slaughter, J.E. and Highhouse, S. (2003) Does matching up features mess up job choice? Boundary conditions on attribute-salience effects, *Journal of Behavioral Decision Making*, **16**, 1–16.
25. Dhar, R. and Sherman, S.J. (1996) The effects of common and unique features in consumer choice, *Journal of Consumer Research*, **23**, 193–203.
26. Simonsohn, U. (2007) Clouds make nerds look good: field evidence of the impact of incidental factors on decision making, *Journal of Behavioral Decision Making*, **20**, 143–152.
27. Ariely, D. and Lowenstein, G. (2006) The heat of the moment: the effect of sexual arousal on sexual decision making, *Journal of Behavioral Decision Making*, **19**, 87–98.
28. Ditto, P.M., Pizaro, D.A. and Epstein, E.B. (2006) Visceral influences on risk-taking behavior, *Journal of Behavioral Decision Making*, **19**, 99–113.
29. Finucane, M.L., Alhakami, A., Slovic, P. and Johnson, S.M. (2000) The affect heuristic in judgments of risks and benefits, *Journal of Behavioral Decision Making*, **13**, 1–17.

30. Bateman, I., Dent, S., Peter, E. and Slovic, P. (2007) The affect heuristic and the attractiveness of simple gambles, *Journal of Behavioral Decision Making*, **20**, 365–380.
31. Simon, D.A., Krawczyk, C., Bleicher, A. and Holyoak, K.J. (2008) The transience of constructed preferences, *Journal of Behavioral Decision Making*, **21**, 1–14.
32. Morwitz, V.G., Greenleaf, E.A. and Johnson, E.J. (1998) Divide and prosper: consumers' reactions to partitioned prices, *Journal of Marketing Research*, **35**, 453–463.

Decisions involving multiple objectives: SMART 3

Introduction

As we saw in the last chapter, when decision problems involve a number of objectives, unaided decision-makers tend to avoid making trade-offs between these objectives. This might lead to the rejection of relatively attractive options because their good performance on some objectives is not allowed to compensate for poor performance elsewhere. For example, a supplier might be rejected because of his high price, in spite of his fast delivery times and excellent after-sales service. These problems can arise when there is too much information to handle simultaneously, so the decision-maker is forced to use simplified mental strategies, or heuristics, in order to make a choice.

This chapter will explore how decision analysis can be used to support decision-makers who have multiple objectives. As we stated in Chapter 1, the central idea is that, by splitting the problem into small parts and focusing on each part separately, the decision-maker is likely to acquire a better understanding of the problem than that gained by taking a holistic view. Also, by requiring a commitment of time and effort, analysis encourages the decision-maker to think deeply about the problem, enabling a rationale that is explicit and defensible to be developed. As a result, the decision-maker should be better able to explain and justify why a particular option is favored.

The methodology outlined in this chapter is underpinned by a set of axioms. We will discuss these towards the end of the chapter, but, for the moment, we can regard them as a set of generally accepted propositions or 'a formalization of common sense' (Keeney[1]). If the decision-maker accepts the axioms, then it follows that the results of the analysis will indicate how he or she should behave if the decision is to be made in a rational way. The analysis is therefore normative or prescriptive; it shows which alternative should be chosen if the decision-maker acts consistently with his or her stated preferences.

The method explained here is normally applied in situations where a particular course of action is regarded as certain (or virtually certain) to lead to a given outcome, so that uncertainty is not a major concern of the analysis (we will discuss techniques for handling risk and uncertainty in later chapters). Nevertheless, there are exceptions to this rule, and we will show later how the method can be adapted to problems involving risk and uncertainty.

The main role of our analysis is to enable the decision-maker to gain an increased understanding of his or her decision problem. If, at the end of the process, no single best course of action has been identified, this does not mean that the analysis was worthless. Often the insights gained may suggest other approaches to the problem or lead to a greater common understanding among a heterogeneous group of decision-makers. They may lead to a complete reappraisal of the nature of the problem or enable a manager to reduce a large number of alternatives to a few, which can then be put forward to higher management with arguments for and against. Although we present the method as a series of stages, the decision-maker is always free at any point to return to an earlier stage or to change the definition of the problem. Indeed, it is likely that this will happen as a deeper understanding of the nature of the problem is gained through the analysis.

Basic terminology

Objectives and attributes

Before proceeding, we need to clarify some of the basic terms we will be using. An *objective* has been defined by Keeney and Raiffa[2] as an indication of the preferred direction of movement. Thus, when stating objectives, we use terms like 'minimize' or 'maximize'. Typical objectives might be to minimize pollution or maximize market share. An *attribute* is used to measure performance in relation to an objective. For example, if our objective is to 'maximize the exposure of a television advertisement', we may use the attribute 'number of people surveyed who recall seeing the advertisement' in order to measure the degree to which the objective was achieved. Sometimes we may have to use an attribute that is not directly related to the objective. Such an attribute is referred to as a *proxy attribute*. For example, a company may use the proxy attribute 'staff turnover' to measure how well they are achieving their objective of maximizing job satisfaction for their staff.

Value and utility

For each course of action facing the decision-maker we will be deriving a numerical score to measure its attractiveness to him. If the decision involves no element of risk and uncertainty, we will refer to this score as the *value* of the course of action.

Alternatively, where the decision involves risk and uncertainty, we will refer to this score as the *utility* of the course of action. Utility will be introduced in Chapter 6.

An office location problem

To illustrate the analysis of decisions involving multiple objectives, consider the following problem. A small printing and photocopying business must move from its existing office because the site has been acquired for redevelopment. The owner of the business is considering seven possible new offices, all of which would be rented. Details of the location of these offices and the annual rent payable are given below:

Location of office		Annual rent ($)
Addison Square	(A)	30 000
Bilton Village	(B)	15 000
Carlisle Walk	(C)	5 000
Denver Street	(D)	12 000
Elton Street	(E)	30 000
Filton Village	(F)	15 000
Gorton Square	(G)	10 000

While the owner would like to keep his costs as low as possible, he would also like to take other factors into account. For example, the Addison Square office is in a prestigious location close to potential customers, but it is expensive to rent. It is also an old, dark building that will not be comfortable for staff to work in. In contrast, the Bilton Village office is a new building that will provide excellent working conditions, but it is several miles from the center of town, where most potential customers are to be found. The owner is unsure how to set about making his choice, given the number of factors involved.

An overview of the analysis

The technique that we will use to analyze the office location problem is based on the simple multi-attribute rating technique (SMART).[3] SMART has been widely applied because of its relative simplicity and transparency, which means that decision-makers from many different backgrounds can easily apply the method and understand its recommendations. Although SMART may not always capture all the detail and complexities of a decision, it can be an excellent method for illuminating the important aspects of the problem and how they relate to each other. Often this is sufficient for a decision to be made with confidence and insight.

The main stages in the analysis are shown below:

Stage 1: *Identify the decision-maker (or decision-makers)*. In our problem we will assume that this is just the business owner, but in Chapter 14 we will look at the application of SMART to problems involving groups of decision-makers.

Stage 2: *Identify the alternative courses of action*. In our problem these are, of course, the different offices the owner can choose.

Stage 3: *Identify the attributes that are relevant to the decision problem*. The attributes that distinguish the different offices will be factors such as rent, size and quality of working conditions. In the next section we will show how a value tree can be useful when identifying relevant attributes.

Stage 4: For each attribute, assign values to *measure the performance of the alternatives on that attribute*. For example, how well do the offices compare when considering the quality of the working conditions they offer?

Stage 5: *Determine a weight for each attribute*. This may reflect how important the attribute is to the decision-maker (although we will discuss the problem of using importance weights later).

Stage 6: *For each alternative, take a weighted average of the values assigned to that alternative*. This will give us a measure of how well an office performs over all the attributes.

Stage 7: Make a provisional decision.

Stage 8: *Perform sensitivity analysis* to see how robust the decision is to changes in the figures supplied by the decision-maker.

Constructing a value tree

Stages 1 and 2 of our analysis have already been completed: we know who the decision-maker is and we have identified the alternatives open to him. The next step is to determine the attributes that the decision-maker considers to be relevant to his problem. Recall that attributes are used to measure the performance of courses of action on the objectives. To do this, we aim to arrive at a set of attributes that will allow us to measure performance on a numeric scale. However, the initial attributes elicited from the decision-maker may be vague (e.g. he might say that he is looking for the office that will be 'the best for his business'), and they may therefore need to be broken down into more specific attributes before measurement can take place. A value tree can be useful here (Figure 3.1).

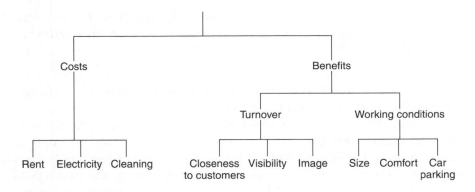

Figure 3.1 – A value tree for the office location problem

We can start constructing the tree by addressing the attributes that represent the general concerns of the decision-maker. Initially, the owner identifies two main attributes, which he decides to call 'costs' and 'benefits'. There is no restriction on the number of attributes that the decision-maker can initially specify (e.g. our decision-maker might have specified 'short-term costs', 'long-term costs', 'convenience of the move' and 'benefits' as his initial attributes). Nor is there any requirement to categorize the main attributes as costs and benefits. In some applications (e.g. Wooler and Barclay[4]), 'the risk of the options' is an initial attribute. Buede and Choisser[5] describe an engineering design application for the US Defense Communications Agency, where the main attributes are 'the effectiveness of the system' (i.e. factors such as quality of performance, survivability in the face of physical attack, etc.) and 'implementation' (i.e. manning, ease of transition from the old system, etc.).

We next need to break down the cost and benefits of the offices into more specific attributes that will make it easier for us to compare the locations. The owner identifies three main costs that are of concern to him: the annual rent, the cost of electricity (for heating, lighting, operating equipment, etc.) and the cost of having the office regularly cleaned. Similarly, he decides that benefits can be subdivided into 'potential for improved turnover' and 'staff working conditions'. However, he thinks that he will have difficulty comparing each office's potential for improving turnover without identifying more specific attributes that will have an impact on turnover. He considers these attributes to be 'the closeness of the office to potential customers', 'the visibility of the site' (much business is generated from people who see the office while passing by) and 'the image of the location' (a decaying building in a back street may convey a poor image and lead to a loss of business). Similarly, the owner feels that he will be better able to compare the working conditions of the offices if he breaks down this attribute into 'size', 'comfort' and 'car-parking facilities'.

Having constructed a value tree, how can we judge whether it is an accurate and useful representation of the decision-maker's concerns? Keeney and Raiffa[2] have suggested five criteria that can be used to judge the tree:

(i) *Completeness*. If the tree is complete, all the attributes that are of concern to the decision-maker will have been included.

(ii) *Operationality*. This criterion is met when all the lowest-level attributes in the tree are specific enough for the decision-maker to evaluate and compare them for the different options. For example, if our decision-maker felt that he was unable to judge the 'image' of the locations on a numeric scale, the tree would not be operational. In this case we could attempt to decompose image further into new attributes that would be capable of being assessed, or we could attempt to find a proxy attribute for image.

(iii) *Decomposability*. This criterion requires that the attractiveness of an option on one attribute can be assessed independently of its attractiveness on other attributes. If the owner feels unable to assess the relative comfort afforded by the offices separately without also considering their size, then decomposability has not been achieved. Decomposability means that the decision-maker can focus on how well the options perform on each attribute separately, unencumbered by the need to think at the same time about their performance on other attributes. This clearly simplifies the assessment process. If we find that we have not achieved decomposability, we will need to look again at the tree to see if we can redefine or regroup these attributes.

(iv) *Absence of redundancy*. If two attributes duplicate each other because they actually represent the same thing, then one of these attributes is clearly redundant. For example, the owner may mistakenly include both 'size' and 'spaciousness' in his tree. If duplicated attributes are not eliminated, then they will be double-counted and hence have undue weight when the final decision is made.

(v) *Minimum size*. If the tree is too large, any meaningful analysis may be impossible. To ensure that this does not happen, attributes should not be decomposed beyond the level where they can be evaluated. Sometimes the size of the tree can be reduced by eliminating attributes that do not distinguish between the options. For example, if all the offices in our problem offered identical car-parking facilities, then this attribute could be removed from the tree.

Sometimes it may be necessary to find compromises between these criteria. For example, to make the tree operational, it may be necessary to increase its size. Often, several attempts at formulating a tree may be required before an acceptable structure is arrived at. This process of modification is well described in an application reported by Brownlow and Watson,[6] where a value tree was being used in a decision problem relating to the transportation of nuclear waste. The tree went through a number of stages of development as new insights were gained into the nature of the problem.

Measuring how well the options perform on each attribute

Having identified the attributes that are of concern to the owner, the next step is to find out how well the different offices perform on each of the lowest level attributes in the value tree. Determining the annual costs of operating the offices is relatively straightforward. The owner already knows the annual rent, and he is able to obtain estimates of cleaning and electricity costs from companies that supply these services. Details of all these costs are given in Table 3.1.

At a later stage in our analysis we will need to trade off the costs against the benefits. This can be an extremely difficult judgment to make. Edwards and Newman[7] consider this kind of judgment to be 'the least secure and most uncomfortable to make' of all the judgments required in decisions involving multiple objectives. Because of this, we will now ignore the costs until the end of our analysis and, for the moment, simply concentrate on the benefit attributes.

In measuring these attributes, our task will be made easier if we can identify variables to represent the attributes. For example, the size of an office can be represented by its floor area in square feet. Similarly, the distance of the office from the town center may provide a suitable approximation for the attribute 'distance from potential customers'. However, for other attributes such as 'image' and 'comfort' it will be more difficult to find a variable that can be quantified. Because of this, there are two approaches that can be used to measure the performance of the offices on each attribute: direct rating and the use of value functions.

Table 3.1 – Costs associated with the seven offices

Office	Annual rent ($)	Annual cleaning costs ($)	Annual electricity costs ($)	Total cost ($)
Addison Square	30 000	3 000	2 000	35 000
Bilton Village	15 000	2 000	800	17 800
Carlisle Walk	5 000	1 000	700	6 700
Denver Street	12 000	1 000	1 100	14 100
Elton Street	30 000	2 500	2 300	34 800
Filton Village	15 000	1 000	2 600	18 600
Gorton Square	10 000	1 100	900	12 000

Direct rating

Let us first consider those attributes that cannot be represented by easily quantifiable variables, starting with the attribute 'image'. The owner is first asked to rank the locations in terms of their image from the most preferred to the least preferred. His rankings are as follows:

(1) Addison Square
(2) Elton Street
(3) Filton Village
(4) Denver Street
(5) Gorton Square
(6) Bilton Village
(7) Carlisle Walk

Addison Square, the best location for image, can now be given a value for image of 100, and Carlisle Walk, the location with the least appealing image, can be given a value of 0. As we explain below, any two numbers could have been used here, as long as the number allocated to the most preferred location is higher than that allocated to the least preferred. However, the use of 0 and 100 makes the judgments that follow much easier, and it also simplifies the arithmetic.

The owner is now asked to rate the other locations so that that the space between the values he gives to the offices represents his strength of preference for one office over another in terms of image. Figure 3.2 shows the values assigned by the owner. It can be seen that the improvement in image between Carlisle Walk and Gorton Square is perceived by the owner to be twice as preferable as the improvement in image between Carlisle Walk and Bilton Village. Similarly, the improvement in image between Carlisle Walk and Addison Square is seen to be 10 times more preferable than the improvement between Carlisle Walk and Bilton Village.

Note that it is the *interval* (or improvement) between the points in the scale that we compare. We cannot say that the image of Gorton Square is twice as preferable as that of the Bilton Village office. This is because the allocation of a zero to represent the image of Carlisle Walk was arbitrary, and we therefore have what is known as an *interval scale*, which allows only intervals between points to be compared. The Fahrenheit and Celsius temperature scales are the most well-known examples of interval scales. We cannot, for example, say that water at 80 °C is twice the temperature of water at 40 °C. You can verify this by converting the temperatures to degrees Fahrenheit to obtain 175 °F and 104 °F respectively. Clearly, the first temperature is no longer twice the second temperature. However, we can say that an increase in temperature

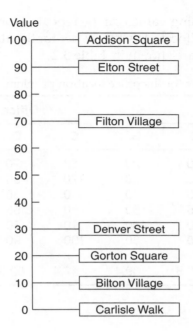

Figure 3.2 – A value scale for office image

from 40 to 80 °C is twice as great as an increase from 40 to 60 °C. You will find that such a comparison does apply, even if we convert the temperatures to degrees Fahrenheit.

Having established an initial set of values for image, these should be checked to see if they consistently represent the preferences of the decision-maker. We can achieve this by asking him, for example, if he is happy that the improvement in image between Elton Street and Addison Square is roughly as preferable as the improvement in image between Gorton Square and Denver Street. Similarly, is he happy that the improvement in image between Carlisle Walk and Denver Street is less preferable than that between Denver Street and Elton Street? The answers to these questions may lead to a revision of the values. Of course, if the owner finds it very difficult to make these sorts of judgment, we may need to return to the value tree and see if we can break the image down into more measurable attributes. Nevertheless, it should be emphasized that the numbers allocated by the owner to the different offices do not need to be precise. As we will see later, the choice of a course of action is generally fairly robust, and it often requires quite substantial changes in the figures supplied by the decision-maker before another option is preferred.

This procedure for obtaining values can be repeated for the other, less easily quantified attributes. The values allocated by the owner for the attributes 'comfort', 'visibility' and 'car-parking facilities' are shown in Table 3.2.

Table 3.2 – Values and weights for the office location problem

Attribute	Weight	Office						
		A	B	C	D	E	F	G
Closeness	32	100	20	80	70	40	0	60
Visibility	26	60	80	70	50	60	0	100
Image	23	100	10	0	30	90	70	20
Size	10	75	30	0	55	100	0	50
Comfort	6	0	100	10	30	60	80	50
Car parking	3	90	30	100	90	70	0	80
Aggregate Benefits		80.8	39.4	47.4	52.3	64.8	20.9	60.2

Value functions

Consider next the benefit attributes that can be represented by easily quantified variables, starting with the owner's relative strength of preference for offices of different sizes. The floor area of the offices is shown below:

		Floor area (ft^2)
Addison Square	(A)	1000
Bilton Village	(B)	550
Carlisle Walk	(C)	400
Denver Street	(D)	800
Elton Street	(E)	1500
Filton Village	(F)	400
Gorton Square	(G)	700

Now it may be that an increase in area from 500 to 1000 ft^2 is very attractive to the owner, because this would considerably improve working conditions. However, the improvements to be gained from an increase from 1000 to 1500 ft^2 might be marginal and make this increase less attractive. To translate the owner's preferences for these floor areas into values on a 0–100 scale, we can proceed as follows.

The owner judges that, the larger the office, the more attractive it is. The largest office, Elton Street, has an area of 1500 ft^2, so we can give 1500 ft^2 a value of 100. In mathematical notation, we can say that $v(1500) = 100$, where $v(1500)$ means 'the value of 1500 ft^2'. Similarly, the smallest offices (Carlisle Walk and Filton Village) both have areas of 400 ft^2, so $v(400) = 0$.

We now need to find the value of the office areas that fall between the most preferred and least preferred areas. We could ask the owner directly to rate the areas of the offices under consideration using the methods of the previous section. However, because areas involving rather awkward numbers are involved, it may be easier to derive what is known as a value function. Several methods can be used to elicit a value function, but one of the most widely applied is *bisection*.

Bisection requires the owner to identify an office area halfway between the least preferred area (400 ft^2) and the most preferred area (1500 ft^2). Note that this area does not necessarily have to correspond to that of one of the offices under consideration. Initially, the owner suggests that the midpoint area would be 1000 ft^2. This implies that an increase in area from 400 to 1000 ft^2 is just as attractive as an increase from 1000 to 1500 ft^2. However, after some thought, he rejects this value. The increases from smaller areas will, he reasons, reduce overcrowding and so be much more attractive than increases from larger areas, which would only lead to minor improvements. He is then offered other candidates for the midpoint position (for example, 900 and 600 ft^2), but rejects these values as well. Finally, he agrees that 700 ft^2 has the midpoint value, so $v(700) = 50$.

Having identified the midpoint value, the decision-maker is now asked to identify the 'quarter-points'. The first of these will be the office area that has a value halfway between the least preferred area (400 ft^2) and the midpoint area (700 ft^2). He decides that this is 500 ft^2, so $v(500) = 25$. Similarly, we ask him to identify an area that has a value halfway between the midpoint area (700 ft^2) and the best area (1500 ft^2). He judges this to be 1000 ft^2, which implies that $v(1000) = 75$. We now have the values for five floor areas, and this enables us to plot the value function for office size, which is shown in Figure 3.3. This value function can now be used to estimate the values for the actual areas of the offices under consideration. For example, the Bilton Village office has an area of 550 ft^2, and the curve suggests that the value of this area is about 30.

A similar method can be applied to the attribute 'closeness to customers'. This attribute has been represented by the variable 'distance from town center', and the value function is shown in Figure 3.4. Note that the greater the distance from the town center, the lower the value will be. The curve also suggests that a move from 0 to 2 miles from the town center is far more damaging to business than a move from 6 to 8 miles. The values identified for the seven offices in terms of 'office area' and 'closeness to customers' are shown in Table 3.2.

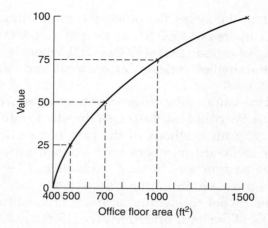

Figure 3.3 – Constructing a value function for office floor area

Determining the weights of the attributes

Having obtained the values shown in Table 3.2, the owner now needs to combine these so that the overall attractiveness of each office can be measured across all of the attributes (except cost). To do this, he needs to assign a weight to each attribute.

A common way of doing this is to assign numbers to reflect the relative importance of the attributes (we will refer to these as 'importance weights'). For example, the owner might consider office floor area to be five times more important than distance from customers and hence give weights of 5 to floor area and 1 to distance from customers.

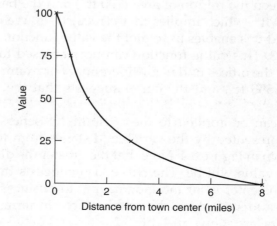

Figure 3.4 – A value function for distance from customers

Unfortunately, this approach can lead to serious problems. To see this, consider the following decision.

Suppose that the choice is between just two offices, X and Y, and that we are evaluating these on only two attributes: office area and distance from customers. The table below shows how the offices perform on these two attributes:

Office	Floor area	Distance from customers
X	400 ft^2	0 miles
Y	402 ft^2	15 miles

The values assigned to the offices would therefore be as follows:

Office	Floor area	Distance from customers
X	0	100
Y	100	0
Weights	5	1

If we assume that the weights of 5 and 1 apply, then the aggregate value for each office can be obtained by multiplying each value by its weight and summing the results, as shown below:

$$\text{Office X: Aggregate value} = (5 \times 0) + (1 \times 100) = 100$$
$$\text{Office Y: Aggregate value} = (5 \times 100) + (1 \times 0) = 500$$

According to this, the decision-maker should choose office Y. This is because it has the largest floor area and therefore performed best on the attribute that was considered to be most important. However, a look at the original figures reveals that Y's floor area exceeds X's by only 2 ft^2! Indeed, the weights imply that the decision-maker is prepared to sacrifice moving 15 miles closer to his customers to gain just two extra square feet of office space, which seems an unlikely proposition.

The problem with importance weights is that they may not take into account the *range* between the least and most preferred options on each attribute (see von Winterfeldt and Edwards[8]). If the options perform very similarly on a particular attribute, so that the range between worst and best is small, then this attribute is unlikely to be important *in the decision*, even though the decision-maker may consider it to be an important attribute per se. Taking this to extremes, suppose that both offices had a floor area of 400 ft^2. In this case, the weight attached to floor area should be zero because this attribute has no importance in discriminating between the two offices.

Fortunately, this problem can be avoided by using *swing weights*. These are derived by asking the decision-maker to compare a change (or swing) from the least preferred to the most preferred value on one attribute with a similar change in another attribute.

The simplest approach is to proceed as follows. Consider the lowest-level attributes on the 'Benefits' branch of the value tree (Figure 3.1). The owner is asked to imagine a hypothetical office with all these attributes at their least preferred levels, that is, an office that is the greatest distance (i.e. 8 miles) from the town center, has the worst position for visibility and has the worst image, the smallest size and so on. Then he is asked, if just one of these attributes could be moved to its best level, which would he choose? The owner selects 'closeness to customers'. After this change has been made, he is asked which attribute he would next choose to move to its best level, and so on, until all the attributes have been ranked. The owner's rankings are as follows:

(1) Closeness to customers
(2) Visibility
(3) Image
(4) Size
(5) Comfort
(6) Car-parking facilities

We can now give 'closeness to customers' a weight of 100. The other weights are assessed as follows. The owner is asked to compare a swing from the least visible location to the most visible, with a swing from the most distant location from customers to the closest location. After some thought, he decides that the swing in 'visibility' is 80% as important as the swing in 'closeness to customers', so visibility is given a weight of 80. Similarly, a swing from the worst 'image' to the best is considered to be 70% as important as a swing from the worst to the best location for 'closeness to customers', so 'image' is assigned a weight of 70. The procedure is repeated for all the other lower-level attributes, and Figure 3.5 illustrates the results. As shown below, the six weights obtained sum to 310, and it is conventional to 'normalize' them so that they add up to 100 (this will make later stages of the analysis easier to understand); normalization is achieved by simply dividing each weight by the sum of the weights (310) and multiplying by 100:

Attribute	Original weights	Normalized weights (to nearest whole number)
Closeness to customers	100	32
Visibility	80	26
Image	70	23
Size	30	10
Comfort	20	6
Car-parking facilities	10	3
	310	100

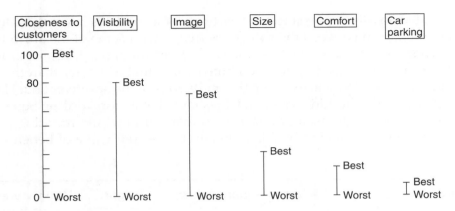

Figure 3.5 – Derivation of swing weights. For example, a swing from the worst to the best location for visibility is considered to be 80% as important as a swing from the worst to the best location for closeness to customers

The weights for the higher-level attributes in the value tree, 'turnover' and 'working conditions', are now found by summing the appropriate lower-level weights, so the weight for turnover is 81 (i.e. 32 + 26 + 23) and the weight for working conditions is 19 (i.e. 10 + 6 + 3). Note that experiments by Pöyhönen et al.[9] and Hämäläinen and Alaja[10] have indicated that the weight people attach to a given attribute is sensitive to whether or not the attribute has been split in the value tree into lower-level attributes. For example, the weight attached to 'car-parking facilities' in the office value tree might have been different if the decision-maker had decided to split this attribute into three subattributes: 'quality of car-park surface', 'security of car park' and 'distance of car park from office'. Because of this, Pöyhönen et al.[9] suggest that it is also worth asking decision-makers what weight they would attach to an attribute if it were split into subattributes. Any inconsistencies between the two sets of weights can then be discussed and, hopefully, resolved.

Aggregating the benefits using the additive model

We now have (1) a measure of how well each office performs on each attribute and (2) weights that enable us to compare the values allocated to one attribute with the values allocated to the others. The next step is to calculate how well each office performs overall by combining the six value scores allocated to that office.

To do this, we will assume that the additive model is appropriate. As we show below, this simply involves adding an office's weighted value scores together to obtain a measure of its overall benefits. The additive model is by far the most widely used, but it is not suitable for all circumstances. In particular, the model is inappropriate where there is an interaction between the values associated with some of the attributes. For example, when choosing a house, an attractive architecture and a pleasant garden may complement each other, leading to a combined value that is greater than the sum of the individual values. We will examine the limitations of the additive model later.

The calculations for the additive model are shown below for Addison Square (each value is multiplied by the weight attached to that attribute; the resulting products are then summed and divided by 100 to obtain the overall value of benefits at that location):

Attribute	Addison Square values	Weight	Value × weight
Closeness to customers	100	32	3200
Visibility	60	26	1560
Image	100	23	2300
Size	75	10	750
Comfort	0	6	0
Car-parking facilities	90	3	270
			8080

It can be seen that the aggregate value for Addison Square is 8080/100, i.e. 80.8. Table 3.2 gives a summary of the values obtained for all the offices and their aggregate values. It can be seen that Addison Square has the highest value for benefits, and Filton Village the lowest. However, so far we have ignored the costs associated with the offices, and the next section shows how these can be taken into account.

Trading benefits against costs

So far we have ignored the costs of the offices because of the difficulties decision-makers often have in making judgments about the trade-off between money and qualitative benefits. If this is not a problem, we can treat cost as just another attribute. In this case we can allocate values to the various costs, with a value of 100 being given to the office with the lowest costs and a value of 0 to the office with the highest. A swing weight can then be elicited for cost, and the office achieving the highest aggregate value would be the one the owner should choose.

However, because our owner does have difficulties in judging the cost–benefit trade-off, we can proceed as follows. In Figure 3.6 the aggregate value of benefits has been plotted against the annual cost for each of the offices. Note that the cost scale has been 'turned round', so that the lower (and therefore more preferable) costs are to the right. This is to make this graph comparable with ones we will meet later in the

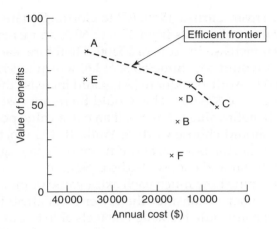

Figure 3.6 – A plot of benefits against costs for the seven offices

book. Clearly, the higher an office appears on the benefits scale, and the further to the right on the cost scale, the more attractive it will be. If we compare Addison Square (A) with Elton Street (E), it can be seen that, while both have similar costs, Addison Square has higher benefits. It would not therefore be worth considering Elton Street, and this office is said to be *dominated* by Addison Square. Similarly, Gorton Square (G) not only has lower costs but also has higher benefits compared with Bilton Village (B), Denver Street (D) and Filton Village (F). Therefore, B, D and F are also dominated offices. Thus, the only locations that are worth considering are Addison Square (A), Gorton Square (G) and Carlisle Walk (C). These non-dominated offices are said to lie on the *efficient frontier*.

The choice between the three offices on the efficient frontier will depend on the relative weight the owner attaches to costs and benefits. If he is much more concerned about benefits, then Addison Square will be his choice. Alternatively, if he is more concerned to keep his costs low, then he should choose Carlisle Walk. Gorton Square would be an intermediate choice. It costs $5300 more per year than Carlisle Walk, but offers slightly higher benefits.

This information may be sufficient for the owner to make a choice. At the very least, it should illuminate his understanding of the decision problem. He may be surprised that Bilton Village has fared so badly or that Carlisle Walk has done so well, and he may wish to check back through the data he has supplied to see why this has happened.

However, it is possible that the decision-maker still feels unable to choose between the three offices on the efficient frontier and thinks that a more formal approach would help him. If this is the case, then the following procedure suggested by Edwards and Newman[7] can be used.

Consider first a move from Carlisle Walk (C) to Gorton Square (G). This would lead to an increase in the value of benefits from 47.4 to 60.2, an increase of 12.8. However, it would also lead to an increase in costs of $5300. Therefore, each one-point increase in the value of benefits would cost him $5300/12.8, which is $414. Similarly, a move from Gorton Square (G) to Addison Square (A) would increase the value of benefits by 20.6 points at an extra cost of $23 000. This would therefore cost $23 000/20.6, which is $1117 for each extra benefit value point. So, if an extra value point is worth less than $414 to the owner, he should choose Carlisle Walk. If it is worth between $414 and $1117, he should choose Gorton Square, and if it is worth paying more than $1117 for each extra value point, he should choose Addison Square.

Now we need to determine how much each extra value point is worth to the owner. To do this, we ask the owner to consider the lower-level attributes in the value tree. We ask him to identify an attribute for which he feels able to put a monetary value on the improvement from the worst position to the best position. We ask him to do this assuming that nothing else changes. For example, how much would he be prepared to pay to improve the size of an office from 400 ft^2 (equivalent to the smallest on his list) to 1500 ft^2 (equivalent to the largest), assuming that no other attributes change? The owner indicates that he is most comfortable in putting a monetary value on the improvement for 'image'. He indicates that he would be prepared to pay an extra $15 000 per year to upgrade the image of an office from one equivalent to the worst image to one equivalent to the best, all else remaining equal. This means that he considers that it would be worth paying $15 000 for a 100-point increase in the value of image. Now the normalized weight of image is 23% of the total weight allocated to the attributes. So an increase of 100 points on the image scale would increase the aggregate value of an office's benefits by 23 points. Therefore, the owner is prepared to pay $15 000 to gain 23 points in the value of aggregate benefits. This implies that he is prepared to pay $15 000/23 or $652 per point. He should therefore choose the Gorton Square office.

Of course, the data we have been dealing with are far less precise than the above analysis might have implied, and it is unlikely that the owner will be 100% confident about the figures that he has put forward. Before making a firm recommendation, we should therefore explore the effect of changes in these figures. This topic is covered in the next section.

Sensitivity analysis

Sensitivity analysis is used to examine how robust the choice of an alternative is to changes in the figures used in the analysis. The owner is worried about the weight of turnover (i.e. 81) relative to working conditions (i.e. 19), and he would like to know what would happen if this weight were changed. Figure 3.7 shows how the value of

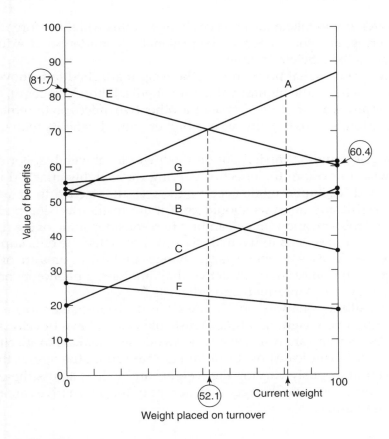

Figure 3.7 – Sensitivity analysis for weight placed on turnover

benefits for the different offices varies with changes in the weight placed on turnover. For example, if turnover had a weight of zero, this would imply that the three turnover attributes would also have zero weights, so the weights for the six lowest-level benefit attributes would now be: closeness to customers 0, visibility 0, image 0, size 30, comfort 20 and car parking 10. These normalize to 0, 0, 0, 50, 33.3 and 16.7 respectively, which would mean that Elton Street (E), for example, would have benefits with a value of 81.7. At the other extreme, if turnover had a weight of 100 (and therefore working conditions a weight of zero), the value of benefits for Elton Street would be 60.4. The line joining these points shows the value of benefits for Elton Street for turnover weights between 0 and 100.

It can be seen that Elton Street gives the highest value of benefits as long as the weight placed on turnover is less than 52.1. If the weight is above this figure, then Addison Square (A) has the highest value of benefits. As the owner assigned a weight of 81 to turnover, it will take a fairly large change in this weight before Elton Street is worth considering, and the owner can be reasonably confident that Addison Square should appear on the efficient frontier.

Figure 3.7 also shows that no change in the weight attached to turnover will make the other offices achieve the highest value for benefits. Filton Village (F), in particular, scores badly on any weight. If we consider the other two offices on the efficient frontier, we see that Gorton Square (G) always has higher valued benefits than Carlisle Walk (C).

Similar analysis could be carried out on the lower level weights. For example, the owner may wish to explore the effect of varying the weights attached to 'closeness to customers' and 'visibility' while keeping the weight attached to 'image' constant. Carrying out sensitivity analysis should contribute to the decision-maker's under-standing of his problem, and it may lead him to reconsider some of the figures he has supplied. In many cases, sensitivity analysis also shows that the data supplied do not need to be precise. As we saw above, large changes in these figures are often required before one option becomes more attractive than another: a phenomenon referred to as 'flat maxima' by von Winterfeldt and Edwards.[8]

Note that sensitivity analysis only allows the decision-maker to investigate the effect of changing one weight at a time. Mustajoki *et al.*[11] have developed a method called interval sensitivity analysis which allows decision-makers to specify ranges for weights and values to indicate how uncertain they are about the figures they have put forward. By simultaneously varying the weights and values across these ranges, the method shows how sensitive the aggregate scores of the alternatives are to combined changes in these figures.

Theoretical considerations

The axioms of the method

In our analysis of the office location problem, we implicitly made a number of as-sumptions about the decision-maker's preferences. These assumptions, which are listed below, can be regarded as the axioms of the method. They represent a set of postulates that may be regarded as reasonable. If the decision-maker accepts these axioms, and if he is rational (i.e. if he behaves consistently in relation to the axioms), then he should also accept the preference rankings indicated by the method. Let us now consider the axioms:

(1) *Decidability*. We assumed that the owner was able to decide which of two options he preferred. For example, we assumed that he could state whether the improve-ment in image between Carlisle Walk and Gorton Square was greater than the

improvement between Carlisle Walk and Bilton Village. It may have been that the owner was very unsure about making this comparison, or he may have refused to make it at all.

(2) *Transitivity*. The owner preferred the image of Addison Square to that of Bilton Village (i.e. A to B). He also preferred the image of Bilton Village to that of Carlisle Walk (i.e. B to C). If transitivity applies, then the owner must therefore also prefer the image of Addison Square to that of Carlisle Walk (i.e. A to C).

(3) *Summation*. This implies that, if the owner prefers A to B and B to C, then the strength of preference of A over C must be greater than the strength of preference of A over B (or B over C).

(4) *Solvability*. This assumption was necessary for the bisection method of obtaining a value function. Here, the owner was asked to identify a distance from the center of town that had a value halfway between the worst and best distances. It was implicitly assumed that such a distance existed. In some circumstances there may be 'gaps' in the values that an attribute can assume. For example, the existence of a zone of planning restrictions between the center of the town and certain possible locations might mean that siting an office at a distance that has a value halfway between the worst and best distances is not a possibility that the decision-maker can envisage.

(5) *Finite upper and lower bounds for value*. In assessing values, we had to assume that the best option was not so wonderful and the worst option was not so awful that values of plus and minus infinity would be assigned to these options.

Assumptions made when aggregating values

In our analysis we used the additive model to aggregate the values for the different attributes. As we pointed out, the use of this model is not appropriate where there is an interaction between the scores on the attributes. In technical terms, in order to apply the model, we need to assume that *mutual preference independence* exists between the attributes.

To demonstrate preference independence, let us suppose that our office location problem only involves two attributes: 'distance from customers' and 'office size'. Our decision-maker is now offered two offices, X and Y. These are the same size (1000 ft^2), but X is closer to customers, as shown below:

Office	Distance from customers	Office floor area
X	3 miles	1000 ft^2
Y	5 miles	1000 ft^2

Not surprisingly, the decision-maker prefers X to Y. Now suppose that we change the size of both offices to 400 ft^2. If, as is likely, the decision-maker still prefers X to Y, his preference for a distance of 3 miles over a distance of 5 miles has clearly been unaffected by the change in office size. This might remain true if we change the size of both offices to any other possible floor area. If this is the case, we can say that 'distance from customers' is preference independent of 'office size' because the preference for one distance over another does not depend on the size of the offices.

If we also find that 'size of office' is preference independent of 'distance from customers', then we can say that the two attributes are *mutually preference independent*. Note that mutual preference independence does not automatically follow. When choosing a holiday destination, you may prefer a warmer climate to a cooler one, irrespective of whether or not the hotel has an open-air or indoor swimming pool. However, your preference between hotels with open-air or indoor swimming pools will probably depend on whether the local climate is warm or cool.

To see what can happen when the additive model is applied to a problem where mutual preference independence does not exist, consider the following problem. Suppose now that our office location decision depends only on the attributes 'visibility' and 'image' and the owner has allocated weights of 40 and 60 to these two attributes. Two new offices, P and Q, are being compared, and the values assigned to the offices for each of these attributes are shown below (0 = worst, 100 = best):

Office	Visibility	Image
P	0	100
Q	100	0

Using the additive model, the aggregate value of benefits for P will be

$$(40 \times 0) + (60 \times 100) = 6000, \text{ i.e. } 60 \text{ after dividing by } 100$$

while the aggregate value of benefits for Q will be

$$(40 \times 100) + (60 \times 0) = 4000, \text{ i.e. } 40 \text{ after dividing by } 100$$

This clearly suggests that the decision-maker should choose office P. However, it may be that he considers image only to be of value if the office is highly visible. Office P's good image is, he thinks, virtually worthless because it is not in a highly visible location, and he might therefore prefer office Q. Thus, if image is not preference independent of visibility, the additive model will not correctly represent the owner's preferences.

How can the absence of mutual preference independence be identified? The most obvious way in which this will reveal itself is in the use of phrases like 'this depends on . . .' when the decision-maker responds to questions. For example, when asked to assign a value to the 'image' of an office, our decision-maker might well have said 'that depends on how visible the office is'.

If mutual preference independence does not exist, it is usually possible to return to the value tree and redefine the attributes so that a set of attributes that are mutually preference independent can be identified. For example, perhaps visibility and image could be replaced with a single attribute 'ability to attract casual customers'.

In the occasional problems where this is not possible, other models are available that can handle the interaction between the attributes. The most well known of these is the multiplicative model. Consider again the case of the house purchase decision where the quality of the architecture and attractiveness of the garden complemented each other. If we let $v(A)$ = the value of the architecture of a given house and $v(G)$ = a value for the attractiveness of the garden, then we might find that the following represented the overall value of the house:

$$\text{Value} = 0.6v(A) + 0.3v(G) + 0.1v(A)v(G)$$

The numbers in the above expression represent the weights (note that they sum to 1), and the last term, which involves multiplying the values together, represents the interaction between architecture and garden. Because the multiplicative model is not widely used, we will not consider it in detail. Longer discussions can be found in Bodily[12] and von Winterfeldt and Edwards.[8]

Conflicts between intuitive and analytic results

It may be that, if the decision-maker had viewed the problem holistically, then he would have ranked his preferences for the offices in a very different order from that obtained through our analysis. This could be because the problem was too large and complex for him to handle as a whole, so that his true preferences were not reflected in his holistic judgments. An analogy can be made with an attempt to answer a mathematical problem by using mental arithmetic rather than a calculator. This view is supported by research suggesting that the correlation of preference rankings derived from holistic judgments with those derived from SMART-type analyses decreases as the number of attributes in the problem gets larger. In other words, the larger the problem, the less reliable holistic judgments may be (see von Winterfeldt and Edwards[8] for a summary of this research).

Alternatively, discrepancies between holistic and analytic results may result when the axioms are not acceptable to the decision-maker. It is possible that the decision-maker could argue the case for a different set of sensible axioms. As long as he behaved consistently with these axioms, we could not argue that his rejection of the results of our analysis was irrational.

Nevertheless, any conflict between holistic and analytic rankings should be examined, as it may suggest that an important element of the problem has not been captured by the analysis. For example, an important attribute may have been left out, or the interaction between two attributes may not have been taken into account. We can, of course, never be certain that a decision model is a faithful representation of the decision-maker's preferences. In a computer model of a traffic system, for example, the model's validity can be assessed by comparing its predictions with the behavior of the real system, but here we are attempting to model the decision-maker's beliefs and attitudes, for which there is no physical analog. This begs the question: at what point do we decide that a decision model is adequate so that further refinements and revisions are not worth carrying out?

One approach to this question is to use Phillips'[13] concept of a *requisite decision model*. We will examine this idea in more detail in Chapter 13 in the context of group decision-making, but, briefly, a model is considered to be requisite when it provides the decision-maker with enough guidance and insight to decide upon a course of action. Thus, at the point where the decision-maker knows what to do next, a requisite model has been achieved. Phillips argues that:

> the modeling process uses the sense of unease among the problem owners about the results of the current model as a signal that further modeling may be needed, or that intuition may be wrong. If exploration of the discrepancy between holistic judgment and model results shows the model to be at fault, then the model is not requisite – it is not yet sufficient to solve the problem. The model can be considered requisite only when no new intuitions emerge about the problem.

Thus, the requisite modeling process does not attempt to obtain an exact representation of the decision-maker's beliefs and preferences, or to prescribe an optimal solution to his problem. However, by exploiting the conflicts between the results of the analysis and his intuitive judgments, it will help him to resolve conflicts and inconsistencies in his thinking. As a deeper understanding of the problem is obtained, the model will be revised and the discrepancy between the analytical and intuitive judgments will be reduced. Eventually, the decision-maker will find that the model provides enough guidance for him to reach a decision.

Value-focused thinking

Earlier we set out the process of applying SMART as a series of stages. Although we emphasized that the application of the method is not a linear process through these stages – decision-makers will move backwards and forwards through the stages as they learn more about their decision problem – the order of the stages we presented implies what is known as 'alternative-focused thinking'. We identify the alternative courses of action (stage 2) before we determine the relevant attributes (stage 3). Keeney[14] has proposed an approach that he calls 'value-focused thinking', which essentially involves a reversal of these two stages. In this approach you first determine your 'values' – that is, what objectives (and hence what attributes) are important to you. Only then do you *create* alternatives that might help you to achieve these objectives. These alternatives are then evaluated in the same way as for alternative-focused thinking.

Keeney's approach is particularly worth considering for major strategic or life-changing decisions where there is a need to think deeply about what you want to achieve in life or what the fundamental values of an organization are.[15] Such decisions imply a need to 'think outside the box'. Typical questions that may stimulate a decision-maker to think about values include: 'what would you like to achieve in this situation?' and 'if you had no limitations at all, what would your objectives be?' Having obtained a preliminary list of objectives, the decision-maker is encouraged to consider why each objective is important. For example, the objective 'minimizing travel distance between home and work' may be important to you for several reasons including your desire to minimize your carbon footprint when traveling to work. It is also a good idea to consider what each objective includes in more detail. Minimizing travel distance between home and work might include factors such as the reduced stress as a result of shorter daily journeys, reduced travel costs, being able to keep fit by walking or cycling to work and being able to spend more time with your family – in addition to your reducing your environmental impact. The intention of this process is to stimulate thinking so that all of your fundamental objectives (in Keeney's words, 'what you care about') become apparent.

Summary

In this chapter we have looked at a method for analyzing decision problems where each alternative had several attributes associated with it. This meant that the performance of each alternative had to be measured on each attribute, and then the attributes themselves had to be 'weighed against' each other before a decision could be made. The central idea was that, by splitting the problem into small parts and focusing on each part separately, the decision-maker was likely to acquire a better understanding of his or her problem than would have been achieved by taking a holistic view. We saw that the method required the decision-maker to quantify his or her strengths of preferences. While this may not have been an easy process, we found that the figures put forward did not need to be exact, although we did try to ensure that they were consistent.

The decision problem presented in this chapter was designed to be amenable to hand calculations. This would, however, be an extremely tedious way of approaching larger problems, and for these it would be necessary to use a computer. Packages available include Hiview (Catalyze Ltd) and V·I·S·A (SIMUL8 Corporation), which both have all the features that are needed to carry out a SMART-type analysis, including a facility that allows the user to construct and modify value trees on-screen.

We stated in the Introduction that this method is normally applied where risk and uncertainty are not major concerns of the decision-maker. However, it is possible to apply the method even in these circumstances by treating risk as an attribute. Wooler and Barclay[4] describe such an application involving a strike-prone production facility. (The analysis involved a group of managers in a decision conference.) A value tree was used to decompose 'risk' into lower-level attributes such as 'risk of strikes' and 'public relations risks', and the various strategies were scored in terms of their performance on these attributes using direct rating (for example, the least risky option was allocated the highest value). A second part of the value tree dealt with the benefits of the strategies, and these were similarly scored. A graph such as Figure 3.7 was then used to display the aggregate risk of strategies against their aggregate benefits (rather than costs against benefits). We will consider a similar approach to risk in the context of a group decision problem in Chapter 14. However, a number of techniques have been specially designed to handle decisions involving a large element of risk and uncertainty, and we will consider these methods in later chapters.

Exercises

Additional exercises can be found on the book's website

(1) Formulate a value tree to identify the attributes that are of concern to you when choosing a vacation.

(2) You need a word-processing package for the personal computer in your office. Because your employer will pay for the package, you are not concerned about the cost, but you would like a package that is as easy to use as possible and that also has a wide range of functions such as a thesaurus, spell checker and graphics. After discussing the matter with a friend who is something of an expert in this field, you identify seven potential packages and allocate values to them to reflect their ease of use and available facilities. These values are shown below (0 = worst, 100 = best):

Package	Ease of use	Facilities available
Super Quill	100	30
Easywrite	90	70
Wordright	50	20
Lexico	0	40
Ultraword	20	100
Keywrite	40	0
Fastwrite	85	55

(a) Plot each package's value for 'ease of use' and 'facilities available' on a graph, and hence determine the packages that lie on the efficient frontier.

(b) Suppose that you judge that a switch from a package with the least facilities available to one with the most facilities is only 60% as attractive as a switch from a package that is the least easy to use to one that is the most easy to use. Assuming that mutual preference independence exists between the two attributes, which package should you choose?

(c) After some reflection, you realize that the extra facilities available on a package will be of little value to you if they are going to be difficult to use. What does this imply about your method of analysis in (b)?

(3) A chemical company is expanding its operations, and a disused woollen mill is to be converted into a processing plant. Four companies have submitted designs for the equipment that will be installed in the mill, and a choice has to be made between them. The manager of the chemical company has identified three attributes that he considers to be important in the decision: 'cost', 'environmental impact' and 'reliability'. He has assessed how well each design performs on each attribute by allocating values on a scale from 0 (the worst design) to 100 (the best). These values are shown below, together with the costs that will be incurred if a design is chosen:

Design	Cost ($)	Benefits	
		Environmental impact	Reliability
A	90 000	20	100
B	110 000	70	0
C	170 000	100	90
D	60 000	0	50

(a) The manager is having difficulty in allocating weights to the two benefit attributes. Assuming that the two weights sum to 100 and that mutual preference independence exists between the attributes, perform a sensitivity analysis to show how the design offering the highest value for aggregate benefits will vary depending upon the weight that has been allocated to 'environmental impact'.

(b) Eventually, the manager decides to allocate 'environmental impact' a weight of 30 and 'reliability' a weight of 70. By plotting the benefits and costs of the designs on a graph, identify the designs that lie on the efficient frontier.

(c) The manager also decides that, if he were offered a hypothetical design that had the lowest reliability and the worst environmental impact, he would be prepared to pay $120 000 to convert that design to one that had the best impact on the environment but that still had the lowest level of reliability. Which design should the manager choose?

(4) A British company has won an important contract to supply components regularly to Poland. Four methods of transport are being considered: (i) air, (ii) sea, (iii) road and ferry and (iv) rail and ferry. The company's distribution manager has identified four relevant attributes for the decision: 'punctuality', 'safety of cargo', 'convenience' and 'costs'. She has also allocated weights of 30 to punctuality, 60 to safety of cargo and 10 to convenience. The manager has then rated the performance of each form of transport on the different attributes. The values she has assigned are shown below, together with the estimated annual cost of using each form of transport:

Form of transport	Benefits			Costs ($)
	Punctuality	Safety	Convenience	
Air	100	70	60	150 000
Sea	0	60	80	90 000
Road and Ferry	60	0	100	40 000
Rail and Ferry	70	100	0	70 000

(a) Determine the form of transport that has the highest valued overall benefits, assuming that mutual preference independence exists between the attributes.

(b) For each form of transport, plot the value of overall benefits against costs and hence identify the forms of transport that lie on the efficient frontier.

(c) If the manager would be prepared to pay $70 000 per year to move from the least safe to the most safe form of transport (all else remaining equal), determine which alternative she should select.

(5) A local authority has to decide on the location of a new waste-disposal facility, and five sites are currently being considered: Inston Common, Jones Wood, Peterton, Red Beach and Treehome Valley. In order to help them to choose between the sites, the managers involved in the decision arranged for a decision analyst to attend one of their meetings. The analyst first got the managers to consider the factors that they thought were relevant to the decision, and, after some debate, four factors were identified:

   (i) The visual impact of the site on the local scenery (for example, a site at Treehome Valley would be visible from a nearby beauty spot).
   (ii) The ease with which waste could be transported to the site (for example, Red Beach is only 2 miles from the main town in the area and is close to a main highway, while Inston Common is in a remote spot and its use would lead to a major increase in the volume of transport using the minor roads in the area).
   (iii) The risk that the use of the site would lead to contamination of the local environment (e.g. because of leakages of chemicals into watercourses).
   (iv) The cost of developing the site.

The decision analyst then asked the managers to assign scores to the sites to show how well they performed on each of the first three attributes. The scores they eventually agreed upon are shown below, together with the estimated cost of developing each site (note that 0 represents the worst and 100 the best score on an attribute; in the case of risk, therefore, a score of 100 means that a site is the least risky):

| | **Benefits** | | | |
Site	Visual impact	Ease of transport	Risk	Costs ($ million)
Inston Common	100	0	60	35
Jones Wood	20	70	100	25
Peterton	80	40	0	17
Red Beach	20	100	30	12
Treehome Valley	0	70	60	20

The decision analyst then asked the managers to imagine a site that had the worst visual impact, the most difficult transport requirements and the highest level of risk. He then asked them which site they would choose if they had a chance of switching from this site to one that had just one of the benefits at its best value? The managers agreed that they would move to a site offering the least risk of contamination. A move to a site with the best visual impact was considered to be 80% as preferable as this, while a move to one with the most convenient transport facilities was 70% as preferable.

(a) Can we conclude from the values that were assigned to the different sites for visual impact that, in terms of visual impact, the Inston Common site is 5 times more preferable than Red Beach? If not, what can we infer from the figures?

(b) An alternative way of allocating weights to the three benefit attributes would have involved asking the managers to allocate a score reflecting the importance of each attribute. For example, they might have judged that risk was five times more important and visual impact three times more important than ease of transport, so that weights of 5, 3 and 1 would have been attached to the attributes. What are the dangers of this approach?

(c) Assuming that mutual preference independence exists between the attributes, determine the value of aggregate benefits for each site.

(d) Plot the aggregate benefits and costs of each site on a graph and hence identify the sites that lie on the efficient frontier.

(e) Although a weight of 80 was finally agreed for visual impact, this was only after much debate, and some managers still felt that a weight of 65 should have been used, while others thought that 95 would have been more appropriate. Perform a sensitivity analysis on the weight assigned to visual impact to examine its effect on the aggregate benefits of the sites, and interpret your results.

(6) As an experiment, a charity decides to use the simple multi-attribute rating technique (SMART) to determine a short list from the seven applicants who have applied for the post of Regional Officer for the Western region. The main criteria that will be used to compare candidates are: the salary they would expect (SALARY) (they have stated this on the application form), their experience of charity work (CHARITY EXP), their managerial experience (MANAGEMENT EXP), their educational qualifications (EDUCATION), their apparent commitment to the charity's work (COMMITMENT) (as gleaned from the application form) and the quality of the ideas they put forward on the form (IDEAS).

(a) When a value tree was used to identify the above attributes, there was some doubt about whether the attributes IDEAS and COMMITMENT met Keeney and Raiffa's criterion of decomposability.[2] Explain what this means and why the concerns might be justified.

(b) The personnel manager ranked all the criteria, except salary, in order of importance, and then assigned weights as follows:

COMMITMENT	100
MANAGEMENT EXP	70
IDEAS	65
CHARITY EXP	55
EDUCATION	10

(Note that, on the basis of the application form, all of the candidates appeared to be equally committed to the charity.) Discuss whether the method the personnel manager used to assess these weights is appropriate.

(c) Candidate A's scores for the non-monetary attributes are given below:

COMMITMENT	100
MANAGEMENT EXP	10
IDEAS	65
CHARITY EXP	0
EDUCATION	10

Using the weights given in part (b), show how the personnel manager obtained a score of 50 (subject to rounding) for this candidate.

(d) The aggregate scores for all the candidates are given below, together with their expected salaries:

Candidate	Aggregate score	Expected salary
A	50	$46 000
B	31	$40 000
C	75	$42 000
D	90	$60 000
E	20	$54 000
F	62	$52 000
G	49	$42 000

Assuming that the personnel manager's model is appropriate, determine the candidates who appear on the efficient frontier and explain the significance of this.

(e) The candidate with the least management experience has only been working in management for 2 years, while the most experienced candidate has 10 years' experience. If the personnel manager reckons that the charity would be prepared to pay $8000 for the 8 years' extra management experience, all else remaining equal, determine which candidate she should recommend for the appointment prior to the interview. State any assumptions you have made.

References

1. Keeney, R.L. (1982) Decision analysis: an overview, *Operations Research*, **30**(5), 803–837.
2. Keeney, R.L. and Raiffa, H. (1976) *Decisions with Multiple Objectives: Preferences and Value Tradeoffs*, John Wiley & Sons, Inc., New York, NY.
3. Edwards, W. (1971) Social utilities, *Engineering Economist*, Summer Symposium Series, **6**.
4. Wooler, S. and Barclay, S. (1988) Strategy for reducing dependence on a strike-prone production facility, in *Strategic Decision Support Systems*, ed. by Humphreys, P., Vari, A., Vecsenyi, J. and Larichev, O., North-Holland, Amsterdam, The Netherlands.
5. Buede, D.M. and Choisser, R.W. (1984) An aid for evaluators of system design alternatives, *Defense Management Journal*, 32–38.
6. Brownlow, S.A. and Watson, S.R. (1987) Structuring multi-attribute value hierarchies, *Journal of the Operational Research Society*, **38**, 309–317.
7. Edwards, W. and Newman, J.R. (1986) Multiattribute evaluation, in *Judgment and Decision Making*, Arkes, H.R. and Hammond, K.R., Cambridge University Press, Cambridge, UK.
8. von Winterfeldt, D. and Edwards, W. (1986) *Decision Analysis and Behavioral Research*, Cambridge University Press, Cambridge.
9. Pöyhönen, M., Vrolijk, H. and Hämäläinen, R.P. (2001) Behavioral and procedural consequences of structural variation in value trees, *European Journal of Operational Research*, **134**, 216–227.
10. Hämäläinen, R.P. and Alaja, S. (2008) The threat of weighting biases in environmental decision analysis, *Ecological Economics*, **69**, 556–569.
11. Mustajoki, J., Hämäläinen, R.P and Lindstedt, M.R.K. (2006) Using intervals for global sensitivity and worst-case analyses in multiattribute value trees, *European Journal of Operational Research*, **174**, 278–292.
12. Bodily, S.E. (1985) *Modern Decision Making*, McGraw-Hill, New York, NY.
13. Phillips, L.D. (1984) A theory of requisite decision models, *Acta Psychologica*, **56**, 29–48.
14. Keeney, R.L. (1992) *Value-Focused Thinking*, Harvard University Press, Cambridge, MA.
15. Wright, G. and Goodwin, P. (1999) Rethinking value elicitation for personal consequential decisions, *Journal of Multi-Criteria Decision Analysis*, **8**, 3–10.

Decisions involving multiple objectives: alternatives to SMART 4

Introduction

Although SMART is a relatively simple method for supporting decision-makers who are faced with problems involving multiple objectives, some of the judgments required by the method can still be quite demanding. In this chapter we consider a number of alternative methods that are designed to make judgments about multi-objective decisions easier. As we shall see, SMARTER simplifies the decision process by using linear value functions and an approximation method to estimate the decision-maker's swing weights. The Even Swaps approach avoids the need to estimate scores or weights altogether. Finally, the analytic hierarchy process (AHP) and MACBETH allow decision-makers to express their preferences using words rather than numbers.

SMARTER

The assessment of value functions and swing weights in SMART can sometimes be a difficult task, and decision-makers may not always be confident about the numbers that they are providing for the decision model. As a result, the model may not accurately reflect the decision-maker's true preferences. Because of this, Edwards and Barron[1] have argued for 'the strategy of heroic approximation'. Underlying this strategy is the idea that, while a very simple decision-making model may only approximate the real decision problem, it is less likely to involve errors in the values elicited from a decision-maker because of the simpler judgments it involves. Consistent with this strategy, Edwards and Barron have suggested a simplified form of SMART that they call SMARTER (SMART Exploiting Ranks).

SMARTER differs from SMART in two ways. First, value functions are normally assumed to be linear. Thus, the assessment of a value function for office floor area over the range 400–1500 ft^2, for example, would involve giving 400 ft^2 a value of 0 and 1500 ft^2 a value of 100, as before, and then simply drawing a straight line, rather than a curve, between these two points on a diagram like Figure 3.3 in Chapter 3. Clearly, this approximation becomes more inaccurate as the curvature of the 'true' value function increases, so, to guard against poor approximations, Edwards and Barron recommend that preliminary checks be made.

For example, we would ask the decision-maker to think about small increases in office floor area. Specifically, would a 100 ft^2 increase in floor area be more attractive if it fell near the bottom of the scale (e.g. 400–500 ft^2), in the middle (e.g. 1000–1100 ft^2) or near the top (e.g. 1400–1500 ft^2), or would it not matter where the increase occurred? If it does not matter, then a linear approximation can be used. Suppose, however, that the decision-maker says that the increase at the lower end of the scale is most appealing, while an increase at the top end of the scale would be least useful. We could then ask how much more desirable the improvement at the bottom is compared with the improvement at the top. As a rule of thumb, if the ratio is less than 2:1, then Edwards and Barron suggest that the linear approximation is probably safe, otherwise we should fall back on methods such as bisection (see Chapter 3) to obtain the value function.

The second difference between SMART and SMARTER relates to the elicitation of the swing weights. Recall that in the office location problem in Chapter 3 the decision-maker was asked to compare and evaluate swings from the worst to the best positions on the different attributes. For example, a swing from the worst to the best position for 'office visibility' was considered to be 80% as important as a swing from the worst to the best position for 'closeness to customers'. In SMARTER we still have to compare swings, but the process is made easier by simply asking the decision-maker to *rank* the swings in order of importance. This avoids the need to estimate a number to represent their relative importance. SMARTER then uses what are known as 'rank order centroid', or ROC, weights to convert these rankings into a set of approximate weights.

While a set of equations, or tables, is needed to obtain the ROC weights, the basic idea is easy to understand. Suppose that the office location decision had involved just two attributes – 'closeness to customers' and 'visibility' – and that the decision-maker had considered the swing in 'closeness to customers' to be more important than the swing in 'visibility'. We know that, after normalization, the two weights will sum to 100. As the swing in 'closeness to customers' is more important, its normalized weight must fall between just over 50 and almost 100. This suggests an approximate weight of 75, and this is indeed what the ROC equations would give us. Clearly, the ROC weight for 'visibility' would be 25.

Table 4.1 shows the ROC weights for decision problems involving up to seven attributes (see Edwards and Barron[1] for more details). In the 'original' office location problem, the decision-maker would have simply ranked the importance of the swings for the six attributes, as shown below; this would have yielded the ROC weights

Table 4.1 – Rank order centroid (ROC) weights

	Number of attributes					
Rank	2	3	4	5	6	7
1	75.0	61.1	52.1	45.7	40.8	37.0
2	25.0	27.8	27.1	25.7	24.2	22.8
3		11.1	14.6	15.7	15.8	15.6
4			6.3	9.0	10.3	10.9
5				4.0	6.1	7.3
6					2.8	4.4
7						2.0

indicated, and these could then have been used to obtain the aggregate benefits of the offices in the normal way (the original normalized SMART weights are also shown below for comparison):

Rank of swing	Attribute	ROC weight	SMART weight
1	Closeness to customers	40.8	32.0
2	Visibility	24.2	26.0
3	Image	15.8	23.0
4	Size	10.3	10.0
5	Comfort	6.1	6.0
6	Car parking	2.8	3.0
		100.0	100.0

How good are the ROC weights as approximations to the weights that might have been obtained in SMART? Edwards and Barron report the results of extensive simulations suggesting that SMART and SMARTER will agree on which option has the highest aggregate benefits in 75–87% of cases. Even when they did not agree, the options identified as having the highest aggregate benefits tended to have very similar scores, suggesting that an option that was 'not too bad' was being picked by SMARTER.

All of this suggests that SMARTER is a technique that is well worth employing. However, we should note some reservations about the method. First, in problems where it has been necessary to separate costs from benefits, you might obtain a different efficient frontier if you use SMARTER rather than SMART. This means we should be very careful before we exclude dominated options from further consideration. In particular, if you were to employ the method suggested by Edwards and Newman for selecting an option from the efficient frontier, then SMART and SMARTER may well suggest that different options should be chosen. This is because the assessment of the worth of a value point to the decision-maker is based on the normalized weights, and differences between the SMART and ROC weights can lead to large discrepancies in this assessment.

These discrepancies become less important if we recall that the main purpose of a decision analysis model is not to tell us what to do in a mechanistic fashion but to yield insights and understanding about the problem in hand. However, this raises another concern about SMARTER, which Edwards and Barron acknowledge. By simplifying the decision-maker's judgmental task, we may be encouraging only a superficial consideration of the problem and hence precluding the very insights that we hope to obtain. Analysts sometimes find that these insights only emerge when the decision-maker is forced to grapple with more demanding judgmental tasks that require deeper thinking about the issues.

Finally, the ROC weights themselves raise a number of concerns. The method through which they are derived involves some sophisticated mathematics, which means that they will lack transparency to most decision-makers. To be told that your implied weight for an attribute is 15.8, without understanding why this is the case, is likely to reduce your sense of ownership of the model that is purporting to represent your decision problem. This may reduce the model's credibility. Furthermore, Belton and Stewart[2] point out that the ratio of the ROC weights between the most and least important attributes is generally very high. For example, in a seven-attribute problem, this ratio is $37/2 = 18.5$ (see Table 4.1). This makes the relative importance of the lowest-ranked attribute so low that, in practice, it would probably be discarded from the analysis.

Both of these problems can be mitigated to some extent by using an alternative weight-approximation method. Several methods exist, but Roberts and Goodwin[3] have recommended the much simpler rank-sum method for problems that involve more than two or three attributes. Rank-sum weights are easily calculated and hence are more transparent. Suppose that three attributes have been ranked. The sum of their ranks will be $1 + 2 + 3 = 6$. The least important attribute is therefore assigned a rank of 1/6, the second-ranked attribute a rank of 2/6 and the highest-ranked attribute a rank of 3/6 (i.e. the weights are 0.167, 0.333 and 0.5). For four attributes, the weights will be 0.1, 0.2, 0.3 and 0.4, and so on.

Even Swaps

As we saw in Chapter 3, trade-offs are one of the most difficult judgments to make when faced with decisions involving multiple objectives. When choosing a holiday, how many extra hours are you prepared to fly in order to sunbathe on a beach where the climate is typically 5 degrees warmer? When choosing a job, will the $8000 extra salary offered by a position 1000 miles away compensate you for the inconvenience of moving house and the end of the social life you are currently enjoying? As we have seen, SMART and SMARTER use swing weights to represent these trade-offs. Hammond et al.[4] have proposed a radically different approach, which they call Even Swaps. In this approach, decision-makers are asked to consider directly how much gain in one attribute they would need to receive in order to compensate them for a loss in another attribute – a so-called swap. As we demonstrate below, Even Swaps uses these swaps progressively to reduce the size of the decision problem until only one option remains.

To illustrate Even Swaps, consider the following decision faced by a manufacturer who has to choose a components supplier from abroad. The choice will be based on four objectives. The manufacturer wants to minimize the annual purchase costs of the components, minimize the average delivery time, minimize the average percentage of defective components in each delivery and receive the best after-sales service from the supplier. The table below shows how the suppliers perform against these objectives (in Even Swaps, this is known as a consequences table):

Supplier location	Annual purchase cost ($)	Average delivery time (days)	Average % defective	After-sales service
Canada	140 000	3	2	Med
Mexico	80 000	4	4	Good
Japan	190 000	5	6	Med
S. Korea	90 000	5	3	Good
China	70 000	8	5	Med
India	75 000	7	4	Poor

To apply Even Swaps we proceed as follows:

(1) *Identify any options that can be eliminated because they are dominated.* If one option performs better than another on all of the attributes, then it is said to dominate the other option. Dominance can also occur if one option performs better than another option on some of the attributes and performs just as well on the remaining attributes. We can usually spot dominance more easily if the options are ranked from best to worst on each attribute, as shown below (1 = best, 6 = worst):

Supplier location	Annual purchase cost ($)	Average delivery time (days)	Average % defective	After-sales service
Canada	5	1	1	3
Mexico	3	2	3	1
Japan	6	3	6	3
S. Korea	4	3	2	1
China	1	6	5	3
India	2	5	3	6

If we study the ranks carefully, we can see that the Japanese supplier performs worse than the Canadian supplier on all of the attributes except after-sales service, where they tie. This means that the Japanese supplier can be eliminated from the decision.

(2) *Identify any options that can be eliminated because they are practically dominated.* If we compare the South Korean supplier with the Mexican supplier, we see that the Mexican supplier is either better than or at least as good as the South Korean on all attributes except average percentage defective. However, here the Korean supplier is only slightly better than the Mexican supplier (offering an average of 3% defectives rather than 4%). The manufacturer judges that this small advantage does not compensate for the $10 000 extra cost of the Korean supplier and the extra day's delivery time. The Mexican supplier is therefore said 'practically' to dominate the Korean supplier, and the latter can be eliminated from further consideration. Our decision has now been reduced to the one below:

Supplier location	Annual purchase cost ($)	Average delivery time (days)	Average % defective	After-sales service
Canada	140 000	3	2	Med
Mexico	80 000	4	4	Good
China	70 000	8	5	Med
India	75 000	7	4	Poor

(3) *Perform Even Swaps so that attributes can be eliminated.* Suppose that the percentage defective rate of all of the suppliers was exactly the same at, say, 5%. This attribute would then be irrelevant to the decision because, whichever supplier we chose, we would end up with the same percentage defective rate. Even Swaps uses this idea to simplify the problem further by eliminating attributes. Consider the Canadian supplier's average percentage defective rate of 2%. Suppose that this rose to 5%. What compensation would the manufacturer require on another attribute so that

the attraction of the Canadian supplier remained unchanged? The manufacturer feels that a reduction in the annual cost of the Canadian supplier to $80 000 would be sufficient compensation for this large deterioration in quality. Thus, in our table, we can replace the Canadian supplier's performance on the attributes with an equally attractive performance, as shown below:

Supplier location	Annual purchase cost ($)	Average delivery time (days)	Average % defective	After-sales service
Canada	80 000 ~~140000~~	3	5 ~~2~~	Med

Suppose that the Mexican supplier's defective rate also went up to 5%. The manufacturer says he would require a reduction in the Mexican supplier's annual costs down to $60 000 to compensate him for this 1% increase in defectives if this supplier is to remain equally attractive to him. He would require the same reduction in costs from the Indian supplier if its defective rate also increased from 4 to 5%. The table below shows these changes:

Supplier location	Annual purchase cost ($)	Average delivery time (days)	Average % defective	After-sales service
Canada	80 000 ~~140000~~	3	5 ~~2~~	Med
Mexico	60 000 ~~80000~~	4	5 ~~4~~	Good
China	70 000	8	5	Med
India	55 000 ~~75000~~	7	5 ~~4~~	Poor

We can now see that the average percentage of defectives is identical for all of the suppliers, so this attribute can now be eliminated. We also note that the Chinese supplier is now dominated by the Mexican supplier, so we can also remove China from our decision. Our considerably simplified decision is shown below:

Supplier location	Annual purchase cost ($)	Average delivery time (days)	After-sales service
Canada	80 000	3	Med
Mexico	60 000	4	Good
India	55 000	7	Poor

We now aim to see how the table would change if the quality of the after-sales service of all the suppliers was changed to 'Good'. The manufacturer judges that, if the quality of the Canadian supplier's after-sales service were improved to this level, then he would be prepared to accept an increase in the average delivery time to 5 days. If the Indian supplier's after-sales service improved from its current 'Poor' level to 'Good', he would accept an increase in the average delivery time to 12 days. Our new table is shown below:

Supplier location	Annual purchase cost ($)	Average delivery time (days)	After-sales service
Canada	80 000	5	Good
Mexico	60 000	4	Good
India	55 000	12	Good

We see that after-sales service no longer discriminates between the suppliers, and also that Canada is now dominated by Mexico. The new version of the decision problem becomes:

Supplier location	Annual purchase cost ($)	Average delivery time (days)
Mexico	60 000	4
India	55 000	12

Finally, the manufacturer indicates that he would require a reduction in the Mexican supplier's annual cost to $30 000 if this supplier's delivery time increased to 12 days. The final table is shown below:

Supplier location	Annual purchase cost ($)	Average delivery time (days)
Mexico	30 000 ~~60000~~	12 ~~4~~
India	55 000	12

Clearly, the Mexican supplier is dominant, and hence this supplier should be chosen.

Even Swaps versus SMART

What are the advantages and disadvantages of using Even Swaps in a decision rather than SMART?

The relative strengths of Even Swaps

(1) *Avoids need to assign scores.* In Even Swaps, the decision process is applied directly to the information in the consequences table. In the above example, the decision-maker dealt directly with costs, delivery times and levels of after-sales service. This avoided the need to assign scores to represent the performance of the options on each attribute on a 0–100 scale, which is a requirement of SMART.

(2) *Avoids need to determine swing weights.* In SMART, decision-makers often have difficulties in understanding the true meaning of the swing weights. Even Swaps avoids this by asking decision-makers to make the sort of trade-offs with which they are likely to be familiar. It has been argued that, because Even Swaps deals with concrete changes in objectives, the trade-offs are easier to think about and are more understandable.[5] Similarly, the idea of dominance, which is central to Even Swaps, is also likely to be well understood by decision-makers.

(3) *Even Swaps may be closer to a natural decision process.* Research suggests that decision-makers who do not have access to decision-aiding technologies often go through a process of progressively simplifying the decision problem until they reach a decision. As we have seen, this principle is also inherent in the Even Swaps procedure. For example, we saw in Chapter 2 that, when faced with complex decisions involving many options and attributes, people often initially use a non-compensatory procedure, such as elimination by aspects, to reduce the number of options that they have to consider to a manageable level.[6] They then apply more cognitively demanding compensatory decision strategies to the remaining options. Other research shows that decision-makers actively restructure decision problems until one alternative is seen to be dominant.[7] This may involve operations such as collapsing two or more attributes into a more comprehensive one, emphasizing an attribute or adding new attributes to the problem representation that will bolster one alternative. Thus, although both SMART and Even Swaps are compensatory methods, the principle of progressive simplification used by Even Swaps has some consistency with the results of psychological studies of unaided choice. By contrast, the SMART approach, which preserves all the alternatives within a choice set, is less close to descriptions of unaided choice.

The relative limitations of Even Swaps

(1) *It is relatively hard to apply without practice.* There is some evidence that people can find Even Swaps harder to use than SMART, especially when they have not had much practice in applying it. In particular, the identification of dominance or practical dominance can be demanding and time consuming if done manually.

Also, for sizeable decision problems, the decision-maker will need to make a very large number of swaps, so that the effort and time required will be substantial.[8,9] In one study that compared Even Swaps with SMART,[10] people made a number of errors when applying the technique. For example, they became confused when bigger values on one attribute were better (e.g. a larger market share) while bigger values on another attribute were worse (e.g. higher costs) and made compensations in the wrong direction. Another study[11] found that decision-makers sometimes tried to make links between the swaps that were made and what they thought was likely to occur in practice. In our supplier example, experience might have taught the decision-maker that better after-sales service is usually associated with a lower delivery time *and* fewer defectives. He therefore might attempt to make a swap where higher costs are compensated for not only by better after-sales service but also by improvements in average delivery time and average number of defectives. Thus, the increase in costs is compensated for many times over. There is also the problem of ensuring that all of the swaps are consistent with each other, but checking consistency is not a simple process in Even Swaps. All of this points to the need for software to support applications of Even Swaps, especially for larger problems. One package, SMART SWAPS,[12] provides guidance by suggesting potential swaps that might be attractive to users based on their initial swaps. It is also designed to trap any errors that the decision-maker might make when applying the swaps.

(2) *The output of the process is less informative.* Even if decision-makers can apply Even Swaps without errors, the output of the process provides less information than SMART. In our supplier example, it only told us which supplier to choose, and we therefore have no idea of how close the other suppliers were to being the best choice. In SMART we would have a list of all the options and their associated scores, so that any option that came a close second could be identified. It is also difficult to perform sensitivity analysis in Even Swaps. To do this, we would have to return to earlier stages in the process and apply different swaps to examine their effects. However, without sensitivity analysis, we cannot tell how robust the recommended choice is to slight changes in the swaps that we made. Decision analysis models can play a valuable role in enabling managers to explore decision problems and in helping them to explain the rationale behind choosing a particular course of action. These benefits will be less easy to achieve when Even Swaps has been used to make a decision.

(3) *Use of Even Swaps may not have a neutral effect on choice.* There is some evidence that using Even Swaps may not have a neutral effect on the alternative that the decision-maker chooses at the end of the process. First, as we have seen, Even Swaps deliberately creates tables where all of the alternatives perform equally well on particular attributes (e.g. in our choice of supplier we created a table where the average percentage defectives of all the suppliers was the same). Normative

decision theory suggests that people should then simply ignore these attributes and base their choice on how the options perform on the remaining attributes. Research suggests that this might not be the case – the attributes where performance is equal can still have an effect on how the remaining attributes are perceived.[13, 14] Under some conditions, these equal performances may make the alternatives look more similar. This dilutes the effect of the attributes where they perform differently. Under other conditions, these equal performances emphasize the importance of the different performances on the remaining attributes.[15–19] In Even Swaps this may have an impact on the identification of practical dominance. For example, in our supplier example, creating equal performances on some of the attributes may have the effect of either diminishing or exaggerating the importance of a three-day difference in the delivery time of two suppliers in the decision-maker's eyes. If the importance is diminished, then this may lead to a decision that practical dominance applies – a decision that results purely from the effect of the eliminated (and now supposedly irrelevant) attributes. Indeed, this raises the possibility that the final choice of an alternative may depend on the order in which the attributes are eliminated during the Even Swaps process.

Second, another study[20] found that the seemingly equivalent preference assessment procedures of *choice* (e.g. 'choose between a store's own-brand cola at 40 cents and a 55 cent Coke') and *matching* (e.g. 'imagine if a store's own-brand cola costs 40 cents: at what price would a Coke be attractive to you?') generate systematically different estimates of a consumer's price-quality trade-offs. This finding of a lack of 'procedural invariance' illustrated the prominence effect, in that people were more likely to prefer the alternative that was superior on the more important attribute in a straightforward choice than in a matching task. This suggests that the more important attribute is more salient in choice than in matching. The process of defining an even swap is essentially a matching task, and thus the use of this process may affect decision-making.

The analytic hierarchy process

The analytic hierarchy process (AHP), which was developed by Thomas Saaty when he was acting as an adviser to the US government, has been very widely applied to decision problems in areas such as economics and planning, energy policy, material handling and purchasing, project selection, microcomputer selection, budget allocations and forecasting.[21] Saaty developed a user-friendly computer package, called EXPERT CHOICE,[22] to support the method. Other software that supports the AHP includes HIPRE 3+ (HIerarchical PREference analysis).[23]

We will use the following problem to demonstrate the application of the AHP. A manager in a food processing company has to choose a new packaging machine to

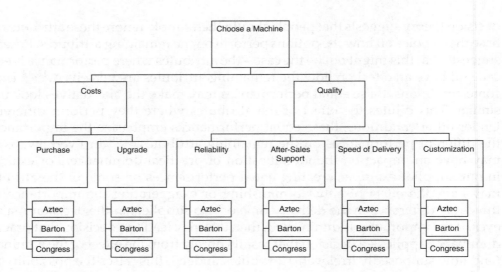

Figure 4.1 – A hierarchy for the packaging machine problem

replace the existing one which is wearing out. The manager has a limited budget for the purchase and has narrowed down the possible options to three: (i) the Aztec, (ii) the Barton and (iii) the Congress. However, the decision is still proving to be difficult because of the variety of attributes associated with the machines, such as the purchase price, reputation for reliability and the quality of after-sales support provided by the different manufacturers.

To apply the AHP, we proceed as follows:

(1) *Set up the decision hierarchy.* This is similar to a value tree in SMART, but the main difference is that the alternative courses of action also appear on the hierarchy at its lowest level. Figure 4.1 shows the decision hierarchy for the packaging machine problem. At the top of the tree is a statement of the general objective of the decision, in our case 'Choose a Machine'. The 'general' attributes associated with the decision problem ('Costs' and 'Quality') are then set out below this. As shown, these attributes can be broken down into more detail at the next level. For example, within 'Quality' the manager wishes to consider the attributes 'Reliability', 'After-Sales Support', 'Speed of Delivery' and 'Customization' (this is the extent to which the manufacturer is able to adapt the machine for the specific requirements of the food company). If necessary, this process of breaking down attributes continues until all the essential criteria for making the decision have been specified. Finally, the alternative courses of action are added to the hierarchy, below each of the lowest level attributes.

(2) *Make pairwise comparisons of attributes and alternatives.* This is used to determine the relative importance of attributes, and also to compare how well the options perform on the different attributes. For example, how much more important is the initial purchase price than the cost of upgrading the machine at a later date? Is the Aztec strongly preferred to the Barton for the quality of after-sales support?

Following each 'split' in the hierarchy, the importance of each attribute is compared, in turn, with every other attribute immediately below that 'split'. Thus, the importance of 'Costs' and the importance of 'Quality' are first compared. Then the four 'Quality' attributes are compared with each other for importance, and so on. Note that the comparisons are pairwise, so that, if there are four attributes, A, B, C and D, we need to make six comparisons: A with B, A with C, A with D, B with C, B with D and, finally, C with D.

Saaty recommends that these pairwise comparisons be carried out using verbal responses. For example, the manager is asked to consider whether 'Costs' and 'Quality' are of equal importance or whether one is more important than the other. The manager indicates that 'Costs' are more important, so he is then asked if costs are:

weakly more important?	(3)
strongly more important?	(5)
very strongly more important?	(7)
extremely more important?	(9)

The method then converts the response to the number shown in brackets. For example, if 'Costs' are 'strongly more important' than 'Quality', then they are assumed to be 5 times more important. Note that intermediate responses are allowed if the decision-maker prefers these (e.g. 'between weakly and strongly more important, which would be converted to a '4'). Also, if decision-makers prefer not to use verbal responses, then they can either make direct numerical inputs, on a scale from 1 ('equally important') to 9, or they can use a graphical facility in EXPERT CHOICE to make these inputs.

Each set of comparisons can be represented in a table (or matrix). From the 'Costs' versus 'Quality' comparison, we obtain Table 4.2.

Table 4.2 – Comparing the importance of 'Costs' and 'Quality'

	Costs	Quality
Costs	1	5
Quality		1

Table 4.3 – Comparing the importance of the 'Quality' attributes

	Reliability	After-Sales Support	Speed of Delivery	Customization
Reliability	1	4	5	4
After-Sales Support		1	3	1/2
Speed of Delivery			1	1/3
Customization				1

Similarly, for the four 'Quality' attributes, the manager's judgments lead to the values in Table 4.3. The numbers in the tables represent how much more important the 'row' attribute is compared with the 'column' attribute. For example, 'Reliability' is four times more important than 'After-Sales Support'. Fractional values therefore indicate that the 'column' attribute is most important. For example, 'Speed of Delivery' is only 1/3 as important as 'Customization'. Note that only 1s appear on the diagonal of the tables, as each attribute must have equal importance with itself. A similar table is obtained from the manager's comparison of the importance of 'Purchase' and 'Upgrade' costs.

Finally, the same process is used to compare the manager's relative *preferences* for the machines with respect to each of the lower-level attributes. For example, he will be asked to consider the purchase costs of the machines and asked whether, *in terms of purchase costs*, the Aztec and Barton are 'equally preferred'. If he indicates that the Barton is preferred, he will then be asked whether it is 'weakly preferred', 'strongly preferred' or 'extremely strongly preferred' (with intermediate responses allowed). This leads to the values in Table 4.4, which shows, for example, that the Aztec is twice as preferable as the Congress on purchase cost.

This process is repeated, yielding a table for each of the lowest-level attributes to represent the manager's preferences for the machines in terms of that attribute.
(3) *Transform the comparisons into weights and check the consistency of the decision-maker's comparisons.* After each table has been obtained, the AHP converts it into a set of weights, which are then automatically normalized to sum to 1. A number

Table 4.4 – Comparing the machines on 'Purchase Cost'

	Aztec	Barton	Congress
Aztec	1	1/3	2
Barton		1	6
Congress			1

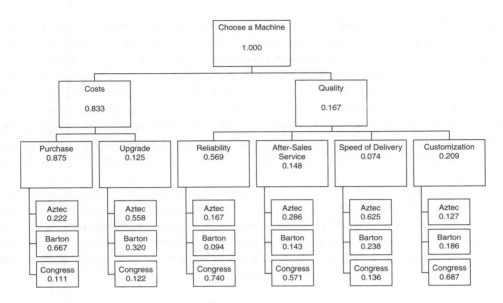

Figure 4.2 – Weights for the packaging machine problem

of conversion methods are possible. Saaty recommends a mathematical approach based on eigenvalues (see Saaty[24] for details of this method). Because this involves a relatively complex mathematical procedure, software such as EXPERT CHOICE is usually needed to perform the calculations. However, later on we will show a simple method for approximating the weights used in the AHP.

Figure 4.2 shows the weights obtained from all the tables in the hierarchy using EXPERT CHOICE. For Table 4.2, where 'Costs' were considered to be 5 times more important than 'Quality', the derivation of the weights is clear (a 5:1 ratio yields weights of 5/6 and 1/6, i.e. 0.833 and 0.167). The derivation is less transparent for the larger tables. For example, for Table 4.3 the weights are 'Reliability' 0.569, 'After-Sales Service' 0.148, 'Speed of Delivery' 0.074 and 'Customization' 0.209, suggesting that the decision-maker considered 'Reliability' to be by far the most important of the 'Quality' attributes.

Along with the weights, the AHP also yields an inconsistency ratio. This is produced automatically by EXPERT CHOICE (see Saaty[24] for details of the method of calculation), but later on we will show a way of getting a good approximation to this ratio by hand calculation. The ratio is designed to alert the decision-maker to any inconsistencies in the comparisons that have been made, with a value of zero indicating perfect consistency. For example, suppose a decision-maker's responses imply that attribute A is twice as important as B, while B is judged to be three times as important as C. To be perfectly consistent, the decision-maker should judge that

A is six times more important than C. Any other response would lead to an index greater than zero. Saaty recommends that inconsistency should only be a concern if the ratio exceeds 0.1 (as a rule of thumb), in which case the comparisons should be re-examined. Obviously, there can be no inconsistency in Table 4.2, as only one comparison was made. For Tables 4.3 and 4.4, the inconsistency ratios were 0.059 and 0 respectively. Values of less than 0.1 were also obtained for all of the other tables in the hierarchy. Saaty stresses, however, that minimizing inconsistency should not be the main goal of the analysis. A set of erroneous judgments about importance and preference may be perfectly consistent, but they will not lead to the 'best' decision.

(4) *Use the weights to obtain scores for the different options and make a provisional decision.* Although EXPERT CHOICE will automatically calculate the scores for the options, it is useful to demonstrate how the score for the Aztec machine was obtained. In Figure 4.2, all of the paths that lead from the top of the hierarchy to the Aztec option are identified. All of the weights in each path are then multiplied together, and the results for the different paths summed, as shown below:

$$\begin{aligned}
\text{Score for Aztec} = {} & 0.833 \times 0.875 \times 0.222 \\
& + 0.833 \times 0.125 \times 0.558 \\
& + 0.167 \times 0.569 \times 0.167 \\
& + 0.167 \times 0.148 \times 0.286 \\
& + 0.167 \times 0.074 \times 0.625 \\
& + 0.167 \times 0.209 \times 0.127 = 0.255
\end{aligned}$$

Note that the Aztec scores well on attributes that are considered to be relatively unimportant, such as 'Upgrade Costs' (which carries only 0.125 of the 0.833 weight allocated to costs) and 'Speed of Delivery' (which carries only 0.074 of the weight allocated to 'Quality', which itself is relatively unimportant). It scores less well on the more important attributes, so its overall score is relatively low. The scores for all three machines are shown below:

Aztec	0.255
Barton	0.541
Congress	0.204

This clearly suggests that the Barton should be purchased.

(5) *Perform sensitivity analysis.* As in any decision model, it is important to examine how sensitive the preferred course of action is to changes in the judgments made by the decision-maker. Many of these judgments will be 'rough and ready', and the decision-maker may be unsure about exactly what judgments to input.

EXPERT CHOICE has a number of facilities for carrying out sensitivity analysis. In dynamic sensitivity analysis, a bar chart shows the weights attached to attributes at a particular level in the hierarchy. By changing the lengths of these bars, the effect on the scores of the alternative courses of action can be examined. Other graphs allow decision-makers to examine the amount of change that can be made to an attribute's weight before the preferred course of action changes.

Performing AHP calculations by hand

If you do not have access to AHP software, then it is possible to obtain approximations of the weights using the following simple procedure. Consider Table 4.3. We first enter the numbers into the lower triangle of the table. For example, as Reliability is four times more important than After-Sales Support, After-Sales Support must be only 1/4 as important as Reliability. This yields the table below:

	Reliability	After-Sales Support	Speed of Delivery	Customization
Reliability	1	4	5	4
After-Sales Support	1/4	1	3	1/2
Speed of Delivery	1/5	1/3	1	1/3
Customization	1/4	2	3	1

Next, we sum the columns of the table and then divide each number in the table by the total of its column. For example, the total of the Reliability column is 1.7. This means that the four values in the Reliability column become 0.588, 0.147, 0.118 and 0.147. The table below shows all the results. Finally, we average the numbers in each row. These averages, which are also shown in the table, can now be used as approximate weights for the four attributes. Similar calculations can be applied to the other tables in the hierarchy.

	Reliability	After-Sales Support	Speed of Delivery	Customization	Average of row
Reliability	0.588	0.545	0.417	0.686	**0.559**
After-Sales Support	0.147	0.136	0.250	0.086	**0.155**
Speed of Delivery	0.118	0.045	0.083	0.057	**0.076**
Customization	0.147	0.273	0.250	0.171	**0.210**

It is also possible to calculate an approximation to the inconsistency ratio by using the following procedure. This may seem involved, but it is easily implemented on a spreadsheet. We will demonstrate the process on Table 4.3:

Step 1: Fill in the lower triangle of the table, as before. Then write the weight for each attribute (or option) at the top of each column. The results are shown below:

	Reliability	After-Sales Support	Speed of Delivery	Customization
Weights	**0.559**	**0.155**	**0.076**	**0.210**
Reliability	1	4	5	4
After-Sales Support	1/4	1	3	1/2
Speed of Delivery	1/5	1/3	1	1/3
Customization	1/4	2	3	1

Step 2: Multiply the weight at the top of each column by each of the numbers in that column. Then sum each row of the resulting table:

	Reliability	After-Sales Support	Speed of Delivery	Customization	Sums
Reliability	0.559	0.620	0.380	0.840	**2.399**
After-Sales Support	0.140	0.155	0.228	0.105	**0.628**
Speed of Delivery	0.112	0.052	0.076	0.070	**0.309**
Customization	0.140	0.310	0.228	0.210	**0.888**

Step 3: Divide each of these sums by the weight for that attribute (or option). Then average the resulting ratios.

	Sums	Weight	Ratio
Reliability	2.399	0.559	**4.291**
After-Sales Support	0.628	0.155	**4.056**
Speed of Delivery	0.309	0.076	**4.078**
Customization	0.888	0.210	**4.221**
		Average ratio	**4.161**

Step 4: An inconsistency index can be calculated using the following formula:

$$\text{Inconsistency index} = \frac{\text{average ratio from step 3} - n}{n - 1}$$

where n is the number of rows in the table we are investigating. In our case, this is 4, so we have

$$\text{Inconsistency index} = \frac{4.161 - 4}{4 - 1} = 0.054$$

Note that, if our table had been perfectly consistent, the average ratio from step 3 would have been 4.0, so our inconsistency index would have had a value of zero.

Step 5: Divide the inconsistency index by the appropriate value from Table 4.5 to obtain the inconsistency ratio. The values in this table were generated by Saaty to estimate the inconsistency indices for random tables. Our inconsistency ratio is therefore $0.054/0.90 = 0.06$. As this is below 0.1, we should have no concerns about inconsistency in this table. Note that this is very close to the 0.059 value produced by EXPERT CHOICE.

Table 4.5 – Random indices for checking the consistency of a table

	n								
	2	3	4	5	6	7	8	9	10
Random index	0	0.58	0.90	1.12	1.24	1.32	1.41	1.45	1.49

The axioms of the AHP

The AHP is based on four axioms:[25]

(1) The *reciprocal axiom* states that, if A and B are options or attributes in the decision hierarchy and A is n times more preferable (or more important or more likely) than B, then B must be $1/n$th as preferable (or important or likely) as A. For example, if Reliability is four times more important that After-Sales Support, then After-Sales Support must be only 1/4 as important as Reliability.

(2) The *homogeneity axiom* states that the elements being compared should not differ by extreme amounts on a criterion. For example, this axiom would be violated if

A were 24 times more important than B. This axiom is reflected in the range of the AHP verbal scale, which runs from 1/9 to 9. As we discuss below, this axiom can be relaxed if this is judged to be absolutely necessary.

(3) The *synthesis axiom* states that judgments about the importance of elements in a hierarchy do not depend on the elements below them. For example, in our hierarchy, judgment about the relative importance of Reliability and After-Sales Support does not depend on the packaging machines that are available. Thus, the relative importance would be the same even if a different set of machines were on offer. This axiom may be violated in many practical applications. For example, suppose that we state that Reliability is four times more important than After-Sales Support and then discover that all of the available machines have extremely high and similar levels of Reliability that far exceed the minimum acceptable level. However, they differ to a considerable extent in the quality of After-Sales Support offered. In this case we may wish to change our mind and judge After-Sales Support as being more important in our choice between the machines. To guard against this danger, it is recommended that a 'bottom-up' approach be applied when evaluating the elements in an AHP hierarchy (i.e. we should start with the alternative courses of action and work upwards). By comparing the machines' performances on Reliability and After-Sales Support first, we would learn about their similarities in reliability, and this would inform our judgment when we came to compare the importance of these two attributes. Alternatively, the analytical network process (ANP)[26] provides a formal approach to this problem, but at the cost of greater mathematical complexity.

(4) The *expectation* axiom states that decision-makers should make sure that their ideas are adequately represented in the decision model. This is similar to the concept of requisite decision modeling in SMART. If the decision-maker's intuitively preferred option differs from the best option suggested by the model, then this indicates that the model should be investigated to identify the reason for the discrepancy. Perhaps the hierarchy is incomplete or the relative importance of attributes is not independent of the options (see the synthesis axiom above). Alternatively, the investigation might reveal that the decision-maker's intuition is at fault because he or she is unable to comprehend a complex decision problem in its entirety.

The AHP versus SMART

It can be seen that the AHP is fundamentally different to SMART in many respects. We next consider the relative strengths of the AHP and then consider the main criticisms that have been made of the technique.

The relative strengths of the AHP

(1) *Simplicity of pairwise comparisons.* The use of pairwise comparisons means that the decision-maker can focus, in turn, on each small part of the problem. Only two attributes or options have to be considered at any one time, so that the decision-maker's judgmental task is simplified. Verbal comparisons are also likely to be preferred by decision-makers who have difficulty in expressing their judgments numerically.

(2) *Redundancy allows consistency to be checked.* The AHP requires more comparisons to be made by the decision-maker than are needed to establish a set of weights. For example, if a decision-maker indicates that attribute A is twice as important as B, and B, in turn, is four times as important as C, then it can be inferred that A is eight times more important than C. However, by also asking the decision-maker to compare A with C, it is possible to check the consistency of the judgments. It is considered to be good practice in decision analysis to obtain an input to a decision model by asking for it in several ways and then asking the decision-maker to reflect on any inconsistencies in the judgments put forward. In the AHP this is carried out automatically.

(3) *Versatility.* The wide range of applications of the AHP is evidence of its versatility. In addition to judgments about importance and preference, the AHP also allows judgments about the relative likelihood of events to be made. This has allowed it to be applied to problems involving uncertainty, and also to be used in forecasting.[27–30] AHP models have also been used to construct scenarios by taking into account the likely behavior and relative importance of key actors and their interaction with political, technological, environmental, economic and social factors (Saaty,[24] p. 130).

Criticisms of the AHP

(1) *Conversion from verbal to numeric scale.* Decision-makers using the verbal method of comparison will have their judgments automatically converted to the numeric scale, but the correspondence between the two scales is based on untested assumptions. If you indicate that A is weakly more important than B, the AHP will assume that you consider A to be 3 times more important, but this may not be the case. In particular, several authors have argued that a multiplicative factor of 5 is too high to express the notion of 'strong' preference.[30]

(2) *Problems of the 1–9 scale.* Experimental work suggests that, when one attribute or option is 'extremely more important' than another, then ratios of 1 to 3 or 1 to 5 are more appropriate than the 1 to 9 ratio assumed by the AHP.[31] However, if a

decision-maker using the verbal scale does wish to incorporate very extreme ratios into the decision model, the restriction of pairwise comparisons with a 1–9 scale is bound to create inconsistencies. For example, if A is considered to be four times more important than B, and B is four times more important than C, then, to be consistent, A should be judged to be 16 times more important than C, but this is not possible with the AHP's verbal scale.

To avoid this problem, Forman and Gass[25] recommend that, when setting up the AHP hierarchy, the decision-maker should attempt to arrange the elements in clusters so that they do not differ in extreme ways (this would also ensure conformance with axiom 2). They argue that this is desirable, anyway, because judgments involving extreme differences are likely to be unreliable. However, where extreme judgments are required, one can avoid verbal judgments altogether and directly input the desired numerical ratios.

(3) *Meaningfulness of responses to questions.* Unlike SMART, weights are elicited in the AHP without reference to the scales on which attributes are measured. For example, a person using SMART to choose a house might be asked to compare the value of reducing the daily journey to work from 80 to 10 miles with the value of increasing the number of bedrooms in the house from 2 to 4. Implicit in this type of comparison is the notion of a trade-off or exchange: 70 fewer miles may be only half as valuable as two extra bedrooms. It can be shown that AHP questions, which simply ask for the relative importance of attributes without reference to their scales, imply weights that reflect the relative value of the *average* score of the options on the different criteria,[32] which is a difficult concept for decision-makers to grasp. This may mean that the questions are interpreted in different and possibly erroneous ways by decision-makers.[32, 33]

(4) *New alternatives can reverse the rank of existing alternatives.* This issue, which is related to the last point, has attracted much attention.[34] Suppose that you are using the AHP to choose a location for a new sales office and the weights you obtained from the method give the following order of preference: 1 Albuquerque, 2 Boston, 3 Chicago. However, before making the decision, you discover that a site in Denver is also worth considering, so you repeat the AHP to include this new option. Even though you leave the relative importance of the attributes unchanged, the new analysis gives the following rankings: 1 Boston, 2 Albuquerque, 3 Denver, 4 Chicago, so the rank of Albuquerque and Boston has been reversed, which may not seem to be intuitively reasonable. If Albuquerque is better than Boston, then surely it is still better than Boston, irrespective of whether or not Denver is available.

These rank reversals cannot occur in SMART, but some analysts have argued that in some circumstances they are desirable.[25] Their arguments are based on what is referred to as dilution. Suppose that two people, Alan and Barbara, work in a sales office. Alan has excellent computing skills but is less good at selling than

Barbara. Barbara knows very little about computers. Alan is therefore rated as the most valued of the two employees because, if he is absent, there is no one to fix computer problems. Subsequently, a third person, Colin, joins the office. While Colin is not as knowledgeable as Alan about computers, he is still quite skilled. Now Barbara is regarded as more valuable than Alan (i.e. their ranks have been reversed). She is a better salesperson and Alan's computer knowledge is now less vital, given that he is no longer the only computer buff in the office. The value of his computing skills has been 'diluted'.

In spite of this example, some research suggests, anyway, that rank reversals occur rarely in applications of the AHP.[25] However, if the decision-maker does want to avoid any danger of such reversals, then it is now possible to choose to run the AHP in what is referred to as 'ideal mode' (the original mode is referred to as 'distributive mode'). The term 'ideal' refers to the fact that the weights of alternatives are assigned relative to the ideal (or the most preferred) alternative. For example, the best option on an attribute might have a weight of 0.6. If it is twice as preferable as the second best option, then this second option will have a weight of 0.3, and so on. Adding further options at a later stage will not change the rankings of these weights because all the weights are compared with a fixed value (the ideal). This is similar to SMART, where the scores given to options on an attribute are also assigned relative to the best performing option, which has a score of 100.

(5) *Number of comparisons required may be large.* While the redundancy built into the AHP is an advantage, it may also require a large number of judgments from the decision-maker. Consider, for example, the office location problem in Chapter 3, which involved seven alternatives and seven attributes (if we simplify the problem to include 'Total Costs' and only lower-level benefit attributes). This would involve 168 pairwise comparisons of importance or preference. In a study by Olson *et al.*,[33] this requirement to answer a large number of questions reduced the attraction of the AHP in the eyes of potential users, even though the questions themselves were considered to be easy.

To address this problem, EXPERT CHOICE has a facility for using a 'ratings' or 'absolute' approach where each of the alternatives is rated on a single scale that the decision-maker can define. For example, we might define a scale for the computer skills of job applicants as 'Excellent', 'Good', 'Average', 'Poor' and 'Very Poor'. The decision-maker can then determine numerical values to represent the 'intensity' of the verbal descriptions. For example, 'Excellent' may be assigned a score of 1, 'Good' a score of 0.7, and so on. Having formulated the scale, each applicant can be rated directly on this scale. This avoids the need to make pairwise comparisons between all of the applicants. For example, if we had ten job applicants, we would only have to make ten direct ratings, rather than 45 pairwise judgments, for each attribute.

MACBETH

MACBETH (Measuring Attractiveness by a Categorical-Based Evaluation TecHnique), which was developed by Carlos Bana e Costa and Jean-Claude Vansnick,[35,36] is similar to the AHP in a number of ways. First, users are asked to compare only pairs of options or attributes at a time, and second, they express their preferences in terms of words rather than numbers. Like the AHP, this results in a table of comparisons that allows the method to inform decision-makers about the consistency of their pairwise judgments.

There are, however, a number of important differences between the methods. Whereas the AHP elicits a ratio for the relative importance or preference between elements of the hierarchy (e.g. Reliability is five times more important than After-Sales Service), MACBETH asks users to compare *differences* in attractiveness. For example, suppose that two packaging machines, the Aztec and the Barton, are compared for the attractiveness of the After-Sales Service they offer. The decision-makers would be asked to decide whether the difference in their attractiveness was 'Very Weak', 'Weak', 'Moderately Strong', 'Strong', 'Very Strong' or 'Extreme'. Alternatively, the decision-maker could indicate that the machines were equally attractive in their After-Sales Service. A similar process is used to obtain the swing weights for the attributes. Once the decision-maker has made these indications, MACBETH uses a mathematical algorithm to check their consistency and generate numerical scores and weights. When inconsistencies are discovered, the method indicates how they have arisen and suggests how greater consistency could be achieved.

Because MACBETH uses the additive value model (see Chapter 3), it is possible to integrate it with SMART. This integrative facility is available in at least one software product (HIVIEW 3). This is useful where decision-makers have problems in directly assigning the numerical scores required by SMART and are more comfortable in expressing their preferences in terms of words. In particular, some decision-makers may have problems in understanding the 0–100 scales used in SMART. For example, a score of zero simply indicates that an option is the worst performer on an attribute, not that it has no value. Similarly, because the zero is defined in this way, the scales used in SMART are interval scales, so an option scoring 50 on an attribute is not necessarily twice as preferable as an option scoring 25. The idea that it is the relative size of differences (or intervals) between scores that is meaningful may be difficult to convey. Macbeth addresses this by asking users to compare these differences in words.

In addition to these advantages, MACBETH includes extensive facilities for examining the robustness of decisions and their sensitivity to changes in the decision-maker's judgments. However, the mathematical algorithm underlying the method means that users have to rely on computer software to implement the technique, and this will reduce the transparency of the process through which the method produces its recommendations. Because of this, in any application of MACBETH, decision-makers should spend time reviewing the outputs of the method to ensure that they agree that their preferences are being accurately represented.

Summary

In this chapter we have reviewed some alternative methods to SMART. We saw that each of these alternatives contains attractive features such as automatic consistency checks on the decision-maker's judgments, avoidance of the need to specify weights or facilities allowing decision-makers to express preferences using words rather than numbers. However, none of the methods was clearly superior to the others on all counts. Because of this, there has been a convergence between some of the techniques in an attempt to embrace the best features of each. For example, verbal judgments can now be used alongside SMART via the MACBETH procedure. Similarly, some commercial software products now include facilities for both SMART and the AHP, allowing decision-makers to have considerable flexibility in the way they tackle different decision problems.

Exercises

Additional exercises can be found on the book's website

(1) The owner of a small business is unhappy with the service she has been receiving from her bank and has decided to move her account to a rival bank. Her decision on which bank to choose will be based not only on the estimated annual bank charges that each bank will levy but also on the following 'benefit attributes':
(a) the proximity of the local branch;
(b) whether the local branch has a small business adviser;
(c) the maximum automatic loan allowed;
(d) whether a telephone banking facility is offered.

The alternative banks are listed below, together with their estimated annual costs and the scores the business owner has allocated for each of the 'benefit attributes':

Bank	Estimated annual charge ($)	Proximity	Small business adviser	Maximum loan	Telephone facility
Central	3000	0	100	40	0
Northern	5000	100	100	80	0
Direct	2000	70	0	100	100
Royal	1000	30	0	0	100
Marks	4000	90	100	20	0

The business owner is then asked to imagine that she has her account with a hypothetical bank that had the lowest scores on all of the 'benefit attributes'. She is then asked to imagine that each attribute could be switched to its best possible value and asked to rank the attractiveness of these possible switches. Her ranks are given as:

Rank	Switch
1	Lowest maximum loan facility to highest
2	No telephone banking facility to existence of this facility
3	Non-availability of small business adviser to availability
4	Least close branch to closest branch

(a) SMARTER has been used to obtain scores to represent the aggregate benefits of the banks, and these are given below:

Bank	Aggregate score
Central	35.4
Northern	62.5
Direct	83.5
Royal	29.0
Marks	30.6

Show how the score of 35.4 for the Central Bank was determined.
(b) By taking into account the estimated annual charges of the banks, determine which banks lie on the efficient frontier. Explain the significance of the efficient frontier.
(c) SMARTER is based on the 'principle of heroic approximation'. Explain how this principle applies to your analysis of the businesswoman's problem, and discuss whether it is likely to be appropriate.
(2) Imagine that you have won a holiday for two people in a magazine competition and you have been given the choice of five holiday destinations. The names and details of these destinations are shown below:

Destination	Flying time (hours)	Typical sunshine (hours per day)	Time to walk to beach (minutes)	Size of place	No. of cultural attractions nearby	Night life
Alucia	4	8	0	Large town	3	Average
Bellonia	9	6	5	Village	1	Quiet
Catin	3	5	12	Isolated	0	Quiet
Dorania	5	9	20	Large town	5	Lively
Estinet	2	5	2	Village	0	Average

Use the Even Swaps method to determine which destination you would choose on the basis of the information that has been supplied.

(3) A motorist is using the AHP to choose a new car from three possible models: an Arrow, a Bestmobile and a Commuter. The choice will be based on just two attributes, 'Cost' and 'Style'. The motorist considers that Cost is 'Weakly More Important' than Style.

When asked to compare the costs of the cars. The motorist makes the following statements: on cost, the Bestmobile is 'Weakly Preferred' to the Arrow, but the Arrow is 'Weakly Preferred' to the Commuter. Also, the Bestmobile is 'Extremely Preferred' to the Commuter.

On style, the Arrow is '*Very* Strongly Preferred' to the Bestmobile, but the Commuter is 'Weakly Preferred' to the Arrow. Also, the Commuter is 'Extremely Preferred' to the Bestmobile.

(a) Construct a hierarchy to represent the decision problem.

(b) Use an appropriate software package, or the approximation method, to calculate the weights for each table in the hierarchy, and hence determine which car should be purchased.

(c) Calculate the inconsistency ratios for the motorist's comparisons of the cars on (i) cost and (ii) style, and interpret your results (use either your software or the approximation method here).

(4) One of the criticisms of the AHP is that the introduction of new alternatives can change the ranking of existing alternatives. Under what circumstances, if any, is this likely to be reasonable?

(5) A manager is hoping to appoint a new assistant and decides to use the AHP to rank the applicants for the job. Then, as a check, she decides to repeat the process using SMART. She is surprised to find that the ranking of the applicants derived from the AHP differs significantly from the ranking suggested by the SMART analysis. Discuss why these differences might have arisen.

References

1. Edwards, W. and Barron, F.H. (1994) SMARTS and SMARTER: improved simple methods for multiattribute utility measurement, *Organizational Behavior and Human Decision Processes*, **60**, 306–325.
2. Belton, V. and Stewart, T.R. (2002) *Multiple Criteria Decision Analysis. An Integrated Approach*, Kluwer Academic Publishers, Norwell, MA.
3. Roberts, R. and Goodwin, P. (2002) Weight approximations in multi-attribute decision models, *Journal of Multi-Criteria Decision Analysis*, **11**, 291–203.
4. Hammond, J.S., Keeney, R.L. and Raiffa, H. (1998) Even Swaps: a rational method for making tradeoffs, *Harvard Business Review*, **76**, 137–150.
5. Kajanus, M., Ahola, J., Kurttila, M. and Pesonen, M. (2001) Application of Even Swaps for strategy selection in a rural enterprise, *Management Decision*, **39**, 394–402.
6. Payne, J. (1982) Contingent decision behaviour, *Psychological Bulletin*, **92**, 382–402.
7. Montgomery, H. (1983) Decision rules and the search for a dominance structure: towards a process model of decision making, in *Analyzing and Aiding Decision Processes*, ed. by Humphreys P.C. *et al.*, North Holland, Amsterdam, The Netherlands, pp. 343–369.
8. Mustajoki, J. and Hämäläinen, R.P. (2005) A preference programming approach to make the Even Swaps method even easier, *Decision Analysis*, **2**, 110–123.
9. Bouyssou, D. and Pirlot, M. (2005) Conjoint measurement tools for MCDM, in *Multiple Criteria Decision Analysis: State of the Art Surveys*, ed. by Figueira, J., Greco, S. and Erhgott, M., Springer, New York, NY, pp. 73–132.
10. Belton, V., Wright, G. and Montibeller, G. (2008) When is swapping better than weighting? An evaluation of the Even Swaps method in comparison with multi attribute value analysis, Working Paper, Department of Management Science, University of Stratchclyde.
11. Luo, C.-M. and Cheng, B.-W. (2006) Applying Even Swaps method to structurally enhance intuitive decision making, *Systemic Practice and Action Research*, **19**, 45–59.
12. Hämäläinen, R. (2003) Decisionarium – aiding decisions, negotiating and collecting opinions on the web, *Journal of Multi-Criteria Decision Analysis*, **12**, 101–110.
13. Dhar, R. and Sherman, S.J. (1996) The effect of common and unique features in consumer choice, *Journal of Consumer Research*, **23**(3), 192–203.
14. Chernev, A. (1997) The effect of common features on brand choice: moderating role of attribute importance, *Journal of Consumer Research*, **23**(4), 304–311.
15. Tversky, A. (1977) Features of similarity, *Psychological Review*, **84**, 327–352.
16. Nisbett, R.E., Zukier, H. and Lemley, R.E. (1981) The dilution effect: nondiagnostic information weakens the implications of diagnostic information, *Cognitive Psychology*, **13**, 248–277.
17. Mellers, B.A. and Biangini, K. (1994) Similarity and choice, *Psychological Review*, **101**, 505–518.
18. Meyer, R.J. and Eagle, T.C. (1982) Context-induced parameter instability in a disaggregate-stochastic model of store choice, *Journal of Marketing Research*, **19**, 62–71.
19. Tversky, A. and Russo, J. (1969) Substitutability and similarity in binary choice, *Journal of Mathematical Psychology*, **6**, 1–12.

20. Carmon, Z. and Simonson, I. (1998) Price-quality tradeoffs in choice versus matching: new insights into the prominence effect, *Journal of Consumer Psychology*, **7**, 323–343.
21. Zahedi, F. (1986) The analytic hierarchy process – a survey of the method and its applications, *Interfaces*, **16**, 96–108.
22. Expert Choice is a product of Expert Choice, Inc., 4922 Ellsworth Avenue, Pittsburgh, PA 15213, USA.
23. Mustajoki, J. and Hämäläinen, R.P. (2000) Web-HIPRE: global decision support by value tree and AHP Analysis, *INFOR*, **38**, 208–220; see also www.hipre.hut.fi
24. Saaty, T.L. (1990) *The Analytic Hierarchy Process*, RWS Publications, Pittsburgh, PA.
25. Forman, E.H. and Gass, S.L. (2001) The analytic hierarchy process – an exposition, *Operations Research*, **49**, 469–486.
26. Saaty, T.L. (1996) *Decision Making with Dependence and Feedback*, RWS Publications, Pittsburgh, PA.
27. Saaty, T.L. and Vargas, L.G. (1991) *Prediction, Projection and Forecasting*, Kluwer Academic Publishers, Norwell, MA.
28. Ulengin, F. and Ulengin, B. (1994) Forecasting foreign exchange rates: a comparative evaluation of the AHP, *Omega*, **22**, 509–519.
29. Wolfe, C. and Flores, B. (1990) Judgmental adjustments of earnings forecasts, *Journal of Forecasting*, **9**, 389–405.
30. Belton, V. and Goodwin, P. (1996) Remarks on the application of the analytic hierarchy process to judgmental forecasting, *International Journal of Forecasting*, **12**, 155–161.
31. Belton, V. and Stewart, T.J. (2002) *Multiple Criteria Decision Analysis. An Integrated Approach*, Kluwer Academic Publishers, Norwell, MA.
32. Belton, V. (1986) A comparison of the analytic hierarchy process and simple multi-attribute value function, *European Journal of Operational Research*, **26**, 7–21.
33. Olson, D.L., Moshkovich, H.M., Schellenberger, R. and Mechitov, A.I. (1995) Consistency and accuracy in decision aids: experiments with four multiattribute systems, *Decision Sciences*, **26**, 723–748.
34. Belton, V. and Gear, T. (1983) On a shortcoming in Saaty's method of analytic hierarchies, *Omega*, **11**, 228–230.
35. Bana e Costa, C.A. and Vansnick, J.-C. (1997) Applications of the MACBETH approach in the framework of the additive-aggregation model, *Journal of Multi-Criteria Decision Analysis*, **6**, 107–114.
36. Bana e Costa, C.A. and Chagas, M.P. (2004) A career choice problem: an example of how to use MACBETH to build a quantitative value model based on qualitative value judgments, *European Journal of Operational Research*, **153**, 323–331.

Introduction to probability 5

Introduction

In the previous chapter we discussed the analysis of decisions where uncertainty was not considered to be a major factor. However, in many problems the decision-maker is not sure what will happen if a particular course of action is chosen. A company that is considering the purchase of an expensive new machine will face uncertainty relating to factors such as the machine's reliability, life span and resale value. Similarly, an individual who has to decide whether or not to purchase household insurance will be uncertain as to whether his home will be burgled, flooded or damaged by fire. In the next chapter we will be looking at how to analyze decisions that involve uncertainty, but before this we need to consider how the concept of probability can be used to provide a measure of uncertainty.

Numbers offer a precise way of measuring uncertainty, and most people will be familiar with the use of odds. While many decision-makers may be happy to use expressions such as '100 to 1 against' or 'evens', odds do have the disadvantage that they are awkward to handle arithmetically when, for example, we want to determine the chances that a number of different outcomes will occur.

Because of this, we will be using the concept of probability in our decision models. Probabilities are measured on a scale that runs from 0 to 1. If the probability of an outcome occurring is zero, then this implies that the outcome is impossible. At the opposite extreme, if it is considered that an outcome is certain to occur, then this will be represented by a probability of 1; the greater the chances of the event occurring, the closer its probability will be to 1. It is worth pointing out that odds can be converted to probabilities. For example, odds of 50 to 1 against imply that there are 50 'chances' that the outcome will not occur and one chance that it will: a total of 51 'chances'. Hence, the chances of the event occurring are, in probability terms, 1 in 51 (or 0.0196). 'Evens' is, of course, represented by the probability of 1/2.

In this chapter we will introduce the main ideas and rules that are used in probability calculations. The ways in which decision analysts elicit subjective probabilities from decision-makers will be described and evaluated in Chapter 11. Throughout the book we will be using the notation $p(\ )$ to mean 'the probability of . . .'. For example, we will write 'the probability of rain' as $p(\text{rain})$.

Outcomes and events

Before proceeding, we need to be clear in our definitions of outcomes and events. Suppose that a company is thinking of simultaneously launching two new products, A and B. The company's marketing manager decides to list all the possible things that can happen if the simultaneous launch goes ahead. His list is shown below:

(1) Both products fail.
(2) Product A succeeds but B fails.
(3) Product A fails but B succeeds.
(4) Both products succeed.

Each of the four possible things that can happen is called an *outcome*. An *event* consists of one or more possible outcomes. For example, the event 'just one product succeeds' consists of the two outcomes 'A succeeds but B fails' and 'A fails but B succeeds'. The event 'at least one product succeeds' consists of the last three outcomes in the list. However, the event 'both products fail' clearly consists of only one outcome.

Approaches to probability

There are three different approaches to deriving probabilities: the classical approach, the relative frequency approach and the subjective approach. The first two methods lead to what are often referred to as objective probabilities because, if they have access to the same information, different people using either of these approaches should arrive at exactly the same probabilities. In contrast, if the subjective approach is adopted, it is likely that people will differ in the probabilities that they put forward.

The classical approach

Consider the following problem. You work for a company that is a rather dubious supplier of electronic components, and you have just sent a batch of 200 components to a customer. You know that 80 of the components are damaged beyond repair, 30 are slightly damaged and the rest are in working order. Moreover, you know that, before he signs the acceptance form, the customer always picks out one component at random and tests it. What are the chances that the customer will select a component that is damaged beyond repair?

The classical approach to probability involves applying the following formula:

Probability of an event occurring

$$= \frac{\text{number of outcomes that represent occurrence of event}}{\text{total number of possible outcomes}}$$

In our problem, the customer could select any one of the 200 components, so there are 200 possible outcomes. In 80 of these outcomes, a component is selected that is damaged beyond repair, so

$$p(\text{selected component is damaged beyond repair}) = 80/200 = 0.40$$

In order to apply the classical approach to a problem, we have to assume that each outcome is equally likely to occur, so in this case we would have to assume that the customer is equally likely to select each component. Of course, this would not be the case if you knew that the customer tended to select a component from the top of the box and you deliberately packed the defective components in the bottom. In most practical situations (e.g. the simultaneous product launch above), the outcomes will not be equally likely, and therefore the usefulness of this approach is limited.

The relative frequency approach

In the relative frequency approach, the probability of an event occurring is regarded as the proportion of times that the event occurs in the long run if stable conditions apply. This probability can be estimated by repeating an experiment a large number of times or by gathering relevant data and determining the frequency with which the event of interest has occurred in the past. For example, a quality control inspector at a factory might test 250 light bulbs and find that only eight are defective. This would suggest that the probability of a bulb being defective is 8/250 (or 0.032). The reliability of the inspector's probability estimate would improve as he gathered more data: an estimate based on a sample of ten bulbs would be less reliable than one based on a sample of 250. Of course, the estimate is only valid if manufacturing conditions remain unchanged. Similarly, if the publisher of a weekly magazine found that circulation had exceeded the break-even level in 35 out of the past 60 weeks, then he might estimate that the probability of sales exceeding the break-even level next week will be 35/60 (or 0.583). Clearly, for this probability estimate to be reliable, the same market conditions would have to apply to every week under consideration; if there is a trend or seasonal pattern in sales, it will not be reliable.

This raises the problem of specifying a suitable reference class. For example, suppose that we wish to determine the probability that Mary, a 40-year-old unemployed computer programmer, will find a job within the next 12 months. By looking at recent past records, we might find that 30% of unemployed people found jobs within a year, and hence estimate that the probability is 0.3. However, perhaps we should only look at those records relating to unemployed female computer programmers of Mary's age and living in Mary's region of the country, or perhaps we should go even further and only look at people with similar qualifications and take into account the fact that Mary has a record of ill health. Clearly, if the data we used were made too specific, it is likely we would find that the only relevant record we had related to Mary herself. It can be seen that there is a conflict between the desirability of having a large set of past data and the need to make sure that the data relate closely to the event under consideration. Judgment is therefore required to strike a balance between these two considerations.

The subjective approach

Most of the decision problems that we will consider in this book will require us to estimate the probability of unique events occurring (i.e. events that only occur once). For example, if a company needs to estimate the probability that a new product will be successful or that a new state-of-the-art machine will perform reliably, then, because of the uniqueness of the situation, the past data required by the relative frequency approach will not be available. The company may have access to data relating to the success or otherwise of earlier products or machines, but it is unlikely that the conditions that applied in these past situations will be directly relevant to the current problem. In these circumstances, the probability can be estimated by using the subjective approach. A subjective probability is an expression of an individual's degree of belief that a particular event will occur. Thus, a sales manager may say: 'I estimate that there is a 0.75 probability that the sales of our new product will exceed $2 million next year'. Of course, such a statement may be influenced by past data or any other information that the manager considers to be relevant, but it is ultimately a personal judgment and as such it is likely that individuals will differ in the estimates they put forward even if they have access to the same information.

Many people are skeptical about subjective probabilities, and yet we make similar sorts of judgment all the time. If you decide to risk not insuring the contents of your house this year, then you must have made some assessment of the chances of the contents remaining safe over the next 12 months. Similarly, if you decide to invest on the stock market, purchase a new car or move to a new house, you must have spent some time weighing up the chances that things will go wrong or go well. In organizations, decisions relating to the appointment of new staff, launching an advertising campaign or changing to a new computer system will require some evaluation of the uncertainties involved. As we argued in the Introduction, by representing this judgment numerically rather than verbally, a much less vague assessment is achieved. The resulting statement can be precisely communicated to others and it enables an individual's views to be challenged and explored.

Some people may be concerned that subjective probability estimates are likely to be of poor quality. Much research has been carried out by psychologists to find out how good people are at making these sorts of judgments. We will review this research in Chapter 10, while in Chapter 11 we will introduce a number of elicitation methods that are designed to help decision-makers to make judgments about probabilities. At this stage, however, it is worth pointing out that such judgments rarely need to be exact. As we shall see, sensitivity analysis often reveals that quite major changes in the probabilities are required before it becomes apparent that the decision-maker should switch from one course of action to another.

Having looked at the three approaches to probability, we now need to consider the concepts and rules that are used in probability calculations. These calculations apply equally well to classical, relative frequency or subjective probabilities.

Mutually exclusive and exhaustive events

Two events are mutually exclusive (or *disjoint*) if the occurrence of one of the events precludes the simultaneous occurrence of the other. For example, if the sales of a product in the USA next year exceed 10 000 units, they cannot also be less than 10 000 units. Similarly, if a quality control inspection of a new TV set reveals that it is in perfect working order, it cannot simultaneously be defective. However, the events of 'dollar rises against the yen tomorrow' and 'the Dow-Jones index falls tomorrow' are not mutually exclusive: there is clearly a possibility that both events can occur together. If you make a list of the events that can occur when you adopt a particular course of action, then this list is said to be *exhaustive* if your list includes *every* possible event.

The addition rule

In some problems we need to calculate the probability that *either* one event *or* another event will occur (if A and B are the two events, you may see 'A or B' referred to as the 'union' of A and B). For example, we may need to calculate the probability that a new product development will take either 3 or 4 years, or the probability that a construction project will be delayed by either bad weather or a strike. In these cases, the addition rule can be used to calculate the required probability, but, before applying the rule, it is essential to establish whether or not the two events are mutually exclusive.

If the events are mutually exclusive then the addition rule is

$$p(\text{A or B}) = p(\text{A}) + p(\text{B})$$

where A and B are the events.

For example, suppose that a manager estimates the following probabilities for the time that a new product will take to launch:

Time to launch product	Probability
1 year	0.1
2 years	0.3
3 years	0.4
4 years	0.2

Suppose that we want to use this information to determine the probability that the launch will take either 1 or 2 years. Clearly, both events are mutually exclusive, so

$$p(\text{launch takes 1 or 2 years}) = p(\text{takes 1 year}) + p(\text{takes 2 years})$$
$$= 0.1 + 0.3 = 0.4$$

Similarly, if we want to determine the probability that the launch will take at least 2 years, we have

$$p(\text{launch takes 2 or 3 or 4 years}) = 0.3 + 0.4 + 0.2 = 0.9$$

Note that the complete set of probabilities given by the manager sum to 1, which implies that the list of possible launch times is exhaustive. In the manager's view it is certain that the launch will take 1, 2, 3 or 4 years.

Let us now see what happens if the addition rule for mutually exclusive events is wrongly applied. Consider Table 5.1. This relates to a tidal river that is liable to cause flooding during the month of April. The table gives details of rainfall during April for the past 20 years and also whether or not the river caused flooding. For example, there was light rainfall and yet the river flooded in four out of the last 20 Aprils.

Suppose that, in order to make a particular decision, we need to calculate the probability that next year there will either be heavy rain or the river will flood. We decide to use the relative frequency approach based on the records for the past 20 years, and

Table 5.1 – The frequency of flooding of a tidal river in April over the last 20 years

	Rainfall		
	Light	**Heavy**	**Total Number of Years**
River flooded	4	9	13
River did not flood	5	2	7
Total	9	11	20

we then proceed as follows:

$$p(\text{heavy rain or flood}) = p(\text{heavy rain}) + p(\text{flood})$$
$$= 11/20 + 13/20 = 24/20 \text{ which exceeds 1!}$$

The mistake we have made is to ignore the fact that heavy rain and flooding are *not* mutually exclusive: they can and have occurred together. This has meant that we have double-counted the nine years when both events did occur, counting them both as heavy rain years and as flood years.

If the events are not mutually exclusive, we should apply the addition rule as follows:

$$p(\text{A or B}) = p(\text{A}) + p(\text{B}) - p(\text{A and B})$$

The last term has the effect of negating the double-counting. Thus, the correct answer to our problem is

$$p(\text{heavy rain or flood}) = p(\text{heavy rain}) + p(\text{flood})$$
$$- p(\text{heavy rain and flood})$$
$$= 11/20 + 13/20 - 9/20 = 15/20 \text{ (or 0.75)}$$

Complementary events

If A is an event, then the event 'A does not occur' is said to be the complement of A. For example, the complement of the event 'project completed on time' is the event 'project not completed on time', while the complement of the event 'inflation exceeds 5% next year' is the event 'inflation is less than or equal to 5% next year'. The complement of event A can be written as $\bar{A}$ (pronounced 'A bar').

As it is certain that either the event or its complement must occur, their probabilities always sum to 1. This leads to the useful expression

$$p(\bar{A}) = 1 - p(A)$$

For example, if the probability of a project being completed on time is 0.6, what is the probability that it will not be completed on time? The answer is easily found:

$$p(\text{not completed on time}) = 1 - p(\text{completed on time})$$
$$= 1 - 0.6 = 0.4$$

Marginal and conditional probabilities

Consider Table 5.2, which shows the results of a survey of 1000 workers who were employed in a branch of the chemicals industry. The workers have been classified on the basis of whether or not they have been exposed in the past to a hazardous chemical and whether or not they have subsequently contracted cancer.

Suppose that we want to determine the probability that a worker in this industry will contract cancer *irrespective* of whether or not he or she was exposed to the chemical. Assuming that the survey is representative, and using the relative frequency approach, we have

$$p(\text{worker contracts cancer}) = 268/1000 = 0.268$$

This probability is called an unconditional or marginal probability because it is not conditional on whether or not the worker was exposed to the chemical (note that it is calculated by taking the number of workers in the margin of the table).

Suppose that now we wish to calculate the probability of a worker suffering from cancer *given that* he or she was exposed to the chemical. The required probability is

Table 5.2 – Results of a survey of workers in a branch of the chemicals industry

	Number of workers		
	Contracted cancer	**Have not contracted cancer**	**Total**
Exposed to chemical	220	135	355
Not exposed to chemical	48	597	645
Total	268	732	1000

known as a *conditional probability* because the probability we are calculating is conditional on the fact that the worker has been exposed to the chemical. The probability of event A occurring given that event B has occurred is normally written as $p(A \mid B)$, so in our case we wish to find p(worker contracts cancer | exposed to chemical). We only have 355 records of workers who were exposed to the chemical, and, *of these*, 220 have contracted cancer, so

$$p(\text{worker contracts cancer}|\text{exposed to chemical}) = 220/355 = 0.620$$

Note that this conditional probability is greater than the marginal probability of a worker contracting cancer (0.268), which implies that exposure to the chemical increases a worker's chances of developing cancer. We will consider this sort of relationship between events next.

Independent and dependent events

Two events, A and B, are said to be *independent* if the probability of event A occurring is unaffected by the occurrence or non-occurrence of event B. For example, the probability of a randomly selected husband belonging to blood group O will presumably be unaffected by the fact that his wife is blood group O (unless like blood groups attract or repel!). Similarly, the probability of very high temperatures occurring in England next August will not be affected by whether or not planning permission is granted next week for the construction of a new swimming pool at a seaside resort. If two events, A and B, are independent, then clearly

$$p(A|B) = p(A)$$

because the fact that B has occurred does not change the probability of A occurring. In other words, the conditional probability is the same as the marginal probability.

   In the previous section we saw that the probability of a worker contracting cancer *was* affected by whether or not he or she had been exposed to a chemical. These two events are therefore said to be *dependent*.

The multiplication rule

We saw earlier that the probability of either event A or B occurring can be calculated by using the addition rule. In many circumstances, however, we need to calculate the probability that *both* A *and* B will occur. For example, what is the probability that both the New York and the London Stock Market indices will fall today, or what is the probability that we will suffer strikes this month at both of our two production plants? The probability of A and B occurring is known as a *joint probability* and joint probabilities can be calculated by using the multiplication rule.

Before applying this rule, we need to establish whether or not the two events are independent. If they are, then the multiplication rule is

$$p(\text{A and B}) = p(\text{A}) \times p(\text{B})$$

For example, suppose that a large civil engineering company is involved in two major projects: the construction of a bridge in South America and a dam in Europe. It is estimated that the probability that the bridge construction will be completed on time is 0.8, while the probability that the dam will be completed on time is 0.6. The teams involved with the two projects operate totally independently, and the company wants to determine the probability that both projects will be completed on time.

As it seems reasonable to assume that the two completion times are independent, we have

$$p(\text{bridge and dam completed on time}) = p(\text{bridge completed on time})$$
$$\times\ p(\text{dam completed on time})$$
$$= 0.8 \times 0.6 = 0.48$$

The use of the above multiplication rule is not limited to two independent events. For example, if we have four independent events, A, B, C and D, then

$$p(\text{A and B and C and D}) = p(\text{A}) \times p(\text{B}) \times p(\text{C}) \times p(\text{D})$$

If the events are not independent, the multiplication rule is

$$p(\text{A and B}) = p(\text{A}) \times p(\text{B|A})$$

because A's occurrence would affect B's probability of occurrence. Thus, we have the probability of A occurring multiplied by the probability of B occurring, given that A has occurred.

To see how the rule can be applied, consider the following problem. A new product is to be test marketed in Florida and it is estimated that there is a probability of 0.7 that the test marketing will be a success. If the test marketing is successful, it is estimated that there is a 0.85 probability that the product will be a success nationally. What is the probability that the product will be both a success in the test marketing and a success nationally?

Clearly, it is to be expected that the probability of the product being a success nationally will depend upon whether it is successful in Florida. Applying the multiplication rule, we have

p(success in Florida and success nationally)
$$= p(\text{success in Florida}) \times p(\text{success nationally}|\text{success in Florida})$$
$$= 0.7 \times 0.85 = 0.59$$

Probability trees

As you have probably gathered by now, probability calculations require clear thinking. One device that can prove to be particularly useful when awkward problems need to be solved is the probability tree and the following problem is designed to illustrate its use.

A large multinational company is concerned that some of its assets in an Asian country may be nationalized after that country's next election. It is estimated that there is a 0.6 probability that the Socialist Party will win the next election, and a 0.4 probability that the Conservative Party will win. If the Socialist Party wins, then it is estimated that there is a 0.8 probability that the assets will be nationalized, while the probability of the Conservatives nationalizing the assets is thought to be only 0.3. The company wants to estimate the probability that their assets will be nationalized after the election.

The probability tree for this problem is shown in Figure 5.1. Note that the tree shows the possible events in chronological order from left to right; we consider first which party will win the election and then whether each party will or will not nationalize the assets. The four routes through the tree represent the four joint events which can occur (e.g. Socialists win and assets are not nationalized). The calculations shown on the tree are explained below.

We first determine the probability that the Socialists will win and the assets will be nationalized, using the multiplication rule for dependent events:

p(Socialists win and assets nationalized)
$$= p(\text{Socialists win}) \times p(\text{assets nationalized}|\text{Socialists win})$$
$$= 0.6 \times 0.8 = 0.48$$

We then determine the probability that the Conservatives will win and that the assets will be nationalized:

p(Conservatives win and assets nationalized)
$$= p(\text{Conservatives win}) \times p(\text{assets nationalized}|\text{Conservatives win})$$
$$= 0.4 \times 0.3 = 0.12$$

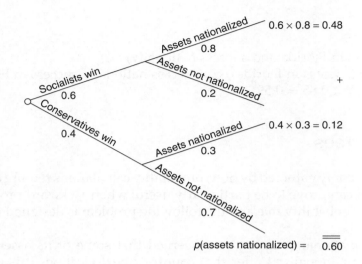

Figure 5.1 – A probability tree

Now we can obtain the overall probability of the assets being nationalized as follows:

$$p(\text{assets nationalized}) = p(\textit{either} \text{ Socialists win and nationalize } \textit{or}$$
$$\text{Conservatives win and nationalize})$$

These two events are mutually exclusive, as we assume that the election of one party precludes the election of the other, so we can simply add the two probabilities we have calculated to get

$$p(\text{assets nationalized}) = 0.48 + 0.12 = 0.60$$

Probability distributions

So far in this chapter we have looked at how to calculate the probability that a *particular* event will occur. However, when we are faced with a decision, it is more likely that we will be concerned to identify all the possible events that could occur if a particular course of action were chosen, together with their probabilities of occurrence. This complete statement of all the possible events and their probabilities is known as a probability distribution. For example, a consortium of business people who are considering setting up a new airline might estimate the following probability distribution

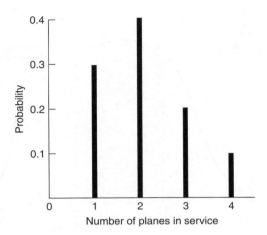

Figure 5.2 – Probability distribution for the number of planes in service by the end of the year

for the number of planes they will be able to have in service by the end of the year (this distribution is illustrated in Figure 5.2):

No. of planes in service	Probability
1	0.3
2	0.4
3	0.2
4	0.1
	1.0

Note that the probabilities sum to 1, as all the possible events have been listed. The 'number of planes in service' is known as an uncertain quantity. If we plotted, on a continuous scale, the values that this quantity could assume, then there would be gaps between the points: it would clearly be impossible for the airline to have 2.32 or 3.2451 planes in service, as the number of planes must be a whole number. This is therefore an example of what is known as a *discrete* probability distribution.

In contrast, in a *continuous* probability distribution the uncertain quantity can take on any value within a specified interval. For example, the time taken to assemble a component on a production line could take on any value between, say, 0 and 30 minutes. There is no reason why the time should be restricted to a whole number of minutes. Indeed, we might wish to express it in thousandths or even millionths of a minute; the only limitation would be the precision of our measuring instruments.

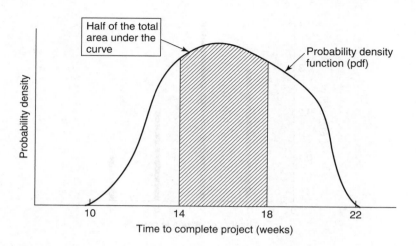

Figure 5.3 – Probability distribution for project completion time

Because continuous uncertain quantities can, in theory, assume an infinite number of values, we do not think in terms of the probability of a particular value occurring. Instead, the probability that the variable will take on a value within a given range is determined (e.g. what is the probability that our market share in a year's time will be between 5 and 10%?). Figure 5.3 shows a probability distribution for the time to complete a construction project. Note that the vertical axis of the graph has been labeled *probability density* rather than probability because we are not using the graph to display the probability that exact values will occur. The curve shown is known as a *probability density function* (pdf). The probability that the completion time will be between two values is found by considering the *area* under the pdf between these two points. As the company is certain that the completion time will be between 10 and 22 weeks, the whole area under the curve is equal to 1. Because half of the area under the curve falls between times of 14 and 18 weeks, this implies that there is a 0.5 probability that the completion time will be between these two values. Similarly, 0.2 (or 20%) of the total area under the curve falls between 10 and 14 weeks, implying that the probability that the completion time will fall within this interval is 0.2. A summary of the probability distribution is shown below:

Project completion time	Probability
10 to under 14 weeks	0.2
14 to under 18 weeks	0.5
18 to under 22 weeks	0.3
	1.0

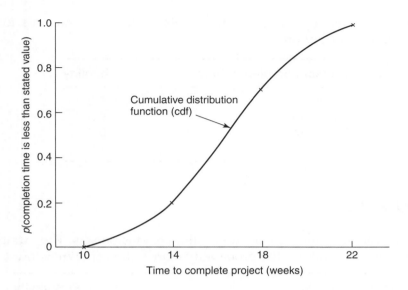

Figure 5.4 – Cumulative distribution function for project completion time

When eliciting a probability distribution, it is sometimes easier to think in terms of the probability of a variable having a value less than a particular figure. For example, 'what is the probability that our market share in a year's time will be less than 10%?' This can be facilitated by deriving the *cumulative distribution function* (cdf), which gives the probability that a variable will have a value less than a particular value. The cdf for the above project is shown in Figure 5.4. It can be seen that there is a 0.2 probability that the completion time will be less than 14 weeks and a 0.7 probability that it will be less than 18 weeks, and it is certain that the time will be less than 22 weeks.

Sometimes it is useful to use continuous distributions as approximations for discrete distributions, and vice versa. For example, when a discrete variable can assume a large number of possible values, it may be easier to treat it as a continuous variable. In practice, monetary values can usually be regarded as continuous because of the very large number of values that can be assumed within a specified range (consider, for example, the possible revenues in the range $0–1 million that could be earned by a company). This might also apply to the sales of a product. For example, the number of tins of baked beans sold must be an integer, but, if sales can range from 0 to 5 million tins, then, again, the uncertain quantity can take on a very large number of possible values. Similarly, it is often convenient to use discrete distributions as approximations to continuous distributions, particularly when constructing decision tree models (see Chapter 7). For example, we might approximate the continuous distribution of project completion times above by using the midpoints of the three intervals to obtain the following discrete distribution:

Project completion time	Probability
12 weeks	0.2
16 weeks	0.5
20 weeks	0.3
	1.0

Expected values

Suppose that a retailer runs a small shop selling television sets. The number of color sets she sells per week follows the probability distribution shown below:

No. of sets sold	Probability
0	0.01
1	0.10
2	0.40
3	0.30
4	0.10
5	0.09
	1.00

If this probability distribution applies to all weeks (e.g. we will assume that there is no trend or seasonal pattern in her sales), then we might be interested in calculating her mean (or average) weekly sales. This is easily done by multiplying each sales level by its probability of occurrence and summing the resulting products, as shown below; the result is known as an expected value:

No. of sets sold	Probability	No. of sets × probability
0	0.01	0.00
1	0.10	0.10
2	0.40	0.80
3	0.30	0.90
4	0.10	0.40
5	0.09	0.45
	1.00	Expected sales = 2.65

It can be seen that an expected value is a weighted average with each possible value of the uncertain quantity being weighted by its probability of occurrence. The resulting figure represents the mean level of sales that would be expected if we looked at the sales records over a large number of weeks. Note that an expected value does not have to coincide with an actual value in the distribution; it is obviously not possible to sell 2.65 sets in a given week.

Although an expected value is most easily interpreted as 'an average value that will result if a process is repeated a large number of times', as we will see in the next chapter, we may wish to use expected values even in unique situations. For example, suppose that a company purchases its main raw material from a country that has just experienced a military coup. As a result of the coup, it is thought that there is some possibility that the price of the material will increase in the very near future, and the company is therefore thinking of purchasing a large supply of the material now. It estimates that there is a 0.7 probability that the price will increase, in which case a saving of $350 000 will be made, and a 0.3 probability that the price will fall because of other world market conditions. In this case, purchasing early will cost $200 000. What is the expected saving of purchasing early? The calculations are shown below:

$$\text{Expected savings} = (0.7 \times \$350\,000) + (0.3 \times -\$200\,000)$$
$$= \$185\,000$$

Note that savings of $185 000 will not be achieved because the company will either save $350 000 or lose $200 000. The figure is simply an average of the two monetary values, taking into account their probabilities of occurrence. The practical use of such a figure is that it allows a decision-maker to evaluate the attractiveness of different options in decision problems that involve uncertainty, the topic of the next chapter.

The axioms of probability theory

If you use subjective probabilities to express your degree of belief that events will occur, then your thinking must conform to the axioms of probability theory. These axioms have been implied by the preceding discussion, but we will formally state them below:

Axiom 1: *Positiveness*. The probability of an event occurring must be non-negative.
Axiom 2: *Certainty*. The probability of an event that is certain to occur is 1. Thus, axioms 1 and 2 imply that the probability of an event occurring must be at least zero and no greater than 1.

Axiom 3: *Unions.* If events A and B are mutually exclusive, then

$$p(\text{A or B}) = p(\text{A}) + p(\text{B})$$

It can be shown that all the laws of probability that we have considered in this chapter can be derived from these three axioms. Note that they are generally referred to as Kolmogoroff's axioms and, as stated above, they relate to situations where the number of possible outcomes is finite.

In the next few chapters we will use subjective probability assessments in our calculations without attempting to evaluate the quality of these judgmental inputs to our analyses. In Chapters 10 and 11 we will consider the degree to which probability judgments comply with the axioms and have validity as predictions of future events.

Summary

As we shall see in the next chapter, probability assessments are a key element of decision models when a decision-maker faces risk and uncertainty. In most practical problems, the probabilities used will be subjective, but they must still conform to the underlying axioms of probability theory. Again, our approach has been normative; probability calculus is designed to show you what your judgments should look like if you accept its axioms and think rationally.

In later chapters we will look at methods that are designed to help the decision-maker to generate coherent assessments and we will examine in detail how good individuals are at making judgments about probabilities. Often the receipt of new information, such as market research results or provisional sales figures, can be used to modify initial probability assessments, and in Chapter 9 we will show how this revision of opinion should be carried out.

Above all, the correct application of the rules and concepts that we have introduced in this chapter requires both practice and clarity of thought. You are therefore urged to attempt the following exercises before reading further.

Exercises

Additional exercises can be found on the book's website

(1) Determine the probability of each of the following events occurring. State the approach to probability that you used and any assumptions that you needed to make.

(a) A person selected from the payroll of a company is a clerical worker, given that there are 350 people on the payroll of whom 120 are clerical workers.

(b) A light bulb selected from a production line is defective if, out of 400 bulbs already tested, eight were defective.

(c) A new-born baby is male.

(d) This month's sales forecast for a product has an error of more than 10% if the forecast had an error of over 10% in 21 out of the last 60 months.

(e) A permanently manned space station is established on Mars by the year 2050.

(2) The following table shows an estimated probability distribution for the sales of a new product in its first week:

Number of units sold	0	1	2	3	4	5
Probability	0.05	0.15	0.20	0.35	0.15	0.10

What is the probability that in the first week:
(a) four or five units will be sold;
(b) at least three units will be sold;
(c) at least one unit will be sold?

(3) The managers of a food company are interested in determining the effect on their sales of a competitor's television advertisements. An analysis of sales records for the last 120 weeks gives the following results:

	Level of sales			Total number of weeks
	Low	Medium	High	
Competitor advertised	32	14	18	64
Competitor did not advertise	21	12	23	56
Total	53	26	41	120

Assuming that these past data are a reliable guide to the future, determine the probability that next week:
(a) the competitor will advertise;
(b) sales will not be high;
(c) medium or high sales will be achieved;

    (d) either the competitor will advertise or only low sales will be achieved;

    (e) either the competitor will not advertise or high sales will be achieved.

(4) (a) With reference to the table in question (3), determine the following probabilities:

      (i) p(next week's sales will be high);

      (ii) p(next week's sales will be high | the competitor advertises);

      (iii) p(next week's sales will be high | the competitor does not advertise);

      (iv) p(next week's sales will be low);

      (v) p(next week's sales will be low | the competitor advertises).

    (b) Do the events 'competitor advertises' and 'high sales' appear to be independent?

(5) Given below are the results of a survey of 100 cars:

Condition of tires	Condition of brakes		
	Faulty	Not faulty	Total
Faulty	25	5	30
Not faulty	15	55	70
Total	40	60	100

    (a) Assuming that the survey is representative of all the cars on the road, what is the probability that a car selected at random will have:

      (i) faulty brakes;

      (ii) faulty tires;

      (iii) either faulty brakes or faulty tires;

      (iv) faulty brakes given that it has faulty tires;

      (v) faulty tires given that it has faulty brakes?

    (b) What conclusion would you draw about the relationship between the events 'faulty tires' and 'faulty brakes'?

(6) Three machines, A, B and C, operate independently in a factory. Machine A is out of action for 10% of the time, while B is out of action for 5% of the time and C for 20% of the time. A rush order has to be commenced at midday tomorrow. What is the probability that at this time:

    (a) all three machines will be out of action;

    (b) none of the machines will be out of action?

(7) A speculator purchases three stocks on the London Stock Exchange. He estimates that the probabilities that each of these stocks will have risen in value by the end of the week are, respectively, 0.6, 0.8 and 0.4.

(a) Assuming that the price changes in the three stocks are independent, determine the probability that all three stocks will have risen in value by the end of the week.

(b) Do you think that it is reasonable to assume that movements in the prices of individual stocks are independent?

(8) The managers of a company are considering the launch of a new product and they are currently awaiting the results of a market research study. It is thought that there is a 0.6 probability that the market research will indicate that sales of the product in its first three years will be high. If this indication is received, then the probability that sales will be high is thought to be 0.8. What is the probability that the market research will indicate high sales and sales will turn out to be high?

(9) An engineer at a chemical plant wishes to assess the probability of a major catastrophe occurring at the plant during the overhaul of a processor as a result of a malfunction in the equipment being used in the overhaul. He estimates that the probability of a malfunction occurring is 0.1. If this happens, there is only a 0.001 probability that a safety device will fail to switch off the equipment. If the safety device fails, the probability of a major catastrophe is estimated to be 0.8. What is the probability that a major catastrophe will occur at the plant during the overhaul as a result of the equipment malfunctioning?

(10) The probability of the Dow-Jones index rising on the first day of trading next week is thought to be 0.6. If it does rise, then the probability that the value of shares in a publishing company will rise is 0.8. If the index does not rise, then the publishing company's shares will only have a 0.3 probability of rising. What is the probability that the publishing company's shares will rise in value on the first day of trading next week?

(11) A car owners' club that offers a rescue service for stranded motorists has to make a decision on the number of breakdown patrols to deploy between midnight and 8 a.m. on weekdays during the summer. The number of requests for assistance received by a local office during these hours follows the probability distribution shown below:

No. of requests received	0	1	2	3	4	5
Probability	0.01	0.12	0.25	0.42	0.12	0.08

(a) Calculate the expected number of requests received and interpret your results.

(b) Is this a discrete or a continuous probability distribution?

(12) You are thinking of selling your house and you reckon that there is a 0.1 probability that you will sell it for $120 000, a 0.5 probability that you will receive $100 000 for it and a 0.4 probability that you will only receive $80 000. What is the expected selling price of the property? Interpret your result.

Decision-making under uncertainty 6

Introduction

In many decisions, the consequences of the alternative courses of action cannot be predicted with certainty. A company that is considering the launch of a new product will be uncertain about how successful the product will be, while an investor in the stock market will generally be unsure about the returns that will be generated if a particular investment is chosen. In this chapter we will show how the ideas about probability that we introduced in Chapter 5 can be applied to problems where a decision has to be made under conditions of uncertainty.

We will first outline a method that assumes the decision-maker is unable, or unwilling, to estimate probabilities for the outcomes of the decision, but that makes extremely pessimistic assumptions about these outcomes. Then, assuming that probabilities can be assessed, we will consider an approach based on the expected value concept that we met in Chapter 5. Because an expected value can be regarded as an average outcome if a process is repeated a large number of times, this approach is arguably most relevant to situations where a decision is made repeatedly over a long period. A daily decision by a retailer on how many items to have available for sale might be an example of this sort of decision problem. In many situations, however, the decision is not made repeatedly, and the decision-maker may only have one opportunity to choose the best course of action. If things go wrong, then there will be no chance of recovering losses in future repetitions of the decision. In these circumstances, some people might prefer the least risky course of action and we will discuss how a decision-maker's attitude to risk can be assessed and incorporated into a decision model.

Finally, we will broaden the discussion to consider problems that involve both uncertainty and more than one objective. As we saw in Chapter 2, problems involving multiple objectives are often too large for a decision-maker to comprehend in their entirety. We will therefore look at a method that is designed to allow the problem to be broken down into smaller parts so that the judgmental task of the decision-maker is made more tractable.

The maximin criterion

Consider the following problem. Each morning a food manufacturer has to make a decision on the number of batches of a perishable product that should be produced. Each batch produced costs $800, while each batch sold earns revenue of $1000. Any batch that is unsold at the end of the day is worthless. The daily demand for the product is either one or two batches, but at the time of production the demand for the day is unknown. The food manufacturer feels unable to estimate probabilities for the two levels of demand. The manufacturer would like to determine the optimum number of batches that he should produce each morning.

Clearly, the manufacturer has a dilemma. If he produces too many batches, he will have wasted money in producing food that has to be destroyed at the end of the day. If he produces too few, he will be forgoing potential profits. We can represent his problem in the form of a *decision table* (Table 6.1). The rows of this table represent the alternative courses of action that are open to the decision-maker (i.e. produce one or two batches), while the columns represent the possible levels of demand, which are, of course, outside the control of the decision-maker. The monetary values in the table show the profits that would be earned per day for the different levels of production and demand. For example, if one batch is produced and one batch demanded, a profit of $1000 − $800 (i.e. $200) will be made. This profit would also apply if two batches were demanded, as a profit can only be made on the batch produced.

Given these potential profits and losses, how should the manufacturer make his decision? (We will assume that he has only one objective, namely to maximize monetary gain so that other possible objectives, such as maximizing customer goodwill or market share, are of no concern.) According to the maximin criterion, the manufacturer should first identify the worst possible outcome for each course of action and then choose the alternative yielding the best of these worst outcomes. If the manufacturer produces one batch, he will make the same profit whatever the demand, so the worst possible outcome is a profit of $200. If he decides to produce two batches, the worst possible outcome is a loss of $600. As shown below, the best

Table 6.1 – A decision table for the food manufacturer
(the figures shown are the daily profits)

Course of action	Demand (no. of batches)	
	1	2
Produce one batch	$200	$200
Produce two batches	−$600	$400

of these worst possible outcomes (the MAXImum of the MINimum possible profits) is associated with the production of one batch per day, so, according to maximin, this should be the manufacturer's decision:

Course of action	Worst possible profit
Produce one batch	$200 − best of the worst possible outcomes
Produce two batches	−$600

Note that, if the outcomes had been expressed in terms of costs rather than profits, we would have listed the highest possible costs of each option and selected the option for which the highest possible costs were lowest. Because we would have been selecting the option with the minimum of the maximum possible costs, our decision criterion would have been referred to as *minimax*.

The main problem with the maximin criterion is its inherent pessimism. Each option is assessed only on its worst possible outcome, so that all other possible outcomes are ignored. The implicit assumption is that the worst is bound to happen, while, in reality, the chances of this outcome occurring may be extremely small. For example, suppose that you were offered the choice of receiving $1 for certain or taking a gamble that had a 0.9999 probability of yielding $1 million and only a 0.0001 probability of losing you $1. The maximin criterion would suggest that you should not take the risk of engaging in the gamble because it would assume, in spite of the probabilities, that you would lose. This is unlikely to be a sensible representation of most decision-makers' preferences. Nevertheless, the extreme risk aversion that is implied by the maximin criterion may be appropriate where decisions involve public safety or possible irreversible damage to the environment. A new cheaper form of food processing that had a one in ten thousand chance of killing the entire population would clearly be unacceptable to most people.

The expected monetary value (EMV) criterion

If the food manufacturer is able and willing to estimate probabilities for the two possible levels of demand, then it may be appropriate for him to choose the alternative that will lead to the highest *expected* daily profit. If he makes the decision on this basis, then he is said to be using the *expected monetary value* or EMV criterion. Recall from Chapter 5 that an expected value can be regarded as an average result that is obtained if a process is repeated a large number of times. This may make the criterion particularly appropriate for the retailer who will be repeating his decision day after day.

Table 6.2 – Another decision table for the food manufacturer
(the figures shown are the daily profits)

	Demand (no. of batches)	
Course of action	**1 (probability 0.3)**	**2 (probability 0.7)**
Produce one batch	$200	$200
Produce two batches	−$600	$400

Table 6.2 shows the manufacturer's decision table again, but this time with the probabilities added.

As we showed in Chapter 5, an expected value is calculated by multiplying each outcome by its probability of occurrence and then summing the resulting products. The expected daily profits for the two production levels are therefore as follows:

Produce one batch

$$\text{Expected daily profit} = (0.3 \times \$200) + (0.7 \times \$200) = \$200$$

Produce two batches

$$\text{Expected daily profit} = (0.3 \times -\$600) + (0.7 \times \$400) = \$100$$

These expected profits show that, in the long run, the highest average daily profit will be achieved by producing just one batch per day, and, if the EMV criterion is acceptable to the food manufacturer, then this is what he should do.

Of course, the probabilities and profits used in this problem may only be rough estimates, or, if they are based on reliable past data, they may be subject to change. We should therefore carry out sensitivity analysis to determine how large a change in these values there would need to be before the alternative course of action would be preferred. To illustrate the process, Figure 6.1 shows the results of a sensitivity analysis on the probability that just one batch will be demanded. Producing one batch will always yield an expected profit of $200, whatever this probability is. However, if the probability of just one batch being demanded is zero, then the expected profit of producing two batches will be $400. At the other extreme, if the probability of just one batch being demanded is 1.0, then producing two batches will yield an expected profit of −$600. The line joining these points shows the expected profits for all the intermediate probabilities. It can be seen that producing one batch will continue to yield the highest expected profit as long as the probability of just one batch being demanded is greater than 0.2. As, currently, this probability is estimated to be 0.3, it

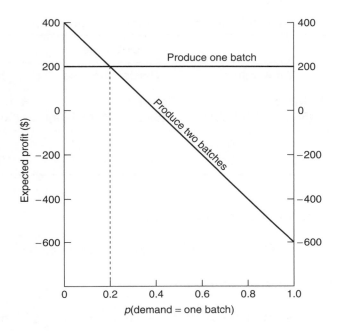

Figure 6.1 – A sensitivity analysis for the food manufacturer's problem

would take only a small change in the estimate for the alternative course of action to be preferred. Therefore, in this case the probability needs to be estimated with care.

Limitations of the EMV criterion

The EMV criterion may have been appropriate for the food manufacturer because he was only concerned with monetary rewards, and his decision was repeated a large number of times so that a long-run average result would have been of relevance to him. Let us now consider a different decision problem.

Imagine that you own a high-technology company that has been given the task of developing a new component for a large engineering corporation. Two alternative, but untried, designs are being considered (for simplicity, we will refer to these as designs 1 and 2) and because of time and resource constraints, only one design can be developed. Table 6.3 shows the estimated net returns that will accrue to your company if each design is developed. Note that these returns depend on how successful the design is. The estimated probabilities of failure, partial success and total success for each design are also shown in the table.

Table 6.3 – Returns and probabilities for the new component problem

	Outcome					
	Total failure		**Partial success**		**Total success**	
Course of action	**Returns ($m)**	**Probability**	**Returns ($m)**	**Probability**	**Returns ($m)**	**Probability**
Choose design 1	−1	0.1	0	0.1	3	0.8
Choose design 2	−6	0.3	1	0.1	10	0.6

The expected returns for design 1 are

$$0.1 \times (-\$1 \text{ m}) + 0.1 \times \$0 + 0.8 \times (\$3 \text{ m}) = \$2.3 \text{ m}$$

while for design 2 the expected returns are

$$0.3 \times (-\$6 \text{ m}) + 0.1 \times (\$1 \text{ m}) + 0.6 \times (\$10 \text{ m}) = \$4.3 \text{ m}$$

Thus, according to the EMV criterion, you should develop design 2, but would this really be your preferred course of action? There is a 30% chance that design 2 will fail and lead to a loss of $6 million. If your company is a small one or facing financial problems, then these sorts of losses might put you out of business. Design 1 has a smaller chance of failure, and, if failure does occur, then the losses are also smaller. Remember that this is a one-off decision, and there is therefore no chance of recouping losses on subsequent repetitions of the decision. Clearly, the risks of design 2 would deter many people. The EMV criterion therefore fails to take into account the attitude to risk of the decision-maker.

This can also be seen in the famous St Petersburg paradox described by Bernoulli. Imagine that you are offered the following gamble. A fair coin is to be tossed until a head appears for the first time. If the head appears on the first throw you will be paid $2, if it appears on the second throw, $4, if it appears on the third throw, $8, and so on. How much would you be prepared to pay to have the chance of engaging in this gamble? The expected returns on the gamble are

$$\$2 \times (0.5) + \$4 \times (0.25) + \$8 \times (0.125) + \ldots, \text{ etc.}$$

which equals

$$1 + 1 + 1 + \ldots \text{ to infinity}$$

so your expected returns will be infinitely large. On this basis, according to the EMV criterion, you should be prepared to pay a limitless sum of money to take part in the gamble. Given that there is a 50% chance that your return will be only $2 (and an 87.5% chance that it will be $8 or less), it is unlikely that many people would be prepared to pay anywhere near the amount prescribed by the EMV criterion!

It should also be noted that the EMV criterion assumes that the decision-maker has a linear value function for money. In reality, an increase in returns from $0 to $1 million may be regarded by the decision-maker as much more preferable than an increase from $9 million to $10 million, yet the EMV criterion assumes that both increases are equally desirable.

A further limitation of the EMV criterion is that it focuses on only one attribute: money. In choosing the design in the problem we considered above, we may also wish to consider attributes such as the effect on company image of successfully developing a sophisticated new design, the spin-offs of enhanced skills and knowledge resulting from the development and the time it would take to develop the designs. All these attributes, like the monetary returns, would probably have some risk associated with them.

In the rest of this chapter we will address these limitations of the EMV criterion. First, we will look at how the concept of single-attribute utility can be used to take into account the decision-maker's attitude to risk (or risk preference) in problems where there is just one attribute. The approach that we will adopt is based on the theory of utility, which was developed by von Neumann and Morgenstern.[1] Then we will consider multi-attribute utility, which can be applied to decision problems that involve both uncertainty and more than one attribute.

However, before we leave this section, we should point out that the EMV criterion is very widely used in practice. Many people would argue that it is even appropriate to apply it to one-off decisions. Although an individual decision may be unique, over time a decision-maker may make a large number of such decisions involving similar monetary sums, so that returns should still be maximized by consistent application of the criterion. Moreover, large organizations may be able to sustain losses on projects that represent only a small part of their operations. In these circumstances it may be reasonable to assume that risk neutrality applies, in which case the EMV criterion will be appropriate.

Single-attribute utility

The attitude to risk of a decision-maker can be assessed by eliciting a *utility function*. This is to be distinguished from the value functions we met in Chapter 3. Value functions are used in decisions where uncertainty is not a major concern, and therefore they do not involve any consideration of risk attitudes. (We will have more to say about the distinction between utility and value from a practical point of view in a later section of this chapter.)

To illustrate how a utility function can be derived, consider the following problem. A businesswoman who is organizing a business equipment exhibition in a provincial town has to choose between two venues: the Luxuria Hotel and the Maxima Center. To simplify her problem, she decides to estimate her potential profit at these locations on the basis of two scenarios: high attendance and low attendance at the exhibition. If she chooses the Luxuria Hotel, she reckons that she has a 60% chance of achieving a high attendance and hence a profit of $30 000 (after taking into account the costs of advertising, hiring the venue, etc.). There is, however, a 40% chance that attendance will be low, in which case her profit will be just $11 000. If she chooses the Maxima Center, she reckons she has a 50% chance of high attendance, leading to a profit of $60 000, and a 50% chance of low attendance, leading to a loss of $10 000.

We can represent the businesswoman's problem in the form of a diagram known as a decision tree (Figure 6.2). In this diagram, a square represents a decision point; immediately beyond this, the decision-maker can choose which route to follow. A circle represents a chance node; immediately beyond this, chance determines, with the indicated probabilities, which route will be followed, so the choice of route is beyond the control of the decision-maker. (We will consider decision trees in much more detail in Chapter 7.) The monetary values show the profits earned by the businesswoman if a given course of action is chosen and a given outcome occurs.

Now, if we apply the EMV criterion to the decision, we find that the business-woman's expected profit is $22 400 (i.e. 0.6 × $30 000 + 0.4 × $11 000) if she chooses

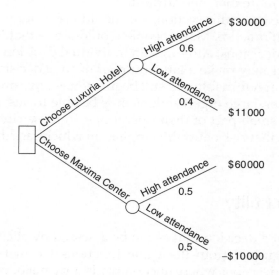

Figure 6.2 – A decision tree for the conference organizer's problem

the Luxuria Hotel, and $25 000 if she chooses the Maxima Center. This suggests that she should choose the Maxima Center, but this is the riskiest option, offering high rewards if things go well but losses if things go badly.

Let us now try to derive a utility function to represent the businesswoman's attitude to risk. We will use the notation $u(\ )$ to represent the utility of the sum of money that appears in the parentheses. First, we rank all the monetary returns that appear on the tree from best to worst and assign a utility of 1.0 to the best sum of money and 0 to the worst sum. As was the case with value functions in Chapter 3, any two numbers could have been assigned here, as long as the best outcome is assigned the higher number. We used 0 and 100 for value functions, but the use of 0 and 1 here will enable us to interpret what utilities actually represent. (If other values were used, they could easily be transformed to a scale ranging from 0 to 1 without affecting the decision-maker's preference between the courses of action.) Thus, so far we have the following:

Monetary sum	Utility
$60 000	1.0
$30 000	Not yet known
$11 000	Not yet known
−$10 000	0

We now need to determine the businesswoman's utilities for the intermediate sums of money. There are several approaches that can be adopted to elicit utilities. The most commonly used methods involve offering the decision-maker a series of choices between receiving given sums of money for certain or entering hypothetical lotteries. The decision-maker's utility function is then inferred from the choices that are made. The method that we will demonstrate here is an example of the *probability-equivalence* approach (an alternative elicitation procedure will be discussed in a later section).

To obtain the businesswoman's utility for $30 000 using this approach, we offer her a choice between receiving that sum for certain or entering a hypothetical lottery that will result in either the best outcome on the tree (i.e. a profit of $60 000) or the worst (i.e. a loss of $10 000) with specified probabilities. These probabilities are varied until the decision-maker is indifferent between the certain money and the lottery. At this point, as we shall see, the utility can be calculated. A typical elicitation session might proceed as follows:

Question: Which of the following would you prefer?

A: $30 000 for certain; or
B: A lottery ticket that will give you a 70% chance of winning $60 000 and a 30% chance of losing $10 000?

Answer: A 30% chance of losing $10 000 is too risky, I'll take the certain money.

We therefore need to make the lottery more attractive by increasing the probability of the best outcome:

Question: Which of the following would you prefer?

A: $30 000 for certain; or
B: A lottery ticket that will give you a 90% chance of winning $60 000 and a 10% chance of losing $10 000?

Answer: I now stand such a good chance of winning the lottery that I think I'll buy the lottery ticket.

The point of indifference between the certain money and the lottery should therefore lie somewhere between a 70% chance of winning $60 000 (when the certain money was preferred) and a 90% chance (when the lottery ticket was preferred). Suppose that, after trying several probabilities, we pose the following question:

Question: Which of the following would you prefer?

A: $30 000 for certain; or
B: A lottery ticket that will give you an 85% chance of $60 000 and a 15% chance of −$10 000?

Answer: I am now indifferent between the certain money and the lottery ticket.

We are now in a position to calculate the utility of $30 000. As the businesswoman is indifferent between options A and B, the utility of $30 000 will be equal to the expected utility of the lottery. Thus

$$u(\$30\,000) = 0.85\ u(\$60\,000) + 0.15\ u(-\$10\,000)$$

As we have already allocated utilities of 1.0 and 0 to $60 000 and −$10 000 respectively, we have

$$u(\$30\,000) = 0.85(1.0) + 0.15(0) = 0.85$$

Note that, once we have found the point of indifference, the utility of the certain money is simply equal to the probability of the best outcome in the lottery. Thus, if the decision-maker had been indifferent between the options that we offered in the first question, her utility for $30 000 would have been 0.7.

We now need to determine the utility of $11 000. Suppose that, after being asked a similar series of questions, the businesswoman finally indicates that she would be indifferent between receiving $11 000 for certain and a lottery ticket offering a 60% chance of the best outcome ($60 000) and a 40% chance of the worst outcome

(−$10 000). This implies that $u(\$11\ 000) = 0.6$. We can now state the complete set of utilities, and these are shown below:

Monetary sum	Utility
$60 000	1.0
$30 000	0.85
$11 000	0.60
−$10 000	0

These results are now applied to the decision tree by replacing the monetary values with their utilities (see Figure 6.3). By treating these utilities in the same way as the monetary values, we are able to identify the course of action that leads to the highest expected utility.

Choosing the Luxuria Hotel gives an expected utility of

$$0.6 \times 0.85 + 0.4 \times 0.6 = 0.75$$

Choosing the Maxima Center gives an expected utility of

$$0.5 \times 1.0 + 0.5 \times 0 = 0.5$$

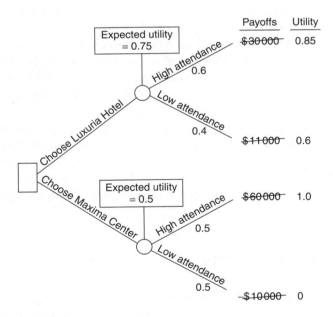

Figure 6.3 – The conference organizer's decision tree with utilities

Thus, the businesswoman should choose the Luxuria Hotel as the venue for her exhibition. Clearly, the Maxima Center would be too risky.

It is useful at this point to establish what expected utilities actually represent. Indeed, given that we have just applied the concept to a one-off decision, why do we use the term *expected* utility? To see what we have done, consider Figure 6.4(a). Here we have the businesswoman's decision tree with the original monetary sums replaced by the lotteries that she regarded as being equally attractive. For example, receiving $30 000 was considered to be equivalent to a lottery offering a 0.85 probability of $60 000 and a 0.15 probability of −$10 000. Obviously, receiving $60 000 is equivalent to a lottery ticket offering $60 000 for certain. You will see that every payoff in the tree is now expressed in terms of a probability of obtaining either the best outcome ($60 000) or the worst outcome (−$10 000).

Now, if the businesswoman chooses the Luxuria Hotel, she will have a 0.6 probability of finishing with a profit which she perceives to be equivalent to a lottery ticket offering a 0.85 probability of $60 000 and a 0.15 probability of −$10 000. Similarly, she will have a 0.4 probability of a profit, which is equivalent to a lottery ticket offering a 0.6 probability of $60 000 and a 0.4 chance of −$10 000. Therefore, the Luxuria Hotel offers her the equivalent of a $0.6 \times 0.85 + 0.4 \times 0.6 = 0.75$ probability of the best outcome (and a 0.25 probability of the worst outcome). Note that 0.75 is the expected utility of choosing the Luxuria Hotel.

Obviously, choosing the Maxima Center offers her the equivalent of only a 0.5 probability of the best outcome on the tree (and a 0.5 probability of the worst outcome). Thus, as shown in Figure 6.4(b), utility allows us to express the returns of all the courses of action in terms of simple lotteries all offering the same prizes, namely the best and worst outcomes, but with different probabilities. This makes the alternatives easy to compare. The probability of winning the best outcome in these lotteries is the expected utility. It therefore seems reasonable that we should select the option offering the highest expected utility.

Note that the use here of the term 'expected' utility is therefore somewhat misleading. It is used because the procedure for calculating expected utilities is arithmetically the same as that for calculating expected values in statistics. It does *not*, however, necessarily refer to an average result that would be obtained from a large number of repetitions of a course of action, nor does it mean a result or consequence that should be 'expected'.

Interpreting utility functions

The businesswoman's utility function has been plotted on a graph in Figure 6.5. If we selected any two points on this curve and drew a straight line between them, then it can be seen that the curve would always be above the line. Utility functions

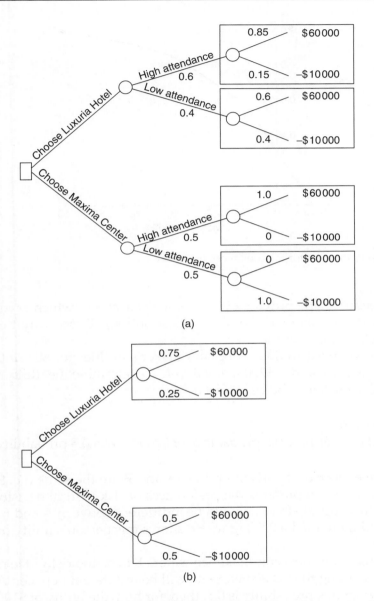

Figure 6.4 – A demonstration of how expected utility reduces the decision to a simple choice between lotteries

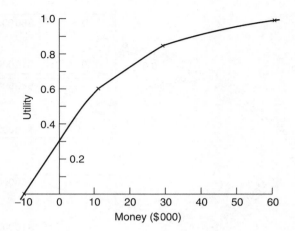

Figure 6.5 – A utility function for the conference organizer

having this *concave* shape provide evidence of *risk aversion* (which is consistent with the businesswoman's avoidance of the riskiest option). To see why this is the case, consider the following example.

Suppose that we need to find a decision-maker's utilities for $0, $1000 and $2000. We set $u($0)$ equal to 0 and $u($2000)$ equal to 1. To determine the utility for $1000, we offer the decision-maker a choice between

A: $1000 for certain; or
B: A lottery ticket offering a 0.5 probability of $2000 and a 0.5 probability of $0.

We see that the expected payoffs of options A and B are the same (i.e. $1000). Recall that the EMV criterion represents the preferences of risk-neutral decision-makers, so a person with this attitude to risk would be indifferent between A and B. Their utility for $1000 would therefore be 0.5. Figure 6.6 shows this person's utility function. Note that it is linear.

However, what if our decision-maker considers B to be too risky? He needs a larger probability of winning the $2000 before he will be indifferent between A and B. If he is indifferent when this probability is 0.8, then, for him, the utility of $1000 will be 0.8. Figure 6.6 also shows this person's utility function. Note that it has a concave shape similar to that of the businesswoman. As this person needed a higher probability of winning the lottery than the risk-neutral person before he was prepared to take the risk of option B, he is said to be risk averse. The extent to which a utility function departs from the diagonal line can be seen to reflect the extent of a decision-maker's risk aversion. An extremely risk-averse person might not have been prepared to consider taking option B until the probability of winning the $2000 was 0.95. His utility function

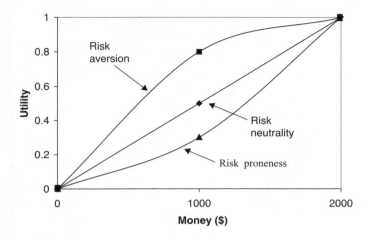

Figure 6.6 – Interpreting the shape of a utility function

would clearly have departed from the diagonal to a much greater extent than that of our decision-maker.

Finally, suppose that another person would be indifferent between A and B if the probability of winning the $2000 were only 0.3. Compared with a risk-neutral person, this person is prepared to take the risk of option B when the probability of winning is much lower. This indicates a risk-seeking attitude (or risk proneness). For this person, the utility of $1000 is 0.3. When the utility function is plotted in Figure 6.6, it can be seen to have a convex shape in that it always falls below the diagonal line.

Utility functions for non-monetary attributes

Utility functions can be derived for attributes other than money. Consider the problem that is represented by the decision tree in Figure 6.7. This relates to a drug company that is hoping to develop a new product. If the company proceeds with its existing research methods, it estimates that there is a 0.4 probability that the drug will take 6 years to develop and a 0.6 probability that development will take 4 years. However, recently a 'short-cut' method has been proposed that might lead to significant reductions in the development time, and the company, which has limited resources available for research, has to decide whether to take a risk and switch completely to the proposed new method. The head of research estimates that, if the new approach is adopted, there is a 0.2 probability that development will take a year, a 0.4 probability that it will take 2 years and a 0.4 probability that the approach will not work and, because of the time wasted, it will take 8 years to develop the product.

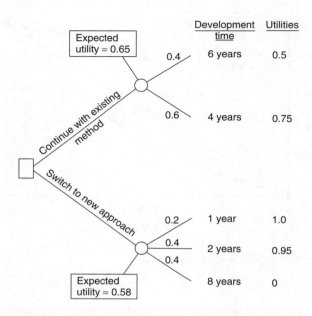

Figure 6.7 – A decision tree for the drug company research department problem

Clearly, adopting the new approach is risky, so we need to derive utilities for the development times. The worst development time is 8 years, so $u(8 \text{ years}) = 0$, and the best time is 1 year, so $u(1 \text{ year}) = 1.0$. After being asked a series of questions, based on the variable probability method, the head of research is able to say that she is indifferent between a development time of 2 years and engaging in a lottery that will give her a 0.95 probability of a 1 year development and a 0.05 probability of an 8 year development time. Thus

$$u(2 \text{ years}) = 0.95 \, u(1 \text{ year}) + 0.05 \, u(8 \text{ years})$$
$$= 0.95(1.0) + 0.05(0) = 0.95$$

By a similar process we find that $u(4 \text{ years}) = 0.75$ and $u(6 \text{ years}) = 0.5$. The utilities are shown on the decision tree in Figure 6.7, where it can be seen that continuing with the existing method gives the highest expected utility. Note, however, that the two results are close, and a sensitivity analysis might reveal that minor changes in the probabilities or utilities would lead to the other alternative being selected. The utility function is shown in Figure 6.8. This has a concave shape indicating risk aversion.

It is also possible to derive utility functions for attributes that are not easily measured in numerical terms. For example, consider the choice of design for a chemical plant. Design A may have a small probability of failure that may lead to pollution of the local environment. An alternative, design B, may also carry a small probability of

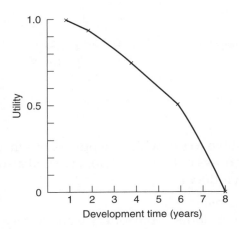

Figure 6.8 – A utility function for product development time

failure that would not lead to pollution but would cause damage to some expensive equipment. If a decision-maker ranks the possible outcomes from best to worst as (i) no failure, (ii) equipment damage and (iii) pollution, then, clearly, u(no failure) $= 1$ and u(pollution) $= 0$. The value of u(equipment damage) could then be determined by posing questions such as which would you prefer:

(1) a design that was certain at some stage to fail, causing equipment damage; or
(2) a design that had a 90% chance of not failing and a 10% chance of failing and causing pollution?

Once a point of indifference was established, u(equipment damage) could be derived.

Ronen *et al.*[2] describe a similar application in the electronics industry, where the decision relates to designs of electronic circuits for cardiac pacemakers. The designs carry a risk of particular malfunctions, and the utilities relate to outcomes such as 'pacemaker not functioning at all', 'pacemaker working too fast', 'pacemaker working too slow' and 'pacemaker functioning OK'.

The axioms of utility

In the last few sections we have suggested that a rational decision-maker should select the course of action that maximizes expected utility. This will be true if the decision-maker's preferences conform to the following axioms:

Axiom 1: The complete ordering axiom
To satisfy this axiom, the decision-maker must be able to place all lotteries in order of preference. For example, if he is offered a choice between two lotteries, the

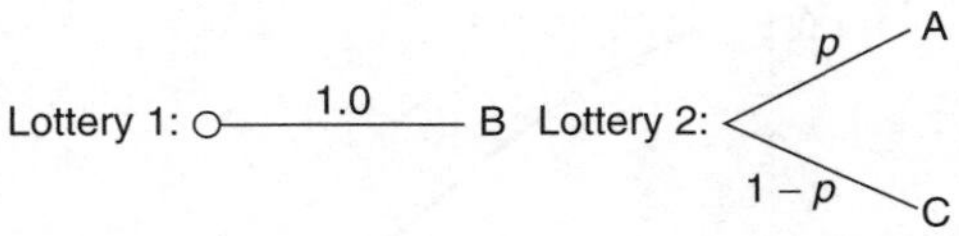

Figure 6.9 – The continuity axiom

decision-maker must be able to say which he prefers or whether he is indifferent between them. (For the purposes of this discussion, we will also regard a certain chance of winning a reward as a lottery.)

Axiom 2: The transitivity axiom

If the decision-maker prefers lottery A to lottery B and lottery B to lottery C, then, if he conforms to this axiom, he must also prefer lottery A to lottery C (i.e. his preferences must be transitive).

Axiom 3: The continuity axiom

Suppose that we offer the decision-maker a choice between the two lotteries shown in Figure 6.9. This shows that lottery 1 offers a reward of B for certain, while lottery 2 offers a reward of A with probability p and a reward of C with probability $1 - p$. Reward A is preferable to reward B, and B in turn is preferred to reward C. The continuity axiom states that there must be some value of p at which the decision-maker will be indifferent between the two lotteries. We obviously assumed that this axiom applied when we elicited the conference organizer's utility for $30 000 earlier in the chapter.

Axiom 4: The substitution axiom

Suppose that a decision-maker indicates that he is indifferent between the lotteries shown in Figure 6.10, where X, Y and Z are rewards and p is a probability. According to the substitution axiom, if reward X appears as a reward in another lottery, it can always be replaced with lottery 2 because the decision-maker regards X and lottery 2 as being equally preferable. For example, the conference organizer indicated that she was indifferent between the lotteries shown in Figure 6.11(a). If the substitution axiom applies, she will also be indifferent between lotteries 3 and 4, which are shown in Figure 6.11(b). Note that these lotteries are identical, except that in lottery 4 we have

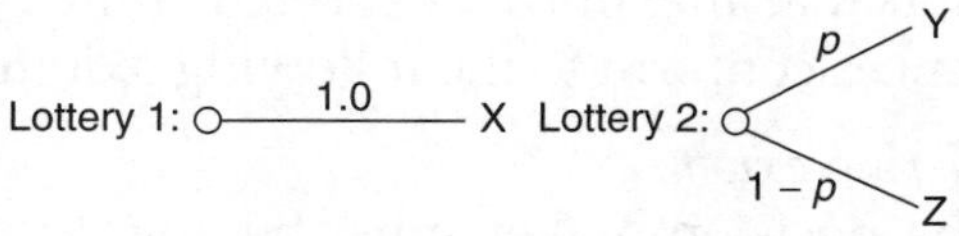

Figure 6.10 – The substitution axiom

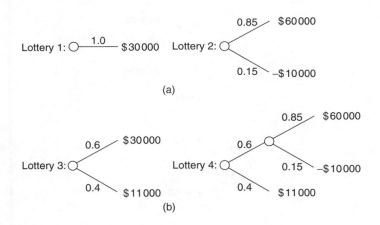

(a)

(b)

Figure 6.11 – Demonstration of the substitution axiom

substituted lottery 2 for the $30 000. Lottery 4 offers a 0.6 chance of winning a ticket in another lottery and is therefore referred to as a compound lottery.

Axiom 5: Unequal probability axiom
Suppose that a decision-maker prefers reward A to reward B. Then, according to this axiom, if he is offered two lotteries that only offer rewards A and B as possible outcomes, he will prefer the lottery offering the highest probability of reward A. We used this axiom in our explanation of utility earlier, where we reduced the conference organizer's decision to a comparison of the two lotteries shown in Figure 6.12. Clearly, if the conference organizer's preferences conform to this axiom, then she will prefer lottery 1.

Axiom 6: Compound lottery axiom
If this axiom applies, then a decision-maker will be indifferent between a compound lottery and a simple lottery that offers the same rewards with the same probabilities. For example, suppose that the conference organizer is offered the compound lottery shown in Figure 6.13(a). Note that this lottery offers a 0.28 (i.e. 0.4×0.7) probability of $60 000 and a 0.72 (i.e. $0.4 \times 0.3 + 0.6$) probability of −$10 000. According to this axiom, she will also be indifferent between the compound lottery and the simple lottery shown in Figure 6.13(b).

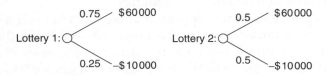

Figure 6.12 – Demonstration of the unequal probability axiom

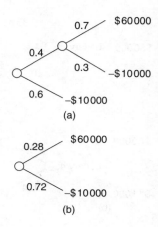

Figure 6.13 – Demonstration of the compound lottery axiom

It can be shown (see, for example, French[3]) that, if the decision-maker accepts these six axioms, then a utility function exists that represents his preferences. Moreover, if the decision-maker behaves in a manner that is consistent with the axioms (i.e. rationally), then he will choose the course of action that has the highest expected utility. Of course, it may be possible to demonstrate that a particular decision-maker does not act according to the axioms of utility theory. However, this does not necessarily imply that the theory is inappropriate in his case. All that is required is that he *wishes* to behave consistently according to the axioms. Applying decision analysis *helps* a decision-maker to formulate preferences, assess uncertainty and make judgments in a coherent fashion. Thus, coherence is the *result* of decision analysis, not a prerequisite.

More on utility elicitation

So far, we have only considered utility assessment based on the probability-equivalence approach. A disadvantage of this approach is that the decision-maker may have difficulty in thinking in terms of probabilities such as 0.90 or 0.95. Because of this, a number of alternative approaches have been developed (for example, Farquahar[4] reviews 24 different methods). Perhaps the most widely used of these is the *certainty-equivalence approach*, which, in its most common form, only requires the decision-maker to think in terms of 50:50 gambles.

To illustrate the approach, let us suppose that we wish to elicit a decision-maker's utility function for monetary values in the range $0–40 000 (so that $u(\$0) = 0$ and $u(\$40\ 000) = 1$). An elicitation session might proceed as follows:

Analyst: If I offered you a hypothetical lottery ticket that gave a 50% chance of $0 and a 50% chance of $40 000, how much would you be prepared to pay for it? Obviously, its expected monetary value is $20 000, but I want to know the minimum amount of money you would just be willing to pay for the ticket.

Decision-maker: (after some thought) $10 000.

Hence

$$u(\$10\,000) = 0.5\ u(\$0) + 0.5\ u(\$40\,000) = 0.5(0) + 0.5(1) = 0.5$$

The analyst would now use the $10 000 as the worst payoff in a new hypothetical lottery:

Analyst: If I now offered you a hypothetical lottery ticket that gave you a 50% chance of $40 000 and a 50% chance of $10 000, how much would you be prepared to pay for it?

Decision-maker: About $18 000.

Hence

$$u(\$18\,000) = 0.5\ u(\$10\,000) + 0.5\ u(\$40\,000)$$
$$= 0.5(0.5) + 0.5(1) = 0.75$$

The $10 000 is also used as the best payoff in a lottery that will also offer a chance of $0:

Analyst: What would you be prepared to pay for a ticket offering a 50% chance of $10 000 and a 50% chance of $0?

Decision-maker: $3000.

Thus

$$u(\$3000) = 0.5\ u(\$0) + 0.5\ u(\$10\,000)$$
$$= 0.5(0) + 0.5(0.5) = 0.25$$

It can be seen that the effect of this procedure is to elicit the monetary values that have utilities of 0, 0.25, 0.5, 0.75 and 1. Thus, we have the following:

Monetary value	$0	$3000	$10 000	$18 000	$40 000
Utility	0	0.25	0.5	0.75	1.0

If we plotted this utility function on a graph, it would be seen that the decision-maker is risk averse for this range of monetary values. The curve could, of course, also be used to estimate the utilities of other sums of money.

While the certainty-equivalence method we have just demonstrated frees the decision-maker from the need to think about awkward probabilities, it is not without its dangers. You will have noted that the decision-maker's first response ($10 000) was used by the analyst in subsequent lotteries, both as a best and worst outcome. This process is known as chaining, and the effect of this can be to propagate earlier judgmental errors.

The obvious question is 'do these two approaches to utility elicitation produce consistent responses?' Unfortunately, the evidence is that they do not. Indeed, utilities appear to be extremely sensitive to the elicitation method that is adopted. For example, Hershey et al.[5] identified a number of sources of inconsistency. Certainty-equivalence methods were found to yield greater risk seeking than probability-equivalence methods. The payoffs and probabilities used in the lotteries and, in particular, whether or not they included possible losses, also led to different utility functions. Moreover, it was found that responses differed depending upon whether the choice offered involved risk being assumed or transferred away. For example, in the certainty-equivalence method we could either ask the decision-maker how much he would be prepared to pay to *buy* the lottery ticket or, assuming that he already owns the ticket, how much he would accept to *sell* it. Research suggests that people tend to offer a lower price to buy the ticket than they would accept to sell it. There is thus a propensity to prefer the status quo, so that people are generally happier to retain a given risk than to take the same risk on (see also Thaler[6]). Finally, the context in which the questions were framed was found to have an effect on responses. For example, Hershey et al.[5] refer to an earlier experiment when the same choice was posed in different ways, the first involving an insurance decision and the second a gamble as shown below:

Insurance formulation
Situation A: You stand a one in a thousand chance of losing $1000.
Situation B: You can buy insurance for $10 to protect you from this loss.

Gamble formulation
Situation A: You stand a one in a thousand chance of losing $1000.
Situation B: You will lose $10 with certainty.

It was found that 81% of subjects preferred B in the insurance formulation, while only 56% preferred B in the gamble formulation.

Tversky and Kahneman[7] provide further evidence that the way in which the choice is framed affects the decision-maker's response. They found that choices involving statements about gains tend to produce risk-averse responses, while those involving losses are often risk seeking. For example, in an experiment, subjects were asked to choose a program to combat a disease that was otherwise expected to kill 600 people. One group was told that Program A would certainly save 200 lives, while Program B offered a 1/3 probability of saving all 600 people and a 2/3 probability of saving nobody. Most subjects preferred A. A second group was offered the equivalent choice, but this time the statements referred to the number of deaths rather than lives saved. They were therefore told that the first program would lead to 400 deaths while the second would offer a 1/3 probability of no deaths and a 2/3 probability of 600 deaths. Most subjects in this group preferred the second program, which clearly carries the higher risk. Further experimental evidence that different assessment methods lead to different utilities can be found in a paper by Johnson and Schkade.[8]

What are the implications of this research for utility assessment? First, it is clear that utility assessment requires effort and commitment from the decision-maker. This suggests that, before the actual elicitation takes place, there should be a preanalysis phase in which the importance of the task is explained to the decision-maker so that he will feel motivated to think carefully about his responses to the questions posed.

Second, the fact that different elicitation methods are likely to generate different assessments means that the use of several methods is advisable. By posing questions in new ways, the consistency of the original utilities can be checked, and any inconsistencies between the assessments can be explored and reconciled.

Third, as the utility assessments appear to be very sensitive both to the values used and the context in which the questions are framed, it is a good idea to phrase the actual utility questions in terms that are closely related to the values that appear in the original decision problem. For example, if there is no chance of losses being incurred in the original problem, then the lotteries used in the utility elicitation should not involve the chances of incurring a loss. Similarly, if the decision problem involves only very high or low probabilities, then the use of lotteries involving 50:50 chances should be avoided.

How useful is utility in practice?

We have seen that utility theory is designed to provide guidance on how to choose between alternative courses of action under conditions of uncertainty, but how useful is utility in practice? Is it really worth going to the trouble of asking the decision-maker a series of potentially difficult questions about imaginary lotteries given that, as we have just seen, there are likely to be errors in the resulting assessments? Interestingly, in a survey of published decision analysis applications over a 20 year period, Corner and Corner[9] found that 2/3 of applications used expected values as the decision criterion and reported no assessment of attitudes to risk. We will summarize here arguments both for and against the application of utility, and then present our own views at the end of the section.

First, let us restate that the *raison d'être* of utility is that it allows the attitude to risk of the decision-maker to be taken into account in the decision model. Consider again the drug research problem that we discussed earlier. We might have approached this in three different ways. First, we could have simply taken the course of action that led to the shortest expected development time. These expected times would have been calculated as follows:

Expected development time of continuing with the existing method
$$= 0.4 \times 6 + 0.6 \times 4 = 4.8 \text{ years}$$
Expected development time of switching to new research approach
$$= 0.2 \times 1 + 0.4 \times 2 + 0.4 \times 8 = 4.2 \text{ years}$$

The adoption of this criterion would therefore suggest that we should switch to the new research approach. However, this criterion ignores two factors. First, it assumes that each extra year of development time is perceived as being equally bad by the decision-maker, whereas it is possible, for example, that an increase in time from 1 to 2 years is much less serious than an increase from 7 to 8 years. This factor could be captured by a *value function*. We could therefore have used one of the methods introduced in Chapter 3 to attach numbers on a scale from 0 to 100 to the different development times in order to represent the decision-maker's relative preference for them. These *values* would then have replaced the actual development times in the calculations above, and the course of action leading to the highest expected value could be selected. However, you will recall from Chapter 3 that the derivation of a value function does not involve any considerations about probability, and it therefore will not capture the second omission from the above analysis, which is, of course, the attitude to risk of the decision-maker. A utility function is therefore designed to allow *both* of these factors to be taken into account.

In spite of this, there are a number of arguments against the use of utility. Perhaps the most persuasive relates to the problems of measuring utility. As Tocher[10] has argued, the elicitation of utilities takes the decision-maker away from the real world of the decision to a world of hypothetical lotteries. Because these lotteries are only imaginary, the decision-maker's judgments about the relative attractiveness of the lotteries may not reflect what he would really do. It is easy to say that you are prepared to accept a 10% risk of losing $10 000 in a hypothetical lottery, but would you take the risk if you were really facing this decision? Others (e.g. von Winterfeldt and Edwards[11]) argue that, if utilities can only be measured approximately, then it may not always be worth taking the trouble to assess them, as a value function, which is more easily assessed, would offer a good enough approximation. Indeed, even Howard Raiffa,[12] a leading proponent of the utility approach, argues:

> Many analysts assume that a value scoring system – designed for trade-offs under certainty – can also be used for probabilistic choice (using expected values). Such an assumption is wrong theoretically, but as I become more experienced I gain more tolerance for these analytical simplifications. This is, I believe, a relatively benign mistake in practice.

Another criticism of utility relates to what is known as Allais's paradox. To illustrate this, suppose that you were offered the choice of options A and B as shown in

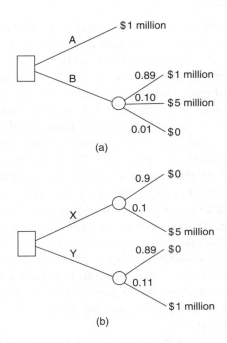

Figure 6.14 – Allais's paradox

Figure 6.14(a). Which would you choose? Experiments suggest that most people would choose A (e.g. see Slovic and Tversky).[13] After all, $1 million for certain is extremely attractive, while option B offers only a small probability of $5 million and a chance of receiving $0.

Now consider the two options X and Y that are shown in Figure 6.14(b). Which of these would you choose? The most popular choice in experiments is X. With both X and Y, the chances of winning are almost the same, so it would seem to make sense to go for the option offering the biggest prize.

However, if you did choose options A and X, your judgments are in conflict with utility theory, as we will now show.

If we let $u(\$5\text{ m}) = 1$ and $u(\$0) = 0$, then selecting option A suggests that $u(\$1\text{ m})$ is greater than $0.89\ u(\$1\text{ m}) + 0.1\ u(\$5\text{ m}) + 0.01\ u(\$0\text{ m})$, i.e. $u(\$1\text{ m})$ exceeds $0.89\ u(\$1\text{ m}) + 0.1$, which implies that $u(\$1\text{ m})$ *exceeds* $0.1/0.11$.

However, choosing X implies that $0.9\ u(\$0) + 0.1\ u(\$5\text{ m})$ exceeds $0.89\ u(\$0) + 0.11\ u(\$1\text{ m})$, i.e. 0.1 exceeds $0.11\ u(\$1\text{ m})$, so that $u(\$1\text{ m})$ is less than $0.1/0.11$.

This paradox has stimulated much debate[14] since it was put forward in 1953. However, we should emphasize that utility theory does not attempt to describe the way in which people make decisions like those addressed above. It is intended as a normative theory that indicates what a rational decision-maker should do *if* he accepts the axioms of the theory. The fact that people make inconsistent judgments does not by itself invalidate the theory. Nevertheless, it seems sensible to take a relaxed view of the problem. Remember that utility theory is designed as simply an aid to decision-making, and if a decision-maker wants to ignore its indications, then that is his prerogative.

Having summarized some of the main arguments, what are our views on the practical usefulness of utility? First, we have doubts about the practice adopted by some analysts of applying utility to decisions where risk and uncertainty are not central to the decision-maker's concerns. Introducing questions about lotteries and probabilities to these sorts of problems seems to us to be unnecessary. In these circumstances, the problem of trading off conflicting objectives is likely to be the main concern, and we would therefore recommend the approach taken in Chapter 3. In important problems that do involve a high level of uncertainty and risk, we do feel that utility has a valuable role to play as long as the decision-maker is familiar with the concept of probability and has the time and patience to devote the necessary effort and thought to the questions required by the elicitation procedure. In these circumstances, the derivation of utilities may lead to valuable insights into the decision problem. In view of the problems associated with utility assessment, we should not regard the utilities as perfect measures and automatically follow the course of action they prescribe. Instead, it is more sensible to think of the utility function as a useful tool for gaining a greater understanding of the problem.

If the decision-maker does not have the characteristics outlined above or only requires rough guidance on a problem, then it may not be worth eliciting utilities. Given the errors that are likely to occur in utility assessment, the derivation of values (as opposed to utilities) and the identification of the course of action yielding the highest expected value may offer a robust enough approach. (Indeed, there is evidence that linear utility functions are extremely robust approximations.) Sensitivity analysis would, of course, reveal just how precise the judgments needed to be (e.g. see Kirkwood[15]).

In the final section of this chapter we extend the application of utility to problems involving more than one attribute. We should point out that multi-attribute utility analysis can be rather complex, and the number of people applying it is not large. In the light of this, and the points made in our discussion above, we have decided to give only an introduction to this area so that a general appreciation can be gained of the type of judgments required.

Multi-attribute utility

So far in this chapter we have focused on decision problems that involve uncertainty and only one attribute. We next examine how problems involving uncertainty and multiple attributes can be handled. In essence, the problem of deriving a multi-attribute utility function is analogous to that of deriving a multi-attribute value function, which we discussed in Chapter 3. Again, the 'divide and conquer' philosophy applies. As we argued before, large multifaceted problems are often difficult to grasp in their entirety. By dividing the problem into small parts and allowing the decision-maker to focus on each small part separately, we aim to simplify his judgmental task. Thus, if certain conditions apply, we can derive a single-attribute utility function for each attribute using the methods of earlier sections and then combine these to obtain a multi-attribute utility function. A number of methods have been proposed for performing this analysis, but the approach we will discuss is associated with Keeney and Raiffa.[16] This approach has been applied to decision problems ranging from the expansion of Mexico City Airport (de Neufville and Keeney[17]) to the selection of sites for nuclear power plants (Kirkwood[18]).

The Decanal Engineering Corporation

To illustrate the approach, let us consider the following problem, which involves just two attributes. The Decanal Engineering Corporation has recently signed a contract to carry out a major overhaul of a company's equipment. Ideally, the customer would like the overhaul to be completed in 12 weeks, and, if Decanal meet the target or does not exceed it by a significant amount of time, it is likely to gain a substantial amount of goodwill from the customer and an enhanced reputation throughout the industry. However, to increase the chances of meeting the target, Decanal would have to hire extra labor and operate some 24 hour working, which would increase its costs. Thus, the company has two conflicting objectives: (1) to minimize the time that the project overruns the target date and (2) to minimize the cost of the project.

For simplicity, we will assume that Decanal's project manager has two options: (1) work normally or (2) hire extra labor and work 24 hour shifts. His estimates of the probabilities that the project will overrun the target date by a certain number of weeks are shown on the decision tree in Figure 6.15. The costs of the project for the two options and for different project durations are also shown on the tree. (Note that, once a given option is chosen, the longer the project takes to complete, the greater will be the costs because labor, equipment, etc., will be employed on the project for a longer period.)

To analyze this problem, we need to derive a multi-attribute utility function that will enable the project manager to compare the two options. This process is simplified if certain assumptions can be made. The most important of these is that of mutual utility independence.

Mutual utility independence

Suppose that the project manager is indifferent between the following alternatives:

A: A project that will certainly overrun by 2 weeks and that will certainly cost $50 000; and

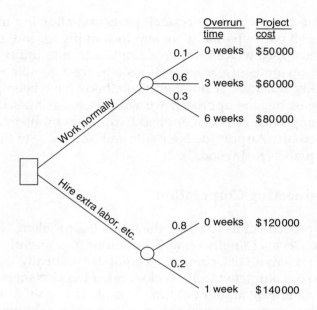

Figure 6.15 – A decision tree for the project manager's problem

B: A gamble that will give him a 50% chance of a project that overruns by 0 weeks (i.e. it meets the target) and that will cost $50 000 and a 50% chance of a project that will overrun by 6 weeks and cost $50 000.

These alternatives are shown in Figure 6.16(a) (note that all the costs are the same).

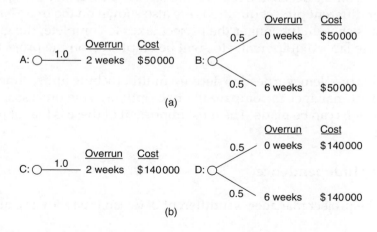

Figure 6.16 – Determining utility independence

Suppose that we now offer the project manager the same two options, but with the project costs increased to $140 000, as shown in Figure 6.16(b). If the project manager is still indifferent between the options, then clearly his preference between the overrun times is unaffected by the change in costs. If this is the case for all possible costs, then overrun time is said to be *utility independent* of project cost. Putting this in more general terms: attribute A is utility independent of attribute B if the decision-maker's preferences between gambles involving different levels of A but the same level of B do not depend on the level of attribute B.

It can be seen that utility independence is analogous to preference independence, which we discussed in Chapter 3, except that we are now considering problems that involve uncertainty. If project cost is also utility independent of overrun time (this will not automatically be the case), then we can say that overrun time and project cost are *mutually utility independent*.

The great advantage of mutual utility independence, if it exists, is that it enables the decision-maker to concentrate initially on deriving utility function for one attribute at a time without the need to worry about the other attributes. If this independence does not exist, then the analysis can be extremely complex (see Keeney and Raiffa[16]), but in very many practical situations it is usually possible to define the attributes in such a way that they do have the required independence.

Deriving the multi-attribute utility function

Assuming that mutual utility independence does exist, we now derive the multi-attribute utility function as follows:

Stage 1: Derive single-attribute utility functions for overrun time and project cost.
Stage 2: Combine the single-attribute functions to obtain a multi-attribute utility function so that we can compare the alternative courses of action in terms of their performance over both attributes.
Stage 3: Perform consistency checks, to see if the multi-attribute utility function really does represent the decision-maker's preferences, and sensitivity analysis to examine the effect of changes in the figures supplied by the decision-maker.

Stage 1

First we need to derive a utility function for project overrun. Using the approach that we discussed earlier in the context of single-attribute utility, we give the best overrun (0 weeks) a utility of 1.0 and the worst (6 weeks) a utility of 0. We then attempt to find the utility of the intermediate values, starting with an overrun of 3 weeks. After

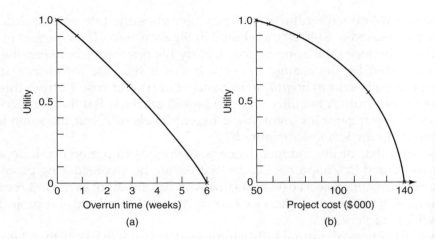

Figure 6.17 – Utility functions for overrun time and project cost

being asked a series of questions, the project manager indicates that he is indifferent between:

A: A project that will certainly overrun by 3 weeks; and
B: A gamble offering a 60% chance of a project with 0 weeks overrun and a 40% chance of a 6 week overrun.

This implies that u(3 weeks overrun) $= 0.6$. By a similar process, the manager indicates that u(1 week overrun) $= 0.9$. The resulting utility function is shown in Figure 6.17(a).

We then repeat the elicitation process to obtain a utility function for project cost. The function obtained from the manager is shown in Figure 6.17(b). Table 6.4 summarizes the utilities that have been elicited for overrun and cost.

Stage 2

We now need to combine these utility functions to obtain the multi-attribute utility function. If the two attributes are mutually utility independent, then it can be shown that the multi-attribute utility function will have the following form:

$$u(x_1, x_2) = k_1 u(x_1) + k_2 u(x_2) + k_3 u(x_1)u(x_2)$$

where x_1 is the level of attribute 1; x_2 is the level of attribute 2; $u(x_1, x_2)$ is the multi-attribute utility if attribute 1 has a level x_1 and attribute 2 has a level x_2; $u(x_1)$ is the single-attribute utility if attribute 1 has a level x_1; $u(x_2)$ is the single-attribute utility if attribute 2 has a level x_2; and k_1, k_2 and k_3 are numbers that are used to 'weight' the single-attribute utilities.

Table 6.4 – The project manager's utilities for overrun and cost

No. of weeks project overruns target	Utility	Cost of project ($)	Utility
0	1.0	50 000	1.00
1	0.9	60 000	0.96
3	0.6	80 000	0.90
6	0.0	120 000	0.55
		140 000	0.00

In stage 1 we derived $u(x_1)$ and $u(x_2)$, so we now need to find the values of k_1, k_2 and k_3. We note that k_1 is the weight attached to the utility for overrun time. In order to find its value, we offer the project manager a choice between the following alternatives:

A: A project where overrun is certain to be at its best level (i.e. 0 weeks), but where the cost is certain to be at its worst level (i.e. $140 000); or

B: A lottery that offers a probability of k_1 that both overrun and cost will be at their best levels (i.e. 0 weeks and $50 000) and a $1 - k_1$ probability that they will both be at their worst levels (i.e. 6 weeks and $140 000).

These options are shown in Figure 6.18. Note that, because we are finding k_1, it is attribute 1 (i.e. overrun) that appears at its best level in the certain outcome.

The decision-maker is now asked what value the probability k_1 must have to make him indifferent between the certain outcome and the lottery. After some thought, he indicates that this probability is 0.8, so $k_1 = 0.8$. This suggests that the 'swing' from the worst to the best overrun time is seen by the project manager to be significant relative to project cost. If he hardly cared whether the overrun was 0 or 6 weeks, it would have taken only a small value of k_1 to have made him indifferent to a gamble where overrun time might turn out to be at its worst level.

To obtain k_2, the weight for project cost, we offer the project manager a similar pair of options. However, in the certain outcome, project cost is now at its best level and the other attribute at its worst level. The probability of the best outcome in the lottery is now k_2. These two options are shown in Figure 6.19.

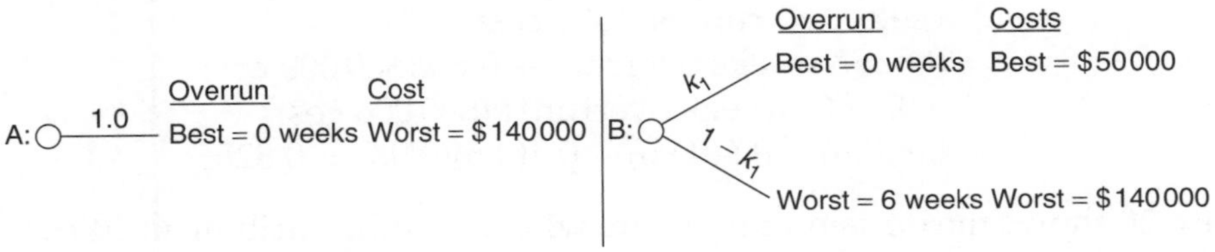

Figure 6.18 – Determining k_1

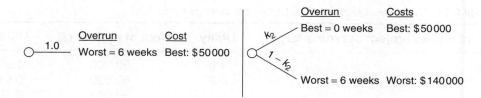

Figure 6.19 – Determining k_2

We now ask the project manager what value k_2 would need to be to make him indifferent between the two options. He judges this probability to be 0.6, so $k_2 = 0.6$. The fact that k_2 is less than k_1 suggests that the project manager sees the swing from the worst to the best cost as being less significant than the swing from the worst to the best overrun time. Having been offered a project that is certain to incur the lowest cost, he requires a smaller probability to tempt him to the lottery where he might gain a project where overrun is also at its best level but where there is also a risk of a project with costs at their worst level.

Finally, we need to find k_3. This is a simple calculation, and it can be shown that

$$k_1 + k_2 + k_3 = 1$$

so

$$k_3 = 1 - k_1 - k_2$$

Thus, in our case, $k_3 = 1 - 0.8 - 0.6 = -0.4$. The project manager's multi-attribute utility function is therefore

$$u(x_1, x_2) = 0.8u(x_1) + 0.6u(x_2) - 0.4u(x_1)u(x_2)$$

We can now use the multi-attribute utility function to determine the utilities of the different outcomes in the decision tree. For example, to find the utility of a project that overruns by 3 weeks and costs $60 000, we proceed as follows. From the single-attribute functions, we know that $u(3$ weeks overrun$) = 0.6$ and $u(\$60\,000$ cost$) = 0.96$. Therefore

$$
\begin{aligned}
u(3 \text{ weeks overrun, } \$60\,000 \text{ cost}) \\
= 0.8\, u(3 \text{ weeks overrun}) + 0.6\, u(\$60\,000 \text{ cost}) \\
-0.4\, u(3 \text{ weeks overrun})u(\$60\,000 \text{ cost}) \\
= 0.8(0.6) + 0.6(0.96) - 0.4(0.6)(0.96) = 0.8256
\end{aligned}
$$

Figure 6.20 shows the decision tree again, with the multi-attribute utilities replacing the original attribute values. By multiplying the probabilities of the outcomes by their utilities, we obtain the expected utility of each option. The results shown on the tree

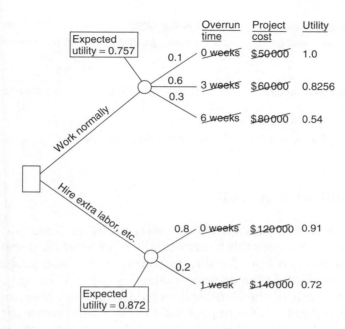

		Overrun time	Project cost	Utility
Expected utility = 0.757	0.1	0 weeks	$50000	1.0
	0.6	3 weeks	$60000	0.8256
	0.3	6 weeks	$80000	0.54
	0.8	0 weeks	$120000	0.91
Expected utility = 0.872	0.2	1 week	$140000	0.72

Figure 6.20 – The project manager's decision tree with utilities

indicate that the project manager should hire the extra labor and operate 24-hour working, as this yields the highest expected utility.

Stage 3

It is important that we should check that the results of the analysis have faithfully represented the project manager's preferences. This can involve tracking back through the analysis and explaining why one option has performed well and another has performed badly. If the decision-maker does not feel that the explanations are consistent with his preferences, then the analysis may need to be repeated. In fact, it is likely that several iterations will be necessary before a consistent representation is achieved, and, as the decision-maker gains a greater understanding of his problem, he may wish to revise his earlier responses.

Another way of checking consistency is to offer the decision-maker a new set of lotteries and to ask him to rank them in order of preference. For example, we could offer the project manager the three lotteries shown in Figure 6.21. The expected utilities of these lotteries are A 0.726, B 0.888 and C 0.620, so if he is consistent then he should rank them in the order B, A, C. We should also carry out sensitivity analysis on the probabilities and utilities by, for example, examining the effect of changes in the values of k_1 and k_2.

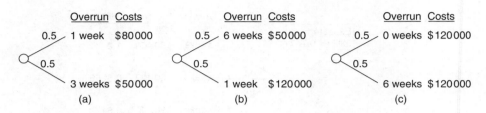

Figure 6.21 – Checking the consistency of the decision maker's responses

Interpreting multi-attribute utilities

In the analysis above, we derived an expected utility of 0.872 for the 'hire extra labor . . .' option, but what does this figure actually represent? We demonstrated earlier that we could use the concept of utility to convert a decision problem to a simple choice between lotteries that the decision-maker regarded as being equivalent to the original outcomes. Each of these lotteries would result in either the best or worst possible outcome, but with different probabilities. The same is true for multi-attribute utility. This time the lotteries will result in either the best outcome on both attributes (i.e. the best/best outcome) or the worst possible outcome on both attributes (i.e. worst/worst). Thus, the expected utility of 0.872 for the 'hire extra labor . . .' option implies that the decision-maker regards this option as being equivalent to a lottery offering a 0.872 chance of the best/best outcome (and a complementary probability of the worst/worst outcome). It therefore seems reasonable that he should prefer this option to the 'work normally' alternative, which is regarded as being equivalent to a lottery offering only a 0.757 chance of the best/best outcome.

Further points on multi-attribute utility

The principles that we applied to the two-attribute problem above can be extended to any number of attributes (see, for example, Bunn,[19] who discusses a problem involving four attributes), although the form of the multi-attribute utility function becomes more complex as the number of attributes increases. Models have also been developed that can handle situations where mutual utility independence does not exist (see Keeney and Raiffa[16]), but the complexities of these models have meant that they have proved to be of little practical value. In any case, as we mentioned earlier, if mutual utility independence does not exist, it is likely that, by redefining the attributes, a new set can be found that does exhibit the required independence (we discussed the analogous problem in Chapter 3 when looking at multi-attribute value functions).

The approach to multi-attribute utility that we discussed above clearly requires a major commitment of time and effort from the decision-maker, and, as the method lacks the 'transparency' of the SMART procedure, which we met in Chapter 3, a non-mathematical person may be suspicious of its results. In all models, a balance has to be struck between the accuracy with which the model represents the real problem and the effort required to formulate the model. If a problem is of major importance, and if the decision-maker is happy to make the necessary judgments, then what Watson and Buede[20] refer to as the 'deep soul searching' engendered by Keeney and Raiffa's approach may lead to valuable insights into the decision problem. In other circumstances, where the decision-maker only requires outline guidance from the model, a less sophisticated approach based, for example, on values rather than utilities may suffice. Sensitivity analysis will provide useful guidance on the robustness of any approximations that are used. Methods and software designed to support decisions where there are multiple objectives are constantly being enhanced (and their range of applications is constantly being extended),[21,22] so it is likely that most decision-makers will find an approach that is suited to their needs.

Summary

In this chapter we have considered a number of methods that enable a decision-maker to make rational decisions when the outcomes of courses of action are not known for certain. The approach based on expected monetary value was relatively simple, but, if the decision-maker does not have a neutral attitude to risk, then the adoption of this criterion may lead to the most preferred course of action not being chosen. We therefore introduced the concept of expected utility to show how the decision-maker's attitude to risk can be incorporated into the decision model. Finally, we showed how the application of utility can be extended to decision problems involving more than one attribute.

Exercises

Additional exercises can be found on the book's website

(1) An entertainment company is organizing a pop concert in London. The company has to decide how much it should spend on publicizing the event, and three options have been identified:

Option 1: Advertise only in the music press;

Option 2: As option 1, but also advertise in the national press;

Option 3: As options 1 and 2, but also advertise on commercial radio.

For simplicity, the demand for tickets is categorized as low, medium or high. The payoff table below shows how the profit that the company will earn for each option depends on the level of demand:

		Demand		
Option	Low	Medium	High	Profits ($000s)
1	−20	−20	100	
2	−60	−20	60	
3	−100	−60	20	

It is estimated that if option 1 is adopted the probabilities of low, medium and high demand are 0.4, 0.5 and 0.1 respectively. For option 2 the respective probabilities are 0.1, 0.3 and 0.6, while for option 3 they are 0.05, 0.15 and 0.8. Determine the option that will lead to the highest expected profit. Would you have any reservations about recommending this option to the company?

(2) A speculator is considering the purchase of a commodity that he reckons has a 60% chance of increasing in value over the next month. If he purchases the commodity and it does increase in value, the speculator will make a profit of about $200 000, otherwise he will lose $60 000.

   (a) Assuming that the expected monetary value criterion is applicable, determine whether the speculator should purchase the commodity.

   (b) Perform a sensitivity analysis on the speculator's estimate of the probability of a price increase, and interpret your result.

   (c) What reservations would you have about applying the expected monetary value criterion in this context?

(3) A team of scientists is due to spend 6 months in Antarctica carrying out research. One major piece of equipment they will be taking is subject to breakdowns caused by the sudden failure of a particular component. Because a failed component cannot be repaired, the team intend to carry a stock of spare units of the component, but it will cost them roughly $3000 for each spare unit they take with them. However, if the equipment breaks down and a spare is not available, a new unit will have to be specially flown in and the team will incur a total cost of $4000 for each unit that is delivered in this way. An engineer who

will be traveling with the team has estimated that the number of spares that will be required during the 6 months follows the probability distribution shown below:

No. of spares required	0	1	2	3
Probability	0.2	0.3	0.4	0.1

Determine the number of spares that the team should carry if their objective is to minimize expected costs.

(4) You are a contestant on a television game show and you have won $5000 so far. You are now offered a choice: either you can keep the money and leave or you can continue into the next round, where you have a 70% chance of increasing your winnings to $10 000 and a 30% chance of losing the $5000 and finishing the game with nothing.

(a) Which option would you choose?

(b) How does your choice compare with that which would be prescribed by the expected monetary value criterion?

(5) A building contractor is submitting an estimate to a potential customer for carrying out some construction work at the customer's premises. The builder reckons that, if he offers to carry out the work for $150 000, there is a 0.2 probability that the customer will agree to the price, a 0.5 probability that a price of $120 000 would eventually be agreed and a 0.3 probability that the customer will simply refuse the offer and give the work to another builder. If the builder offers to carry out the work for $100 000, he reckons that there is a 0.3 probability that the customer will accept this price, a 0.6 probability that the customer will bargain so that a price of $80 000 will eventually be agreed and a 0.1 probability that the customer will refuse the offer and take the work elsewhere.

(a) Determine which price the builder should quote in order to maximize the expected payment he receives from the customer.

(b) Suppose that, after some questioning, the builder is able to make the following statements:

'I am indifferent between receiving $120 000 for certain or entering a lottery that will give me a 0.9 probability of $150 000 and a 0.1 probability of winning $0.'

'I am indifferent between receiving $100 000 for certain or entering a lottery that will give me a 0.85 probability of winning $150 000 and a 0.15 probability of winning $0.'

'I am indifferent between receiving $80 000 for certain or entering a lottery that will give me a 0.75 probability of winning $150 000 and a 0.25 probability of winning $0.'

  (i) Sketch the builder's utility function and comment on what it shows.

  (ii) In the light of the above statements, which price should the builder now quote to the customer and why?

(6) (a) Use the following questions to assess your own utility function for money values between $0 and $5000. You should assume that all sums of money referred to will be received immediately.

  (i) You are offered either a sum of money for certain or a lottery ticket that will give you a 50% chance of winning $5000 and a 50% chance of winning $0. Write down below the certain sum of money that would make you indifferent between whether you received it or the lottery ticket. $......(we will refer to this sum of money as X). The utility of X is 0.5.

  (ii) You are now offered a lottery ticket that offers you a 50% chance of $......(enter X here) and a 50% chance of $0. Alternatively, you will receive a sum of money for certain. Write down below the certain sum of money that would make you indifferent between whether you received it or the lottery ticket.

$......

The utility of this sum of money is 0.25.

  (iii) Finally, you are offered a sum of money for certain or a lottery ticket that will give you a 50% chance of $5000 and a 50% chance of $......(enter X here). Write down below the certain sum of money that would make you indifferent between whether you received it or the lottery ticket.

$......

The utility of this sum of money is 0.75.

(b) Plot your utility function and discuss what it reveals.

(c) Discuss the strengths and limitations of the assessment procedure that was used in (a).

(7) A company is planning to re-equip one of its major production plants, and one of two types of machine, the Zeta and the Precision II, is to be purchased. The prices of the two machines are very similar, so the choice of machine is to be based on two factors: running costs and reliability. It is agreed that these two factors can be represented by the following variables: average weekly operating costs and number of breakdowns in the first year of operation. The company's production manager estimates that the following probability distributions apply to the two machines (it can be assumed that the probability distributions for operating costs and number of breakdowns are independent):

Zeta			
Average weekly operating costs ($)	Prob.	No. of breakdowns	Prob.
20 000	0.6	0	0.15
30 000	0.4	1	0.85

Precision II			
Average weekly operating costs ($)	Prob.	No. of breakdowns	Prob.
15 000	0.5	0	0.2
35 000	0.5	1	0.7
		2	0.1

Details of the manager's utility functions for operating costs and number of breakdowns are shown below:

Average weekly operating costs ($)	Utility	No. of breakdowns	Utility
15 000	1.0	0	1.0
20 000	0.8	1	0.9
30 000	0.3	2	0
35 000	0		

(a) The production manager's responses to questions reveal that, for him, the two attributes are mutually utility independent. Explain what this means.

(b) The production manager also indicates that, for him, $k_1 = 0.7$ (where attribute 1 = operating costs) and $k_2 = 0.5$. Discuss how these values could have been determined.

(c) Which machine has the highest expected utility for the production manager?

(8) The managers of the Lightning Cycle Company are hoping to develop a new bicycle braking system. Two alternative systems have been proposed, and, although the mechanics of the two systems are similar, one design will use mainly plastic components while the other will use mainly metal ones. Ideally, the design chosen would be the lightest and the most durable but, because some of the technology involved is new, there is some uncertainty about what the characteristics of the resulting product would be.

The leader of Lightning's research and development team has estimated that, if the plastic design is developed, there is a 60% chance that the resulting system would add 130 grams to a bicycle's weight and would have a guaranteed lifetime of 1 year. He also reckons that there is a 40% chance that a product with a 2-year lifetime could be developed, but this would weigh 180 grams.

Alternatively, if the metal design is developed, the team leader estimates that there is a 70% chance that a product with a 2-year guaranteed life and weighing 250 grams could be developed. However, he estimates that there is a 30% chance that the resulting product would have a guaranteed lifetime of 3 years and would weigh 290 grams.

It was established that, for the team leader, weight and guaranteed lifetime were mutually utility independent. The following utilities were then elicited from him:

Weight (grams)	Utility	Guaranteed lifetime (years)	Utility
130	1.0	3	1.0
180	0.9	2	0.6
250	0.6	1	0
290	0		

After further questioning, the team leader indicated that he would be indifferent between the following alternatives:

A: A product that was certain to weigh 130 grams but that had a guaranteed lifetime of only 1 year; or

B: A gamble that offered a 0.7 probability of a product with a weight of 130 grams and a guaranteed lifetime of 3 years and a 0.3 probability of a product with a weight of 290 grams and a guaranteed lifetime of 1 year.

Finally, the team leader said that he would be indifferent between alternatives C and D below:

C: A product that was certain to weigh 290 grams but that had a guaranteed lifetime of 3 years; or

D: A gamble that offered a 0.9 probability of a product with a weight of 130 grams and a guaranteed lifetime of 3 years and a 0.1 probability of a product with a weight of 290 grams and a guaranteed lifetime of 1 year.

(a) What do the team leader's responses indicate about his attitude to risk and the relative weight that he attaches to the two attributes of the proposed design?

(b) Which design should the team leader choose, given the above responses?

(c) What further analysis should be conducted before a firm recommendation can be made to the team leader?

References

1. von Neumann, J. and Morgenstern, O. (1944) *The Theory of Games and Economic Behavior*, Princeton University Press, Princeton, NJ.
2. Ronen, B., Pliskin, J.S. and Feldman, S. (1984) Balancing the failure modes in the electronic circuit of a cardiac pacemaker: a decision analysis, *Journal of the Operational Research Society*, **35**(5), 379–387.
3. French, S. (1988) *Decision Theory: an Introduction to the Mathematics of Rationality*, Ellis Horwood, Chichester, UK.
4. Farquahar, P.H. (1984) Utility assessment methods, *Management Science*, **30**(11), 1283–1300.
5. Hershey, J.C., Kunreuther, H.C. and Schoemaker, P.J.H. (1982) Sources of bias in assessment procedures for utility functions, *Management Science*, **28**(8), 936–954.
6. Thaler, R.H. (1983) Illusions and mirages in public policy, in *Judgment and Decision Making*, ed. by Arkes H.R. and Hammond K.R., Cambridge University Press, Cambridge, UK.
7. Tversky, A. and Kahneman, D. (1981) The framing of decisions and the psychology of choice, *Science*, **211**(30 January), 453–458.
8. Johnson, E.J. and Schkade, D.A. (1989) Bias in utility assessments: further evidence and explanations, *Management Science*, **35**(4), 406–424.
9. Corner, J.L. and Corner, P.D. (1995) Characteristics of decisions in decision analysis practice, *Journal of the Operational Research Society*, **46**, 304–314.
10. Tocher, K.D. (1977) Planning systems, *Philosophical Transactions of the Royal Society of London*, **A287**, 425–441.
11. von Winterfeldt, D. and Edwards, W. (1986) *Decision Analysis and Behavioral Research*, Cambridge University Press, Cambridge, UK.
12. Raiffa, H. (1982) *The Art and Science of Negotiation*, Harvard University Press, Cambridge, MA.
13. Slovic, P. and Tversky A. (1974) Who accepts Savage's axiom?, *Behavioral Science*, **19**, 368–373.
14. Indeed, a whole debate has been organized around paradoxical choice and the psychological acceptability of the axioms of expected utility theory and its variants. See, for example, Stigum, B.P. and Wenstop, F. (eds) (1983) *Foundations of Risk and Utility Theory with Applications*, Reidel, Dordrecht, Netherlands.
15. Kirkwood, C.W. (2004) Approximating risk aversion in decision analysis applications, *Decision Analysis*, **1**, 51–67.
16. Keeney, R.L. and Raiffa, H. (1976) *Decisions with Multiple Objectives: Preferences and Value Tradeoffs*, John Wiley & Sons, Inc., New York, NY.
17. De Neufville, R. and Keeney, R.L. (1972) Systems evaluation through decision analysis: Mexico City Airport, *Journal of Systems Engineering*, **3**(1), 34–50.
18. Kirkwood, C.W. (1982) A case history of nuclear power plant site selection, *Journal of the Operational Research Society*, **33**, 353–363.
19. Bunn, D.W. (1982) *Analysis for Optimal Decisions*, John Wiley & Sons, Ltd, Chichester, UK.
20. Watson, S.R. and Buede, D.M. (1987) *Decision Synthesis*, Cambridge University Press, Cambridge, UK.

21. Wallenius, J., Dyer, J.S., Fishburn, P.C., Steuer, R.E., Zionts, S. and Deb, K. (2008) Multiple criteria decision making, multiattribute utility theory: recent accomplishments and what lies ahead, *Management Science*, **54**, 1336–1349.
22. Montibeller, G., Belton, V., Ackermann, F. and Ensslin, L. (2008) Reasoning maps for decision aid: an integrated approach for problem-structuring and multi-criteria evaluation, *Journal of the Operational Research Society*, **59**, 575–589.

Decision trees and influence diagrams 7

Introduction

When they are first encountered, some decision problems appear to be overwhelmingly complex. Any attempt at clear thinking can be frustrated by the large number of interrelated elements that are associated with the problem, so that, at best, the unaided decision-maker can have only a hazy perception of the issues involved. In these circumstances, decision trees and influence diagrams can be extremely useful in helping people to gain an understanding of the structure of the problems that confront them.

We have already introduced some very simple decision trees in Chapter 6, but here we will extend the idea to show how multistage problems can be modeled. Decision problems are multistage in character when the choice of a given option may result in circumstances that will require yet another decision to be made. For example, a company may face an immediate decision relating to the manufacturing capacity that should be provided for a new product. Later, when the product has been on the market for several years, it may have to decide whether to expand or reduce the capacity. This later decision will have to be borne in mind when the initial decision is being made, as the costs of converting from one capacity level to another may vary. A decision to invest now in a very small manufacturing plant might lead to high costs in the future if a major expansion is undertaken. This means that the decisions made at the different points in time are interconnected.

As we shall see, decision trees can serve a number of purposes when complex multistage problems are encountered. They can help a decision-maker to develop a clear view of the structure of a problem and make it easier to determine the possible scenarios that can result if a particular course of action is chosen. This can lead to creative thinking and the generation of options that were not previously being considered. Decision trees can also help a decision-maker to judge the nature of the information that needs to be gathered in order to tackle a problem, and, because they are generally easy to understand, they can be an excellent medium for communicating one person's perception of a problem to other individuals.

The process of constructing a decision tree is usually iterative, with many changes being made to the original structure as the decision-maker's understanding of the problem develops. Because the intention is to help the decision-maker to think about the problem, very large and complex trees, which are designed to represent every possible scenario that can occur, can be counterproductive in many circumstances. Decision trees are models, and as such are simplifications of the real problem. The simplification is the very strength of the modeling process because it fosters the understanding and insight that would be obscured by detail and complexity. Nevertheless, in rare circumstances, highly complex trees may be appropriate, and software developments mean that their structuring and analysis can now be facilitated with relative ease. For example, Dunning et al.[1] used software to apply a decision tree with over 200 million paths to a 10 year scheduling problem faced by the New York Power Authority. Similarly, Beccue[2] used a tree with around half-a-million scenarios to help a pharmaceutical company to make decisions relating to the development and marketing of a new drug.

Influence diagrams offer an alternative way of structuring a complex decision problem, and some analysts find that people relate to them much more easily. Indeed, Howard[3] has called them 'The greatest advance I have seen in the communication, elicitation and detailed representation of human knowledge ... the best tool I know of for crossing the bridge from the original opaque situation in the person's mind to a clear and crisp decision basis.' As we will show later, influence diagrams can be converted to decision trees, and we will therefore regard them in this chapter as a method for eliciting decision trees. However, some computer programs now exist that use complex algorithms to enable the influence diagram to be used not just as an initial elicitation tool but as a means for identifying the best sequence of decisions.

Constructing a decision tree

You may recall from earlier chapters that two symbols are used in decision trees. A square is used to represent a decision node and, because each branch emanating from this node presents an option, the decision-maker can choose which branch to follow. A circle, on the other hand, is used to represent a chance node. The branches that stem from this sort of node represent the possible outcomes of a given course of action, and the branch that is followed will be determined not by the decision-maker but by circumstances that lie beyond his or her control. The branches emanating from a circle are therefore labeled with probabilities that represent the decision-maker's estimate of the probability that a particular branch will be followed. Obviously, it is not sensible to attach probabilities to the branches that stem from a square.

The following example will be used to demonstrate how a decision tree can be used in the analysis of a multistage problem. An engineer who works for a company

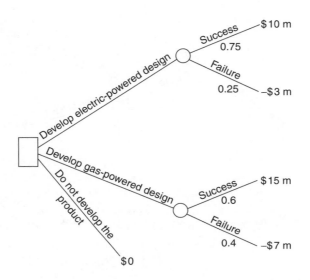

Figure 7.1 – An initial decision tree for the food-processor problem

that produces equipment for the food-processing industry has been asked to consider the development of a new type of processor and to make a recommendation to the company's board. Two alternative power sources could be used for the processor, namely gas and electricity, but for technical reasons each power source would require a fundamentally different design. Resource constraints mean that the company will only be able to pursue one of the designs and, because the processor would be more advanced than others that have been developed, it is by no means certain that either design would be a success. The engineer estimates that there is a 75% chance that the electricity-powered design would be successful and only a 60% chance that the gas-powered design would be a success.

Figure 7.1 shows an initial decision tree for the problem, with estimated payoffs in millions of dollars. After considering this tree, the engineer realizes that, if either design failed, then the company would still consider modifying the design, although this would involve more investment and would still not guarantee success. He estimates that the probability that the electrical design could be successfully modified is only 30%, although the gas design would have an 80% chance of being modified successfully. This leads to the new tree shown in Figure 7.2. Note that the decision problem is now perceived to have two stages. At stage 1 a decision has to be made between the designs or not developing the problem at all. At stage 2 a decision *may* have to be made on whether the design should be modified.

After some reflection, the engineer agrees that this tree is a satisfactory representation of the options facing the company. Other alternatives such as switching to the development of a gas-powered design if the electrical design is not successful are not considered to be feasible, given the resources available to the company.

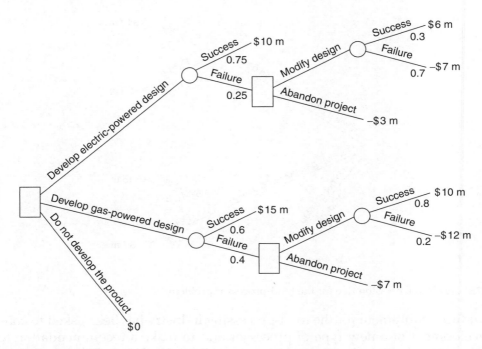

Figure 7.2 – A new decision tree for the food-processor problem

Determining the optimal policy

It can be seen that our decision tree consists of a set of *policies*. A policy is a plan of action stating which option is to be chosen at each decision node that might be reached under that policy. For example, one policy would be: choose the electrical design; if it fails, modify the design. Another policy would be: choose the electrical design; if it fails, abandon the project.

We will now show how the decision tree can be used to identify the optimal policy. For simplicity, we will assume that the engineer considers that monetary return is the only attribute that is relevant to the decision, and we will also assume that, because the company is involved in a large number of projects, it is neutral to the risk involved in this development and therefore the expected monetary value (EMV) criterion is appropriate. Considerations of the timing of the cash flows and the relative preference for receiving cash flows at different points in time will also be excluded from our analysis (this issue is dealt with in Chapter 8).

The technique for determining the optimal policy in a decision tree is known as the *rollback method*. To apply this method, we analyze the tree from right to left by considering the later decisions first. The process is illustrated in Figure 7.3. Thus, if

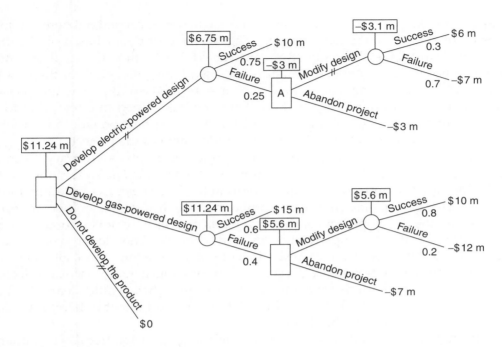

Figure 7.3 – Rolling back the decision tree

the company chose the electrical design and it failed (i.e. if the decision node labeled with an A was reached), what would be the best course of action? Modifying the design would lead to an expected return of (0.3 × $6 m) + (0.7 × −$7 m), which equals −$3.1 m. As this is worse than the −$3 m payoff that would be achieved if the design were abandoned, abandoning the design would be the best course of action. Two bars are therefore placed over the inferior branch, and the 'winning' payoff is moved back to the decision node where it is now treated as a payoff for the 'failure' branch. This means that the expected payoff of the electrical design is (0.75 × $10 m) + (0.25 × −$3 m), which equals $6.75 m.

The same analysis is applied to the section of the tree that represents the gas-powered design. It can be seen that, if this design fails, the best option is to modify it. Hence, the expected payoff of the gas design is $11.24 m. This exceeds the expected payoff of the electrical design and the $0 payoff of not proceeding with the development. Two bars are therefore placed over the branches representing these options, and the $11.24 m is moved back to the initial decision node. The optimum policy is therefore to develop the gas-powered design and, if it fails, to modify the design.

It can be seen that the rollback method allows a complex decision problem to be analyzed as a series of smaller decision problems. We should, of course, now apply sensitivity analysis to the probabilities and payoffs using the method we introduced in the previous chapter. For brevity, this analysis will not be carried out here. It should also be pointed out that the decision tree suggests the best policy based on the information that is available at the time it is constructed. By the time the engineer knows whether or not the gas-powered design is successful, his perception of the problem may have changed, and he would then, of course, be advised to review the decision. For example, if the design fails, the knowledge he has gained in attempting to develop the equipment may lead him to conclude that modification would be unlikely to succeed, and he might then recommend abandonment of the project.

Note also that the planning period that the tree represents is arbitrary. Even if a successful gas design is developed, this surely will not be the end of the story, as this choice of design is bound to have ramifications in the future. For example, any money earned from the design may well be reinvested in research and development for future products, and the developments of these products may or may not be successful, and so on. Moreover, if the company chooses to develop its knowledge of gas, rather than electric, technology, this may restrict its options in the long term. However, any attempt to formulate a tree that represents every possible consequence and decision that may arise over a period stretching into the distant future would clearly lead to a model that was so complex that it would be intractable. Judgment is therefore needed to determine where the tree should end.

Clearly, the calculations involved in analyzing a large decision tree can be rather tedious. Because of this, a number of computer packages have been developed that will display and analyze decision trees and influence diagrams and allow them to be easily modified. For example, DPL, produced by Syncopation Software, is a Microsoft® Windows® application that links to Microsoft Excel, while PrecisionTree®, produced by the Palisade Corporation, allows decision trees and influence diagrams to be developed in Excel spreadsheets. Other software products that support decision tree analysis include TreeAge Pro (TreeAge Software Inc.) and TreePlan® (Decision Toolworks™) which also works within Excel.

Decision trees and utility

In the previous section we made the assumption that the decision-maker was neutral to risk. Let us now suppose that the engineer is concerned that his career prospects will be blighted if the development of the processor leads to a great loss of money for the company. He is therefore risk averse, and his utility function for the monetary sums involved in this problem is shown in Figure 7.4.

The procedure for analyzing the tree when utilities are involved is exactly the same as that which we used for the EMV criterion. Figure 7.5 shows the decision tree, with the utilities replacing the monetary values. After applying the rollback method, it can be seen that now the optimum policy is to develop the electric-powered design, and,

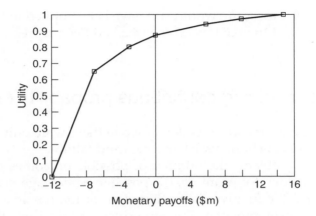

Figure 7.4 – The engineer's utility function

if it fails, to abandon the project. Note, however, that the closeness of the expected utilities suggests that sensitivity analysis should be applied to the tree before a firm decision is made.

If the engineer had wished to include other attributes besides money in his decision model, then multi-attribute utilities would have appeared at the ends of the tree.

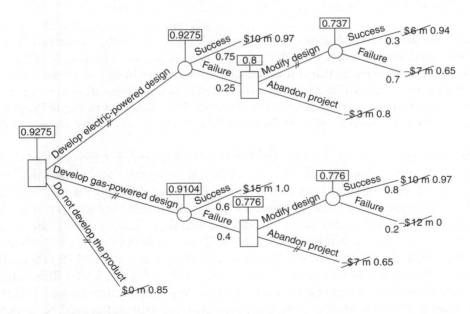

Figure 7.5 – Apply the rollback method to a decision tree involving utilities

However, the rollback procedure would still have been applied in the same way. This would also be the case if the payoffs on the tree had been represented as net present values (see Chapter 8).

Decision trees involving continuous probability distributions

In the decision problem that we considered above there were only two possible outcomes for each course of action, namely success and failure.

However, in some problems the number of possible outcomes may be very large or even infinite. Consider, for example, the possible percentage market share a company might achieve after an advertising campaign or the possible levels of cost that may result from the development of a new product. Variables like these could be represented by continuous probability distributions, but how can we incorporate such distributions into our decision tree format? One obvious solution is to use a discrete probability distribution as an approximation. For example, we might approximate a market share distribution with just three outcomes: high, medium and low. A number of methods for making this sort of approximation have been suggested, and we will discuss the *extended Pearson–Tukey (EP-T) approximation* here. This was proposed by Keefer and Bodily,[4] who found it to be a very good approximation to a wide range of continuous distributions. The method is based on earlier work by Pearson and Tukey[5] and requires three estimates to be made by the decision-maker:

(i) The value in the distribution that has a 95% chance of being exceeded. This value is allocated a probability of 0.185.
(ii) The value in the distribution that has a 50% chance of being exceeded. This value is allocated a probability of 0.63.
(iii) The value in the distribution that has only a 5% chance of being exceeded. This value is also allocated a probability of 0.185.

To illustrate the method, let us suppose that a marketing manager has to decide whether to launch a new product and wishes to represent on a decision tree the possible sales levels that will be achieved in the first year if the product is launched. To apply the EP-T approximation to the sales probability distribution, we would need to obtain the three estimates from the decision-maker. Suppose that she estimates that there is a 95% chance that first-year sales will exceed 10 000 units, a 50% chance that they will exceed 15 000 units and a 5% chance that they will exceed 25 000 units. The resulting decision tree is shown in Figure 7.6(a), while Figure 7.6(b) illustrates how the discrete distribution has been used to approximate the continuous distribution.

Of course, in many decision trees the probability distributions will be dependent. For example, in our product launch example one might expect second-year sales to

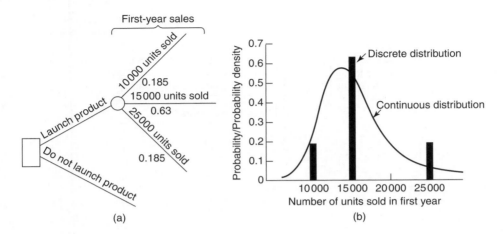

Figure 7.6 – The extended Pearson–Tukey (EP-T) approximation method

be related to the sales that were achieved in the first year. In this case, questions like the following would need to be asked to obtain the distribution for second-year sales: 'Given that first-year sales were around 25 000 units, what level of sales in the second year would have a 50% chance of being exceeded?'

As Keefer and Bodily point out, the EP-T approximation does have its limitations. It would be inappropriate to use it where the continuous probability distribution had more than one peak (or mode), and the approximation would probably not be a good one if the shape of the continuous distribution was very asymmetric. Moreover, in some decision problems a subsequent decision depends upon the achievement of a particular level of a variable. For example, in our product launch problem, the manager may decide to discontinue the product after the first year if sales do not reach 12 000 units. In this case, clearly attention should be focused on the probability of this critical sales level being reached, rather than on the three points used in the EP-T approximation. Nevertheless, in general, there are clear advantages in using this approximation. Above all, it is simple, and each distribution requires only three estimates to be made, which has the obvious effect of reducing the decision-maker's judgmental task.

Assessment of decision structure

As we have seen, decision trees are the major analytical structures underlying the application of decision analysis to problems involving uncertainty. In the examples that we have used so far in this book we have either given a decision-tree representation or used a case example where the individual pieces in the jigsaw were sufficient and

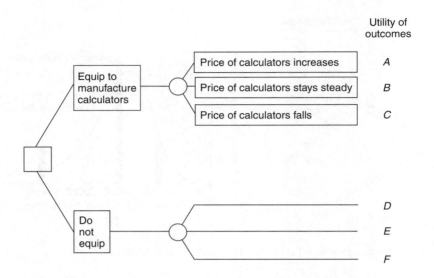

Figure 7.7 – One decision-analytic representation of the calculator problem

necessary to complete the case analysis for subsequent computations. Real-life decision problems may, at first pass, contain *pieces from many different jigsaws*. The trick is to know which pieces are missing (and so need to be obtained) or which are either redundant or not relevant to the problem analysis in hand.

Consider the following 'real-life' decision problem that we would like you to attempt to represent in the form of a decision tree:

> Imagine that you are a businessman and you are considering making electronic calculators. Your factory can be equipped to manufacture them, and you recognize that other companies have profited from producing them. However, equipping the factory for production will be very expensive and you have seen the price of calculators dropping steadily. What should you do?

Well, what is the correct decision-analytic representation? Figure 7.7 presents one representation which may or may not match yours. Figure 7.8 is a more elaborate and perhaps more realistic representation of the problem.

Do you agree? Actually, as you have probably guessed, there is no *obviously* right or wrong representation of any problem that is in any way related to real life. Although expected utility may be an optimal decision principle, there is no normative technique for eliciting the *structure* of the decision problem from the decision-maker. It is really a matter of the decision analyst's judgment as to whether the elicited tree is a fair representation of the decision-maker's decision problem. Once a structure is agreed, then the computation of expected utility is fairly straightforward. Structuring

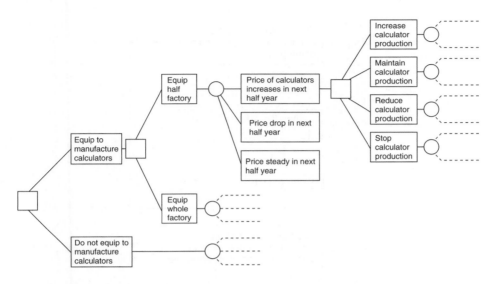

Figure 7.8 – Toward the correct decision-analytic representation of the calculator problem?

is therefore a major problem in decision analysis for, if the structuring is wrong, then it is a necessary consequence that assessments of utilities and probabilities may be inappropriate and the expected utility computations may be invalid.

Figure 7.9 presents a description of the typical phases in a decision analysis of a problem that the decision-maker wishes to resolve with the help of the practitioner of decision analysis – the decision analyst.

Stages 1 and 2 of the decision process are iterative, and the structure of the decision problem emerges from discussions between the decision-maker and the analyst. Once a structure for the decision representation has been agreed and probabilities and utilities are elicited (stage 3), the expected utility for the various acts under consideration can be computed (stage 4) and the act that has the maximal expected utility is chosen (stage 5).

What determines the decision analyst's provisional representation of the decision problem? Generally, it will be based upon past experience with similar classes of decision problems and, to a significant extent, intuition. To quote von Winterfeldt:[6]

> Often the analyst decides on a specific structure and later finds it unmanageable . . . knowing about the recursive nature of the structuring process, it is good decision analysis practice to spend much effort on structuring and to keep an open mind about possible revisions.

However, problem representation is an art rather than a science, as Fischhoff[7] notes:

> Regarding the validation of particular assessment techniques we know . . . next to nothing about eliciting the structure of problems from decision-makers.

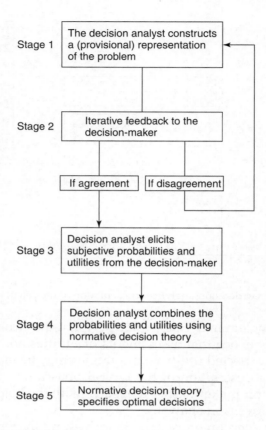

Figure 7.9 – Phases of a decision analysis

Keeney[8] has fewer reservations:

> Often the complex problems are so involved that their structure is not well understood. A simple decision tree emphasizing the problem structure, which illustrates the main alternatives, uncertainties and consequences, can usually be drawn up in a day. Not only does this often help in defining the problem, but it promotes client and colleague confidence that perhaps decision analysis can help. It has often been my experience that sketching out a simple decision tree with a client in an hour can lead to big advances in the eventual solution to a problem.

Many decision-makers report that they feel the process of problem representation is perhaps more important than the subsequent computations. Humphreys[9] has labeled the latter the 'direct value' of decision analysis, and the former the 'indirect value'. Decision analysis provides the decision-maker with a convincing rationale for choice, improves communication and permits direct and separate comparisons of different people's conceptions of the structure of the problem, and of the assessment of decomposed elements within their structures, thereby raising consciousness about the root of any conflict.

However, some studies have illustrated that the decision-makers' estimates, judgment and choices are affected by the way knowledge is elicited.

This research has direct relevance for the decision analyst's attempts at structuring. In one study, Fischhoff et al.[10] investigated the estimation of failure probabilities in decision problem representations called fault trees. These fault trees are essentially similar to decision trees, with the exception that events rather than acts and events are represented. Figure 7.10 gives a fault tree representation for the event 'a car fails to start'. This is the full version of the fault tree that Fischhoff produced from the use of several car-repair reference texts.

In several experiments, Fischhoff presented various 'full' and 'pruned' fault trees to members of the public. For example, three of the first six subevents in Figure 7.10 would be omitted from the presentation to be implicitly included under the seventh subevent, 'all other problems'. Fischhoff asked:

> For every 100 times that a trip is delayed due to a 'starting failure' estimate, on average, how many of the delays are caused by the 7(4) factors?

Fischhoff found that the amount of probability placed on 'all other problems' did not increase significantly when it contained three of the other main subevents. In a subsequent experiment, the importance of 'all other problems' was emphasized:

> In particular we would like you to consider its [the fault tree's] completeness. That is, what proportion of the possible reasons for a car not starting are left out, to be included in the category 'all other problems'?

However, focusing subjects' attention on what was missing only partially improved their awareness. Fischhoff labeled this insensitivity to the incompleteness of the fault tree 'out of sight, out of mind'. The finding was confirmed with technical experts and garage mechanics. Neither self-rated degree of knowledge nor actual garage experience has any significant association with subjects' ability to detect what was missing from the fault tree.

Another finding from the study was that the perceived importance of a particular subevent or branch of the fault tree was increased by presenting it in pieces (i.e. as two separate branches). The implications of this result are far reaching. Decision trees constructed early in the analyst/decision-maker interaction may be incomplete representations of the decision problem facing the decision-maker.

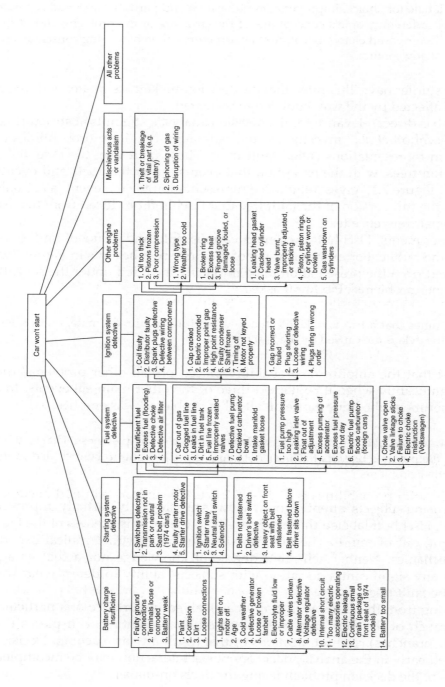

Figure 7.10 – A possible fault tree for discovering why a car will not start (adapted from Fischhoff, B., Slovic, P. and Lichtenstein (1978) Fault Trees: Sensitivity of Estimated Failure Probabilities to Problem Representation, *Journal of Experimental Psychology: Human Perception and Performance*, **4**: 2; 330–344. Copyright 1978 © American Psychological Association. By permission of the authors)

Eliciting decision tree representations

What methods have been developed to help elicit decision tree representations from decision-makers? One major method, much favored by some decision analysts, is that of *influence diagrams*,[11] which are designed to summarize the dependencies that are seen to exist among events and acts within a decision. Such dependencies may be mediated by the flow of time, as we saw in our examples of decision trees. As we shall see, a close relationship exists between influence diagrams and the more familiar decision trees. Indeed, given certain conditions, influence diagrams can be converted into trees. The advantage of starting with influence diagrams is that their graphic representation is more appealing to the intuition of decision-makers who may be unfamiliar with decision technologies. In addition, influence diagrams are more easily revised and altered as the decision-maker iterates with the decision analyst. Because of their strict temporal ordering of acts and events, decision trees need to be completely respecified when additional acts and events are inserted into preliminary representations. We will illustrate the applicability of influence diagrams through a worked example. First, however, we will present the basic concepts and representations underlying the approach.

Figure 7.11 presents the key concepts. As with the decision tree, event nodes are represented by circles and decision nodes by squares. Arrowed lines between nodes indicate the influence of one node on another. For example, an arrow pointing to an event node indicates that the likelihood of events (contained in the node) is influenced *either* by a prior decision *or* by the occurrence (or not) of prior events. Alternatively, an arrow pointing to a decision node indicates that the decision is influenced *either* by a prior decision *or* by the occurrence (or not) of prior events. The whole set of interconnected decisions and events is called an influence diagram.

Figure 7.12(a) gives one exemplar influence diagram for the calculator production problem, and Figure 7.13 gives the decision tree representation of this influence diagram. Two conditions must be met in order for an influence diagram to be represented as a decision tree. First, the diagram must contain no circles of influence arrows (loops). A loop would show that a node (variable) both influences and is influenced by another node. Such a relationship could not be represented by the left-to-right ordering of influences represented by a decision tree. Second, as decision trees are conventionally used to aid a *single* decision-maker who is knowledgeable about *all* temporally prior acts and events, then those nodes that have *direct* influence (shown by direct arrows) on a particular decision must be a subset of the influences on subsequent decisions. If such an ordering is not represented in an influence diagram (for example, the combination of Figures 7.12(a) and (b)), then at least two decision trees need to be developed to represent the diagram.

Obviously, a decision tree representation must preserve the ordering represented by the arrows in an influence diagram, and the tree must not have an event node as

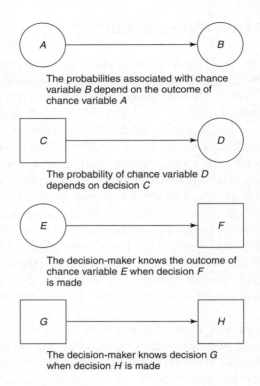

The probabilities associated with chance
variable *B* depend on the outcome of
chance variable *A*

The probability of chance variable *D*
depends on decision *C*

The decision-maker knows the outcome of
chance variable *E* when decision *F*
is made

The decision-maker knows decision *G*
when decision *H* is made

Figure 7.11 – Definitions used in influence diagrams

a predecessor of a decision node for which it is not directly linked by an arrow in the
influence diagram. If the tree did, it would imply that the decision depends on the
event node, which, from the influence diagram, is not the case.

One step-by-step procedure for turning an influence diagram into a decision tree is
as follows:

(1) Identify a node with no arrows pointing into it (as there can be no loops, at least
one node will be such).
(2) If there is a choice between a decision node and an event node, choose the decision
node.
(3) Place the node at the beginning of the tree and 'remove' the node from the influence
diagram.
(4) For the now-reduced diagram, choose another node with no arrows pointing into
it. If there is a choice, a decision node should be chosen.
(5) Place this node next in the tree and 'remove' it from the influence diagram.
(6) Repeat the above procedure until all the nodes have been removed from the
influence diagram.

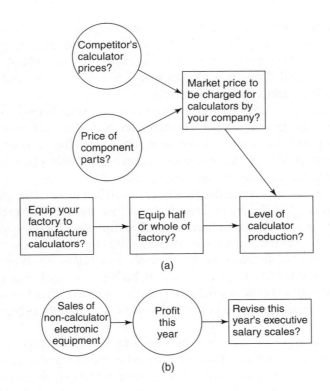

(a)

(b)

Figure 7.12 – Influence diagram

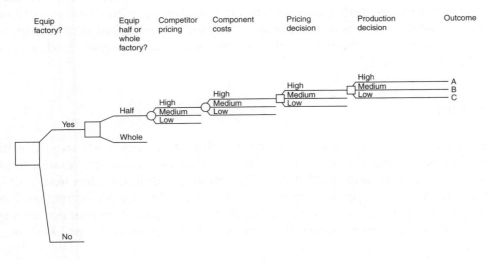

Figure 7.13 – Decision tree derived from influence diagram

For practice, try this procedure on the content of Figure 7.12(a). You should achieve the decision tree represented in Figure 7.13. To complete the tree, the possible choices at each decision node and the possible events at each event node must now be specified. Finally, subjective probabilities must be assessed for the events, and utilities must be assigned to the endpoints in the decision tree.

Very complex decision trees can be represented as one-page influence diagrams. However, the use of influence diagrams to construct decision trees where subsequent events and acts depend on the initial decision (i.e. where the resulting decision tree is asymmetric) is more problematic. In these instances, the influence diagram approach to decision tree structuring can be used as a guide only.

From our overview of influence diagrams you will have seen that such diagrams aid subsequent structuring of decision trees. They allow the easy insertion of additional acts and events as the decision-maker talks through the decision problem with the decision analyst (see stages 1 and 2 in Figure 7.9.). *By themselves, influence diagrams do not aid in the creation of decision options or in the recognition of event possibilities.* Such creation and recognition activities perhaps may be best thought of as creative behavior. As we have seen, Fischhoff *et al.* found that people seem to suffer from 'out of sight, out of mind' bias when evaluating the completeness of decision-tree-type representations of knowledge.

In other words, individual decision-makers may be inappropriately content with decision problem representations that are created early in the decision-maker/analyst interaction. One major way to combat this tendency is to subject initial problem representations to outside critique by other people who have knowledge of the decision problem domain. Such critiques are readily available in the context of decision conferencing, where those individuals with a stake in a key decision interact with the aid of a decision analyst who acts to facilitate a decision. We will deal with this approach in detail in Chapter 13, where we will focus on the advantages and disadvantages of group decision-making.

Summary

In this chapter we have illustrated the construction of decision trees and the rollback method for identifying the optimal policy. We described an approximation method for dealing with continuous probability distributions within decision trees and summarized some practical applications of decision trees within decision analysis. Finally, we analyzed the process of generating decision tree representation of decision problems and advocated the influence diagram as a key technique to facilitate decision structuring.

In spite of the benefits of using decision trees, some decision analysts counsel against using them too early in the decision process before a broad perspective of the decision problem has been obtained. For example, Chapman and Ward[12] argue that decision trees should often be embedded in a more wide-ranging analysis that includes assessments of the sources of uncertainty (we deal with this in Chapters 8 and 12) and exploration of the decision-maker's objectives (see Chapter 3). We broadly agree with this view and have therefore presented decision trees in this book as just one of many potentially useful decision-aiding tools – unlike most other decision analysis texts, which focus almost exclusively on decision trees.

Exercises

Additional exercises can be found on the book's website

(1) A company has to decide whether to invest money in the development of a microbiological product. The company's research director has estimated that there is a 60% chance that a successful development could be achieved in 2 years. However, if the product had not been successfully developed at the end of this period, the company would abandon the project, which would lead to a loss in present value terms of $3 million. (Present value is designed to take the company's time preference for money into account. The concept is explained in Chapter 8.)

In the event of a successful development, a decision would have to be made on the scale of production. The returns generated would depend on the level of sales that could be achieved over the period of the product's life. For simplicity, these have been categorized as either high or low. If the company opted for large-volume production and high sales were achieved, then net returns with a present value of $6 million would be obtained. However, large-scale production followed by low sales would lead to net returns with a present value of only $1 million.

On the other hand, if the company decided to invest only in small-scale production facilities, then high sales would generate net returns with a present value of $4 million, and low sales would generate net returns with a present value of $2 million. The company's marketing manager estimates that there is a 75% chance that high sales could be achieved.

(a) Construct a decision tree to represent the company's decision problem.
(b) Assuming that the company's objective is to maximize its expected returns, determine the policy that it should adopt.
(c) There is some debate in the company about the probability that was estimated by the research director. Assuming that all other elements of the problem remain the same, determine how low this probability would have to be before the option of not developing the product should be chosen.
(d) Before the final decision is made, the company is taken over by a new owner who has the utilities shown below for the sums of money involved in the decision. (The owner has no interest in other attributes that may

be associated with the decision, such as developing a prestige product or maintaining employment.) What implications does this have for the policy that you identified in (b) and why?

Present value of net returns	New owner's utility
−$3 m	0
$0 m	0.6
$1 m	0.75
$2 m	0.85
$4 m	0.95
$6 m	1.0

(2) A large machine in a factory has broken down and the company that owns the factory will incur costs of $3200 for each day the machine is out of action. The factory's engineer has three immediate options:

Option 1: He can return the machine to the supplier who has agreed to collect, repair and return it free of charge, but not to compensate the company for any losses they might incur while the repair is being carried out. The supplier will not agree to repair the machine if any other person has previously attempted to repair it. If the machine is returned, the supplier will guarantee to return it in working order in 10 days' time.

Option 2: He can call in a specialist local engineering company. They will charge $20 000 to carry out the repair, and they estimate that there is a 30% chance that they will be able to return the machine to working order in 2 days. There is, however, a 70% chance that repairs will take 4 days.

Option 3: He can attempt to carry out the repair work himself, and he estimates that there is a 50% chance that he could mend the machine in 5 days. However, if at the end of 5 days the attempted repair has not been successful, he will have to decide whether to call in the local engineering company or to make a second attempt at repair by investigating a different part of the mechanism. This would take two further days, and he estimates that there is a 25% chance that this second attempt would be successful. If he fails at the second attempt, he will have no alternative other than to call in the local engineering company. It can be assumed that the probability distribution for the local engineering company's repair time will be unaffected by any work that the factory engineer has carried out.

Assuming that the engineer's objective is to minimize expected costs, what course(s) of action should he take?

(3) Westward Magazine Publishers are thinking of launching a new fashion magazine for women in the under-25 age group. Their original plans were to launch in April of next year, but information has been received that a rival publisher is planning a similar magazine. Westward now have to decide whether to bring their launch forward to January of next year, although this would cost an additional $500 000. If the launch is brought forward, it is estimated that the chances of launching before the rival are about 80%. However, if the launch is not brought forward, it is thought that there is only a 30% chance of launching before the rival.

For simplicity, the management of Westward have assumed that the circulation of the magazine throughout its life will be either high or low. If Westward launch before the rival, it is thought that there is a 75% chance of a high circulation. However, if the rival launches first, this probability is estimated to be only 50%.

If the rival does launch first, then Westward could try to boost sales by increasing their level of advertising. This would cost an extra $200 000, but it is thought that it would increase the probability of a high circulation to 70%. This increased advertising expenditure would not be considered if Westward's magazine were launched first. Westward's accountants have estimated that a high circulation would generate a gross profit over the magazine's lifetime of $4 million. A low circulation would bring a gross profit of about $1 million. It is important to note, however, that these gross profits do *not* take into account additional expenditure caused by bringing the launch forward or by increased advertising.

(a) Draw a decision tree to represent Westward's problem.

(b) Assuming that Westward's objective is to maximize expected profit, determine the policy that they should choose. (For simplicity, you should ignore Westward's preference for money over time; for example, the fact that they would prefer to receive a given cash inflow now rather than in the future.)

(c) In reality, Westward have little knowledge of the progress that has been made by the rival. This means that the probabilities given above for beating the rival (if the launch is, or is not, brought forward) are very rough estimates. How sensitive is the policy you identified in (b) to changes in these probabilities?

(4) The risk of flooding in land adjacent to the River Nudd has recently increased. This is because of a combination of high spring tides and the development by farmers of more efficient drainage systems in the nearby hills, which means that, after heavy rainfall, water enters the river more quickly. A tidal barrier is being constructed at the mouth of the river, but the Hartland River Authority

has to decide how to provide flood protection in the 2 years before the barrier is completed. Flooding is only likely to occur during the spring high-tide period, and the height of the river at this time cannot be predicted with any certainty. In the event of flooding occurring in any one year, the Authority will have to pay out compensation of about $2 million. Currently, the Authority is considering three options.

First, it could do nothing and hope that flooding will not occur in either of the next 2 years. The river's natural banks will stop flooding as long as the height of the water is less than 9.5 feet. It is estimated that there is a probability of 0.37 that the height of the river will exceed this figure in any one year.

Alternatively, the Authority could erect a cheap temporary barrier to a height of 11 feet. This barrier would cost $0.9 million to erect, and it is thought that there is a probability of only 0.09 that the height of the river would exceed this barrier. However, if the water did rise above the barrier in the first year, it is thought that there is a 30% chance that the barrier would be damaged, rendering it totally ineffective for the second year. The Authority would then have to decide whether to effect repairs to the barrier at a cost of $0.7 million or whether to leave the river unprotected for the second year.

The third option would involve erecting a more expensive barrier. The fixed cost of erecting this type of barrier would be $0.4 million, and there would be an additional cost of $0.1 million for each foot in the barrier's height. For technical reasons, the height of this barrier would be either 11 or 13 feet, and it is thought that there would be no chance of the barrier being damaged if flooding did occur. The probability of the river's height exceeding the 13-foot barrier in any one year is estimated to be only 0.004.

(a) Draw a decision tree to represent the River Authority's problem.
(b) Determine the optimum policy for the Authority, assuming that their objective is to minimize expected costs. (For simplicity, you should ignore time preferences for money.)

(5) An engineering company is about to undertake a major overhaul of a factory's machinery for a customer. The overhaul will be carried out on a Saturday and Sunday, but, if it is not completed by the Monday morning, the factory will experience serious production losses. In this event, the engineering company has agreed to compensate the customer by paying a penalty of $20 000.

The manager of the engineering company has to decide how many engineers to include in the overhaul team. Each engineer in the team will be paid $480 for working over the weekend, but, because of the nature of the work, only teams of 10, 15 or 20 engineers can be considered. The manager estimates that the chances of a ten-person team completing the overhaul by the Monday morning is only 0.4. A 15-person team has, he estimates, a 0.6 probability of meeting the deadline, while a 20-person team has a 0.9 probability of completing the work in time for Monday morning.

(a) Assuming that the manager wants to minimize expected costs, how large a team should he choose?

(b) Having made a provisional decision about the size of the team, the manager hears that a piece of specialized equipment will be available for hire on the Sunday, at short notice. The cost of hiring this equipment would be $4400, and it would require at least 15 engineers to operate it. However, it is virtually certain that the overhaul would be completed on time if the equipment were used.

Before making a decision on whether to hire the equipment, the manager will review the progress that has been made on the Saturday evening. He reckons that there is a 0.5 probability that a 15-person team would be behind schedule by Saturday evening, while there is only a 0.2 probability that a 20-person team would be in this position. He then calculates the probabilities of the overhaul overrunning the deadline if the equipment is not hired, given the position on Saturday evening. These probabilities are shown below:

	15-person team, position on Saturday evening	
	Behind schedule	Not behind schedule
p(overhaul exceeds deadline if equipment not hired)	0.6	0.2

	20-person team, position on Saturday evening	
	Behind schedule	Not behind schedule
p(overhaul exceeds deadline if equipment not hired)	0.2	0.075

How many people should the manager now include in the team, and should he hire the equipment on the Saturday evening?

(6) The Bonsante Drug Company is aiming to develop a new drug that will alleviate the symptoms of arthritis with few side effects. The earlier the company can develop, test and market the drug, the greater will be the returns it will earn in a market that it is thought will be worth billions of pounds.

Two alternative technologies for developing the drug are being considered, and, given the resources available to the company, only one of these approaches can be pursued at a given time. The first approach is based on a substance called HMP acid, and it is estimated that there is a 0.4 probability that this approach would lead to development of the drug in 5 years, with a 0.6 probability that the development would take 7 years.

There is more uncertainty about the development time of the second approach, which is based on a derivative of the chemical zylogen. It is estimated that the use of this chemical has a 0.3 probability of leading to completion of development in as little as 3 years. If development has not been completed in this period, then a decision would have to be made between switching to the HMP acid technology or attempting to modify the zylogen approach. It is thought that the modification has a 0.8 probability of leading to completion after a further 2 years.

If the modification has still not led to completion after the further 2 years, a decision would then have to be made between switching to the HMP acid approach or persevering with zylogen for a further 7 years, by which time it is assumed that successful development is certain to have been achieved.

Assuming that the objective of Bonsante's directors is to minimize the expected *development time* of the drug, determine their optimum policy.

(7) (a) Use an influence diagram to represent the following decision problem, stating any assumptions you have made.

ABC Chemicals are planning to start manufacturing a new pharmaceutical product. Initially, they must decide whether to go for large-scale or small-scale production. Having made this decision, the profits that they make will also depend on (i) the state of the economy over the next 2 years, (ii) whether or not a rival manufacturer launches a similar product and (iii) the amount that ABC decides to spend on advertising the product (this decision will itself be influenced by the scale of production that ABC opt for, whether a rival product is launched and the state of the economy).

(b) Use your influence diagram to derive the outline of a decision tree that could be used to represent ABC's problem.

(8) Draw an influence diagram for the following problem.

Hatton's mail order company is planning to install a new computer system next year. Two possible systems are being considered: the Gamma II and the Elite. The Gamma II will mean that the company incurs higher initial costs than the Elite, but the total costs associated with the chosen system over its lifetime will also depend on whether the company decides to expand the computer system at some future date (the Gamma II system would cost less to expand). The expansion decision will be influenced by the level of sales achieved by the company over the next 3 years, while the level of sales will, in turn, be influenced by the size of the market and the amount of competition that Hatton's has to face. It is thought that the size of the market will itself be influenced by the performance of the economy (e.g. a continued recession would depress the market). It is also thought that, if the recession continues, a number of rivals will go out of business, so the severity of competition will be less.

References

1. Dunning, D.J., Lockfort, S., Ross, Q.E., Beccue, P.C. and Stonebraker, J.S. (2001) New York Power Authority used decision analysis to schedule refueling of its Indian Point 3 nuclear power plant, *Interfaces*, **31**, 121–135.
2. Beccue, P. (2001) Choosing a development strategy for a new product at Amgen, *Interfaces*, **31**, 62–64.
3. Howard, R.A. (1988) Decision analysis: practice and promise, *Management Science*, **34**(6), 679–695.
4. Keefer, D.L. and Bodily, S.E. (1983) Three point approximations for continuous random variables, *Management Science*, **29**(5), 595–609.
5. Pearson, E.S. and Tukey, J.W. (1965) Approximating means and standard deviations based on distances between percentage points of frequency curves, *Biometrika*, **52**(3–4), 533–546.
6. von Winterfeldt, D.V. (1980) Structuring decision problems for decision analysis, *Acta Psychologica*, **45**, 73–93.
7. Fischhoff, B. (1980) Decision analysis: clinical art or clinical science?, in *Human Decision Making*, ed. by Sjoberg, L., Tyszka, T. and Wise, J.A., Doxa, Bodafors, Sweden.
8. Keeney, R. (1980) Decision analysis in the geo-technical and environmental fields, in *Human Decision Making*, ed. by Sjoberg, L., Tyszka, T. and Wise, J.A., Doxa, Bodafors, Sweden.
9. Humphreys, P. (1980) Decision aids: aiding decisions, in *Human Decision Making*, ed. by Sjoberg, L., Tyszka, T. and Wise, J.A., Doxa, Bodafors, Sweden.
10. Fischhoff, B., Slovic, P. and Lichtenstein, S. (1978) Fault trees: sensitivity of estimated failure probabilities to problem representation, *Journal of Experimental Psychology: Human Perception and Performance*, **4**, 330–344.
11. Howard, R.A. (1989) Knowledge maps, *Management Science*, **35**, 903–923; see also Oliver, R.M. and Smith, J.Q. (eds) (1990) *Influence Diagrams, Belief Nets and Decision Nets*, John Wiley & Sons, Ltd, Chichester, UK.
12. Chapman, C. and Ward, S. (2002) *Managing Project Risk and Uncertainty. A Constructively Simple Approach to Decision Making*, John Wiley & Sons, Ltd, Chichester, UK.

Applying simulation to decision problems 8

Introduction

When the payoff of a decision depends upon a large number of factors, estimating a probability distribution for the possible values of this payoff can be a difficult task. Consider, for example, the problem of estimating a probability distribution for the return that might be generated by a new product. The return on the investment will depend upon factors such as the size of the market, the market share that the product will achieve, the costs of launching the product, manufacturing and distribution costs and the life of the product. We could, of course, ask the decision-maker to estimate the probability distribution directly (for example, we might ask questions such as: 'What is the probability that the investment will achieve a return of over 10% per annum?'). However, it is likely that many people would have difficulty in making this sort of judgment, as all the factors that might influence the return on the investment, and the large number of ways in which they could interrelate, would have to be considered at the same time.

The decision analysis approach to this problem is to help the decision-maker by initially dividing the probability assessment task into smaller parts (a process sometimes referred to as 'credence decomposition'). Thus, we might ask the decision-maker to estimate individual probability distributions for the size of the market, the market share that will be achieved, the launch costs and so on.

The problem is that, having elicited these distributions, we then need to determine their combined effect in order to obtain a probability distribution for the return on the investment. In most practical problems there will be a large number of factors, and also the possible values that each of the factors can assume may be very large or infinite. Consider, for example, the possible levels of the costs of launch, manufacturing and distribution that we might experience. All of this means that there will be a large or infinite number of combinations of circumstances that could affect the return on the investment. In such situations it is clearly impractical to use an approach such as a probability tree to calculate the probability of each of these combinations of circumstances occurring.

One answer to our problem is to use a versatile and easily understood technique called Monte Carlo simulation. This involves the use of a computer to generate a large number of possible combinations of circumstances that might occur if a particular course of action is chosen. When the simulation is performed, the more likely combination of circumstances will be generated most often, while very unlikely combinations will rarely be generated. For each combination, the payoff that the decision-maker would receive is calculated and, by counting the frequency with which a particular payoff occurred in the simulation, a decision-maker is able to estimate the probability that the payoff will be received. Because this method also enables the risk associated with a course of action to be assessed, it is often referred to as *risk analysis* (although some authors use the term to include methods other than simulation, such as mathematical assessment of risk). Monte Carlo simulation is demonstrated in the next section.

Monte Carlo simulation

As we stated earlier, a computer is normally used to carry out Monte Carlo simulation, but we will use the following simplified problem to illustrate how the technique works. A company accountant has estimated that the following probability distributions apply to his company's inflows and outflows of cash for the coming month:

Cash inflows ($)	Probability (%)	Cash outflows ($)	Probability (%)
50 000	30	50 000	45
60 000	40	70 000	55
70 000	30		100
	100		

The accountant would like to obtain a probability distribution for the net cash flow (i.e. cash inflow–cash outflow) over the month. He thinks that it is reasonable to assume that the outflows and inflows are independent.

Of course, for a simple problem like this we could obtain the required probability distribution by calculation. For example, we could use a probability tree to represent the six combinations of inflows and outflows and then calculate the probability of each combination occurring. However, as most practical problems are more complex than this, we will use the example to illustrate the simulation approach. The fact that we can calculate the probabilities exactly for this problem will have the advantage of enabling us to assess the reliability of estimates that are derived from simulation.

In order to carry out our simulation of the company's cash flows, we will make use of *random numbers*. These are numbers that are produced in a manner analogous to those that would be generated by spinning a roulette wheel (hence the name Monte Carlo simulation). Each number in a specified range (e.g. 00–99) is given an equal chance of being generated at any one time. In practical simulations, random numbers are normally produced by a computer, although, strictly speaking, most computers generate what are referred to as pseudorandom numbers because the numbers only have the appearance of being random. If you had access to the computer program that is being used to produce the numbers and the initial value (or seed), then you would be able to predict exactly the series of numbers that was about to be generated.

Before we can start our simulation, we need to assign random numbers to the different cash flows so that, once a particular random number has been generated, we can determine the cash flow that it implies. In this example, we will be using the 100 random numbers between 00 and 99. For the cash inflow distribution, we therefore assign the random numbers 00 to 29 (30 numbers in all) to an inflow of $50 000 which has a 30% probability of occurring. Thus, the probability of a number between 00 and 29 being generated mirrors exactly the probability of the $50 000 cash inflow occurring. Similarly, we assign the next 40 random numbers (30 to 69) to a cash inflow of $60 000, and so on, until all 100 numbers have been allocated.

Cash inflow ($)	Probability (%)	Random numbers
50 000	30	00–29
60 000	40	30–69
70 000	30	70–99

The process is repeated for the cash outflow distribution, and the allocations are shown below.

Cash inflow ($)	Probability (%)	Random numbers
50 000	45	00–44
70 000	55	45–99

We are now ready to perform the simulation run. Each simulation will involve the generation of two random numbers. The first of these will be used to determine the cash inflow, and the second the cash outflow. Suppose that a computer generates the random numbers 46 and 81. This implies a cash inflow of $60 000 and an outflow of $70 000, leading to a net cash flow for the month of −$10 000. If we repeat this process a large number of times, then it is to be expected that the more likely combinations of

Table 8.1 – Ten simulations of monthly cash flows

Random number	Cash inflow ($)	Random number	Cash outflow ($)	Net cash flow ($)
46	60 000	81	70 000	−10 000
30	60 000	08	50 000	10 000
14	50 000	88	70 000	−20 000
35	60 000	21	50 000	10 000
09	50 000	73	70 000	−20 000
19	50 000	77	70 000	−20 000
72	70 000	01	50 000	20 000
20	50 000	46	70 000	−20 000
75	70 000	97	70 000	0
16	50 000	43	50 000	0

cash flows will occur most often, while the unlikely combinations will occur relatively infrequently. Thus, the probability of a particular net cash flow occurring can be estimated from the frequency with which it occurs in the simulations. Table 8.1 shows the results of ten simulations. This number of repetitions is far too small for practical purposes, but the experiment is designed simply to illustrate the basic idea.

If we assume for the moment that this small number of repetitions is sufficient to give us estimates of the probabilities of the various net cash flows occurring, then we can derive the probability distribution shown in Table 8.2. For example, as a net cash flow of −$20 000 occurred in four of our ten simulations, we estimate that the probability of this net cash flow occurring is 4/10. Note that the table also shows the probability distribution that we would have derived if we had used a probability tree to calculate the probabilities. The discrepancies between the two distributions show that the result based on only ten simulations gives a poor estimate of the real distribution. However, as more simulations are carried out, we can expect this estimate to improve. This is

Table 8.2 – Estimating probabilities from the simulation results

Net cash flow ($)	Number of simulations resulting in this net cash flow	Probability estimate based on simulation	Calculated probability
−20 000	4	4/10 = 0.4	0.165
−10 000	1	1/10 = 0.1	0.220
0	2	2/10 = 0.2	0.300
10 000	2	2/10 = 0.2	0.180
20 000	1	1/10 = 0.1	0.135

Table 8.3 – The effect of the number of simulations on the reliability of the probability estimates

	Probability estimates based on			
Net cash flow ($)	50 simulations	1000 simulations	5000 simulations	Calculated probability
−20 000	0.14	0.164	0.165	0.165
−10 000	0.18	0.227	0.216	0.220
0	0.42	0.303	0.299	0.300
10 000	0.12	0.168	0.184	0.180
20 000	0.14	0.138	0.136	0.135

shown in Table 8.3, which compares the 'real' distribution with estimates based on 50, 1000 and 5000 simulations that were carried out on a computer.

How many simulations are needed to give an acceptable level of reliability? This question can be answered by using relatively complex iterative statistical methods, but a simpler approach is to start off with a run of several hundred simulations and then increase the length of the runs until there is virtually no change in the estimates produced by the simulation. However, in some situations it is important to assess the probability of rare extreme events occurring because of the potentially huge impact that they can have. A small number of simulations will be insufficient to generate these events, so in these situations hundreds of thousands of simulations are advisable. Modern software products (see later) should produce the results of such simulations fairly quickly.

Applying simulation to a decision problem

The Elite Pottery Company

We will now show how simulation can be applied to a decision problem. The Elite Pottery Company is planning to market a special product to commemorate a major sporting event that is due to take place in a few months' time. A large number of possible products have been considered, but the list has now been winnowed down to two alternatives: a commemorative plate and a figurine. In order to make a decision between the plate and the figurine, the company's managing director needs to estimate the profit that would be earned by each product (the decision will be made solely on the basis of profit, so that other objectives such as achieving a prestigious company image, increasing public awareness of the company, etc., are not considered to be important). There is some uncertainty about the costs of manufacturing the products and the levels of sales, although it is thought that all sales will be made in the very short period that coincides with the sporting event.

The application of simulation to a problem like this involves the following stages:

(1) Identify the factors that will affect the payoffs of each course of action.
(2) Formulate a model to show how the factors are related.
(3) Carry out a preliminary sensitivity analysis to establish the factors for which probability distributions should be assessed.
(4) Assess probability distributions for the factors that were identified in stage 3.
(5) Perform the simulation.
(6) Apply sensitivity analysis to the results of the simulation.
(7) Compare the simulation results for the alternative courses of action and use these to identify the preferred course of action.

We will now show how each of these stages can be applied to the Elite Pottery Company problem.

Stage 1: Identify the factors

We first need to identify the factors that we think will affect the profit of each product. For brevity, we will focus on those that might affect the potential profit of the commemorative plate. A tree diagram may be helpful in identifying these factors, as it enables them to be subdivided until the decision-maker feels able to give a probability distribution for the possible values that the factor might assume. Figure 8.1 shows a tree for this problem. Of course, it might have been necessary to extend the tree further, perhaps by subdividing fixed costs into different types, such as advertising and production set-up costs, or breaking sales into home and export sales. It is also worth noting that subsequent analysis will be simplified if the factors can be identified

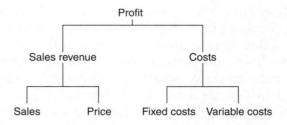

Figure 8.1 – Identifying the factors that will affect the profit earned by the commemorative plate

in such a way that their probability distributions can be considered to be independent. For example, we will assume here that variable costs and sales are independent. However, in practice, there might be a high probability of experiencing a variable cost of around $7 per plate if less than 10 000 plates are sold, while we might expect costs of around $5 if more than 10 000 are sold because of savings resulting from the bulk purchase of materials, etc. It is possible to handle dependence, as we will show later, but it does add complications to the analysis.

Stage 2: Formulate a model

The next step is to formulate a model to show how the factors we have identified affect the variable of interest, in this case profit. For Elite's problem, the following simple model is thought to be appropriate:

$$\text{Profit} = (\text{price} - \text{variable cost}) \times \text{sales} - \text{fixed costs}$$

Of course, this is only a model, and therefore almost certainly a simplification of the real problem. In practice, a large number of factors and relationships that we have not included in the model may affect profit. For example, at higher sales levels, more breakages may occur because of increased pressure on the workforce. Similarly, fixed costs may only remain at a particular level up to a certain number of sales when new equipment and machinery may be required. However, if we tried to include every possible factor and relationship in the model, it would become too complicated to handle and the valuable insights that can be gained by building and analyzing the model might be lost. Therefore, a balance has to be struck between the need to keep the model simple and understandable and the need to provide a reasonable and plausible representation of the real problem.

Stage 3: Preliminary sensitivity analysis

Although we may be uncertain about the values that the factors might assume, this uncertainty may not be important in the case of all the factors. For example, we might find that there would be little change in profit if fixed costs changed from their lowest to their highest possible value. If this were the case, time might be wasted in eliciting a probability distribution for fixed costs, and a single figure representing the most likely value would suffice. Sensitivity analysis can be helpful in screening out those factors that do not require a probability distribution. This analysis can be carried out as follows:

Table 8.4 – Estimates of lowest, highest and most likely values for the Elite Pottery problem

Factor	Most likely value	Lowest possible value	Highest possible value
Variable costs	$13	$8	$18
Sales	22 000 units	10 000 units	30 000 units
Fixed costs	$175 000	$100 000	$300 000

(i) Identify the lowest, highest and most likely values that each factor can assume. The values put forward for the factors in Elite's problem are shown in Table 8.4. (It is assumed that the price of the plate will be fixed at $25, so there is no uncertainty associated with this factor.)

(ii) Calculate the profit that would be achieved if the first factor was at its lowest value and the remaining factors were at their most likely values.

   Thus, if variable costs are at their lowest possible value of $8 and the remaining factors are at their most likely value, we have

$$\text{Profit} = (\$25 - \$8) \times 22\ 000 - \$175\ 000 = \$199\ 000$$

(iii) Repeat (ii), but with the first factor at its highest possible value. Thus, we have

$$\text{Profit} = (\$25 - \$18) \times 22\ 000 - \$175\ 000 = -\$21\ 000$$

(iv) Repeat stages (ii) and (iii) by varying, in turn, each of the other factors between their lowest and highest possible values while the remaining factors remain at their most likely values.

Figure 8.2 shows the results of the preliminary sensitivity analysis. This diagram, which is often referred to as a *tornado diagram*, indicates that each of the factors is crucial to our analysis in that a change from its lowest to its highest possible value will have a major effect on profit. It is therefore well worth spending time in the careful elicitation of probability distributions for all these factors. (Note that some software products also produce tornado diagrams after the simulation has been run, to identify where the major sources of uncertainty are. These packages use more sophisticated statistical methods, such as correlation and multiple regression analysis, to obtain the diagram.)

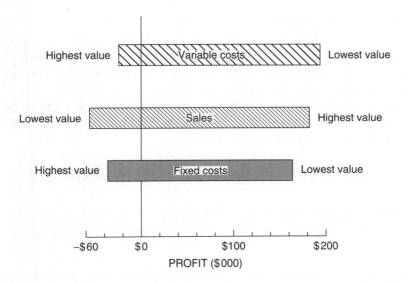

Figure 8.2 – Tornado diagram showing the effect on profit if each factor changes from its lowest to its highest possible value

Stage 4: Assess probability distributions

Figure 8.3 shows the probability distributions that were obtained for variable costs, sales and fixed costs. Techniques for eliciting probability distributions are discussed in Chapter 11.

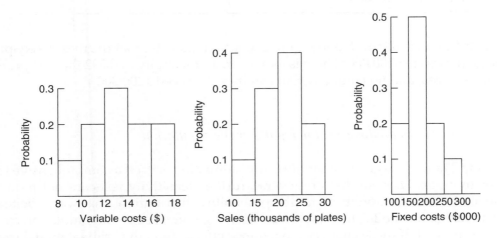

Figure 8.3 – Probability distributions for variable costs, sales and fixed costs

Stage 5: Perform the simulation

Simulation can now be used to obtain a probability distribution for the profit that the plate will earn. A computer was programmed to carry out the simulation, which involved the generation of three random numbers. These yielded values for variable costs, sales and fixed costs respectively. For example, in the first simulation the computer produced variable costs of $13.2, sales of 26 500 and fixed costs of $125 000, and the resulting profit was calculated as follows:

$$\text{Profit} = (\$25 - \$13.2) \times 26\ 500 - \$125\ 000 = \text{£}187\ 700$$

This process was then repeated until 500 simulations had been carried out. The profits generated by these simulations and the resulting probability distribution are shown below:

Profit ($)	No. of simulations	Probability
−200 000 to under −100 000	26	26/500 = 0.052
−100 000 to under 0	120	120/500 = 0.240
0 to under 100 000	213	213/500 = 0.426
100 000 to under 200 000	104	104/500 = 0.208
200 000 to under 300 000	34	34/500 = 0.068
300 000 to under 400 000	3	3/500 = 0.006
	500	1.000

Mean profit = $51 800

This distribution is illustrated in Figure 8.4, which indicates that the most likely profit range is from $0 to $100 000. There is, however, a probability of 0.292 that the product will make a loss, and it is unlikely that profits will exceed $200 000.

Stage 6: Sensitivity analysis on the results of the simulation

Hertz and Thomas[1] argue that Monte Carlo simulation is itself a comprehensive form of sensitivity analysis, so that, in general, further sensitivity tests are not required. However, if there are doubts about the probability distributions that were elicited or the structure of the model, then the effects of changes in these on the simulation results can be examined. If these changes have minor effects, then the original model can be assumed to be adequate.

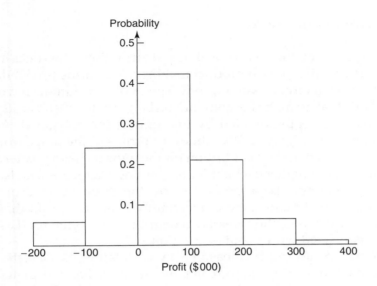

Figure 8.4 – Probability distribution for profit earned by the commemorative plate

Stage 7: Compare alternative courses of action

Recall that Elite Pottery had to make a decision between the production of the commemorative plate and the figurine. The factors that it was thought would affect the profit on the figurine were also identified, and a simulation was carried out. This resulted in the probability distribution shown below:

Profit on figurine ($)	Probability
−300 000 to under −200 000	0.06
−200 000 to under −100 000	0.10
−100 000 to under 0	0.15
0 to under 100 000	0.34
100 000 to under 200 000	0.18
200 000 to under 300 000	0.08
300 000 to under 400 000	0.05
400 000 to under 500 000	0.04
	1.00

Mean profit = $62 000

To choose between the two products, their profit probability distributions need to be compared. This comparison can be made in a number of ways.

Plotting the two distributions

By inspecting graphs of the two probability distributions, the decision-maker can compare the probabilities of each product making a loss or the probabilities that each product would reach a target level of profit. The two distributions have been plotted in Figure 8.5. Note that, to make the comparison between the distributions easier, their histograms have been approximated by line graphs (or polygons). Although both distributions have their highest probabilities for profits in the range from $0 to under $100 000, it can be seen that the distribution for the figurine has a greater spread. Thus, while the figurine has a higher probability of yielding a large loss, it also has a higher probability of generating a large profit. Clearly, the greater spread of the figurine's distribution implies that there is more uncertainty about the profit that will actually be achieved. Because of this, the spread of a distribution is often used as a measure of the risk that is associated with a course of action.

A distribution's spread can be measured by calculating its *standard deviation* (the larger the standard deviation, the greater the spread). For the plate the standard deviation of profits is $99 080, while for the figurine it is $163 270.

Determining the option with the highest expected utility

Because the two products offer different levels of risk, utility theory can be used to identify the preferred option. However, unlike the examples we encountered in

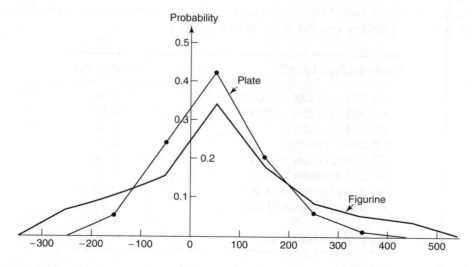

Figure 8.5 – A comparison of the profit probability distributions of the commemorative plate and the figurine

Chapter 6, each option has a very large number of possible outcomes. One way around this problem is to find a mathematical function that will approximate the decision-maker's utility function. A computer can then be used to calculate the utility for each profit generated in the simulation run. The resulting utilities would then be averaged to give the expected utility.

Stochastic dominance

Sometimes the alternative with the highest expected utility can be identified by a short-cut method that is based on a concept known as stochastic dominance. This exists where the expected utility of one option is greater than that of another for an entire class of utility functions. This means that we can be sure that the option will be preferred without going to the trouble of eliciting the decision-maker's complete utility function; all we need to establish is that the utility function has some basic characteristics.[2]

Stochastic dominance can be recognized by plotting the cumulative probability distribution functions (cdfs). As we saw in Chapter 5, the cdf shows the probability that a variable will have a value less than any given value. First- and second-degree stochastic dominance are the two most useful forms that the cdfs can reveal.

First-degree stochastic dominance

This concept requires some very unrestrictive assumptions about the nature of the decision-maker's utility function. When money is the attribute under consideration, the main assumption is simply that higher monetary values have a higher utility. To illustrate the application of first-degree stochastic dominance, consider the following simulation results, which relate to the profits of two potential products, P and Q:

Product P			Product Q		
Profit ($m)	Prob.	Cumulative prob.	Profit ($m)	Prob.	Cumulative prob.
0 to under 5	0.2	0.2	0 to under 5	0	0
5 to under 10	0.3	0.5	5 to under 10	0.1	0.1
10 to under 15	0.4	0.9	10 to under 15	0.5	0.6
15 to under 20	0.1	1.0	15 to under 20	0.3	0.9
			20 to under 25	0.1	1.0

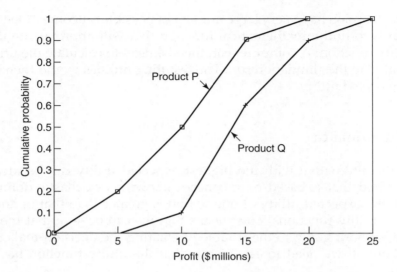

Figure 8.6 – First-degree stochastic dominance

The cdfs for the two products are plotted in Figure 8.6. It can be seen the cdf for product Q is always to the right of that for product P. This means that, for any level of profit, Q offers the smallest probability of falling below that profit. For example, Q has only a 0.1 probability of yielding a profit of less than $10 million, while there is a 0.5 probability that P's profit will fall below this level. Because Q's cdf is always to the right of P's, we can say that Q exhibits first-degree stochastic dominance over P. Thus, as long as the weak assumptions required by first-degree stochastic dominance apply, we can infer that product Q has the highest expected utility.

Second-degree stochastic dominance

When the cdfs for the options intersect each other at least once, it may still be possible to identify the preferred option if, in addition to the weak assumptions we made for first-degree stochastic dominance, we can also assume that the decision-maker is risk averse (i.e. his utility function is concave) for the range of values under consideration. If this assumption is appropriate, then we can make use of second-degree stochastic dominance. To demonstrate this, let us compare the following simulation results, which have been generated for two other potential products, R and S:

Product R			Product S		
Profit ($m)	Prob.	Cumulative prob.	Profit ($m)	Prob.	Cumulative prob.
0 to under 5	0.1	0.1	0 to under 5	0.3	0.3
5 to under 10	0.3	0.4	5 to under 10	0.3	0.6
10 to under 15	0.4	0.8	10 to under 15	0.2	0.8
15 to under 20	0.2	1.0	15 to under 20	0.1	0.9
20 to under 25	0	1.0	20 to under 25	0.1	1.0

The cdfs for the two products are shown in Figure 8.7. It can be seen that, for profits between $0 and $15 million, R is the dominant product, while S dominates for the range $15–25 million. To determine which is the dominant product overall, we need to compare both the lengths of the ranges for which the products are dominant and the extent to which they are dominant within these ranges (i.e. the extent to which one curve falls below the other). This comparison can be made by comparing area X, which shows the extent to which R dominates S, with area Y, the extent to which S dominates R. As area X is larger, we can say that product R has second-degree stochastic dominance over product S. Again, as long as our limited assumptions about the form of the decision-maker's utility function are correct, we can conclude that R has a higher expected utility than S.

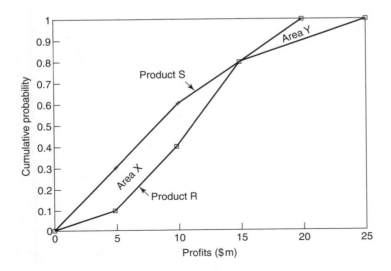

Figure 8.7 – Second-degree stochastic dominance

Of course, there are bound to be situations where the cdfs intersect each other several times. In these cases we would have to add areas together to establish the extent to which one option dominates the other.

The mean–standard deviation approach

When a decision problem involves a large number of alternative courses of action, it is helpful if inferior options can be screened out at an early stage. In these situations, the mean–standard deviation approach can be useful. This has mainly been developed in connection with portfolio theory, where a risk-averse decision-maker has to choose between a large number of possible investment portfolios (see Markowitz[3]).

To illustrate the approach, let us suppose that a company is considering five alternative products, which are code named A to E. For each product, a simulation has been carried out and the mean and standard deviation of that product's profits have been calculated. The results are plotted in Figure 8.8. The company's manager would like to maximize the expected (or mean) return, and, being risk averse, she would also like to minimize the risk or uncertainty that her company faces. If we compare products A and B, we see that, while they offer the same expected return, product B is much more risky. Product A is therefore said to dominate B. B is

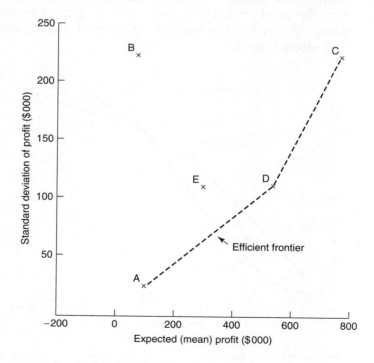

Figure 8.8 – The mean–standard deviation screening method

also dominated by C, which for the same level of risk offers higher expected profits. For the same reason, D dominates E. The non-dominated products, A, C and D, are therefore said to lie on the efficient frontier, and only these products would survive the screening process and be considered further. The choice between A, C and D will depend on how risk averse the decision-maker is. Product A offers a low expected return but also a low level of risk, while, at the other extreme, C offers high expected returns but a high level of risk. The utility approach, which we discussed above, could now be used to compare these three products.

Note that, for the mean–standard deviation screening process to be valid, it can be shown that a number of assumptions need to be made. First, the probability distributions for profit should be fairly close to the normal distribution shape shown in Figure 8.9(a) (in many practical situations this is likely to be the case: see Hertz and Thomas[1]). Second, the decision-maker should have a utility function that not only indicates risk aversion but that also has (at least approximately) a quadratic form. This means that the function can be represented by an equation of the form

$$U(x) = c + bx + ax^2$$

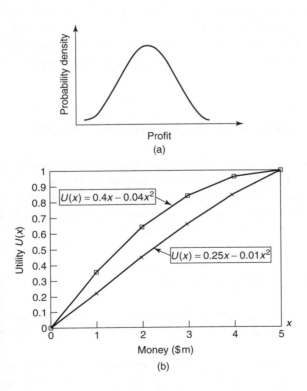

Figure 8.9 – (a) A normal probability distribution for profit; (b) examples of quadratic utility functions

where x is a given sum of money, $U(x)$ is the utility of this sum of money and a, b and c are other numbers that determine the exact nature of the utility function.

For example, Figure 8.9(b) shows the utility functions

$$U(x) = 0 + 0.4x - 0.04x^2$$

and

$$U(x) = 0 + 0.25x - 0.01x^2$$

(where x denotes monetary sums in millions of dollars) for monetary values between $0 and $5 million. Of course, not all utility functions have a quadratic form, but, as Markowitz[3] argues, 'the quadratic nevertheless shows a surprising flexibility in approximating smooth, concave curves'.

Having considered the different ways in which the results of simulations can be compared, how was a decision made in the case of the Elite Pottery Company? First, it was established that the Managing Director's utility function for profit was concave (i.e. he was risk averse). Second, a plot of the cumulative probability distributions for the profits earned by the plate and the figurine showed that the figurine had second-degree stochastic dominance over the plate. Thus, while the figurine had a slightly higher probability of yielding a loss, it could also generate much larger profits than the plate, and this was sufficient for it to have the highest expected utility, even though the manager was risk averse. A decision was therefore made to go ahead with production of the figurine.

Applying simulation to investment decisions

The techniques that we have outlined in this chapter have been most widely applied in the area of investment appraisal. In this section we will briefly discuss the commonly used net present value (NPV) approach to investment appraisal, and then show how Monte Carlo simulation can be used to improve on the 'standard' NPV method, which is based on single-figure estimates of cash flows.

The net present value (NPV) method

We will give only a brief overview of the net present value method here. More detailed explanations can be found in accountancy textbooks (e.g. Balakrishnan *et al.*[4] and Drury[5]).

When money is invested in a project, a commitment of funds is generally required immediately. However, the flow of funds earned by the investment will occur at various points of time in the future. Receiving $1000 in, say, a year's time is less attractive than receiving $1000 now. The $1000 received now could be invested, so that in a year's time it will have earned interest. Similarly, $1000 due to be received in 2 years' time will be less attractive than $1000 that will be received 1 year from now. This implies that money that will be earned in the future should be *discounted* so that its value can be compared with sums of money that are being held now. The process involved is referred to as 'discounting to present value'. For example, we might judge that the $1000 due in 1 year is only equivalent to receiving $909 now, while the $1000 due in 2 years has only the same value as receiving $826 now.

The severity with which we discount future sums of money to their present value is reflected in the discount rate. Determining the appropriate discount rate for a company's potential investment projects is, ultimately, a matter of judgment and preference. However, many attempts have been made to make the choice of a discount rate as 'objective' as possible, making this a complex area that is beyond the scope of this text. For many situations it will be convenient to let the discount rate reflect the opportunity cost of the capital that is being invested (i.e. the rate of return that could be earned on the best alternative investment). Thus, if we are only considering two mutually exclusive projects A and B and we could earn a 12% return on project A, then the discount rate for project B would be 12% because, if we invest in B, we will be forgoing the 12% return that A would have generated. Having determined the appropriate discount rate, the process of discounting future sums of money is very straightforward. It simply involves multiplying the sum of money by a *present value factor*, which can be obtained from published tables.

The following simple example illustrates the net present value approach to investment appraisal. A company has to choose between two new machines, the Alpha and the Beta. Both machines would cost $30 000 and have an expected lifetime of 4 years. Estimates of the annual cash inflows that each machine would generate are given below, together with estimates of the cash outflows that would be experienced for each year of the machine's operation (for simplicity, we will assume that all the cash flows occur at the year end):

Alpha machine

Time of cash flow	Year 1	Year 2	Year 3	Year 4
Cash inflows ($)	14 000	15 000	15 000	14 000
Cash outflows ($)	2 000	4 000	6 000	7 000

Beta machine

Time of cash flow	Year 1	Year 2	Year 3	Year 4
Cash inflows ($)	8 000	13 000	15 000	21 500
Cash outflows ($)	4 000	4 000	5 000	5 000

Table 8.5 – Calculating the NPVs for the Alpha and Beta machines

Time of cash flow	Cash inflow ($)	Cash outflow ($)	Net cash flow ($)	Present value factor	Discounted cash flow ($)
(a) Alpha machine					
Now	0	30 000	−30 000	1.0000	−30 000
Year 1	14 000	2 000	12 000	0.9091	10 909
Year 2	15 000	4 000	11 000	0.8264	9 090
Year 3	15 000	6 000	9 000	0.7513	6 762
Year 4	14 000	7 000	7 000	0.6830	4 781
				Net present value (NPV) =	$1 542
(b) Beta machine					
Now	0	30 000	−30 000	1.0000	−30 000
Year 1	8 000	4 000	4 000	0.9091	3 636
Year 2	13 000	4 000	9 000	0.8264	7 438
Year 3	15 000	5 000	10 000	0.7513	7 513
Year 4	21 500	5 000	16 500	0.6830	11 270
				Net present value (NPV) =	−$143

Table 8.5 shows the calculations that are involved in determining the net present value of the two potential investments. First, the net cash flow is determined for each year. These net cash flows are then discounted by multiplying by the appropriate present value factor. (The present value factors used in Table 8.5 are based on the assumption that a 10% discount rate is appropriate.) Finally, these discounted cash flows are summed to give the net present value of the project. It can be seen that, according to the NPV criterion, the Alpha machine offers the most attractive investment opportunity.

While this approach to investment appraisal is widely used, the NPV figures are obviously only as good as the estimates on which the calculations are based. In general, there will be uncertainty about the size of the future cash flows and about the lifetime of the project. Expressing the cash flow estimates as single figures creates an illusion of accuracy, but it also means that we have no idea how reliable the resulting NPV is. For example, it may be that the year 1 cash inflow for the Beta machine could be anything from $2000 to $14 000, and we have simply used the mid-range figure, $8000, as our estimate. If the actual flow did turn out to be near $14 000, then our estimated NPV would be very misleading.

Our analysis would therefore be more realistic if we could incorporate our uncertainty about the cash flows into the analysis. The result would be a probability distribution for the NPV that would indicate the range within which it would be likely to lie and the probability of it having particular values. From this we could assess the chances of the project producing a negative NPV or the probability that the NPV from one project will exceed that of a competing project. In the following section we will show how simulation can be used to obtain a probability distribution for the NPV.

Using simulation

We first apply simulation to the Alpha machine. It was thought that the following factors would affect the return on this investment:

  (i) the price of the machine;
 (ii) the revenue resulting from the machine's output in years 1 to 4;
(iii) maintenance costs in years 1 to 4;
(iv) the scrap value of the machine at the end of year 4.

The price of the machine was known to be $30 000, but, because there was uncertainty about the other factors, probability distributions were elicited from the company's management. The shapes of these distributions are shown in Figure 8.10 (for simplicity, it was assumed that the distributions were independent).

Random numbers were then used to sample a value from each distribution, using the methods that we outlined earlier, and the NPV was calculated for this set of values. For example, the first simulation generated the following values:

	Purchase costs = $30 000
Year 1 revenue = $24 500	Maintenance costs = $2 150
Year 2 revenue = $14 200	Maintenance costs = $3 820
Year 3 revenue = $17 320	Maintenance costs = $4 340
Year 4 revenue = $16 970	Maintenance costs = $9 090
Scrap value = $1 860	

This led to an NPV of $8328. The process was then repeated until 500 simulations had been carried out. Figure 8.11 shows the resulting probability distribution for the net present value. It can be seen that the NPV could be between about −$20 000 and $36 000. Moreover, although the expected (mean) NPV was $7364, there was roughly a 20% probability that the NPV would be negative.

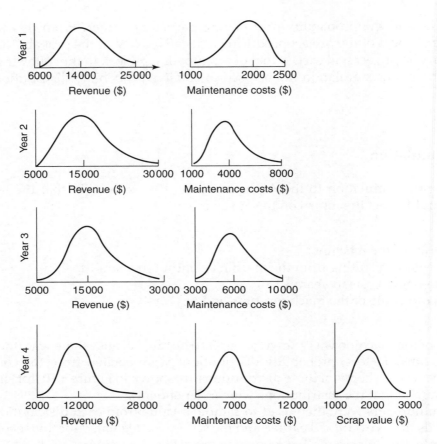

Figure 8.10 – Probability distributions for the Alpha machine (vertical axes represent probability density)

A similar simulation was carried out for the Beta machine, and the resulting distribution is also displayed in Figure 8.11. While this machine has a higher probability (about 30%) of yielding a negative NPV, its distribution is much tighter than that of the Alpha machine. For example, in contrast to the Alpha machine, there is little chance of the NPV being below −$5000.

It can be seen that simulation enables a more informed choice to be made between investment opportunities. By restricting us to single-value estimates, the conventional NPV approach yields no information on the level of uncertainty that is associated with different options. Hespos and Strassman[6] have shown how the simulation approach can be extended to handle investment problems involving sequences of decisions using a method known as stochastic decision tree analysis.

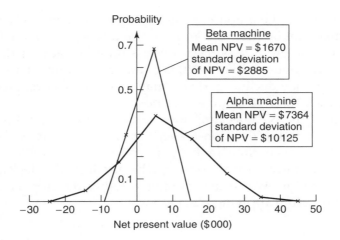

Figure 8.11 – Probability distributions for the NPVs of the Alpha and Beta machines

Utility and net present value

In order to help a decision-maker to choose between a number of alternative invest-ment projects, we could obtain a utility function for net present value. This would involve giving the highest possible NPV a utility of 1 and the lowest possible NPV a utility of 0 and using questions involving lotteries to determine the utilities of inter-mediate NPVs. The decision-maker would then be advised to choose the investment project that had the highest expected utility. How justified would we be in converting NPVs to utilities? As we will demonstrate below, using NPVs requires some strong assumptions about the decision-maker's preferences.

First, the use of the NPV approach implies that the decision-maker's relative strength of preference for receiving money in any two adjacent years is the same, whatever those years are. For example, if a 10% discount rate is used, it implies that $1 receivable in 1 year's time is equivalent to receiving about $0.91 today. Similarly, $1 receivable in 10 years' time is equivalent to receiving $0.91 in 9 years' time. Now it may well be that a decision-maker has a very strong relative preference for receiving money now rather than in a year's time, while his or her relative preference between receiving a sum in 9 as opposed to 10 years is much weaker.

Second, if we consider the decision-maker's relative preference for sums of money between the *same* pair of years, it can be seen that the NPV method assumes a constant rate of trade-off between the years. For example (again assuming a 10% discount rate), it assumes that you would be prepared to give up the promise of $1 in a year's time in order to receive $0.91 today, and that you would be prepared to go on making this exchange, irrespective of the amount of money that is transferred from next year to this. Again, this may not be the case. You may be desperate for $10 000 now and be prepared to give up the promise of $3 in a year's time for each $0.91 you can receive today. Once you have obtained your $10 000, however, your relative preference for money received now may decline, and you may then only be prepared to give up the promise of $1 for each $0.91 you can receive now.

Clearly, if either of the NPV assumptions is *seriously* violated, then the NPV will not accurately represent the decision-maker's preferences between sums of money arriving at different points in time. In this case, converting the NPVs to utilities might not lead to a ranking of investment options, which reflects the decision-maker's true preferences. It is therefore worth questioning whether the implicit assumptions of NPV are reasonable before applying the method.

Modeling dependence relationships

So far we have assumed, for simplicity, that all the probability distributions in our models are independent. In reality, it is possible that the value of some variables will depend upon the value of others. For example, in the Alpha and Beta machine problem it is possible that the maintenance costs will be related to sales revenue, as high sales revenue implies high production levels and hence more wear and tear on machinery. Similarly, the year 2 sales revenue may be closely related to that achieved in year 1, as, for example, high sales in year 1 may signify that the product is popular and hence increase the probability of high sales in subsequent years.

Some commercial risk analysis packages (see later for examples) allow users to model dependencies like these by inputting a correlation coefficient to show the strength of association between the two factors. This coefficient always has a value between −1 and +1. Positive values indicate that higher values of one factor are associated with higher values of the other (e.g. higher production levels are likely to be associated with higher machine maintenance costs). Negative coefficients imply an inverse relationship (e.g. higher advertising expenditure by competitors is associated with lower sales for our company). The closer the coefficient is to either −1 or +1, the stronger is the association.

In practice, it may be possible to determine the appropriate correlation coefficient for the simulation model by analyzing past data. Where this is not possible, the correlation can be estimated judgmentally. However, this needs to be done with care because, as we shall see in Chapter 10, biases can occur in the assessment of covariation. In particular, prior beliefs and expectations can lead people to see associations where none exists, or to overestimate the degree of association when it is weak. Conversely, if the judgment is based on observations with no expectation of an association, then moderately strong associations that do exist are likely to be missed, while correlations for strong associations are likely to be underestimated.[7]

Summary

In this chapter we have shown that simulation can be a powerful tool when the direct calculation of probabilities in a decision problem would be extremely complex. Moreover, because the approach does not involve advanced mathematics, the methods involved and the results of analyses are accessible to decision-makers who are not trained mathematicians or statisticians. Obviously, the application of simulation requires the use of a computer, and a number of specialist computer packages are available. These include @RISK (developed by the Palisade Corporation), Oracle® Crystal Ball and Risk Solver (developed by FrontLine Systems), all of which run with Microsoft® Excel (see Sugiyama[8] for a review of these products).

While computers excel at the rapid calculation of a large number of simulation results, we should not forget that the judgments of the decision-maker are still the crucial inputs to the decision model. This means that, as always, care should be taken in the design of the model and in the elicitation of probabilities and utilities. The process of initially dividing the problem into small parts should help the decision-maker in this task. Nevertheless, it is important to be aware of any assumptions and simplifications that are inherent in the model being used.

Exercises

(1) A small retail store sells a particular brand of monochrome and color television sets. Each monochrome set that is sold earns a profit of $100, while each color set earns $200 profit. The manager of the store estimates that the weekly demands for each type of set follow the probability distributions shown below (it can be assumed that the demands for each type of set are independent, as is the week-to-week demand):

| | Probability | |
Demand per week	Monochrome sets	Color sets
0	0.2	0.4
1	0.5	0.6
2	0.3	

(a) Determine the possible total profits that can be earned in any given week by selling television sets, and *calculate* the probability of each of these profits being earned.

(b) The following two-digit random numbers have been generated by a computer. Use these numbers to simulate the demand for the two types of set for a 10 week period and hence calculate the profit that will be earned in each week (the first set of numbers should be used for monochrome sets and the second for color):

Monochrome	71	82	19	50	67	29	95	48	84	32
Color		36	44	64	92	39	21	18	55	77	73

(c) Use your simulation results to estimate the probability of particular profits being earned in a given week. How close are these probabilities to those that you calculated in (a)?

(2) The managers of a food company are about to install a number of automatic vending machines at various locations in a major city. A number of types of machine are available, and the managers would like to choose the design that will minimize the profit that will be lost because the machine is out of order. The following model is to be used to represent the lost profit:

> Cost of lost profit per month
> = (number of breakdowns per month)
>   × (time to repair machine after each breakdown in hours)
>   × (profit lost per hour)

One machine that is being considered is the Supervend, and the following probability distributions have been estimated for this machine:

Number of breakdowns per month	Prob.	Repair time (hours)	Prob.	Average profit lost per hour	Prob.
0	0.5	1	0.45	$10	0.7
1	0.3	2	0.55	$20	0.3
2	0.2				

(a) Use a table of random numbers, or the random number button on a calculator, to simulate the operation of a machine for 12 months, and hence estimate a probability distribution for the profit that would be lost per month if the machine were purchased.

(b) Explain why the model is likely to be a simplification of the real problem.

(3) Trentware plc is a medium-sized pottery manufacturer that is based in the English Potteries. The company has fared badly over the last 10 years, mainly as a result of Japanese competition, and recently this has led to major changes at the senior management level. The new managing director is determined to increase the company's market share, and you are a member of the ambitious new management team which intends to extend the company's range of tableware designs. Trentware's immediate objective is to launch a new high-quality product for the Christmas market in 18 months' time. Over 30 possible designs have been subjected to both technical analysis (to assess their production implications) and extensive market research. As a result of this analysis, the number of potential designs has now been winnowed down to six. Some of these designs are thought to offer more risk than others because of changes in fashion, similarities to competing products and possible production problems. Now one design has to be selected from the six remaining. Risk analysis has been applied to each of these six designs, and some of the main results are given below:

Design	1	2	3	4	5	6
Mean NPV (£0000)	50	21	20	46	−49	60
Standard deviation of NPV (£0000)	3	2	29	8	31	30

(a) You have been asked to explain to a colleague who is unfamiliar with risk analysis how these results are likely to have been derived. Draft some notes for your colleague, and include in your notes an evaluation of the usefulness of the technique.

(b) Compare the risk analysis results for the six designs, and discuss how a decision could be made between them.

(4) (This exercise is really designed to be carried out by a group of people, with each individual using a different set of random numbers. The individual results can then be combined by using the table at the end of the question.)

An equipment hire company has to decide whether to buy a specialized piece of earth-digging machinery for $6000. The machine would be sold after 2 years. The main factors that it is thought will affect the return on the investment are:

(i) the revenue generated by hiring the machine out for a day: it is certain that this will be $40;

(ii) the number of days for which the machine will be hired out in year 1 and in year 2;

(iii) the costs of having the machine available for hire (e.g. maintenance and repair costs) in year 1 and in year 2;

(iv) the price that will be obtained for the machine when it is sold at the end of year 2.

For each factor, the following probability distributions have been estimated:

No. of days hired out in year 1	Prob. (%)	No. of days hired out in year 2
under 100	30	(This is assumed to
100 to under 200	50	have the same
200 to under 300	20	distribution as
		year 1)

Annual costs ($)	Prob. in year 1 (%)	Prob. in year 2 (%)
1000 to under 2000	50	30
2000 to under 3000	30	40
3000 to under 4000	20	30

Selling price ($)	Prob. (%)
1000 to under 2000	40
2000 to under 3000	60

Carry out one simulation of a possible combination of circumstances and calculate the NPV for your simulation. Use a discount rate of 10%.

The results for the *entire group* can then be entered into the following table:

Net present value ($)	No. of simulations resulting in NPVs in this range	Probability
−15 000 to under 0	. . . .	. . . .
0 to under 5 000	. . . .	. . . .
5 000 to under 10 000	. . . .	. . . .
10 000 to under 15 000	. . . .	. . . .

Therefore, the most likely range for the NPV appears to be ...... and the probability of a negative NPV appears to be ....

(5) The managers of a chemical company have to decide whether to extend their existing plant or replace it with completely new equipment. A simulation of the two alternatives gives the following probability distributions of net present value:

	Probabilities	
NPV ($m)	Extend existing plant	Replace with new equipment
−3 to under −2	0.05	0.00
−2 to under −1	0.05	0.05
−1 to under 0	0.15	0.15
0 to under 1	0.29	0.26
1 to under 2	0.22	0.21
2 to under 3	0.14	0.18
3 to under 4	0.10	0.10
4 to under 5	0.00	0.05

(a) Compare the two distributions and, stating any necessary assumptions, determine the option that the management should choose.

(b) After the above simulations have been carried out, a third possible course of action becomes available. This would involve the movement of some of the company's operations to a new site. A simulation of this option generated the following probability distribution. Is this option worth considering?

NPV ($m)	Probability
−2 to under −1	0.05
−1 to under 0	0.05
0 to under 1	0.40
1 to under 2	0.40
2 to under 3	0.04
3 to under 4	0.03
4 to under 5	0.03

(6) A publisher is considering launching a new magazine for women in the 18–25-year-old age group. It is thought to be vital to the long-term success of the

magazine that its sales should reach break-even point within its first year. When asked to make an estimate of the risk of this target *not* being achieved, the marketing manager, after some thought, states that she thinks the risk is only about 1 in 10.

(a) Sketch out the key features of a risk analysis model that might be appropriate for this estimate, and explain how the estimate would be obtained from the model.

(b) Suppose that your risk analysis model suggests that the risk of not achieving the target is about 1 in 4. Explain why the estimate from the model might differ from the 'holistic' estimate of the marketing manager, and discuss how the conflict might be resolved.

References

1. Hertz, D.B. and Thomas, H. (1983) *Risk Analysis and its Applications*, John Wiley & Sons, Ltd, Chichester, UK.
2. For a theoretical treatment of stochastic dominance, see Hadar, J. and Russell, W.R. (1969) Rules for ordering uncertain prospects, *The American Economic Review*, March, 25–34.
3. Markowitz, H.M. (1959) *Portfolio Selection*, John Wiley & Sons, Inc., New York, NY.
4. Balakrishnan, R., Sivaramakrishnan, K. and Sprinkle, G. (2009) *Managerial Accounting*, John Wiley & Sons, Inc., New York, NY.
5. Drury, C. (2008) *Management and Cost Accounting*, 7th edition, South Western Cengage Learning, London, UK.
6. Hespos, R.F. and Strassman, P.A. (1965) Stochastic decision trees in the analysis of investment decisions, *Management Science*, **10**, B244–B259.
7. Jennings, D.L., Amabile, T.M. and Ross, L. (1982) Informal covariation assessment: data-based versus theory-based judgments, in *Judgment Under Uncertainty: Heuristics and Biases*, ed. by Kahneman, D., Slovic, P. and Tversky, A., Cambridge University Press, Cambridge, UK.
8. Sugiyama, S. (2008) Monte Carlo simulation/risk analysis on a spreadsheet: review of three software packages, *Foresight: The International Journal of Applied Forecasting*, **9**, Spring.

Revising judgments in the light of new information $\quad$ 9

Introduction

Suppose that you are a marketing manager working for an electronics company that is considering the launch of a new type of pocket calculator. On the basis of your knowledge of the market, you estimate that there is roughly an 80% probability that the sales of the calculator in its first year would exceed the break-even level. You then receive some new information from a market research survey. The results of this survey suggest that the sales of the calculator would be unlikely to reach the break-even level. How should you revise your probability estimate in the light of this new information?

You realize that the market research results are unlikely to be perfectly reliable: the sampling method used, the design of the questionnaire and even the way the questions were posed by the interviewers may all have contributed to a misleading result. Perhaps you feel so confident in your own knowledge of the market that you decide to ignore the market research and to leave your probability unchanged. Alternatively, you may acknowledge that, because the market research has had a good track record in predicting the success of products, you should make a large adjustment to your initial estimate.

In this chapter we will look at the process of revising initial probability estimates in the light of new information. The focus of our discussion will be Bayes' theorem, which is named after an English clergyman, Thomas Bayes, whose ideas were published posthumously in 1763. Bayes' theorem will be used as a normative tool, telling us how we *should* revise our probability assessments when new information becomes available. Whether people actually do revise their judgments in the manner laid down by the theorem is an issue that we will discuss in Chapter 15.

Of course, new information, be it from market research, scientific tests or consultants, can be expensive to obtain. Towards the end of the chapter we will show how the potential benefits of information can be evaluated so that a decision can be made as to whether it is worth obtaining it in the first place.

Bayes' theorem

In Bayes' theorem, an initial probability estimate is known as a *prior probability*. Thus, the marketing manager's assessment that there was an 80% probability that sales of the calculator would reach break-even level was a prior probability. When Bayes' theorem is used to modify a prior probability in the light of new information, the result is known as a *posterior probability*.

We will not put forward a mathematical proof of Bayes' theorem here. Instead, we will attempt to develop the idea intuitively and then show how a probability tree can be used to revise prior probabilities. Imagine that you are facing the following problem.

A batch of 1000 electronic components was produced last week at your factory, and it was found, after extensive and time-consuming tests, that 30% of them were defective and 70% 'OK'. Unfortunately, the defective components were not separated from the others, and all the components were subsequently mixed together in a large box. You now have to select a component from the box to meet an urgent order from a customer. What is the prior probability that the component you select is 'OK'? Clearly, in the absence of other information, the only sensible estimate is 0.7.

You then remember that it is possible to perform a 'quick and dirty' test on the component, although this test is not perfectly reliable. If the component is 'OK', then there is only an 80% chance it will pass the test and a 20% chance that it will wrongly fail. On the other hand, if the component is defective, then there is a 10% chance that the test will wrongly indicate that it is 'OK' and a 90% chance that it will fail the test. Figure 9.1 shows these possible outcomes in the form of a tree. Note that, because the

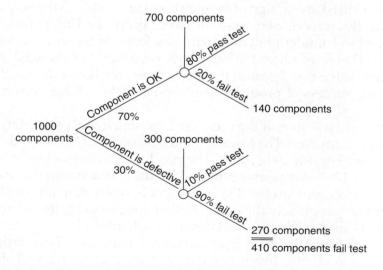

Figure 9.1 – Tree diagram for the components problem

test is better at giving a correct indication when the component is defective, we say that it is *biased*.

When you perform the quick test, the component fails. How should you revise your prior probability in the light of this result? Consider Figure 9.1 again. Imagine each of the 1000 components we start off with traveling through one of the four routes of the tree. Seven hundred of them will follow the 'OK' route. When tested, 20% of these components (i.e. 140) would be expected wrongly to fail the test. Similarly, 300 components will follow the 'defective' route and, of these, 90% (i.e. 270) would be expected to fail the test. In total, we would expect 410 (i.e. 140 + 270) components to fail the test. Now the component you selected is one of these 410 components. Of these, only 140 are 'OK', so your posterior probability that the component is 'OK' should be 140/410, which is 0.341, i.e.

$$p(\text{component OK} \mid \text{failed test}) = 140/410 = 0.341$$

Note that the test result, although not perfectly reliable, has caused you to revise your probability of the component being 'OK' from 0.7 down to 0.341.

Obviously, we would not wish to work from first principles for every problem we came across, and we therefore need to formalize the application of Bayes' theorem. The approach that we will adopt, which is based on probability trees, is very similar to the method we have just applied, except that we will think solely in terms of probabilities rather than numbers of components.

Figure 9.2 shows the probability tree for the components problem. Note that events for which we have prior probabilities are shown on the branches on the left of the tree. The branches to the right represent the new information and the conditional probabilities of obtaining this information under different circumstances. For example, the probability that a component will fail the test given that it is 'OK' is 0.2 [i.e. $p(\text{fails test} \mid \text{'OK'}) = 0.2$]. Given that our component did fail the test, we are not interested in the branches labeled 'component passes test', and in future diagrams we will exclude irrelevant branches.

We now calculate the probability of a component failing the test. First we determine the probability that a component will be 'OK' *and* will fail the test. This is, of course, a joint probability and can be found by applying the multiplication rule:

$$p(\text{OK and fails test}) = 0.7 \times 0.2 = 0.14$$

Next we determine the probability that a component will be defective *and* will fail the test:

$$p(\text{defective and fails test}) = 0.3 \times 0.9 = 0.27$$

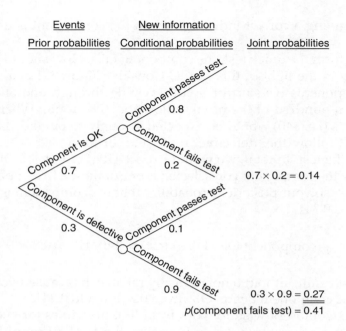

Figure 9.2 – Applying Bayes' theorem to the components problem

Now a component can fail the test either if it is 'OK' or if it is defective, so we add the two joint probabilities to obtain

$$p(\text{fails test}) = 0.14 + 0.27 = 0.41$$

The posterior probability is then found by dividing the appropriate joint probability by this figure. As we want to determine the posterior probability that the component is 'OK', we select the joint probability that emanates from the 'component is OK' part of the tree, i.e. 0.14. Thus, the posterior probability is 0.14/0.41, which is, of course, 0.341.

The steps in the process that we have just applied are summarized below:

(1) Construct a tree with branches representing all the possible events that can occur, and write the prior probabilities for these events on the branches.
(2) Extend the tree by attaching to each branch a new branch that represents the new information that you have obtained. On each branch, write the conditional probability of obtaining this information given the circumstance represented by the preceding branch.

(3) Obtain the joint probabilities by multiplying each prior probability by the conditional probability that follows it on the tree.
(4) Sum the joint probabilities.
(5) Divide the 'appropriate' joint probability by the sum of the joint probabilities to obtain the required posterior probability.

To see if you can apply Bayes' theorem, you may find it useful to attempt the following problem before proceeding. A worked solution follows the question.

Example

An engineer makes a cursory inspection of a piece of equipment and estimates that there is a 75% chance that it is running at peak efficiency. He then receives a report that the operating temperature of the machine is exceeding 80 °C. Past records of operating performance suggest that there is only a 0.3 probability of this temperature being exceeded when the machine is working at peak efficiency. The probability of the temperature being exceeded if the machine is not working at peak efficiency is 0.8. What should be the engineer's revised probability that the machine is operating at peak efficiency?

Answer

The probability tree for this problem is shown in Figure 9.3. It can be seen that the joint probabilities are:

$$p(\text{at peak efficiency and exceeds } 80\,^{\circ}\text{C}) = 0.75 \times 0.3 = 0.225$$
$$p(\text{not at peak efficiency and exceeds } 80\,^{\circ}\text{C}) = 0.25 \times 0.8 = 0.2$$

so the sum of the joint probabilities is $0.225 + 0.2 = 0.425$, and the required posterior probability is $0.225/0.425 = 0.529$.

Another example

So far, we have only applied Bayes' theorem to situations where there are just two possible events. The following example demonstrates that the method of handling a problem with more than two events is essentially the same.

A company's sales manager estimates that there is a 0.2 probability that sales in the coming year will be high, a 0.7 probability that they will be medium and a 0.1 probability that they will be low. She then receives a sales forecast from her assistant,

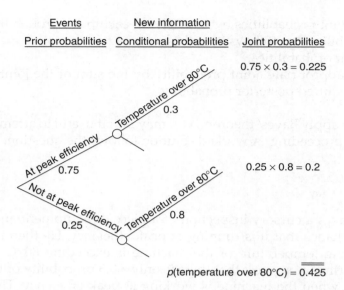

Figure 9.3 – Applying Bayes' theorem to the equipment operating problem

and the forecast suggests that sales will be high. By examining the track record of the assistant's forecasts, she is able to obtain the following probabilities:

p(high sales forecast given that the market will generate high sales) = 0.9
p(high sales forecast given that the market will generate only medium sales) = 0.6
p(high sales forecast given that the market will generate only low sales) = 0.3

What should be the sales manager's revised estimates of the probability of (a) high sales, (b) medium sales and (c) low sales?

The tree for this problem is shown in Figure 9.4. The joint probabilities are

p(high sales occur and high sales forecast) = 0.2 × 0.9 = 0.18
p(medium sales occur and high sales forecast) = 0.7 × 0.6 = 0.42
p(low sales occur and high sales forecast) = 0.1 × 0.3 = 0.03

so the sum of the joint probabilities is 0.63, which means that we obtain the following posterior probabilities:

p(high sales) = 0.18/0.63 = 0.2857
p(medium sales) = 0.42/0.63 = 0.6667
p(low sales) = 0.03/0.63 = 0.0476

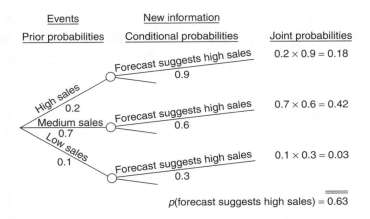

Figure 9.4 – Applying Bayes' theorem to the sales manager's problem

The effect of new information on the revision of probability judgments

It is interesting to explore the relative influence that prior probabilities and new information have on the resulting posterior probabilities. Suppose that a geologist is involved in a search for new sources of natural gas in southern England. In one particular location he is asked to estimate, on the basis of a preliminary survey, the probability that gas will be found in that location. Having made his estimate, he will receive new information from a test drilling.

Let us first consider a situation where the geologist is not very confident about his prior probabilities and where the test drilling is very reliable. The 'vaguest' prior probability distribution that the geologist can put forward is to assign probabilities of 0.5 to the two events 'gas exists at the location' and 'gas does not exist at the location'. Any other distribution would imply that the geologist was confident enough to make some commitment in one direction. Clearly, if he went to the extreme of allocating a probability of 1 to one of the events, this would imply that he was perfectly confident in his prediction. Suppose that, having put forward the prior probabilities of 0.5 and 0.5, the result of the test drilling is received. This indicates that gas is present, and the result can be regarded as 95% reliable. By this we mean that there is only a 0.05 probability that it will give a misleading indication. (Note that we are assuming, for simplicity, that the test drilling is *unbiased*, i.e. it is just as likely wrongly to indicate gas when it is not there as it is wrongly to indicate the absence of gas when it is really present.) Figure 9.5 shows the probability tree and the calculation of the posterior probabilities. It can be seen that these probabilities are identical to the probabilities

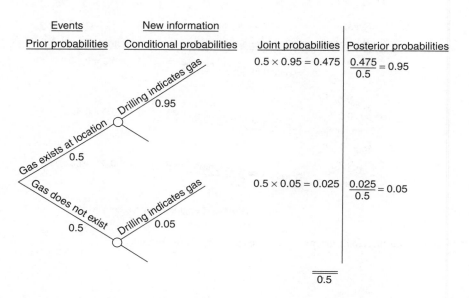

Figure 9.5 – The effect of vague prior probabilities and very reliable information

of the test drilling giving a correct or misleading result. In other words, the posterior probabilities depend only upon the reliability of the new information. The 'vague' prior probabilities have had no influence on the result.

A more general view of the relationship between the 'vagueness' of the prior probabilities and the reliability of the new information can be seen in Figure 9.6. In the figure, the horizontal axis shows the prior probability that gas will be found, while the vertical axis represents the posterior probability when the test drilling has indicated that gas will be found. For example, if the prior probability is 0.4 and the result of the test drilling is 70% reliable, then the posterior probability will be about 0.61.

The graph shows that, if the test drilling has only a 50% probability of giving a correct result, then its result will not be of any interest and the posterior probability will equal the prior, as shown by the diagonal line on the graph. By considering the distance of the curves from the diagonal line, it can be seen that, the more reliable the new information, the greater will be the modification of the prior probabilities. For any given level of reliability, however, this modification is relatively small either where the prior probability is high, implying that the geologist has a strong belief that gas will be found and the test drilling confirms his belief, or where the prior probability is very small, implying that he strongly believes that gas will not be found. In the latter case, so strong is his disbelief that he severely restricts the effect of the disconfirming evidence from the test drilling.

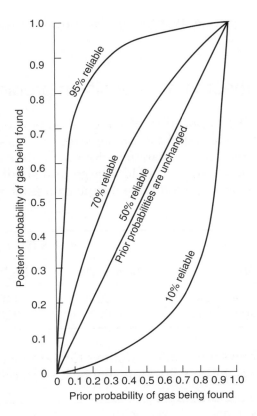

Figure 9.6 – The effect of the reliability of new information on the modification of prior probabilities for the gas-exploration problem

At the extreme, if your prior probability of an event occurring is zero, then the posterior probability will also be zero. Whatever new information you receive, no matter how reliable it is, you will still refuse to accept that the event is possible. In general, assigning prior probabilities of 0 or 1 is unwise. You may think that it is impossible that San Marino will become a nuclear power by the year 2020. However, if you hear that seismic instruments have detected signs of nuclear testing there, then you should allow yourself some chance of being persuaded by this information that the event might just be possible. Assigning a very small but non-zero prior probability might therefore be wiser.

Ironically, if the new information has less than a 0.5 chance of being reliable, its result is of interest, and, the more unreliable it is, the greater the effect it will have on the prior probability. For example, if the test drilling is certain to give the wrong indication, then you can be sure that the opposite of what has been indicated is the true situation!

Applying Bayes' theorem to a decision problem

We will now consider the application of Bayes' theorem to a decision problem, a process that is sometimes referred to as *posterior analysis*. This simply involves the use of the posterior probabilities, rather than the prior probabilities, in the decision model.

A retailer has to decide whether to hold a large or a small stock of a product for the coming summer season. A payoff table for the courses of action and outcomes is shown below:

	Profits ($)	
Decision	Low sales	High sales
Hold small stocks	80 000	140 000
Hold large stocks	20 000	220 000

The following table shows the retailer's utilities for the above sums of money (it can be assumed that money is the only attribute that he is concerned about):

Profit	$20 000	$80 000	$140 000	$220 000
Utility	0	0.5	0.8	1.0

The retailer estimates that there is a 0.4 probability that sales will be low and a 0.6 probability that they will be high. What level of stocks should he hold?

A decision tree for the retailer's problem is shown in Figure 9.7(a). It can be seen that his expected utility is maximized if he decides to hold a small stock of the commodity.

Before implementing his decision, the retailer receives a sales forecast that suggests that sales will be high. In the past when sales turned out to be high, the forecast had correctly predicted high sales on 75% of occasions. However, in seasons when sales turned out to be low, the forecast had wrongly predicted high sales on 20% of occasions. The underlying market conditions are thought to be stable enough for these results to provide an accurate guide to the reliability of the latest forecast. Should the retailer change his mind in the light of the forecast?

We can use Bayes' theorem to modify the retailer's prior probabilities in the light of the new information. Figure 9.7(b) shows the probability tree and the appropriate calculations. It can be seen that the posterior probabilities of low and high sales are

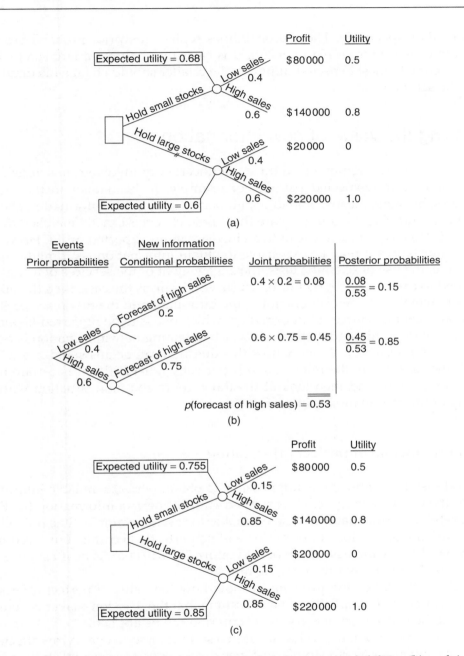

Figure 9.7 – (a) A decision tree for the retailer's problem based on prior probabilities; (b) applying Bayes' theorem to the retailer's problem; (c) a decision tree for the retailer's problem using posterior probabilities

0.15 and 0.85 respectively. These probabilities replace the prior probabilities in the decision tree, as shown in Figure 9.7(c). It is clear that holding a large stock would now lead to the highest expected utility, so the retailer should change his mind in the light of the sales forecast.

Assessing the value of new information

New information can remove or reduce the uncertainty involved in a decision and thereby increase the expected payoff. For example, if the retailer in the previous section was, by some means, able to obtain perfectly accurate information about the summer demand, then he could ensure that his stock levels exactly matched the level of demand. This would clearly lead to an increase in his expected profit. However, in many circumstances it may be expensive to obtain information, as it might involve, for example, the use of scientific tests, the engagement of the services of a consultant or the need to carry out a market research survey. If this is the case, then the question arises as to whether it is worth obtaining the information in the first place or, if there are several potential sources of information, which one is to be preferred (sometimes the process of determining whether it is worth obtaining new information is referred to as *preposterior analysis*). To show how this question can be answered, we will first consider the case where the information is perfectly reliable (i.e. it is certain to give a correct indication) and then look at the much more common situation where the reliability of the information is imperfect.

The expected value of perfect information

In many decision situations it is not possible to obtain perfectly reliable information, but nevertheless the concept of the expected value of perfect information (EVPI) can still be useful. It might enable a decision-maker to say, for example: 'It is unlikely that this consultant's predictions of our sales will be perfectly accurate, but, even if they were, he would only increase my expected returns by $10 000. As he is asking a fee of $15 000, it is clearly not worth engaging him.'

We will use the following problem to show how the value of perfect information can be measured. For simplicity, we will assume that the decision-maker is neutral to risk, so that the expected monetary value criterion can be applied.

A year ago, a major potato producer suffered serious losses when a virus affected the crop at the company's North Holt farm. Since then, steps have been taken to eradicate the virus from the soil, and the specialist who directed these operations estimates, on the basis of preliminary evidence, that there is a 70% chance that the eradication program has been successful.

The manager of the farm now has to decide on his policy for the coming season, and he has identified two options:

(1) He could go ahead and plant a full crop of potatoes. If the virus is still present, an estimated net loss of $20 000 will be incurred. However, if the virus is absent, an estimated net return of $90 000 will be earned.
(2) He could avoid planting potatoes at all and turn the entire acreage over to the alternative crop. This would almost certainly lead to net returns of $30 000.

The manager is now informed that Ceres Laboratories could carry out a test on the farm that will indicate whether or not the virus is still present in the soil. The manager has no idea as to how accurate the indication will be or the fee that Ceres will charge. However, he decides initially to work on the assumption that the test is perfectly accurate. If this is the case, what is the maximum amount that it would be worth paying Ceres to carry out the test?

A decision tree for the farm manager's problem is shown in Figure 9.8. In the absence of information from the test, he should plant a full crop of potatoes, as his expected

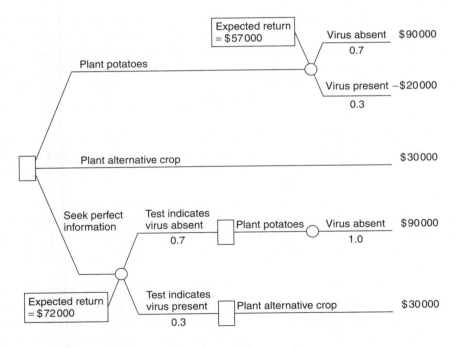

Figure 9.8 – Determining the expected value of perfect information

Table 9.1 – Calculating the expected value of perfect information

Test indication	Prob.	Best course of action	Payoff ($)	Prob. × payoff ($)
Virus is absent	0.7	Plant potatoes	90 000	63 000
Virus is present	0.3	Plant alternative	30 000	9 000

Expected payoff with perfect information = 72 000
Best expected payoff without perfect information = 57 000

Expected value of perfect information (EVPI) = 15 000

return if he follows this course of action will be

$$0.7 \times \$90\,000 + 0.3 \times -\$20\,000 = \$57\,000$$

which exceeds the $30 000 return he will receive if he plants an alternative crop.

Now we need to determine the expected value of the perfect information that will be derived from the test. To do this, we need to consider each of the possible indications the test can give, how probable these indications are and how the manager should respond to each indication.

The calculations are summarized in Table 9.1. First, the test might indicate that the virus is absent from the soil. The specialist has said that there is a 70% chance that the virus is absent, so, because the test is assumed to be perfectly accurate, the manager can assume that there is a probability of 0.7 that the test will give this indication. If the test does indicate that the virus is absent, then the manager would earn $90 000 by planting potatoes and $30 000 by planting the alternative crop, so the best decision would be to plant potatoes.

Alternatively, the test might indicate that the virus is still present. There is a 0.3 probability that it will give this indication. In this case, the manager would lose $20 000 if he planted potatoes, so the best decision would be to plant the alternative crop and earn a net return of $30 000.

To summarize: there is a 0.7 probability that the test will indicate that the virus is absent, in which case the manager would earn net returns of $90 000, and a 0.3 probability that the test will indicate that the virus is present, in which case he will earn $30 000. This means that his expected returns if he buys the perfect information will be $72 000.

As we saw earlier, without the test, the manager should plant potatoes when he would earn an expected return of $57 000. So the expected increase in his returns resulting from the perfect information (i.e. the expected value of perfect information) would be $72 000 − $57 000, which equals $15 000. Of course, we have not yet considered the fee that Ceres would charge. However, we now know that, if their test is perfectly accurate, it would not be worth paying them more than $15 000. It is likely that their test will be less than perfect, in which case the information it yields will be of less value. Nevertheless, the EVPI can be very useful in giving an upper bound to the value of new information. We emphasize that our calculations are based on the assumption that the decision-maker is risk neutral. If the manager is risk averse or risk seeking, or if he also has non-monetary objectives, then it may be worth him paying more or less than this amount. We make the same assumption in the next section, where we consider how to calculate the value of information that is not perfectly reliable.

The expected value of imperfect information

Suppose that, after making further enquiries, the farm manager discovers that the Ceres test is not perfectly reliable. If the virus is still present in the soil the test has only a 90% chance of detecting it, while if the virus has been eliminated there is a 20% chance that the test will incorrectly indicate its presence. How much would it now be worth paying for the test? To answer this question, it is necessary to determine the expected value of imperfect information (EVII). As with the expected value of perfect information, we will need to consider the possible indications the test will give, what the probabilities of these indications are and the decision the manager should take in the light of a given indication.

The new decision tree for his problem is shown in Figure 9.9. If the manager decides not to buy the test, then the decision is the same as before: he should plant potatoes, because the expected return on this option is $57 000. If he decides to buy the test, then he will obviously wait for the test result before making the decision. The values missing from Figure 9.9, and represented by question marks, are the probabilities of the test giving each of the two indications and the probabilities of the virus being present or absent in the light of each indication.

Let us first consider the situation where the test indicates that the virus is present. We first need to calculate the probability of the test giving this indication, using the probability tree in Figure 9.10(a). The prior probability of the virus being present and the test correctly indicating this is 0.3×0.9, which is 0.27. Similarly, the probability of the virus being absent and the test incorrectly indicating its presence is 0.7×0.2, which is 0.14. This means that the total probability that the test will indicate that the virus is present is $0.27 + 0.14$, which is 0.41. We can now put this probability onto the decision tree (Figure 9.11).

We can also use the probability tree in Figure 9.10(a) to calculate the posterior probabilities of the virus being present or absent if the test gives an indication of its presence. Using Bayes' theorem, it can be seen that these probabilities are 0.66 and 0.34 respectively. These probabilities can also be added to the decision tree.

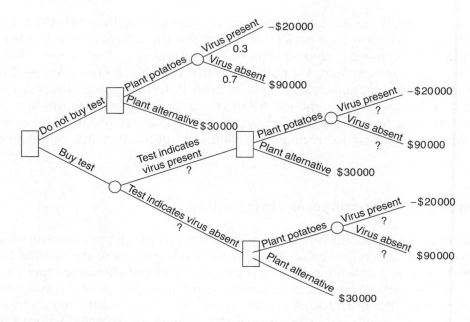

Figure 9.9 – Deciding whether or not to buy imperfect information

We next consider the situation where the test indicates that the virus has been eliminated. Figure 9.10(b) shows the appropriate calculations. The probability of the test giving this indication is 0.59 (we knew that it would be $1 - 0.41$ anyway), and the posterior probabilities of the presence and absence of the virus are 0.05 and 0.95 respectively. Again, these probabilities can now be added to the decision tree.

Let us now determine the expected payoff of buying the test by rolling back this part of the tree. If the test indicates that the virus is present, then the best decision is to plant the alternative crop and earn $30 000. However, if the test indicates the absence of the virus, then clearly the best decision is to plant the potato crop, as the expected payoff of this course of action is $84 500. This means that, if the manager buys the test, there is a 0.41 probability that it will indicate the presence of the virus, in which case the payoff will be $30 000, and a 0.59 probability that it will indicate the absence of the virus, in which case the expected payoff is $84 500. Thus, we have

the expected payoff *with* the imperfect information
    from the text $= 0.41 \times \$30\,000 + 0.59 \times 84\,500$ $= \$62\,155$
the expected payoff without the test $= \$57\,000$
so the expected value of imperfect information $= \$5\,155$

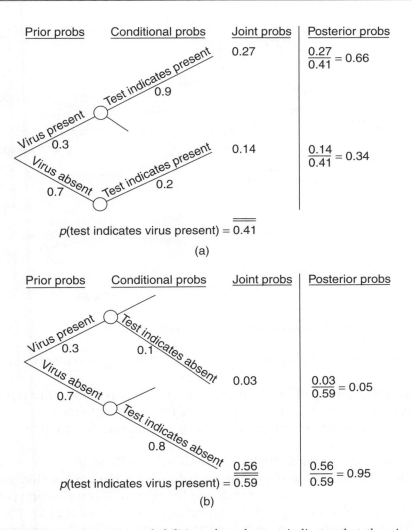

Figure 9.10 – (a) Revising the prior probabilities when the test indicates that the virus is present; (b) revising the prior probabilities when the test indicates that the virus is absent

It would not, therefore, be worth paying Ceres more than $5155 for the test. You will recall that the expected value of perfect information was $15 000, so the value of information from this test is much less than that from a perfectly reliable test. Of course, the more reliable the new information, the closer its expected value will be to the EVPI.

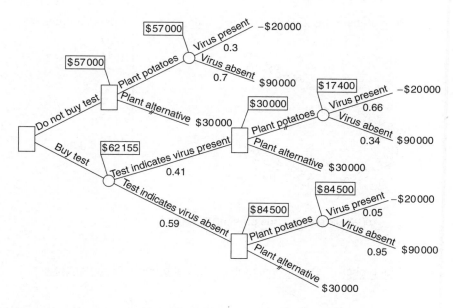

Figure 9.11 – Determining the expected value of imperfect information

A summary of the main stages in the above analysis is given below:

(1) Determine the course of action that would be chosen using only the prior probabilities, and record the expected payoff of this course of action.
(2) Identify the possible indications that the new information can give.
(3) For each indication:
    (a) determine the probability that this indication will occur;
    (b) use Bayes' theorem to revise the probabilities in the light of this indication;
    (c) determine the best course of action in the light of this indication (i.e. using the posterior probabilities) and the expected payoff of this course of action.
(4) Multiply the probability of each indication occurring by the expected payoff of the course of action that should be taken if that indication occurs, and sum the resulting products. This will give the expected payoff with imperfect information.
(5) The expected value of the imperfect information is equal to the expected payoff with imperfect information (derived in stage 4) less the expected payoff of the course of action that would be selected using the prior probabilities (which was derived in stage 1).

There is an alternative way of looking at the value of information. New information can be regarded as being of no value if you would still make the same decision regardless of what the information told you. If the farm manager were to go ahead and plant a crop of potatoes whatever the test indicated, then there would clearly be no point in buying the test. Information has value if some of its indications would cause you to take a different decision to the one you would take without the benefit of the information. Let us calculate the expected value of the imperfect information derived from the test using this approach by again referring to Figure 9.11.

The decision based on the prior probabilities was to plant a crop of potatoes. If the test indicated the presence of the virus, then you would make a different decision, that is, you would plant an alternative crop. Had you stayed with the prior decision, your expected payoff would have been $17 400, while planting the alternative crop yields $30 000.

This means that the new information has stopped you from taking the inferior course of action and thereby increased your expected payoff by $12 600. However, if the test indicates that the virus is absent, you would make the same decision as you would without the information from the test, so the expected value of the information in this case is $0. Given the probabilities of the two test indications, the expected value of the imperfect information is

$$0.41 \times \$12\ 600 + 0.59 \times \$0 = \$5166$$

(The difference between this and the previous result is caused by rounding errors.)

As usual, the importance of sensitivity analysis cannot be understated, and in this respect spreadsheet packages are particularly useful. If the calculations for the EVII are carried out on a spreadsheet in the first place, then it is relatively easy to examine the effect of variations in the inputs to the model. It would then be possible to make statements like: 'I estimate that the proposed market research will be 90% reliable. Sensitivity analysis tells me that it would still be worth carrying out, even if its relia- bility was as low as 75%, so I am fairly confident that we should go ahead and carry out the research.'

Clearly, it is easier to identify the expected value of perfect as opposed to imperfect information, and we recommend that, in general, calculating the EVPI should be the first step in any information evaluation exercise. The EVPI can act as a useful screen, as some sources of information may prove to be too expensive, even if they were to offer perfectly reliable data, which is unlikely.

Summary

In this chapter we have discussed the role that new information can play in revising the judgments of a decision-maker. Bayes' theorem shows the decision-maker how his or her judgments should be modified in the light of new information, and we showed that this revision will depend both upon the 'vagueness' of the prior judgment and the reliability of the new information. Of course, receiving information is often a sequential process. Your prior probability will reflect the information you have received up to the point in time when you make your initial probability assessment. As each new installment of information arrives, you may continue to revise your probability. The posterior probability you had at the end of last week may be treated as the prior probability this week, and be revised in the light of this week's information.

   We also looked at how the value of new information can be assessed. The expected value of perfect information was shown to be a useful measure of the maximum amount that it would be worth paying for information. Calculating the expected value of imperfect information was seen to be a more involved process, because the decision-maker also has to judge the reliability of the information. Because of this, we stressed the importance of sensitivity analysis, which allows the decision-maker to study the effect of changes in these assessments.

Exercises

Additional exercises can be found on the book's website

(1) The sales of a magazine vary randomly: in 70% of weeks they are classified as being 'high', while in 30% of weeks they are classified as 'low'.
   (i) Write down prior probabilities of high and low sales in the coming week
   ....
   (ii) You are now given the sales figures for Monday and these show low sales. In the past:
      • in weeks when sales turned out to be high, Monday had low sales on only 20% of occasions;
      • in weeks when sales turned out to be low, Monday had low sales on 60% of occasions.
   Revise your prior probabilities in the light of Monday's sales figures.

(2) In January, a sales manager estimates that there is only a '30% chance' that the sales of a new product will exceed 1 million units in the coming year. However, he is then handed the results of a sales forecast. This suggests that the sales will exceed 1 million units. The probability that this indication will be given when sales will exceed 1 million units is 0.8. However, the probability that the forecast will give this indication when sales will not exceed 1 million units is 0.4. Revise the sales manager's estimate in the light of the sales forecast.

(3) The probability of a machine being accidentally overfilled on a given day is 0.05. If the machine is overfilled, there is a 0.8 probability that it will break down during the course of the day. If the machine is not overfilled, the probability of a breakdown during the day is only 0.1. Yesterday the machine broke down. What is the probability that it had been accidentally overfilled?

(4) A mining company is carrying out a survey in a region of Western Australia. On the basis of preliminary results, the company's senior geologist estimates that there is a 60% probability that a particular mineral will be found in quantities that would justify commercial investment in the region. Further research is then carried out, and this suggests that commercially viable quantities of the mineral will be found. It is estimated that this research has a 75% chance of giving a correct indication. Revise the senior geologist's prior probability in the light of the research results.

(5) A company that manufactures compact discs has found that demand for its product has been increasing rapidly over the last 12 months. A decision now has to be made as to how production capacity can be expanded to meet this demand. Three alternatives are available:

   (i) expand the existing plant;

   (ii) build a new plant in an industrial development area;

   (iii) subcontract the extra work to another manufacturer.

The returns that would be generated by each alternative over the next 5 years have been estimated using three possible scenarios:

   (i) demand rising at a faster rate than the current rate;

   (ii) demand continuing to rise at the current rate;

   (iii) demand increasing at a slower rate or falling.

These estimated returns, which are expressed in terms of net present value, are shown below (net present values in $000s):

	Scenario		
Course of action	Demand rising faster	Demand rising at current rate	Demand increasing slowly or falling
Expand	500	400	−150
Build new plant	700	200	−300
Subcontract	200	150	−50

  (a) The company's marketing manager estimates that there is a 60% chance that demand will rise faster than the current rate, a 30% chance that it will continue to rise at the current rate and a 10% chance that it will increase at a slower rate or fall. Assuming that the company's objective is to maximize expected net present value, determine:

     (i) the course of action that it should take;

     (ii) the expected value of perfect information.

(b) Before the decision is made, the results of a long-term forecast become available. These suggest that demand will continue to rise at the present rate. Estimates of the reliability of this forecast are given below:

p(forecast predicts demand increasing at current rate when actual demand will rise at faster rate) $= 0.3$

p(forecast predicts demand increasing at current rate when actual demand will continue to rise at current rate) $= 0.7$

p(forecast predicts demand increasing at current rate when actual demand will rise at a slower rate or fall) $= 0.4$

Determine whether the company should, in the light of the forecast, change from the decision you advised in (a).

(c) Discuss the limitations of the analysis you have applied above, and suggest ways in which these limitations could be overcome.

(6) The managers of a soft drinks company are planning their production strategy for next summer. The demand for their products is closely linked to the weather, and an analysis of weather records suggests the following probability distribution for the June to August period:

Weather conditions	Probability
Hot and dry	0.3
Mixed	0.5
Cold and wet	0.2
	1.0

The table below shows the estimated profits ($000s) that will accrue for the different production strategies and weather conditions:

	Weather conditions		
Production strategy	Hot and dry	Mixed	Cold and wet
Plan for high sales	400	100	−100
Plan for medium sales	200	180	70
Plan for low sales	110	100	90

(a) On the basis of the information given, determine:
  (i) the course of action that will maximize expected profits;
 (ii) the expected value of perfect information.
  Discuss the practical implications of your result.
(b) A long-range weather forecast suggests that next summer's weather conditions will, in general, be cold and wet. The reliability of the forecast is indicated by the following probabilities, which are based on past performance:

$$p(\text{cold, wet conditions forecast when} \\ \text{weather will be hot and dry}) = 0.3$$

$$p(\text{cold, wet conditions forecast when} \\ \text{weather will be mixed}) = 0.4$$

$$p(\text{cold, wet conditions forecast when} \\ \text{weather will be cold and wet}) = 0.6$$

In the light of the long-range weather forecast, should the company change from the course of action you recommended in (a)?

(7) A company has just received some 'state-of-the-art' electronic equipment from an overseas supplier. The packaging has been damaged during delivery, and the company must decide whether to accept the equipment. If the equipment itself has not been damaged, it could be sold for a profit of $10 000. However, if the batch is accepted and it turns out to be damaged, a loss of −$5000 will be made. Rejection of the equipment will lead to no change in the company's profit. After a cursory inspection, the company's engineer estimates that there is a 60% chance that the equipment has not been damaged. The company has another option. The equipment could be tested by a local specialist company. Their test, however, is not perfectly reliable and has only an 80% chance of giving a correct indication.

How much would it be worth paying for the information from the test? (Assume that the company's objective is to maximize expected profit.)

(8) The managers of Red Valley Auto Products are considering the national launch of a new car-cleaning product. For simplicity, the potential average sales of the product during its lifetime are classified as being either high, medium or low, and the net present value of the product under each of these conditions is estimated to be $80 million, $15 million and −$40 million respectively. The company's marketing manager estimates that there is a 0.3 probability that average sales will be high, a 0.4 probability that they will be medium and a 0.3

probability that they will be low. It can be assumed that the company's objective is to maximize expected net present value.

(a) On the basis of the marketing manager's prior probabilities, determine:
  (i) whether the product should be launched;
  (ii) the expected value of perfect information.

(b) The managers have another option. Rather than going immediately for a full national launch, they could first test market the product in their Northern sales region. This would obviously delay the national launch, and this delay, together with other outlays associated with the test marketing, would lead to costs having a net present value of $3 million. The test marketing would give an indication as to the likely success of the national launch, and the reliability of each of the possible indications that could result are shown by the conditional probabilities in the table below (e.g. if the market for the product is such that high sales could be achieved, there is a probability of 0.15 that test marketing would in fact indicate only medium sales):

	Test marketing indication		
Actual national sales	High national sales	Medium national sales	Low national sales
High	0.80	0.15	0.05
Medium	0.25	0.60	0.15
Low	0.10	0.30	0.60

Calculate the expected value of imperfect information, and hence determine whether the company should test market the product.

Heuristics and biases in probability assessment

10

Introduction

Methods designed to help managers with decisions involving uncertainty often require estimates of probabilities. Many of these estimates will be based on judgment
because of the unavailability of suitable statistical data. This raises the question,
how good are people at estimating probabilities? Over the past 30 years or so, this
question has been the subject of a great deal of research by psychologists, and in
this chapter we will look at the results of their work.

Before proceeding, you might find it interesting to assess your own ability to estimate
probabilities by answering the following questionnaire. We will give you the answers
in the course of the subsequent discussion.

Test your judgment

(1) In 2007, approximately what percentage of people in the USA (aged 12 or over)
were victims of robbery according to the official statistics?
(2) Consider the chances of a randomly selected US citizen dying as a result of the
following causes in the course of a year (as estimated in 2005):
  (i) assault by a sharp object, such as a knife;
  (ii) a fall;
  (iii) firearm discharge;
  (iv) being bitten or struck by a dog;
  (v) being an occupant in a car that is involved in an accident.
Rank these causes of death from the most to the least likely.
(3) Eight per cent of people interviewed for jobs at a company have a criminal
record. Given below are the notes made by the interviewer on one applicant,
Jim X. These notes have been randomly selected from the files of interviewed
candidates.

Jim had an unshaven, scruffy appearance. Though his clothes looked expensive, they did not fit him well. He never made eye contact during the interview and he had a strange, hard look about him. When I cracked a joke he failed to laugh. His handshake was weak and I noticed a scar on the back of his hand. He said he had no hobbies or family and his general demeanor was unfriendly, and even a little contemptuous.

Estimate the probability, on a 0–100 scale, that Jim X has a criminal record.

(4) A box contains 100 light bulbs, of which half are defective. A quality control inspector is about to select six bulbs randomly from the box. Which of the following sequences is most likely to occur:

	1st bulb	2nd bulb	3rd bulb	4th bulb	5th bulb	6th bulb
A	Defective	OK	Defective	OK	Defective	OK
B	Defective	Defective	Defective	OK	OK	OK
C	OK	OK	Defective	OK	Defective	Defective

(5) A man has been driving for 40 years without having a road accident. A friend tells him that the chances of him being involved in an accident in the next 5 years must be high because the probability of an individual driving for 45 years without an accident is low. Is this thinking correct?

(6) In the British National Lottery, people choose six numbers (from 1 to 49) which they hope will be randomly selected in the draw. When the lottery started, a newspaper advised: '... sometimes week after week, a certain number may resolutely refuse to put in an appearance. It becomes "overdue", and you could reason that therefore it is bound to turn up soon – the so-called cold number system.'

Would choosing 'cold numbers' increase your chances of winning the lottery?

(7) During the summer, a brewery's sales of canned beer are largely influenced by chance factors, such as the weather and the number of people watching sporting events. In the first week of August, exceptional sales of 1.2 million cans were achieved. In the absence of other information, would you judge that it is more likely that sales for the following week will be:
(a) higher;
(b) about the same; or
(c) lower than 1.2 million cans?

(8) David is 28 years old, tall, slim and powerfully built. He is popular with his colleagues at work, who like his ready sense of humor, and he spends his lunchtimes jogging in the nearby park. While relaxing at home, he prefers to wear a track suit and recently he took out a subscription to a cable television channel devoted

entirely to sport. He takes little interest in reading or in the arts or current affairs. Which is more likely:

(a) David is a librarian;

(b) David is a librarian who regularly plays basketball?

(9) Which of the following scenarios is most likely to occur:

(a) a decline in the share of the global market of the US computer manufacturing industry during the second decade of the twenty-first century;

(b) a decline in the share of the global market of the US computer manufacturing industry during the second decade of the twenty-first century as a result of competition from Asian countries such as, China, Japan, Malaysia and South Korea?

(10) (a) Was the population of Egypt in 2006 (excluding Egyptians living abroad) higher or lower than 15 million?

(b) Estimate Egypt's population in 2006 (excluding Egyptians living abroad).

(11) An electronic safety system, which will automatically shut off machinery in the event of an emergency, is being proposed for a factory. It would consist of 150 independent components, each of which must work if the entire system is to be operational. On any day, each component would be designed to have a 99.5% probability of working. Estimate the probability that the entire safety system would be operational on any given day if a decision were made to install it.

(12) Currently, ten people work in an office, and each has a 5% probability of leaving during the next year. Estimate the probability that at least one of these people will leave within the next 12 months. (Assume that the chance of any one person leaving is independent of whether the others stay or leave.)

(13) For each of the ten quantities listed below, (i) write down your best estimate of that quantity and (ii) put a lower and upper bound around your estimate so that you are 90% confident that your range will include the true value of that quantity:

(a) the air distance, in miles or kilometers, from Moscow to Cape Town;

(b) the population of Canada, as recorded by the country's 2006 census;

(c) the area of Greenland in square miles or square kilometers;

(d) the year the ballpoint pen was first patented by Biro;

(e) the year that the H.J. Heinz food manufacturing company was founded;

(f) the distance (in miles or kilometers) between Earth and Mars when Mars is at its closest to Earth;

(g) the US inflation rate (as measured by the Consumer Price Index) over the 20 year period between December 1988 and December 2008;

(h) the year that Louis Braille, inventor of the Braille communication system, was born;

(i) the average depth of the Pacific Ocean in feet or meters (to the nearest thousand);

(j) the length, in miles or kilometers, of the river Danube.

(14) The following table summarizes the results of a survey of the reliability of two makes of personal computer (a cheap brand and an expensive brand):

	Cheap brand	Expensive brand
Required repair in year following purchase	120	40
Did not require repair	24	8

Would you conclude that the cost of the computers is associated with their chances of requiring repair in the year after purchase?

Heuristics and biases

Much of our understanding of how people make judgments about probabilities has come from the work of Tversky and Kahneman[1] who published their findings in a series of papers starting in the early 1970s. The central theme of this work is that people use simple mental strategies, or *heuristics*, to cope with the complexities of making estimates of probabilities. While these heuristics can sometimes provide good estimates and reduce the effort required by the decision-maker, they can also lead to systematically biased judgments. Three main heuristics identified by Tversky and Kahneman are (i) availability, (ii) representativeness and (iii) anchoring and adjustment. We consider these, and their associated biases, next.

The availability heuristic

Suppose that you are asked to assess the probability that a retail business will fail within the next year. If you use the availability heuristic, you will search your mind in an attempt to recall examples of shops failing, or you will try to imagine circumstances that will lead to the demise of the business. If instances of shops failing are easily recalled, or the circumstances leading to closure are easily imagined, then you will judge the probability of failure to be high. People using the availability heuristic therefore judge the probability of the occurrence of events by how easily these events are brought to mind. Events that are vivid, recent, emotionally salient, unusual or highlighted by the media are readily recalled or envisaged and therefore assigned high probabilities. Events that are less available to the mind are assumed to be less likely.

Availability can be a reliable heuristic. Frequently occurring events are usually easier to recall, so the higher probabilities estimated for them should be reliable. However, the ease with which an event can be recalled or imagined sometimes has no relationship to the true probability of the event occurring. For example, some events are easily recalled because their occurrence had major, newsworthy, consequences even though the event itself was unusual and rare, for example the 9/11 terrorist attack on the US homeland. This can lead to biased estimates. Some of the biases associated with the availability heuristic are discussed next.

Biases associated with the availability heuristic

1. When ease of recall is not associated with probability

Easily recalled events are not necessarily highly probable. In Britain a study by the Association of Chief Police Officers in 1996 found that elderly people were rarely victims of violent crime. Yet the perception of elderly people was that the risk of their being attacked was frighteningly high. Although rare, when they do occur, attacks on old people are headline news, and instances of such crimes are therefore easily and vividly recalled. Similarly, studies[2] in the USA found that, although people's estimates of the probability of death by various causes were moderately accurate, there were some serious misperceptions that were closely associated with recent reports of deaths by these causes in newspapers. For example, the probabilities of death by animal bites and stings were grossly overestimated. Similarly, accidents and disease were thought to be equally likely causes of death. In reality, diseases cause 15 times more deaths than accidents.

2. Ease of imagination is not related to probability

Easily imagined events are not necessarily highly probable. The civil engineer in charge of a construction project may find it easy to imagine all of the circumstances that could lead to the delay of the project, such as strikes, adverse weather conditions, geological problems and interruptions in the supply of materials and equipment. The result could be a gross overestimate of the risk of the project overrunning the deadline. Conversely, risks may sometimes be underestimated because the dangers associated with a course of action are difficult to imagine.

Test your judgment: answer to questions 1 and 2

Were your probability estimates in the questionnaire distorted by ease of recall, the extent to which events are reported in the media or ease of imagination?

Q1. Approximately two people in every 1000 (aged 12 or over) were victims of robbery in the USA in 2007 (i.e. 0.2%). *(Source: US Department of Justice, Bureau of Justice Statistics.)*

Q2. The causes of death ranked from most likely to least likely are:
   (1) a fall (probability: 1/15 085);
   (2) being an occupant in a car that is involved in an accident (probability: 1/20 331);
   (3) assault by a sharp object, such as a knife (probability: 1/141 396);
   (4) firearm discharge (probability: 1/1 341 661);
   (5) being bitten or struck by a dog (probability: 1/8 985 062).

(Source: National Safety Council.)

---

3. Illusory correlation

Suppose that you are a manager of a factory and you are considering whether you are more likely to obtain defective goods from a domestic or a foreign supplier. Before thinking about your answer, you may already have some preconceptions, for example that foreign goods tend to be less reliable. In this case, you are likely to find it easy to recall or imagine instances of the co-occurrence of the events 'foreign supplier' and 'goods defective'. You find it less easy to recall the many reliable goods that you have received from foreign suppliers and the defective ones that you have received from domestic suppliers. The result can be an illusory correlation, that is, an overestimation of the frequency with which the two events occur together. In decision analysis models, illusory correlation is of concern when conditional probabilities, e.g. p(goods defective | foreign supplier), have to be estimated.

In a well-known demonstration of illusory correlation, Chapman and Chapman[3] conducted an experiment in which naive judges were given information on several hypothetical mental patients. This information consisted of a diagnosis and a drawing made by a patient. Later, the judges were asked to estimate how frequently certain characteristics referred to in the diagnosis, such as suspiciousness, had been accompanied by features of the drawing, such as peculiar eyes. It was found that the judges significantly overestimated the frequency with which, for example, suspiciousness and peculiar eyes had occurred together. Indeed, this illusory correlation survived even when contradictory evidence was presented to the judges. This research demonstrates the powerful and persistent influence that preconceived notions (in this case that suspiciousness is associated with the eyes) can have on judgments about relationships.

The representativeness heuristic

Suppose that you are considering the following questions. What is the probability that Peter, who you met at last night's conference party, is a salesman? What is the probability that the defective circuit board that you have just been supplied was manufactured at your Pittsburgh factory? What is the probability that your sales graph shows that sales are simply varying randomly, rather than following a cyclical pattern?

In all of these questions you have to judge the probability that a person or object belongs to a particular category, or that events originate from a particular process. If you use the representativeness heuristic, you will answer these questions by judging how representative the object, person or event is of the category or process. For example, Peter was a streetwise extrovert who talked quickly and wore smart clothes. If you judge him to be representative of what salesmen are like, that is, if he fits your stereotypical view of a salesman, then you would assume that his chances of being a salesman are high. Similarly, the peaks and troughs in your sales graph may appear to be typical and representative of what you perceive to be a random pattern, so you judge that it is unlikely that there is a regular cycle in your sales.

Biases associated with the representativeness heuristic

1. Ignoring base-rate frequencies

If you find that only 10% of the delegates at your conference party were salespeople, then this should clearly be considered when you estimate the probability of Peter being a salesman. Unfortunately, judgments based on how typical Peter is of salesmen often make no reference to this statistical information (or base-rate frequency). This tendency to ignore base-rate frequencies was demonstrated by Tversky and Kahneman in a series of experiments where participants were asked to judge the probability that individuals had particular occupations. In a typical experiment, two groups of participants were given the following description of a person:

> This is a brief personality description of Tom W, written by a psychologist when Tom was at his senior year at high school. Tom W is of high intelligence, although lacking in true

creativity. He has a need for order and clarity and for neat and tidy systems in which every detail finds its appropriate place. His writing is rather dull and mechanical, occasionally enlivened by somewhat corny puns and by flashes of imagination of the sci-fi type. He has a strong drive for competence. He seems to have little feel or sympathy for other people and does not enjoy interacting with others. Self-centered, he nonetheless has a deep moral sense.

One group was told that the personality description had been chosen, at random, from those of 30 engineers and 70 lawyers. The other group was told that it had been selected randomly from descriptions of 70 engineers and 30 lawyers. Each participant was then asked to assess the probability that Tom W was an engineer?

If the participants had taken into account the number of engineers and lawyers from which the description had been selected, then the first group should have given a lower probability of Tom W being an engineer than the second. In fact, the two groups gave essentially the same estimates, indicating that they had ignored the statistical base-rate information in favor of the descriptive information – even though the base-rate information should, logically, have been given primacy. They appeared to base their probability estimates only on how representative Tom W seemed to be of an engineer, and typically they stated that it was more probable that he was an engineer. Other experiments by Tversky and Kahneman showed that this tendency to ignore base rates prevailed even when the descriptive information given was totally uninformative, although base rates were properly utilized when no individuating descriptions were given.

Descriptive or individuating information has a large impact on choice. We are much more willing to contribute resources to save a 'real' person than a statistical person – the so-called 'identified victim effect'.[4] Here, people were asked if they were willing to contribute money to treat a sick child. The simple addition of a picture and name of the child to a description of the child's illness elicited more, and higher, donations. In a study of the decision-making of physicians[5] – who might be expected to be more detached – the physicians were more likely to spend time and hospital resources on a particular known patient than when allocating resources across a group of similar patients who were unknown, personally, to the physician.

Test your judgment: answer to question 3

Q3. To what extent was your estimate influenced by the low-reliability personality sketch and the extent to which this appeared to be representative of someone with a criminal record? The base rate would suggest that the probability should be close to 8%.

---

2. Expecting sequences of events to appear random

When a sequence of events is generated by a random process, people expect the sequence to represent the characteristics of randomness. For example, if a coin is about to be thrown six times, they would tend to expect the sequence H-H-H-T-T-T to be less likely to occur than the sequence T-H-H-T-H-T, which appears to be more representative of a random process (of course, both sequences are equally likely). The belief is that even short sequences of events should manifest the essential characteristics of the random process that is generating them. Runs, where the same result is repeated, are expected to be short, and a frequent alternation between the events is expected. In fact, short random sequences will often contain several repetitions of the same event. For example, of the 64 possible, and equally likely, sequences that can be generated by six throws of a fair coin, 38 have runs of the same result coming up on three or more consecutive throws.

Biases like this can lead to errors in forecasts based on judgment. For example, Eggleton[6] asked subjects to produce forecasts of artificially generated monthly production costs. The subjects perceived the series where there was a systematic alternation between high and low costs to be random, while they thought that the truly random series contained systematic patterns. Indeed, reading systematic patterns in random events, and hence overreacting to the latest sales or cost figure, is a common problem in judgmental forecasting.[7,8]

Test your judgment: answer to question 4

Q4. Did you choose C because you thought it appeared to be more representative of randomness? In fact, all of the sequences are equally likely to occur.

---

3. Expecting chance to be self-correcting

If a fair coin is tossed and a long sequence of heads appears, many people will think that the occurrence of a tail on the next throw is highly probable because the tail is overdue. In a random process, after all, one would expect the occurrences of heads and tails to be equally frequent. The phenomenon can also be seen in newspaper articles about lotteries that advise readers to identify cold numbers, that is, numbers that have not been drawn for a long period and therefore must have a higher probability of appearing in the next draw. Of course, coins and lotteries have no memories, so there is no reason at all why they should correct for earlier sequences of results. This bias is another consequence of the belief that random sequences of events should be representative of what a random process is perceived to look like.

Test your judgment: answers to questions 5 and 6

Q5. This thinking is false. At the start of his driving career there may have been a high probability of the driver having an accident at some time during the 45 year period. But, given that 40 of these years are now in the past, there is no reason why an accident should become more likely in order to 'correct' for the 40 accident-free years. You may argue that the driver's chances of an accident have increased because 40 accident-free years have bred complacency, or because he is losing his faculties as he grows older, but this was not the basis for the argument given in the question.

Q6. No.

---

4. Ignoring regression to the mean

In the nineteenth century, the British scientist Sir Francis Galton found that relatively tall fathers tended to have sons who were shorter than them. Short fathers, on the other hand, had sons taller than them. In both cases the sons tended to be closer than their fathers to the mean height of adult males. Galton referred to this phenomenon, whereby events that are above or below the average tend to be followed by events closer to the average, as regression to the mean. The phenomenon can be widely observed in many situations. If you give somebody an intelligence test and they perform exceptionally well, it is likely that they will perform less well if you retest them. A month of exceptionally high sales, assuming there has been no fundamental change in the market conditions or your marketing strategy, will almost certainly be followed by a month of poorer sales, while the reverse will also be true. As Plous[9] points out, athletes and teams who appear on the cover of the US magazine *Sports Illustrated* usually experience a deterioration in performance after the magazine has been published. A cover appearance usually follows an exceptional performance, so closer to average performance is likely in the subsequent period. In all of these cases the unusual event is probably a result of a particularly favorable (or unfavorable) combination of chance factors that is unlikely to recur in the following period.

Unfortunately, regression to the mean is widely ignored or misunderstood. According to Tversky and Kahneman, people assume that, when an event follows an extreme event, it will be maximally representative of the extreme event. In other words, people expect extremes to be followed by similar extremes. They expect extremely tall fathers to have sons as tall as them and extremely high sales in one month to be followed by the same level of sales in the following month.

Failure to recognize regression to the mean can have important consequences. Tversky and Kahneman describe the case of the flight instructors who praised trainee pilots after exceptionally smooth landings and admonished them after rough landings. As a result of regression to the mean, exceptionally smooth landings tended to be followed by poorer landings on the next flight, while rough landings were followed by better landings. This led to the mistaken belief, by the flight instructors, that criticism was more effective than praise.

Test your judgment: answer to question 7

Q7. Because of regression to the mean, lower sales were most likely.

---

5. The conjunction fallacy

Consider the following question which is taken from a study by Tversky and Kahneman:[10]

> Linda is 31 years old, single, outspoken and very bright. She majored in philosophy. As a student, she was deeply concerned with issues of discrimination and social justice, and also participated in anti-nuclear demonstrations. Which is most likely:
>
> (a) Linda is a bank teller;
> (b) Linda is a bank teller who is active in the feminist movement?

Almost 90% of people in the study thought that it was more probable that Linda was a bank teller who was active in the feminist movement. Yet this answer is wrong. There must be more bank tellers in the population, of all kinds, than bank tellers who are specifically active in the feminist movement. The conjunction (or co-occurrence) of two events (in this case 'bank teller' and 'feminist') cannot be more probable than each event on its own. It is more likely that your boss is a female than it is that your boss is female *and* married. Similarly, your car is more likely to be red than red *and* less than 2 years old.

So why did 90% of subjects in the experiment get it wrong? It appears that they were approaching the problem by judging how representative each of the options (a and b) was of Linda, given the way she was described. As the description was designed to be more typical of a feminist than a bank teller, a feminist bank teller seemed to be the most representative of the two options.

The conjunction fallacy will have important implications when we consider scenario planning in Chapter 16. The more detailed and plausible a scenario is, the more likely it will appear to be, even though more specific scenarios must have a lower probability of occurring than general ones. For example, if a company is formulating possible scenarios for a time period 5 years from now, the detailed scenario 'War in the Middle-East between Israel and a neighboring state leads to rocketing oil prices and economic recession in both Western Europe and the USA' may *seem* more probable because of the causal links that are described than the general scenario 'Economic recession occurs in both Western Europe and the USA'.

Test your judgment: answers to questions 8 and 9

Q8. (a) is most likely.
Q9. Scenario (a) is most likely.

The anchoring and adjustment heuristic

Judgment is widely used to make estimates of values such as how long a job will take to complete or what next month's sales level will be. Often these estimates start with an initial value which is then adjusted to obtain the final estimate. Typical initial values might be how long the last job took to complete or this month's level of sales. Unfortunately, the adjustment from these initial values is often insufficient; a phenomenon known as anchoring. We investigate the effects of this next.

Biases associated with anchoring and adjustment

1. Insufficient adjustment

Tversky and Kahneman demonstrated the anchoring effect in an experiment in which subjects were asked to estimate various quantities, such as the percentage of African nations that were members of the United Nations. Before the estimate was elicited, a wheel of fortune was spun to generate a random number between 0 and 100, and the subjects were asked whether the required percentage was above or below the generated number. They were then asked to make their estimate by moving upwards or downwards from the random number. Remarkably, the random number had a substantial effect on subjects' estimates, with lower estimates being associated with lower random numbers. Later studies[11] have shown that even ridiculously extreme anchors can still exert an effect (for example, one study asked subjects whether the mean temperature in San Francisco was higher or lower than 558 °F).

In many of the studies, participants are directed, in some way, to an inappropriate anchor. But what if the anchor is, obviously, irrelevant? One study[11] had people estimate the points scored by a fictitious, but plausibly named, American soccer player whose jersey number was either displayed as '54' or '94'. The study found that the higher the incidental anchor, the higher were the projected points scored. In a real-world study,[12] one of two advertisements was placed at the end of a supermarket aisle. One read 'Snickers bars – buy 18 for your freezer!', while the alternative read 'Snickers bars – buy them for your freezer!' The actual sales of Snickers bars were found to be 38% higher with the first advertisement.

In decision-making, anchoring can be a problem in the estimation of costs, payoffs, project durations and probabilities. Forecasts that are used in the decision process may be biased by forecasters anchoring on the current value and making insufficient adjustment for the effect of future conditions.

Test your judgment: answer to question 10

This question tried to tempt you to anchor on the figure of 15 million. Did it succeed?

Q10. (a) Higher; (b) 72.6 million. *(Source: Egypt State Information Service.)*

---

2. Overestimating the probability of conjunctive events

As we saw earlier, the co-occurrence of events is referred to as a conjunctive event. Typical examples might be 'the main machine *and* the back-up machine both fail today' or 'you get promoted *and* win the lottery *and* write a best-selling novel all within the next 12 months'. Each of the individual events that might co-occur is called an elementary event (for example, 'getting promoted' is an elementary event). Research[13] suggests that people tend to overestimate the probability of conjunctive events occurring because they anchor on the probability of one of the elementary events and make insufficient adjustment from this. Consider the following example.

For a communication system to work, each of seven independent relay centers must be operational. Each center has a 0.9 probability of being operational at any given moment. You are about to send a message through the system. Estimate the probability that your message will reach its destination.

It is likely that you will anchor on the 0.9 probability of one of the centers being operational. If this is the case, you will overestimate the true probability of your message getting through, which (from the multiplication rule – see Chapter 5) is

$$0.9 \times 0.9 \times 0.9 \times 0.9 \times 0.9 \times 0.9 \times 0.9, \text{ i.e. only } 0.48$$

As Tversky and Kahneman point out, the estimation of conjunctive events is particularly important in planning. Projects such as the development of a new product or the completion of a construction project on time involve a series of elementary events, all of which must succeed for the undertaking as a whole to be successful. While the individual probability of each of the elementary events succeeding may be high, the overall probability of success may be low. The tendency of people to overestimate probabilities for conjunctive events may therefore lead to unjustified optimism that the project will succeed.

Test your judgment: answer to question 11

Q11. Did you anchor on the 99.5% probability? The correct answer is that the proposed safety system would only have a 47% probability of being operational on any given day.

---

3. Underestimating probabilities for disjunctive events

Disjunctive events can be expressed in the form '*either* X *or* Y occurs'. Examples would be '*either* the ignition system *or* the cooling system in your car fails this week' and '*either* bad weather *or* supplier problems cause delays in the project'. When asked to estimate the probability of a disjunctive event, it appears that, once again, people anchor on one of the elementary events. With disjunctive events, this leads to a tendency to underestimate the probability.[13] As the estimation of risk often involves probability assessments for disjunctive events, this bias can be a serious concern.

To illustrate this, suppose that a chemical plant will leak dangerous fumes if at least one of ten independent subsystems fails. Each subsystem is designed to have only a 1/100 chance of failure in the course of a year. An estimate of the probability of a leakage occurring in the next 12 months is required. Most people would be likely to anchor on the 1/100 probability of an individual subsystem failing and produce an estimate close to it. In fact, the correct probability is just under 1/10.

Test your judgment: answer to question 12

Q12. Did you anchor on the 5% probability? The probability of at least one person leaving is 40%.

---

4. Overconfidence

Suppose that you are a maintenance manager and you are asked to provide optimistic and pessimistic estimates of how long the overhaul of a machine will take. You are told that your estimates should be such that there is a 99% chance that the actual time will fall between the optimistic and pessimistic estimates. First you consider the most likely time and estimate this to be 30 hours. You then adjust from this to estimate the pessimistic time, 36 hours, and the optimistic time, 27 hours. This means you are 99% certain that the overhaul will take between 27 and 36 hours. However, when the machine overhaul takes place, you are surprised to find that it takes 44 hours – way outside your range. Were you unlucky or was there something wrong with your estimation method?

Unfortunately, a number of research studies[14] suggest that ranges estimated in this way are likely to be too narrow; that is, people tend to be overconfident about the chances that their estimated range will include the true value. Tversky and Kahneman argue that this is because they start with an initial value, in this case the most likely overhaul time, and then anchor onto it. In consequence, the adjustments to the upper and lower limits of the range are too small to give the stated probability of including the true value. For example, in a study by Alpert and Raiffa,[15] subjects were asked to provide estimates of various quantities in the form of ranges that were to have a 90% probability of including the true value. In fact, only about 57% of the quantities actually fell within the estimated ranges.

As we shall see in Chapter 11, overconfidence is of particular concern when probability distributions have to be estimated. There is a danger that, when estimating maximum and minimum possible levels of quantities such as costs or sales, decision-makers will estimate ranges that are too narrow to include all of the possibilities. The elicitation methods that we outline in that chapter are designed to avoid this problem by (i) discouraging decision-makers from anchoring on a particular quantity and (ii) encouraging them to widen their estimated range by imagining circumstances where the true quantity might fall outside it.

Test your judgment: answer to question 13

Q13. Were you overconfident in your estimates? The true values of the quantities are given below:
   (a) 6300 miles or 10 139 kilometers;
   (b) 31 241 030 (*Source: Statistics Canada*);
   (c) 839 781 square miles or 2 174 865 square kilometers;
   (d) 1938;
   (e) 1876;
   (f) 35 million miles or 56 million kilometers;
   (g) 74.46% (*Source: US Department of Labor, Bureau of Labor Statistics*);
   (h) 1809;
   (i) 14 000 feet or 43 000 meters;
   (j) 1770 miles or 2848 kilometers.
   If your 90% confidence was justified, we would typically expect nine of your ten ranges to include the true value. If fewer of your ranges achieved this, then this suggests that you were overconfident.

Other judgmental biases

A large number of other biases in probability estimation have been documented by researchers (see, for example, Hogarth and Makridakis[16] and Plous[9]). We consider next two of these which are likely to be most troublesome in the formulation of decision analysis models. A third well-known bias, 'conservatism', will be discussed in Chapter 15.

1. Believing desirable outcomes are more probable

Much research has suggested that people tend to view desirable outcomes as more probable than those that are undesirable. In one study,[17] college students were asked to estimate how likely they were, relative to other students of the same age and sex, to experience various positive and negative events in their lives. Typically, students considered that they were 15% more likely to experience positive events, such as owning their own home, but 20% less likely to have negative events in their lives, such as suffering a heart attack before they reached the age of 40. Another study[18] found that approximately one-third of independent inventors continued to spend time on projects – even after receiving highly diagnostic advice to cease their effort. Inventors appear to be more overconfident and inappropriately optimistic than people in general. However, the causes of such overconfidence are deeper. Arkes and Hutzel[19] asked participants to imagine that they were the president of an airline company that had invested $100 million in a research project to build an airplane that could not be detected by radar. The project was stated to be 90% completed. Participants were also told that another firm was beginning to market a similar airplane that was faster and more fuel efficient, and were then asked to estimate the chance of commercial success for their own airplane. In this scenario, the chances of success were estimated as 41%, on average, whereas, if respondents were told that their own company had not yet invested any money at all in the development project, then the chances of success were, on average, estimated at 34%. Here, the earlier commitment of resources for the development of the airplane was the cause of the increased expressed optimism. The $100 million was difficult to write off, even though the competitor appeared to have a superior product. In fact, participants were eager to commit another $11 million to complete the development of their airplane. As such, optimism and escalation of commitment appear to be caused by the desire to justify – both to ourselves and to others – our past investments, and to avoid the appearance of having wasted these prior allocations of resources.

By contrast, when couples undergo a program of costly fertility treatments, the progress after each treatment is all-or-nothing – because a baby cannot be part conceived. In such a situation, after repeated failures and with uncertain chances of future success, quitting the program early is the norm.[20] However, such pessimistic de-escalation of commitment is suboptimal, as the expected return of repeated attempts outweighs, for most couples, the continuing costs.

2. Biased assessment of covariation

Earlier in the chapter we discussed illusory correlation and Tversky and Kahneman's explanation that people often see non-existent associations between events because they can easily recall or imagine the events occurring together. Several researchers have found that a similar bias can occur when people are presented with tables showing the number of times that events either occurred or failed to occur together. Consider, for example, the problem of estimating the probability that a patient has a disease, given that a particular symptom is present. Suppose that you are given the information below, which is based on the records of 27 patients:

| | No. of patients | |
	Illness present	Illness absent
Symptom present	12	6
Symptom absent	6	3

Would you conclude that there is a relationship between the symptom and the disease? Research by Arkes *et al.*[21] suggests that many people would conclude that there was. Yet if we calculate the conditional probabilities, we find

$$p(\text{illness present}|\text{symptom present}) = 12/18 = 2/3$$
$$p(\text{illness present}|\text{symptom absent}) = 6/9 = 2/3$$

which shows that the presence or absence of the symptom has no effect on the probability of having the illness. This study, and others (e.g. Smedslund[22]), suggested that people only consider the frequency of cases where both symptom and disease are present. In other words, they only consider the number in the top left-hand corner cell of the above table. The large value in this cell creates the illusion of a relationship. Data in the other cells are ignored, even though they are crucial to any accurate assessment of the strength of the relationship.

Test your judgment: answer to question 14

Q14. There is no evidence that the cost of the computers is associated with their chances of needing repair in the first year.

The probability that the cheap brand will require repair in the first year is $120/144 = 5/6$, while the probability for the expensive brand is $40/48$, which also equals $5/6$.

While people often see non-existent association between variables, they can also miss associations that do exist, even when these associations are strong. This is often because they have no prior expectation that the two variables will be related.[23]

Is human probability judgment really so poor?

The above discussion may give the impression that human judgments about probability are fundamentally flawed, but is this really the case? Over the last decade much of the work on heuristics and biases has been questioned. Most criticisms have centered on the fact that the research has largely been based on inexperienced decision-makers carrying out artificial tasks in psychological laboratories, rather than real-world decision-makers making real decisions. We review these arguments next.

1. Subjects in studies may be unrepresentative of real decision-makers

Beach et al.[24] have pointed out that people who typically take part in experiments designed to assess human judgment are undergraduate students who may be unrepresentative of real decision-makers. Real decision-makers may have acquired skills in probability estimation as a result of regular experience of carrying out the task, and they are also likely to have expertise relevant to the decision problem. For example, a sales manager is likely to have expertise on the market for a product, so that any probability judgments will be informed by this expertise. Undergraduates will usually have no special knowledge that they can bring to the estimation task, and the task of estimating probabilities may be unfamiliar to them.

In spite of this argument, as Ayton[25] points out, it is not difficult to find examples of biases in experts' judgments. For example, real estate agents' valuations of houses were found to be influenced by the house seller's asking (or listing) price.[26] Changes in this led to different valuations. Similarly, professional forecasters have suffered from the conjunction fallacy when comparing the relative probability of general and detailed scenarios.[27] More recently, Tetlock[28] collected 82 361 political and economic forecasts from experts, asking them to estimate probabilities for various future events. He found that they performed worse than chance.

2. Laboratory tasks may be untypical of real-world problems

The tasks used in psychological studies have often involved general knowledge questions, or paper and pencil exercises, similar to some of those in the questionnaire at the start of this chapter. The way that subjects approach these tasks may be very different from the way they tackle judgmental tasks in real-world decision problems. This criticism is supported by the work of Payne,[29] Payne et al.[30] and Einhorn and Hogarth,[31] who suggest that judgment in laboratory tasks may not be generalizable to real-world decision-making. These researchers found that even seemingly minor changes in the nature and context of a judgmental task can result in major changes in the way that a problem is viewed and tackled.

3. Tasks may be misunderstood by subjects

Beach *et al.*[24] have argued that many of the tasks used in psychological research are misunderstood by subjects or viewed in a different light to those expected by the experimenter. For example, in a study designed to assess the ability of judgmental forecasts to extrapolate an artificial sales graph with an upward linear trend,[32] it was found that subjects tended to underestimate the extent to which the sales would grow. However, the experimenters pointed out that subjects may have viewed this not as an assessment of their ability to extrapolate trends in graphs but as a test of their knowledge of the way sales behave in the real world. In many situations, sales do not continue to increase at the same rate; instead, the rate of increase lessens as the market ceiling is approached.

4. Subjects may be poorly motivated

As we indicated earlier, many psychological studies have involved undergraduates as subjects. Where these subjects lacked expertise relating to the experimental task, this may also have affected motivation. As Beach *et al.* point out, the effort that subjects are prepared to invest in a judgmental task is likely to be reduced if the task is not perceived to be within their own particular area of expertise. Also, the absence of actual or potential users of probability judgments made in the laboratory may serve to reduce motivation.[33] Moreover, in many studies there were no rewards for good judgment, so that there may have been little incentive to reflect deeply on the task. This is unlikely to be the case in a real decision where your income, reputation, job or even your life may depend upon the quality of your judgments.

5. Citation bias

Beach *et al.*[24] identified what they termed a 'citation bias' in the psychological literature. Of the 3500 articles on judgment and reasoning published between 1972 and 1981, only 84 were empirical studies. Of these, 47 reported poor performance and 37 found good performance. However, poor performance results were cited by authors on average six times more often than were results showing good performance.

6. Real-world studies suggest better performance

Relatively little research has focused on probability judgments made in real decisions. The most extensive studies have been carried out on the judgmental probability forecasts made by the National Weather Service in the United States. Murphy and colleagues[33] have evaluated these probabilities and found that, for certain categories of weather, they were more accurate than the available objective statistical techniques (accuracy here is measured by the calibration of the probabilities (see Chapter 11) and by special scoring rules[34]). In this case, the forecasters have a very large amount of information available, including the output from statistical techniques. They also receive detailed feedback and have an opportunity to gain experience of making forecasts over a wide range of meteorological conditions. Furthermore, they have considerable practice in quantifying their internal state of uncertainty. These circumstances may well be ideal for the relatively successful application of judgmental, as compared with purely statistical, forecasting. However, as we will discuss later, they are not the circumstances in which managers usually make judgments about the probability of events, which are likely to contain unique characteristics such as predicting the future market share for an innovative product or the profitability of a company's products in an ever-changing business environment.

Nevertheless, accurate probability judgments have been demonstrated in several real-world situations apart from weather forecasting. These include horse racing,[35] prediction of future interest rates by bankers[36] and prediction of the success of R&D projects.[37] Weiss et al.[38] have developed a way of evaluating the quality of expert judgment – and thus enabling the selection of an appropriate expert – when outcome information on the quality of the expert's predictions is not available. Their method scores an expert's judgment in terms of both (i) consistency in the use of a set of predictive cues for a (repeated) single prediction and (ii) consistency of the overall prediction. The method has much in common with ensuring consistency in probability assessment as a necessary but not sufficient condition for subsequent accuracy – a topic that we will discuss further in the next chapter.

Human judgment is particularly widely used in sales and economic forecasting,[39,40] although forecasts tend to be single-point estimates (e.g. 'September's sales will be 450 units') rather than probabilities. Judgment is used here either on its own or in combination with statistical forecasts and there is much evidence to suggest that it can be useful and accurate.[41] In reviews of research in this area, Bunn and Wright[42] and Lawrence et al.[43] suggest that judgmental forecasting will generally outperform statistical methods when the judge has important information that was not available to the statistical method. This information is likely to relate to unusual events that are too rare to include in a statistical model, but that have a profound effect on the variable to be forecast (e.g. a strike at a rival company that will lead to a massive, but temporary, increase in our sales) and soft information (e.g. strong rumors that a rival is about to launch an expensive advertising campaign).

A number of real-world studies support the conclusion of these reviews. These include studies of forecasts made by managers of company earnings,[44] workloads at a public warehouse[45] and the sales of consumer products.[46, 47] All of this, of course, does not necessarily suggest that these judgments did not suffer from the use of heuristics, and the consequent biases, that we discussed earlier, nor does it say that the judgments could not be improved.[48–50] It does, however, show that human judgment can have a valuable role to play in many real decision-making contexts, and that its accuracy can outperform that of statistical methods.

7. People think in terms of frequencies not probabilities

Gerd Gigerenzer has argued that observed bias in probabilistic reasoning is not an error, as probability theory simply does not apply to *single* events. For example, he would argue that assessment of the probability (in 1986) that Saddam Hussein would invade Kuwait within the next 5 years is *not* a sensible question to pose, whereas assessment of the probability that a 17-year-old motorbike rider will make an insurance claim for a road accident *is*, because there is historic relative frequency information on claims by such riders. Gigerenzer[51] focuses on the usefulness of a distinction between single-event probabilities and frequencies, and draws on evidence from both the history of probability and from experimental work in the psychological laboratory. He argues that empirical demonstrations of errors are not stable, and that observed cognitive biases can disappear when the task of assessing single-event probabilities is changed to that of assessing frequencies. In one example, he restates the famous 'Linda' problem, which we discussed earlier. Recall that the original Linda problem was:

> Linda is 31 years old, single, outspoken and very bright. She majored in philosophy. As a student, she was deeply concerned with issues of discrimination and social justice, and also participated in anti-nuclear demonstrations. Which is most likely:
>
> (a) Linda is a bank teller;
> (b) Linda is a bank teller who is active in the feminist movement?

Recall that, in the above formulation of the Linda problem, about 90% of individuals who were given it responded that (b) was more probable than (a) – a demonstration of the conjunction fallacy. However, Gigerenzer showed that, if the words 'which of the alternatives is more probable?' are replaced with the words 'There are 100 people who fit the description above. How many of them are (a) bank tellers and

(b) bank tellers and active in the feminist movement?' then the percentage of individuals who violate the conjunction law drops to less than 25%. Clearly, instructions to assess a frequency (i.e. how many?) facilitates more accurate thinking than instructions to assess a subjective probability (i.e. which of the alternatives is more probable?). Consider also a gambler betting on the spin of a roulette wheel. If the roulette wheel has produced an outcome of red for the last ten spins, then the gambler may feel that her subjective probability of black on the next spin should be higher than that for red. However, ask the same gambler the relative proportions of red to black on spins of the wheel and she may well answer 50:50. As the roulette ball has no memory, it follows that the latter, relative frequency, assessment will produce the more veridical answer. Gigerenzer argues that the untrained mind has a frequentist design. Just as it would be unrealistic to expect one's pocket calculator accurately to compute the answer to arithmetic problems entered with Roman numerals, so it may be unreasonable to judge the general competence of human judgment on the performance of problems *requiring* the assessment of subjective probabilities rather than frequencies. Put simply, Gigerenzer argues that we are not equipped to reason about uncertainty using single-event probabilities, but we can reason successfully about uncertainty with frequencies. In another demonstration of this, Sniezek and Buckley[52] gave subjects a series of general knowledge questions with two alternative answers, one of which was correct. The subjects had to select the answer that they thought was correct and then estimate the probability that their selection was the correct one. Their results showed the same general overconfidence that has been reported in other studies. However, when they asked respondents simply to state the number of times they had picked the right answer for the total number of two alternative questions to which they had responded, individuals' frequency estimates were well calibrated. This was in spite of the fact that the *same* individuals were, generally, overconfident in their subjective probability assessments for individual questions.

Kahneman and Lovallo[53] have similarly argued that we tend to see forecasting problems as unique when they would be better seen as examples of a broader *class* of events. They claim that the natural tendency in thinking about a particular problem, such as the probability of success of a new business venture, is to pay particular attention to the particular characteristics of the specific problem in hand and reject analogies to other instances of the same general type of event as superficial.

They cite a study by Cooper, Woo and Dunkelberger[54] which showed that, when entrepreneurs were interviewed about the probabilities of their businesses being successful, their estimates were not related to objective predictors such as whether they had a college education, what their prior supervisory experience was and the amount of initial capital that they were investing. In spite of the fact that the overall survival rate for new businesses was as low as 33%, more than 80% of them described their chances of success as 70% or better. In such a case, Gigerenzer's advice would be to ask the individual entrepreneurs to estimate the proportion of new businesses that survive (he would argue that they would be able to make good estimates of this relative frequency) and use this as an estimate of an individual's business surviving.

Comparison of studies of the calibration of probability assessments concerning *unique* individual events with those where assessments have been made for *repetitive* predictions of weather events reveals a general finding of relatively poor calibration in the former contrasted with good calibration in the latter. Bolger and Wright[55] have argued that this differential forecasting performance is due, in part, to the existence of rapid and meaningful feedback to the weather forecasters in terms of both the relative frequency of probability predictions *and* the predicted event's occurrence. Such prediction–feedback frequency information may well be ideal for the achievement of frequentist-based accuracy. However, such ideal conditions for probability assessment are not common in many management situations, which tend to be characterized by the need to judge the likelihood of unique events. In summary, we advocate that, in assessing a subjective probability, you attempt to locate a reference class of previous forecasts that you have made that are similar to the event that you now need to forecast. If the event is, say, demand for a set number of batches of perishable food (page 116), attendance at a conference in a provincial town (page 122) or successful development of a new type of processor (page 159), then you should first consider whether

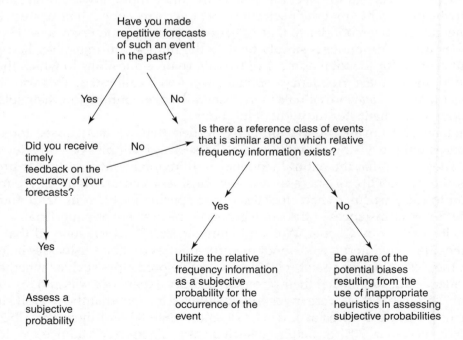

Figure 10.1 – A methodology for choosing how to develop a subjective probability assessment

or not you have made repetitive forecasts of such events in the past. If you have, and have received timely feedback on the accuracy of your forecasts, then the assessment task is likely to be like that of weather forecasting, where good calibration is a general finding. If not, then you should consider whether there is a historic, relative frequency reference class that you can use. For example, if you are considering the likelihood that a newly hired worker will stay for at least a year, then you should consider the number of workers who have been hired in your organization at that grade (i.e. identify the reference class) and then calculate how many in, say, the last 5 years have remained for at least 1 year.

If a reference class of previous forecasts or historic frequencies is not obvious, then be aware that the only way to assess the likelihood of the event is to use judgmental heuristics, and that such heuristics *can* lead to bias – as we have documented in this chapter. Figure 10.1 summarizes this conclusion.

Exercises

Additional exercises can be found on the book's website

(1) Identify the heuristics that decision-makers might use in making estimates in the situations listed below. Explain how biases might emanate from the use of these heuristics.
   (a) Members of an interview panel making estimates of the probability that a candidate would be a successful appointment.
   (b) A marketing manager of a company manufacturing computer peripherals making a forecast of the number of new orders that will be obtained next month.
   (c) A sales executive estimating the correlation between the sales of a product and advertising expenditure.
   (d) A manager of an international construction company making an estimate of the risk of civil unrest in a country that was formerly part of the Soviet Union and where the company is considering making investments.
   (e) A company doctor estimating the degree of association between the exposure/non-exposure of workers to a chemical pollutant and the incidence of a particular respiratory illness among these workers.
   (f) The manager of a manufacturing company estimating the relative probability of (i) a strike at the company's Pittsburgh plant in the next year and (ii) the company experiencing a long-term loss of market share following a strike over pay at its Pittsburgh plant in the next year.

(2) The employees of a leading mail-order computer software company are secretly thinking of breaking away to form their own rival company. This would require an investment of $3 million and the employees will make the decision largely

on the basis of the net present value of this investment. To help them with their decision, a risk-analysis model has been formulated. Development of the model involved estimating a large number of probabilities including those set out below:

(a) Probability distributions for the size of the market (measured in total turnover) for each of the next 5 years – following the recent launch of a major new international software product, the employees have experienced a buoyant market over the last few months.

(b) Probability distributions of the market share that could be obtained by the new company in each of the next 5 years – these distributions were obtained by first estimating a most likely value and then determining optimistic and pessimistic values.

(c) The probability that magazine advertising costs would increase over the next 5 years – this was considered to be less likely than an increase in advertising costs resulting from increased costs of paper and an associated fall in the number of computer magazines.

Discuss the heuristics that the employees might have employed to estimate these probabilities and any biases that might have emanated from the use of these heuristics.

(3) A chemical plant is due for a major overhaul, and the manager has to make an assessment of a number of uncertainties associated with the project. These include the time the overhaul will take to complete (after 35 days, the losses of production caused by the overhaul could have serious consequences for the company) and the risks that there will be leakage of dangerous chemicals into local watercourses during the cleaning process. The following extracts have been taken from the manager's draft report, which details plans for the overhaul:

(i) 'I assessed the most likely duration of the overhaul to be 30 days. I then tried to take an optimistic view and assumed that, if all goes well, we could finish the work 5 days earlier than this (i.e. in 25 days). I then took a pessimistic perspective and estimated that the longest the project will take is 34 days. I am therefore certain that we should complete the overhaul within 35 days.'

(ii) 'Essentially the overhaul will be split into eight independent phases. I think the chances of us completing each phase without a pollution problem are high, say 90%. Overall, I therefore estimate that we have almost a 90% chance of avoiding a pollution problem during the project.'

(iii) 'There must be a high chance that there will be no serious corrosion in the main pump. The last five pumps we've inspected at other plants were all corroded and the chances of getting six corroded pumps in a row must be very low indeed.'

(iv) 'I'm mindful of the theft of equipment we had last week at our Briston plant. If we don't take appropriate security precautions I am virtually certain that we will lose important equipment in this way during the overhaul, with possible disastrous effects on our ability to complete the project within 35 days.'

(v) 'I estimated the probability of the West boiler requiring repair to be about 10%'. (On a later page:) 'Given the likelihood of seepage into the pipe feeding the West boiler, there must be a high chance of this boiler being corroded. I therefore reckon that there is a 50:50 chance that we will have to repair this boiler as a result of the seepage and corrosion.'

Comment on these extracts from the report in the light of Tversky and Kahneman's work on heuristics and biases.

(4) Consider the problem of assessing the probability that a named 17-year-old male automobile driver will be involved in a road traffic accident in the next 12 months. Would it be more prudent to be guided in your judgment by the base rate of accidents for 17-year-old male drivers, as the auto insurers are, or by your personal knowledge of the particular driver?

(5) To what extent is it reasonable to conclude that human judgment in relation to probability estimation is fundamentally flawed.

References

1. Much of their work is reviewed in Tversky, A. and Kahneman, D. (1974) Judgment under uncertainty: heuristics and biases, *Science*, **185**, 1124–1131. For a collection of papers on heuristics and biases, see Kahneman, D., Tversky, A. and Slovic, P. (eds) (1982) *Judgment under Uncertainty: Heuristics and Biases*, Cambridge University Press, Cambridge, UK.

2. Lichtenstein, S., Slovic, P., Fischhoff, B., Layman, M. and Coombs, B. (1978) Judged frequency of lethal events, *Journal of Experimental Psychology: Human Learning and Memory*, **4**, 551–578.

3. Chapman, L.J. and Chapman, L.P. (1969) Illusory correlation as an obstacle to the use of valid psychodiagnostic signs, *Journal of Abnormal Psychology*, **74**, 271–280.

4. Kogut, T. and Ritov, I. (2005) The identified victim effect: an identified group or just a single individual?, *Journal of Behavioral Decision Making*, **18**, 157–167.

5. Redelmeier, D.A. and Tversky, A. (1990) The discrepancy between medical decisions for individual patients and for groups, *New England Journal of Medicine*, **332**, 1162–1164.

6. Eggleton, I.R.C. (1982) Intuitive time-series extrapolation, *Journal of Accounting Research*, **20**, 68–102.

7. O'Connor, M., Remus, W. and Griggs, K. (1993) Judgemental forecasting in times of change, *International Journal of Forecasting*, **9**, 163–172.

8. Goodwin, P. and Fildes, R. (1999) Judgmental forecasts of time series affected by special events: does providing a statistical forecast improve accuracy?, *Journal of Behavioral Decision Making*, **12**, 37–53.

9. Plous, S. (1993) *The Psychology of Judgment and Decision Making*, McGraw-Hill, New York, NY.

10. Tversky, A. and Kahneman, D. (1982) Judgments of and by representativeness, in *Judgment under Uncertainty: Heuristics and Biases*, ed. by Kahneman, D., Tversky, A. and Slovic, P., Cambridge University Press, Cambridge, UK.

11. Critcher, C.R. and Gilovich, T. (2008) Incidental environmental anchors, *Journal of Behavioral Decision Making*, **21**, 242–252.

12. Warsink, B., Kent, R.J. and Hoch, S.J. (1998) Anchoring and adjustment model of purchase quality decisions, *Journal of Marketing Research*, **35**, 71–81.

13. See, for example, Bar-Hillel, M. (1973) On the subjective probability of compound events, *Organizational Behavior and Human Performance*, **9**, 396–406.

14. See Lichtenstein, S., Fischhoff, B. and Phillips, L.D. (1982) Calibration of probabilities: the state of the art to 1980, in *Judgment under Uncertainty: Heuristics and Biases*, ed. by Kahneman, D., Tversky, A. and Slovic, P., Cambridge University Press, Cambridge, UK.

15. Alpert, M. and Raiffa, H. (1982) A progress report on the training of probability assessors, in *Judgment under Uncertainty: Heuristics and Biases*, ed. by Kahneman, D., Tversky, A. and Slovic, P., Cambridge University Press, Cambridge, UK.

16. Hogarth, R.M. and Makridakis, S. (1981) Forecasting and planning: an evaluation, *Management Science*, **227**, 115–138.

17. Weinstein, N.D. (1980) Unrealistic optimism about future life events, *Journal of Personality and Social Psychology*, **39**, 806–820.

18. Astebro, T., Jeffrey, S.A. and Adomdza, G.K. (2007) Inventor perseverance after being told to quit, *Journal of Behavioral Decision Making*, **20**, 253–272.

19. Arkes, H.R. and Hutzel, L. (2000) The role of probability of success estimates in the sunk cost effect, *Journal of Behavioral Decision Making*, **13**, 295–306.

20. Zikmund-Fisher, B.J. (2004) De-escalation after repeated negative feedback: emergent expectations of failure, *Journal of Behavioral Decision Making*, **17**, 365–379.

21. Arkes, H.R., Harkness, A.R. and Biber, D. (1980) Salience and the judgment of contingency, Paper presented at the Midwestern Psychological Association, St Louis, MO (36) (as cited in Arkes, H.R. and Hammond, K.R. (eds) (1986) *Judgment and Decision Making*, Cambridge University Press, Cambridge, UK).

22. Smedslund, J. (1963) The concept of correlation in adults, *Scandinavian Journal of Psychology*, **4**, 165–173.

23. Hamilton, D.L. and Rose, T. L. (1980) Illusory correlation and the maintenance of stereotypic beliefs, *Journal of Personality and Social Psychology*, **39**, 832–845.

24. Beach, L.R., Christensen-Szalanski, J. and Barnes, V. (1987) Assessing human judgment: has it been done, can it be done, should it be done?, in *Judgmental Forecasting*, ed. by Wright, G. and Ayton, P., John Wiley & Sons, Ltd, Chichester, UK.

25. Ayton, P. (1998) How bad is human judgement?, in *Forecasting with Judgment*, ed. by Wright, G. and Goodwin, P., John Wiley & Sons, Ltd, Chichester, UK.

26. Northcraft, G.B. and Neale, M.A. (1987) Experts, amateurs, and real-estate: an anchoring-and-adjustment perspective on property pricing decisions, *Organizational Behavior and Human Decision Processes*, **39**, 84–97.
27. Tversky, A. and Kahneman, D. (1983) Extensional versus intuitive reasoning: the conjunction fallacy in probability judgment. *Psychological Review*, **90**, 293–315.
28. Tetlock, P.E. (2005) *Expert Political Judgment*, Princeton University Press, Princeton, NJ.
29. Payne, J.W. (1982) Contingent decision behavior, *Psychological Bulletin*, **92**, 382–402.
30. Payne, J.W., Bettman, J.R. and Johnson, E.J. (1993) *The Adaptive Decision Maker*, Cambridge University Press, Cambridge, UK.
31. Einhorn, H.J. and Hogarth, R.M. (1981) Behavioral decision theory: processes of judgment and choice, *Annual Review of Psychology*, **32**, 52–88.
32. Lawrence, M.J. and Makridakis, S. (1989) Factors affecting judgmental forecasts and confidence intervals, *Organizational Behavior and Human Decision Processes*, **42**, 172–187.
33. Murphy, A.H. and Brown, B.G. (1985) A comparative evaluation of objective and subjective weather forecasts in the United States, in *Behavioral Decision Making*, ed. by Wright, G., Plenum, New York, NY.
34. Brier, G.W. (1950) Verification of forecasts expressed in terms of probability, *Monthly Weather Review*, **75**, 1–3.
35. Hoerl, A. and Falein, H.K. (1974) Reliability of subjective evaluation in a high incentive situation, *Journal of the Royal Statistical Society*, **137**, 227–230.
36. Kabus, I. (1976) You can bank on uncertainty, *Harvard Business Review*, May–June, 95–105.
37. Balthasar, H.U., Boschi, R.A.A. and Menke, M.M. (1978) Calling the shots in R and D, *Harvard Business Review*, May–June, 151–160.
38. Weiss, D.J., Shanteau, J. and Harries, P. (2006) People who judge people, *Journal of Behavioral Decision Making*, **19**, 441–454.
39. Fildes, R. and Goodwin, P. (2007) Against your better judgment? How organizations can improve their use of management judgment in forecasting, *Interfaces*, **37**, 570–576.
40. Sanders, N.R. and Manrodt, K.B. (1994) Forecasting practices in US corporations: survey results, *Interfaces*, **24**, 92–100.
41. Mathews, B.P. and Diamantopolous, A. (1992) Judgemental revision of sales forecasts: the relative performance of judgementally revised versus non-revised forecasts, *Journal of Forecasting*, **11**, 569–576.
42. Bunn, D. and Wright, G. (1991) Interaction of judgmental and statistical forecasting: issues and analysis, *Management Science*, **37**, 501–518.
43. Lawrence, M., Goodwin, P., O'Connor, M. and Önkal, D. (2006) Judgemental Forecasting: a review of progress over the last 25 years, *International Journal of Forecasting*, **22**, 493–518.
44. Armstrong, J.S. (1983) Relative accuracy of judgemental and extrapolative methods in forecasting annual earnings, *Journal of Forecasting*, **2**, 437–447.
45. Sanders, N.R. and Ritzman, L.P. (1992) The need for contextual and technical knowledge in judgemental forecasting, *Journal of Behavioral Decision Making*, **5**, 39–52.
46. Edmundson, R.H., Lawrence, M.J. and O'Connor, M.J. (1988) The use of non-time series information in sales forecasting: a case study, *Journal of Forecasting*, **7**, 201–211.

47. Fildes, R., Goodwin, P., Lawrence, M. and Nikolopoulos, K. (2009) Effective forecasting and judgmental adjustments: an empirical evaluation and strategies for improvement in supply-chain planning, *International Journal of Forecasting*, **25**, 3–23.

48. Goodwin, P. and Wright, G. (1993) Improving judgmental time series forecasting: a review of the guidance provided by research, *International Journal of Forecasting*, **9**, 147–161.

49. Goodwin, P. and Wright, G. (1994) Heuristics, biases and improvement strategies in judgmental time series forecasting, *Omega International Journal of Management Science*, **22**, 553–568.

50. Goodwin, P. (1996) Statistical correction of judgmental point forecasts and decisions, *Omega International Journal of Management Science*, **24**, 551–559.

51. Gigerenzer, G. (1994) Why the distinction between single event probabilities and frequencies is important for psychology (and vice versa), in *Subjective Probability*, ed. by Wright, G. and Ayton, P., John Wiley & Sons, Ltd, Chichester, UK.

52. Sniezek, J. and Buckley, T. (1991) Confidence depends on level of aggregation, *Journal of Behavioral Decision Making*, **4**, 263–272.

53. Kahneman, D. and Lovallo, D. (1993) Timid choices and bold forecasts: a cognitive perspective on risk taking, *Management Science*, **39**, 17–31.

54. Cooper, A., Woo, C. and Dunkelberger, W. (1988) Entrepreneurs' perceived chances for success, *Journal of Business Venturing*, **3**, 97–108.

55. Bolger, F. and Wright, G. (1994) Assessing the quality of expert judgment: issues and analysis, *Decision Support Systems*, **11**, 1–24.

Methods for eliciting probabilities 11

Introduction

At the end of the last chapter we gave advice on how to approach probability estimation. This was based on recent research evidence that people prefer to think in terms of the relative frequencies with which events occur, rather than probabilities. Nevertheless, it may not always be possible to assess frequencies for an event when there are no past instances of that event or similar events occurring. In fact, many of the future uncertainties facing managers concern unique, or relatively unique, events – such as the likely success of a new advertising campaign or new product launch. A number of techniques have been developed to assist decision-makers with the task of making probability judgments, and in this chapter we will examine some of the more widely used methods.

Before we begin the chapter, we would like to ask you a few questions that involve assessing probabilities.

Probability assessment

(1) What single probability number, on a scale from 0.0 to 1.0, best equates to your understanding of the term 'very probable'?
(2) What single probability number equates to your understanding of the word 'probable'?
(3) What single probability number equates to your understanding of the word 'possible'?
(4) What is the probability, on a scale from 0.0 to 1.0, that it will be raining tomorrow, at precisely 12 noon, over the building that you are now in?
(5) What is the probability, on a scale from 0.0 to 1.0, that it will be raining the day after tomorrow, at precisely 12 noon, over the building that you are now in, given that it does rain at 12.00 tomorrow?

(6) What is the probability, on a scale from 0.0 to 1.0, that it will be raining both tomorrow and the day after, at precisely 12 noon, over the building that you are now in?

(7) What is the probability of throwing a '6' on a single throw of a fair dice?

(8) What is the probability of throwing a '6' or a '4' on a single throw of a fair dice?

(9) What is the probability of throwing a '6' and then another '6' on two successive throws of a fair dice?

(10) What is the probability of drawing an 'ace' from a pack of 52 playing cards?

(11) What is the probability of drawing an 'ace' from a pack of 52 playing cards and then, having replaced the card in the pack and shuffled the pack, a second 'ace'?

(12) What is the probability of drawing an 'ace' from a pack of 52 playing cards and then, on the next draw from the now smaller pack, a second 'ace'?

Issues with verbal probability expressions

There are a number of ways in which uncertainty can be measured and expressed. The simplest method involves the use of words such as 'unlikely', 'almost impossible', 'probable', 'doubtful' and 'expected'. Unfortunately, it has been found that different people attach very different meanings to these expressions, and even individuals are not consistent over time in their use of them. For example, Moore and Thomas[1] discuss an experiment at a business school where a large number of executives were asked to rank ten words or phrases in decreasing order of uncertainty. The ranking of the word 'likely' ranged from second to seventh, while the ranking for 'unlikely' ranged from third to tenth.

If you are like most of the participants who answered our first question, you will have responded somewhere in the range between 0.6 and 0.95. Some individuals attach a high numerical probability to the term 'very probable', and some less so. Imagine if a manager said it was very probable that a particular report would be completed and on his superior's desk at the start of business the next morning. Perhaps the junior meant there was a 60% chance it would be ready, but the senior understood this to be 95%. Clearly, verbal probability expressions are open to misinterpretation. Terms like 'probable' and 'possible' mean, to some people, a numerical probability as low as 0.01 – indicating that there is thought to be *some* probability, or possibility, that an event will happen. Your numerical equivalents for these two probability expressions were likely to be somewhat higher, yet they would still probably be different from those that other people would provide.

In addition to the different interpretations that people place on verbal probability statements, the context within which a statement is made can also affect the way it is understood. For example, consider the prediction that 'this winter you will probably develop a common cold'. Compare this with the prediction that 'this winter you will probably develop a lung infection'. When people are asked to provide the numerical equivalent of 'probably' in each of these contexts, the number provided is lower in the latter context – presumably because the prior probability of the former is higher than that of the latter. Also, when students were asked to evaluate statements about negative events, e.g. 'a small chance of having to repeat a year's studies', as opposed to positive events, e.g. 'a small chance of becoming the parent of a highly talented child', individual students felt that the same verbal probability expression had a lower numerical probability when addressed to their own, negatively portrayed, future than when attached to a prediction of someone else's future. The converse was true for positively portrayed futures.[2] Clearly, verbal expressions of probability are fraught with difficulties in interpretation. Numerical estimates, although relatively infrequent in everyday conversations, may allow the expression and communication of uncertainty in a less ambiguous manner.

Coherence in probability judgments

Turn now to your answers to questions 7 to 12. The true answers are, respectively, $1/6$, $2/6$, $1/36$, $1/52$, $(4/52) \times (4/52)$ and $(4/52 \times 3/51)$. You will probably have got these answers right – showing that you can appreciate the probability concept as applied to the world of dice and playing cards. Now turn to your answers to questions 4, 5 and 6. If you considered that the chances of rain on the second day are independent of whether or not it rains on the first day, then the task is similar to that posed in question 11. Hence, your answers to question 4 and to question 5 should multiply together to give whatever your answer was to question 6. Alternatively, if you considered that the chances of rain on the second day would be influenced by whether or not it rained on the first day, then the task, for you, was similar to that posed in question 12 – in that you saw the events as dependent upon one another. Nevertheless, your answers to question 4 and to question 5 should still multiply together to give your answer to question 6. For most people who were asked to complete these questions, the answer given to question 6 was *not* the product of the answers previously given to questions 4 and 5. In short, answers to questions that deal with dice and playing cards usually show *coherence* according to the probability laws that we detailed in Chapter 5, but subjective probabilities assessed for future events often show *incoherence* according to these laws. We will return to this issue shortly. For the moment it is important to recognize that, even if a person is coherent, for example by giving 0.5, 0.5 and 0.25 as responses to the three weather questions, another person can be equally coherent by, for example, giving 0.2, 0.2 and 0.04 as responses. In such a situation, whose judgments of subjective probability should we take as our weather predictions? We will return to this issue later in this chapter.

Two barriers to improving probability assessments through learning

Professional weather forecasters in the USA are well known for the accuracy of their forecasts, which are expressed as probabilities (e.g. 'there is a 0.7 probability that it will rain in Manhattan tomorrow'). We will discuss later how this 'accuracy' can be measured, but there are a number of conditions that are conducive to the weather forecasters' accuracy. First, they get plenty of practice in carrying out forecasting tasks, as they have to make these forecasts on a daily basis. Second, and probably most importantly, they get regular, speedy and unambiguous feedback, which tells them how accurate their forecasts were. This enables them to learn and hence become expert in the process of producing probability estimates. Unfortunately, these conditions are likely to be absent when many business decisions are made. These decisions will involve assessing probabilities for one-off events, so there is no opportunity for learning through the regular estimation of these probabilities and the subsequent feedback on their accuracy. Moreover, under these conditions, two further barriers to learning are likely to be present.[3]

(1) *Confirmation bias.* People usually have a desire to seek out evidence that confirms their current beliefs and to discount any disconfirming evidence indicating that they may be wrong. If you believe that a new product you have been responsible for developing has a high probability of success, you will tend to focus on information that supports your belief and interpret any new information in a way that confirms that you are right. This clearly inhibits your ability to learn when new information is available.

In some cases, the actions we take in our search for confirmatory evidence mean that we are unable to learn from any feedback that we do receive about the outcomes of events. Einhorn[3] gives the following example:

> Imagine that you are a waiter in a busy restaurant and, because you cannot give good service to all the people at your station, you make a judgment regarding which people will leave good or poor tips. You then give good or bad service depending on your judgment. If the quality of service, in itself, has an effect on the size of the tip, outcome feedback will 'confirm' the predictions ('they looked cheap and left no tip – just as I thought'). The extent of such self-fulfilling prophecies is much greater than we think and represents a considerable obstacle to learning from outcome feedback.

(2) *Hindsight bias*. In 1972, President Nixon made a historic visit to China. Before the visit, psychology and statistics students were asked to estimate probabilities for 15 possible outcomes of the visit.[4] For example, 'President Nixon will meet Mao at least once' and 'President Nixon will announce that his trip was successful'. The students were unaware that, after the visit had been completed and widely reported in the media, they would be called back and asked to recall their probabilities. If an event had occurred, most of the students wrongly recalled that they had assigned it a higher probability than they had. The reverse was true when an event had not occurred. This tendency to look back and think that our predictions were more accurate than they really were is called 'hindsight bias'. In retrospect, everything looks much more predictable than it really was (Fischhoff[5] termed this the 'I-knew-it-all-along' effect). As a result of this bias, we can develop an exaggerated view of how good we are at making probability judgments. This, in turn, limits our ability to learn from experience, so that our probability estimates do not improve.

One antidote to hindsight bias is to ask people to think of reasons why an event might or might not have occurred. This increases their sensitivity to the possibility that the event could have turned out differently, and helps to make them aware that it was not, in fact, quite so easy to predict.

Preparing for probability assessment

These problems suggest that it is worth taking care with the assessment of probabilities when an important decision is being made. It has been found that probability assessment techniques are employed most effectively when they are administered by an analyst who uses them as part of an interview with the decision-maker (see Spetzler and Stäel von Holstein[6] and Shephard and Kirkwood[7]). Spetzler and Stäel von Holstein recommend that the interview carried out by the analyst should involve three phases before the probabilities are quantified: motivating, structuring and conditioning.

Motivating

This phase is designed to introduce the decision-maker to the task of assessing probabilities and to explain the importance and purpose of the task. Sensitivity analysis should be used by the analyst to identify those probabilities that need to be assessed with precision. At this stage, the possibility that assessments may be subject to deliberate biases should be explored (e.g. a manager may overestimate the probability of high costs in the hope that, when costs turn out to be low, he will be seen in a good light).

Deliberate bias is, of course, an undesirable characteristic of an input to an analysis whose intended outcome is improved decision-making.

Structuring

In the structuring phase, the quantity to be assessed should be clearly defined and structured. For example, asking the decision-maker vague questions about 'the value of shares in the USA in 2012' is unlikely to lead to reliable responses. 'The value of the Dow Jones index at the end of trading on Friday 29 June 2012' is obviously a less ambiguous quantity. It is also important at this stage to agree on a scale of measurement with which the decision-maker feels comfortable: if he thinks of sales in terms of 'numbers of boxes sold per week', then it would be inappropriate to force him or her to assess a probability distribution for 'the number of tons sold per week'.

When the decision-maker thinks that the quantity to be assessed depends on other factors, it may be simpler to restructure the assessment task, possibly by making use of a probability tree (see Chapter 5 and the last section of this chapter). For example, it may be that the development time for a new product will depend upon whether two companies can agree to collaborate on the basic research. In this case the decision-maker will probably find it easier to give two separate assessments: one based on the assumption that the collaboration takes place, and the other on the assumption that it does not.

Conditioning

The objective of this phase is to identify and thereby avoid the biases that might otherwise distort the decision-maker's probability assessments. It involves an exploration of how the decision-maker approaches the task of judging probabilities. For example, are last year's sales figures being used as a basis for this year's estimates? If they are, there may be an anchoring effect. To what extent are the assessments based too heavily on the information that is most readily available, such as yesterday's news, without taking a longer-term view? More generally, the heuristics and biases identified in Chapter 10 should be borne in mind by the decision analyst as he works through the assessment process with the decision-maker.

Assessment methods

A number of different methods have been developed for assessing probabilities. Some of these require a direct response from the decision-maker in the form of a probability or quantity, while others allow the probability to be inferred by observing the decision-maker's choice between bets.

Assessment methods for individual probabilities

Direct assessments

The simplest way to elicit a probability from a decision-maker is to pose a direct question such as 'What is the probability that the product will achieve a break-even sales level next month?' Unfortunately, many people would feel uncomfortable with this sort of approach, and they might be tempted to give a response without sufficient thought. Asking the individual to mark a point on a scale that runs from 0 to 1 might be preferred because at least the scale enables the probability to be envisaged. Other people prefer to give their assessments in terms of odds which can then easily be converted to probabilities, as we showed in Chapter 5. For example, odds of 25 to 1 against the occurrence of an event are equivalent to a probability of 1/26 or 0.038.

The probability wheel

A probability wheel is a device like that shown in Figure 11.1, consisting of a disk with two differently colored sectors, the size of which can be adjusted, and a fixed pointer. To see how the device might be used, let us suppose that a manager needs to assess the probability that a rival will launch a competing product within the next week. We could adjust the wheel so that the white sector takes up 80% of its area and ask her to choose between the following two hypothetical gambles:

Bet 1: If the rival launches the product within the next week, you will win $100 000. If the rival does not launch the product, you will win nothing.
Bet 2: If, after spinning the wheel once, the pointer is in the white sector, you will win $100 000. If it is pointing towards the black sector, you will win nothing.

If the manager says that she would choose bet 2, then this implies that she thinks that the probability of the rival launching the product in the next week is less than

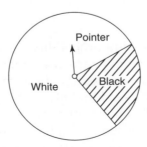

Figure 11.1 – A probability wheel

80%. The size of the white sector could then be reduced and the question posed again. Eventually, the manager should reach a point where she is indifferent between the two bets. If this is achieved when the white sector takes up 30% of the wheel's area, this clearly implies that she estimates that the required probability is 0.3.

Note that the use of the probability wheel allowed an assessment to be made without directly asking the manager to state the probability. It is therefore an example of an indirect assessment method.

The wheel also has the advantage that it enables the decision-maker to visualize the chance of an event occurring. However, because it is difficult to differentiate between the sizes of small sectors, the probability wheel is not recommended for the assessment of events that have either a very low or a very high probability of occurrence (we will deal with this issue later). The analyst should also ensure that the rewards of the two bets are regarded as being equivalent by the decision-maker. For example, if, in bet 1 above, $100 000 will be paid if the rival launches within the next *year*, then this would imply that the decision-maker would have to wait a year before any winnings could be paid. She would probably regard this as being less attractive than a bet on the probability wheel where any winnings would be paid instantly. It is also a good idea to use a large monetary prize in the bets so that the preference between them is not influenced by other attributes that may be imposed by the assessor. The large payoff gives the monetary attribute a big weight compared with the others.

A number of devices similar to the probability wheel have also been used in probability assessment. For example, the decision-maker may be asked to imagine an urn filled with 1000 colored balls (400 red and 600 blue). He or she would then be asked to choose between betting on the event in question occurring or betting on a red ball being drawn from the urn (both bets would offer the same rewards). The relative proportion of red and blue balls would then be varied until the decision-maker was indifferent between the two bets, at which point the required probability could be inferred.

Assessment methods for probability distributions

The probability method

There is evidence[8] that, when assessing probability distributions, individuals tend to be overconfident, so that they quote too narrow a range within which they think the uncertain quantity will lie. Some assessment methods fail to counteract this tendency. For example, if a decision-maker is asked initially for the median value of the distribution (this is the value that has a 50% chance of being exceeded), then this can act as an anchor. As we saw in Chapter 10, it is likely that he will make insufficient adjustments from this anchor when assessing other values in the distribution. For example, the value that has only a 10% chance of being exceeded might be estimated to be closer to the median than it should be, and the result will be a distribution that is too 'tight'.

Because of this, the following procedure,[9] which we will refer to as the probability method, is recommended:

Step 1: Establish the range of values within which the decision-maker thinks that the uncertain quantity will lie.

Step 2: Ask the decision-maker to imagine scenarios that could lead to the true value lying *outside* the range.

Step 3: Revise the range in the light of the responses in step 2.

Step 4: Divide the range into six or seven roughly equal intervals.

Step 5: Ask the decision-maker for the cumulative probability at each interval. This can either be a cumulative 'less than' distribution (e.g. what is the probability that the uncertain quantity will fall below each of these values?) or a cumulative 'greater than' (e.g. what is the probability that the uncertain quantity will exceed each of these values?), depending on which approach is easiest for the decision-maker.

Step 6: Fit a curve, by hand, through the assessed points.

Step 7: Carry out checks as follows.
   (i) Split the possible range into *three* equally likely intervals and find out if the decision-maker would be equally happy to place a bet on the uncertain quantity falling in each interval. If he is not, then make appropriate revisions to the distribution.
   (ii) Check the modality of the elicited distribution (a mode is a value where the probability distribution has a peak). For example, if the elicited probability distribution has a single mode (this can usually be recognized by examining the cumulative curve and seeing if it has a single inflection), ask the decision-maker if he does have a single best guess as to the value the uncertain quantity will assume. Again revise the distribution, if necessary.

Graph drawing

Graphs can be used in a number of ways to elicit probability distributions. In one approach, the analyst produces a set of graphs, each representing a different probability density function (pdf), and then asks the decision-maker to select the graph that most closely represents his or her judgment. In other approaches, the decision-maker might be asked to draw a graph to represent either a probability density function or a cumulative distribution function (cdf).

The *method of relative heights* is one well-known graphical technique that is designed to elicit a probability density function. First, the decision-maker is asked to identify the most likely value of the variable under consideration, and a vertical line is drawn on a graph to represent this likelihood. Shorter lines are then drawn for other possible values to show how their likelihoods compare with that of the most likely value.

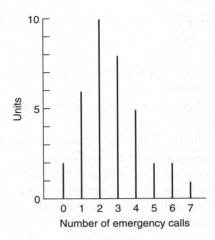

Figure 11.2 – The method of relative heights

To illustrate the method, let us suppose that a fire department has been asked to specify a probability distribution for the number of emergency calls it will receive on a public holiday. The chief administrator of the department considers that two is the most likely number of calls. To show this, the analyst draws on a graph a line that is ten units long (see Figure 11.2). Further questioning reveals that the administrator thinks that three requests are about 80% as likely as two, so this is represented by a line eight units long. The other lines are derived in a similar way, so that the likelihood of seven requests, for example, is considered to be only 10% as likely as two, and it is thought to be extremely unlikely that more than seven requests will be received. To convert the line lengths to probabilities, they need to be normalized so that they sum to 1. This can be achieved by dividing the length of each line by the sum of the line lengths, which is 36, as shown below (note that the probabilities do not sum exactly to 1 because of rounding):

Number of requests	Length of line	Probability
0	2	2/36 = 0.06
1	6	6/36 = 0.17
2	10	10/36 = 0.28
3	8	8/36 = 0.22
4	5	5/36 = 0.14
5	2	2/36 = 0.06
6	2	2/36 = 0.06
7	1	1/36 = 0.03
	36	1.00

The method of relative heights can also be used to assess probability density functions for continuous distributions. In this case the analyst will normally elicit the relative likelihood of a few values and then fit a smooth pdf curve across the tops of the lines.

A comparison of the assessment methods

Which method of probability assessment is the best? A number of experiments have been carried out to compare the methods, but these have not identified one single best method (see, for example, Seaver *et al.*[10] or Wallsten and Budescu[11]). Indeed, the main implication of these studies is that a variety of different methods should be used during the elicitation process. Nevertheless, certain types of approach will obviously be more acceptable than others to particular individuals. For example, some people may be happy to give direct assessments, while others will prefer the indirect approach.

Bunn and Thomas[12] argued that the use of devices such as probability wheels might be most appropriate for 'people who do not accept that psychological feelings [about probabilities] can be quantified'. Indeed, Spetzler and Stäel von Holstein[6] found that many people have difficulty in making direct judgments, and even those who feel capable of assessing probabilities in this way were often subsequently found to lack confidence in their responses. Most subjects, they claim, prefer the probability wheel. For this reason, they recommend that interviews should generally start with assessments based on this device, while other methods should be used at a later stage as consistency checks (by consistency checks we mean testing to see if an assessment obtained by different methods or approaches is firm). Our view is that, when a probability distribution has to be assessed, the *probability method* is usually the best approach to adopt because, as we argued earlier, it tends to overcome the tendency of decision-makers to estimate distributions that have too narrow a range.

Consistency and coherence checks

Consistency checks are, of course, a crucial element of probability assessment. The use of different assessment methods will often reveal inconsistencies which can then be fed back to the decision-maker. These inconsistencies should act as a stimulant to more intense thought, which, hopefully, will result in greater insight and improved judgment. Indeed, the axioms of probability theory give no guidance as to which is the best method for the elicitation of subjective probability. Empirical research in the psychological laboratory has shown that sometimes the indirect methods are inconsistent with direct methods, and sometimes they are not. Some investigators have demonstrated consistency between probability estimates inferred from wagers and direct estimates.[13] Others have shown that statistically naive subjects were inconsistent between direct and indirect assessment methods, whereas statisticians were not.[14] Generally, direct odds estimates, perhaps because they have no upper or lower limit, tend to be more extreme than direct probability estimates. If probability estimates derived by different methods for the same event are inconsistent, which method should be taken as the true index of degree of belief?

One way to answer this question is to use a single method of assessing subjective probability that is most consistent with itself. In other words, there should be high agreement between the subjective probabilities, assessed at different times by a single assessor for the same event, given that the assessor's knowledge of the event is unchanged. Unfortunately, there has been relatively little research on this important problem. One review[15] evaluated the results of several studies using direct estimation methods. Test–retest correlations were all above 0.88, with the exception of one study using students assessing odds – here the reliability was 0.66. It was concluded that most of the subjects in all experiments were very consistent when using a single assessment method.

The implications of this research for decision analysis are not clear cut. The decision analyst should be aware that different assessment techniques are likely to lead to different probability forecasts when these are converted to a common metric.

One useful *coherence* check is to elicit from the decision-maker not only the probability that an event will occur but also the probability that it will not occur. The two probabilities should, of course, sum to 1. Another variant of this technique is to decompose the probability of the event not occurring into the occurrence of other possible events. If the events are seen by the probability assessor as mutually exclusive, then the addition rule (Chapter 5) can be applied to evaluate the coherence of the assessments. Such checks are practically useful and are reinforced by the results of laboratory-based empirical studies of subjective probability assessment, where subjective probabilities attached to sets of mutually exclusive and exhaustive events have often been shown to sum to less than or more than 1. For example, Wright and Whalley[16] found that most untrained probability assessors followed the additivity axiom in simple two-outcome assessments involving the probabilities of an event happening and not happening. However, as the number of mutually exclusive and exhaustive events in a set was increased, more subjects became supra-additive, and supra-additive to a greater degree, in that their assessed probabilities tended to add to more than 1. With the number of mutually exclusive and exhaustive events in a set held constant, more subjects were supra-additive, and supra-additive to a greater degree, in the assessment of probabilities for an event set containing individuating information. In this study, the individuating background information was associated with the possible success of a racehorse in a race that was about to start. It consisted simply of a record of that horse's previous performances. It seems intuitively reasonable that most probabilistic predictions are based, in the main, on one's knowledge and not to any large extent on abstract notions such as additivity. Individuating information about the likelihood of an event's occurrence may psychologically disassociate an event from its event set. As we saw earlier in Chapter 10, a similar phenomenon has been noted by Tversky and Kahneman[17], and the term 'representativeness' was coined to refer to the dominance of individuating information in intuitive prediction.

A recent study[18] asked respondents four questions such as 'What is the chance that you will die of lung cancer? Place an estimate between 0% and 100% in the space below.' Another question asked 'What is the chance that you will die from each of the following . . .?' Here, nine possible causes of death were stated, including lung cancer. Respondents were told that, because the list included all possible causes of death (a catch-all of all possible causes was the ninth alternative), then responses should add to 100%. This instruction ensured additivity in the assessed probabilities. The results revealed that the average answer to death from lung cancer in the first question was 15%, while the average answer to the same component of the second question was 10%. For smokers, the two answers averaged at 30% and 17% respectively. The use of frequency estimates (e.g. 'How many people will die of lung cancer if they smoke two packs a day?' and 'How many people will die from each of the following causes if they smoke two packs a day . . .?') produced similar results. Clearly, the way that a target probability assessment is elicited can result in very different numerical assessments.

In short, judgmental forecasts should be monitored for additivity and any incoherence should be resolved. However, a simple normalization may not be a quick and easy solution to incoherence. Lindley *et al.*[19] outlined a major problem:

> Suppose that I assess the probabilities of a set of mutually exclusive and exhaustive events to be
>
> $$0.001, \ 0.250, \ 0.200, \ 0.100, \ 0.279$$
>
> It is then pointed out to me that these probabilities sum to 0.830 and hence that the assessment is incoherent. If we use the method . . . with the probability metric, we have to adjust the probabilities by adding 0.034 to each ($= (1/5)(1 - 0.830)$) to give
>
> $$0.035, \ 0.284, \ 0.234, \ 0.134, \ 0.313$$
>
> The problem is that the first event, which I originally regarded as very unlikely, has had its probability increased by a factor of 35! Though still small it is no longer smaller than the others by two orders of magnitude.

Obviously, other methods of allocating probability shortfalls can be devised, but our view is that the best solution to such problems is for the decision analyst to show the decision-maker his or her incoherence and so allow *iterative* resolution of departures from this (and other) axioms of probability theory. Such iteration can involve the analyst plotting the responses on a graph (e.g. as a cumulative distribution function) and establishing whether the decision-maker is happy that this is an accurate reflection of his or her judgments. Finally, the decision-maker can be offered a series of pairs of bets. Each pair can be formulated so that the respondent will be indifferent between them if he or she is behaving consistently with assessments that were made earlier.

Assessing the validity of probabilities

The probabilities we have assessed may be both consistent and coherent, but are they necessarily valid predictions of the chances of future events occurring? For example, consider again a person estimating the probability of rain in a given place on two successive days. They may be coherent in that their estimate of 0.04 is the product of their estimates of it raining on each day (0.2×0.2) and consistent in that they produced the same estimate when different methods were employed to elicit their probability. However, another person may also have produced coherent and consistent probabilities and arrived at a probability estimate of 0.25 that it will rain in the specified place on the two successive days. Clearly, both probabilities cannot be valid, so consistency and coherence do not guarantee validity. This raises the question as to which, if any, of the two probabilities is valid.

A major measure of the validity of subjective probability estimates is known as *calibration*. For example, suppose that you study the records of a television weather forecaster and find that in the last 3 months in his evening broadcast he made the following forecast on each of 20 days: 'The probability of it raining tomorrow in this region is 60%.' You then look at what happened on each of the 20 days that followed these forecasts. If it rained on 12 of these 20 days (i.e. 60% of the days), then the forecaster was perfectly calibrated. Thus, for perfect calibration, if you look back at occasions when you stated a probability of x%, the event should have occurred on exactly x% of these occasions. Of course, on other days the weatherman will have used different probabilities such as 10% or 20%. We can display his calibration for all of the probabilities he has used on a calibration curve (see Figure 11.3). If his probabilities are perfectly calibrated, they will follow the diagonal line. The lower curve indicates a tendency to estimate probabilities that are too high (e.g. on occasions when a probability of 0.4 was estimated, the event only occurred 20% of the time), while the upper curve would indicate probabilities that are too low.

Although calibration is a useful measure, it can be manipulated by a forecaster. For example, suppose that a long history of weather records shows that in a particular part of the world it rains on 28% of days. A television weather forecaster could simply quote a probability of 0.28 every time he makes the forecast – never varying from this figure. In the long run he will be perfectly calibrated, as it will rain on 28% of the days when he makes this forecast. However, his forecast will be uninformative because he

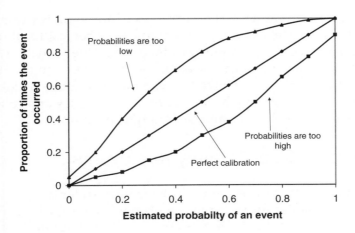

Figure 11.3 – Calibration curves

makes no effort to distinguish between days when rain is highly likely and days when fine weather is assured. Indeed, there would be no point in tuning in to watch the forecaster, as you will always know what his forecast will be. Because of this, a number of additional measures have been devised to assess the validity of probability forecasts. The most well known of these is the Brier score.[20] This is calculated as follows:

$$\text{Brier score (BS)} = 1 - (x - p)^2$$

where $x = 1$ if the event occurs and $x = 0$ if it does not, and p is the probability estimate.

The score ranges from 0 to 1, with 1 representing the most 'accurate' judgment. If another weather forecaster estimates that the probability of rain tomorrow in a particular place is 0.3 and it *does* rain, then her Brier score will be

$$1 - (1 - 0.3)^2 = 0.51$$

Because it has rained she would have achieved a higher score if she had put forward a higher probability. For example, probabilities of 0.7, 0.9 and 1 would have led to Brier scores of 0.91, 0.99 and 1 respectively, with the latter being the highest possible score. Of course, putting forward a probability of 1 is highly risky because, if it does not rain, the lowest Brier score of 0 would be obtained. The Brier score is known to be a strictly proper scoring rule because it can be shown that it rewards honest judgments. A weather forecaster who deliberately tried to manipulate his score by misrepresenting what he really believed was the true probability would not obtain the maximum score in the long run.

Although we have just calculated Brier scores for a single occurrence of an event, both calibration and the Brier score are intended to assess the validity of a person's probabilities over a larger number of occurrences of an event. For example, we could calculate a weather forecaster's average Brier score over her last 100 forecasts. For people who need to make regular probability estimates (e.g. the probability that a product will be out of stock at the end of each week), the Brier score can be a useful measure of the quality of their estimates. However, when managers are making forecasts for one-off events, we have to rely on the attributes of consistency and coherence to make an (imperfect) assessment of how valid their judgments are.

Assessing probabilities for very rare events

Assessment techniques that differ from those we have so far discussed are generally required when probabilities for very rare events have to be assessed. Such events are often of interest because of the disastrous consequences that may be associated with their occurrence. The catastrophic failure of a nuclear power plant, the collapse of a dam or the release of toxic fumes from a chemical factory are obvious examples of these events.

Because of the rarity of such events, there is usually little or no reliable past data that can support a relative frequency approach to the probability assessment, and subjective estimates may be subject to biases that result from the use of the availability heuristic. For example, it may be easy to imagine circumstances that would lead to the event occurring even though these circumstances are extremely improbable. Moreover, as von Winterfeldt and Edwards[21] point out, rare events are newsworthy almost by definition, and widespread reports of their occurrence may have the effect of intensifying the availability bias. Decision-makers are also likely to have problems in conceiving the magnitudes involved in the probability assessment. It is difficult to distinguish between probabilities such as 0.0001 and 0.000001, yet the first probability is a 100 times greater than the second.

Obviously, a probability wheel would be of little use in assessing probabilities like these. There are, however, a number of ways in which the problems of assessing very low probabilities can be tackled. Event trees and fault trees allow the problem to be decomposed so that the combinations of factors that may cause the rare event to occur can be identified. Each of the individual factors may have a relatively high (and therefore more easily assessed) probability of occurrence. A log-odds scale allows the individual to discriminate more clearly between very low probabilities. We will examine each of these approaches below.

Event trees

Event trees are the same as the probability trees that we met in Chapter 5. Figure 11.4 shows a simplified tree for a catastrophic failure at an industrial plant. Each stage

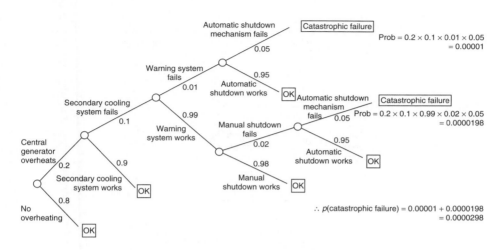

Figure 11.4 – An event tree

of the tree represents a factor that might, in combination with others, lead to the catastrophe. Rather than being asked to perform the difficult task of directly estimating the probability of catastrophic failure, the decision-maker is asked instead to assess the probability that each factor will contribute to it. Then, by using the multiplication and addition rules of probability, the overall probability of failure can be calculated (note that, for simplicity, here it has been assumed that all the factors operate independently). Of course, it is important to try to ensure that the tree is as complete as possible so that all possible causes of the event in question are included (see Chapter 7). However, it may be difficult or impossible to assess subjective probabilities for such events as human error, deliberate sabotage and, by definition, unforeseen weaknesses in a system.

Fault trees

Sometimes it is easier to consider the problem from a different point of view. In contrast to event trees, fault trees start with the failure or accident and then depict the possible causes of that failure. For example, suppose that a decision-maker wants to assess the probability that a vital pipeline in a chemical plant will fracture within the next 12 months. Figure 11.5 shows a fault tree for his problem. He considers that a fracture would occur if there is either a defective weld or excess pressure in the pipeline. Because either event on its own would be sufficient to cause the fracture, these two events are connected to the 'pipeline fracture' node by an 'or' symbol. The excess pressure in turn, however, would only occur if there was *both* a regulator failure *and* a

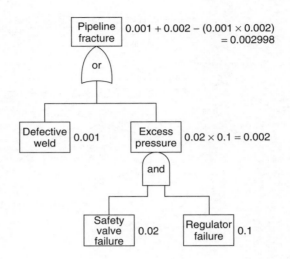

Figure 11.5 – A fault tree

failure in the safety valve, so an 'and' symbol connects these two events to the 'excess pressure' node.

The decision-maker can now assess probabilities for the lowest level events (these probabilities are shown on the tree) and then work up the tree until he eventually obtains the probability of the pipeline fracturing. As the safety valve and regulator failures are considered to be independent, their probabilities can be multiplied to obtain the probability of excess pressure. This probability can then be added to the probability of a weld being defective to obtain the probability of the pipe fracture occurring. (Note that, as excess pressure and a defective weld are not mutually exclusive events, the very low probability of them both occurring has been subtracted from the sum – see Chapter 5.) Of course, in practice, most fault trees will be more extensive than this one. Indeed, the decision-maker in this problem may wish to extend the tree downwards to identify the possible causes of safety valve or regulator failure in order to make a better assessment of these probabilities.

Using a log-odds scale

Because people generally have problems in distinguishing between probabilities such as 0.001 and 0.0001, some analysts prefer to use what is known as a log-odds scale to elicit the probabilities of rare events. You will recall that odds represent the probability that an event will occur divided by the probability that it will not. By converting

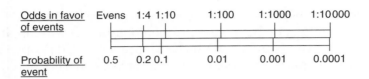

Figure 11.6 – A log-odds scale

probabilities to odds and then taking the logarithms of the results, we arrive at a scale like that shown in Figure 11.6 (this figure shows the scale only for probabilities below 0.5). An analyst using the scale would ask the decision-maker to mark the point that represents his or her assessment of the likelihood of the event occurring. Note that the effect of using log-odds is to spread out the ends of the probability scale, making assessment of very high and low probabilities clearer. The scale also ranges from minus to plus infinity, which makes it very difficult for individuals to assert that particular events are impossible or certain to occur. According to Bunn and Thomas,[12] the log-odds scale appears to correspond to the internal scale that individuals use when assessing odds.

Communicating probability estimates

Probability judgments are made by one person but will often be used by others. People tend to prefer to receive extreme confidence estimates (i.e. high probabilities) because confidence is a cue to the knowledge or competence of the person providing the estimate. However, such knowledge or competence can only be evaluated with hindsight – when the forecast outcomes are known. Nevertheless, we tend to use a person's stated confidence as a rough guide to whether the forecaster will be correct in her forecasts.[22] But, of course, a well-calibrated person may, appropriately, not express extreme confidence. Context also plays a part in our interpretation of probability forecasts. In one study,[23] participants read about a woman who was told by her doctor that, because of a blood condition, she had a 30% chance of developing a disease related to malaria on an upcoming trip. Those who read that the trip was to India expressed greater certainty that she would, in fact, get the disease than those who read that the trip's destination was Hawaii. In another study, these researchers added either pessimistic or optimistic reasons to a surgeon's 'bottom-line' probability estimate of a successful operation. Here, the bottom-line estimate did not serve as such – those who read the pessimistic reasons were less sure of a successful outcome than those who read the optimistic reasons. Also, use of the frequency format can increase the 'imaginability' of low-probability events. A recent study[24] asked participants to consider negative events (being scarred by laser surgery) and positive events (winning the lottery) which were presented either (i) with an attached probability of 0.01 or (ii) with an equivalent attached frequency – '20 people out of 2000'. In the latter case, participants were more frightened of laser surgery and more confident of winning the lottery.

Summary

In this chapter we have described the process by which a decision analyst elicits subjective probability assessments from the decision-maker. Within the analyst's toolbox of techniques are indirect and direct methods for both discrete and continuous assessments. Consistency and coherence checks are used extensively to monitor the assessment process, as validity is a more problematic criterion when probabilities for one-off events are being assessed. The chapter concluded with a description of elicitation methods that are used for very rare events, and introduced issues to do with the communication of probabilities.

Exercises

(1) Use the probability wheel and direct estimate methods to elicit a colleague's subjective probabilities for the outcomes of a forthcoming sports event (e.g. a snooker tournament). Check for consistency between the assessment methods and use the addition rule to evaluate the coherence of the probabilities that your colleague has assessed.

(2) Use the probability method to elicit a colleague's subjective probability distribution for his or her marks in the next decision analysis assignment.

(3) Repeat the above exercise for predictions of the starting salary distribution in his or her first employment after completing the current educational course of study.

(4) An electricity company supplies power to consumers in the eastern region of a country. When the demand for power exceeds the capacity of the cheapest generating station, a second station is brought 'on line'. One of the company's managers makes a daily judgment about the probability that the second station will be required at least once in the following day. The records of his judgments are given below for a period of 600 days:

	Probability assessed by manager				
	0	**0.2**	**0.5**	**0.8**	**1.0**
Number of days this probability judgment was made	40	160	180	120	100
Number of days second station was used	8	50	110	110	100

(a) Plot a calibration curve for the manager and interpret the result.
(b) Calculate the manager's average Brier score.
(c) Suppose that the manager had simply quoted a probability of 0.5 on all 600 days. What would his Brier score have been?

References

1. Moore, P.G. and Thomas, H. (1988) *The Anatomy of Decisions*, 2nd edition, Penguin, Harmondsworth, UK.
2. Smits, T and Hoorens, V. (2005) How probable is probable? It depends on whom you are asking, *Journal of Behavioral Decision Making*, **18**, 83–96.
3. Einhorn, H.J. (1980) Overconfidence in judgment, in *New Directions for Methodology of Social and Behavioral Science: No. 4*, ed. by Shweder, R.A. and Fiske, D.W., Jossey-Bass, San Francisco, CA.
4. Fischhoff, B. and Beyth, R. (1975) 'I knew it would happen'. Remembered probabilities of once-future things, *Organizational Behavior and Human Performance*, **13**, 1–16.
5. Fischhoff, B. (1975) Hindsight? Foresight: the effect of outcome knowledge on judgment under uncertainty, *Journal of Experimental Psychology: Human Perception and Performance*, **1**, 288–299.
6. Spetzler, C.S. and Stäel von Holstein, C.A. (1975) Probability encoding in decision analysis, *Management Science*, **22**, 340–352.
7. Shephard, G.G. and Kirkwood, C.W. (1994) Managing the judgmental probability elicitation process: a case study of analyst/manager interaction, *IEEE Transactions on Engineering Management*, **41**, 414–425.
8. Lichtenstein, S., Fischhoff, B. and Phillips, L.D. (1981) Calibration of probabilities: state of the art to 1980, in *Judgment under Uncertainty: Heuristics and Biases*, ed. by Kahneman, D., Slovic, P. and Tversky, A., Cambridge University Press, New York, NY.
9. For more details of the probability approach, see Stäel von Holstein, C.A. and Matheson, J. (1979) *A Manual for Encoding Probability Distributions*, SRI International, Menlo Park, CA.

10. Seaver, D.A., von Winterfeldt, D. and Edwards, W. (1978) Eliciting subjective probability distributions on continuous variables, *Organizational Behavior and Human Performance*, **21**, 379–391.

11. Wallsten, T.S. and Budescu, D.V. (1983) Encoding subjective probabilities: a psychological and psychometric review, *Management Science*, **29**, 151–173.

12. Bunn, D.W. and Thomas, H. (1975) Assessing subjective probability in decision analysis, in *The Role and Effectiveness of Theories of Decision in Practice*, ed. by White, D.J. and Bowen, K.C., Hodder & Stoughton, London, UK.

13. For example, Beach, L.R. and Phillips, L.D. (1967) Subjective probabilities inferred from estimate and bets, *Journal of Experimental Psychology*, **75**, 354–359.

14. For example, Winkler, R.L. (1967) The assessment of prior distributions in Bayesian analysis, *Journal of the American Statistical Association*, **62**, 776–800.

15. Phillips, L.D., Hays, W.L. and Edwards, W. (1966) Conservatism in complex probabilistic inference, *IEEE Transactions in Human Factors in Electronics*, **7**, 7–18.

16. Wright, G. and Whalley, P.C. (1983) The supra-additivity of subjective probability, in *Foundation of Risk and Utility Theory with Applications*, ed. by Stigum, B. and Wenstop, F., Dordrecht: Reidel.

17. Tversky, A. and Kahneman, D. (1974) Judgment under uncertainty: heuristics and biases, *Science*, **185**, 1124–1131.

18. Windschitl, P.D. (2002) Judging the accuracy of likelihood judgment: the case of smoking risk, *Journal of Behavioral Decision Making*, **15**, 19–35.

19. Lindley, D.V., Tversky, A. and Brown, R.V. (1979) On the reconciliation of probability assessments, *Journal of the Royal Statistical Society*, **142**, 146–180; see also Ayton, P. and Wright, G. (1987) Assessing and improving judgmental probability forecasts, *Omega*, **15**, 191–196, and Wright, G., Ayton, P. and Whalley, P.C. (1985) A general purpose aid to judgmental probability forecasting, *Decision Support Systems*, **1**, 333–340.

20. Brier, G.W. (1950) Verification of forecasts expressed in terms of probability. *Monthly Weather Review*, **78**, 1–3.

21. von Winterfeldt, D. and Edwards, W. (1986) *Decision Analysis and Behavioral Research*, Cambridge University Press, New York, NY.

22. Price, P.C. and Stone E.R. (2004) Intuitive evaluation of likelihood judgment producers, *Journal of Behavioral Decision Making*, **17**, 39–57.

23. Flugstad, A.R. and Windschitl, P.D. (2003) The influence of reasons on interpretations of probability forecasts, *Journal of Behavioral Decision Making*, **16**, 107–126.

24. Newell, B.R., Mitchell, C.J. and Hayes, B.K. (2008) Getting scarred and winning lotteries: effects of exemplar cuing and statistical format on imagining low-probability events, *Journal of Behavioral Decision Making*, **21**, 317–335.

Risk and uncertainty management 12

Introduction

In earlier chapters we have shown how decision models can help managers to gain insights into decision problems that involve substantial elements of risk. However, the risks themselves have been treated as being unchangeable, and we have assumed that the manager simply has to accept them and make the best decision in the light of them. This is not the way that many managers view their role.[1] In fact, rather than passively accepting risks, managers see it as their duty to take actions to reduce them. Indeed, many managers would go further than this and say that their role is also to identify opportunities.

With this perspective, the development of the decision model is seen as only part of a process that is designed to stimulate further thinking on how risks can be modified or how the chosen course of action can be made to yield even better returns than the current model indicates.[2] As Chapman and Ward[3] point out, the two goals of reducing risk and pursuing opportunities need to be balanced – some opportunities will lead to increased risk, while reducing risk may be achieved at the expense of forgoing new opportunities. The term 'uncertainty management' is being increasingly used to describe the process of achieving this balance, and decision models can provide a structure for this process. For example, a model may indicate that we should go ahead and launch a new product but that this is associated with a 20% risk of a net present value (NPV) of −$15 million. The model can now be used for identifying the sources of uncertainty and selecting those that provide the best prospects for taking actions to reduce risk or discovering new opportunities. Creativity techniques like brainstorming can then be employed to complement the decision analysis so that new potential solutions emerge. Perhaps production equipment, which may need to be upgraded after only a few years, can be rented from the manufacturer rather than purchased outright; perhaps the product can be jointly marketed in an overseas market with a local company so that risk there is shared or perhaps the product's design can be modified to allow easy upgrading without the need for substantial retooling if competition necessitates design modifications.

This chapter uses a case study to illustrate how a decision model can be employed to provide a structured approach to uncertainty management. In addition, we will give an outline of brainstorming to show how it can be used to elicit creative uncertainty management solutions from management teams.

The Two Valleys Company

The Two Valleys Company is diversifying into the production of an electronic product and has to decide where to locate its manufacture. Two suitable factories are available to be rented. The factory at Callum Falls is large enough to cope with any foreseeable level of demand, but the alternative location at Littleton would only have the capacity to produce 5 million units of the product per year.

A value tree (see Chapter 3) was used to identify the attributes relevant to the decision problem. These attributes included quality of local transport infrastructure, environmental impact, availability of a skilled labor force and financial return. It was evident that both sites performed very similarly on nearly all of the attributes, except for financial return. There was also considerable uncertainty about the return that could be achieved at each site.

Demand for the product could come from two sources. First, there is the possibility of signing a contract with a major customer for the supply of 1 million units of the product per year. This customer would receive a discount of $0.20 on the normal price of the product, which would be set at $5 per unit, but the customer would not be willing to sign the contract until after the production facility had been set up. Second, the product would be sold on the open market.

Exploring sources of uncertainty

As a first step to managing this uncertainty, an exploratory tree was formulated to represent the factors that contributed to the uncertainty of financial return. This is shown in Figure 12.1. Table 12.1 shows the estimated ranges of values of these factors and their most likely values.

Probability distributions were then estimated for the costs and level of open-market demand. It was also estimated that there was a 0.6 probability that the contract would be signed. A risk-analysis simulation model (see Chapter 8) was then used to generate cumulative probability distributions for the annual profit of each site. These are shown in Figure 12.2.

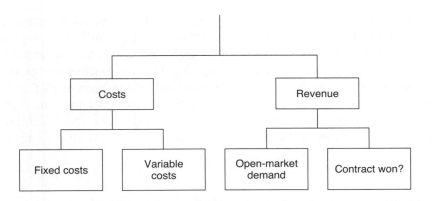

Figure 12.1 – Sources of uncertainty at the Two Valleys Company

Table 12.1 – Estimated values for uncertain factors

	Location					
	Callum Falls			Littleton		
Factor	Lowest	Most likely	Highest	Lowest	Most likely	Highest
Annual fixed costs ($m)	6	7.5	9	2	4	6
Variable cost per unit ($)	2.7	3.0	3.3	3.2	3.5	3.8
Annual demand (units in millions)	1	4	7	(as for Callum Falls)		
p (contract won?)	0	0.6	1	(as for Callum Falls)		

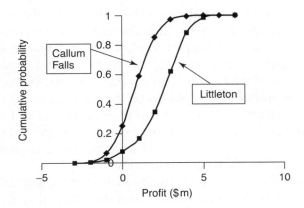

Figure 12.2 – Cumulative probability distributions for annual profit at the two sites

The simulation shows that Littleton exhibits first-order stochastic dominance over Callum Falls. In addition, its expected annual profit is $2.38 million, as opposed to only $1.52 million for Callum Falls. However, although Littleton is the preferred location in terms of annual profit, it is not a risk-free option. The simulation revealed that it has an 8% probability of generating a loss, and this could be as high as $2.8 million.

The managers wanted to investigate the possibility of reducing this risk, and also to explore the possibility of taking actions that would make the Littleton site even more profitable by increasing the payoffs that are associated with the higher levels of demand.

Identifying possible areas for uncertainty management

A structured method of risk management first allows the manager to identify and evaluate the most promising areas where risk might be reduced or payoffs enhanced.[1] This can involve the following approach.

1. Calculate the effect of perfect control

This can be achieved by first looking at the option that the decision model suggests should be preferred and then determining how the probability distribution of the annual profit would change if the decision-maker were able to exercise control over the events that the model assumed were uncertain. Of course, in reality it is very unlikely that the decision-maker will have perfect control, but the results of the calculations will provide some guidance on whether it is worth devoting effort to try to improve the probabilities or values associated with these uncertain events.

Table 12.1 shows that in the Two Valleys problem the managers were uncertain about (i) annual fixed costs, (ii) variable costs, (iii) whether the contract was agreed with the major customer and (iv) the level of open-market demand. Suppose that actions could be taken to ensure that the contract was agreed. By how much would this increase the expected annual profit, and what would the probability distribution of profit now look like? If we increase the probability of obtaining the contract to 1.0 and carry out a new simulation, this reveals that the expected profit associated with Littleton increases to $2.7 million – an increase of just $320 000 on the current expected payoff. In addition, the risk of a loss decreases from 5.7 to 2.9%. Littleton's limited capacity means that its dependence on winning the contract is relatively low.

We can carry out similar analyses on the other uncertain quantities, changing each in turn to its most favorable value while assuming the other quantities cannot be controlled. What if the managers could take actions to ensure that the fixed costs of Littleton were at their lowest possible value of $2 million? What if they were able to

Table 12.2 – Results of risk management actions

Action	Increase in expected profit	Risk of a loss	Lowest possible profit
Do nothing	$0.0	8.0%	−$2.8m
Contract signed	$0.32m	2.9%	−$2.4m
Fixed costs at lowest	$1.98m	0.2%	−$1.8m
Highest possible demand	$0.95m	0	$0.33m
Variable costs at lowest	$1.22m	1.8%	−$2.0m

ensure that open-market demand would be equivalent to the highest possible level of demand that Littleton could cope with (5 million units, or 4 million units if the contract is signed)? What if they could ensure that variable costs will be at their lowest possible level? Table 12.2 summarizes the results of simulations that were run to determine the effect of these actions.

The results suggest that trying to reduce fixed and variable costs or increase demand has the greatest potential for increasing expected profit and reducing the chances of incurring a loss. In contrast, looking into ways that might increase the chances of the contract being accepted and efforts to reduce variable costs are likely to be less productive.

Obtaining these results involves a lot of effort. Each action that is being evaluated requires a new simulation run, and in a complex problem involving a large number of uncertain quantities this could be extremely time consuming. A quicker method that is available on most risk-analysis packages involves the generation of a tornado diagram. As discussed in Chapter 8, this will show the effect on the profit if each of the uncertain quantities in turn varies between its lowest and highest possible values, while all of the other factors are held at their most likely values. For example, if fixed costs are at their lowest value of $2 million, but the other factors are at their most likely values (variable costs per unit $3.5, annual demand 4 million units and p(contract signed) $=$ 0.6), then the annual profit can be found as follows:

$$\begin{aligned} &\text{Annual profit} \\ &= \text{demand(price} - \text{variable costs)} + p(\text{contract}) \\ &\quad \times \text{contract sales(discounted price} - \text{variable costs)} - \text{fixed costs} \\ \\ &= 4\,000\,000(5 - 3.5) + 0.6 \times 1\,000\,000(4.8 - 3.5) - 2\,000\,000 \\ &= \$4.78 \text{ million} \end{aligned}$$

Note that, in this calculation, we have used the *expected* sales that will be achieved from the contract (0.6 × 1 million) rather than the most likely sales level, which is of course

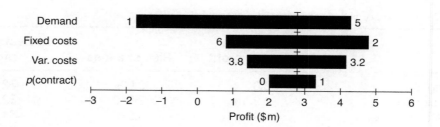

Figure 12.3 – Tornado diagram for Littleton

1 million. This is because the contract sales will turn out to be one of two extremes, 0 or 1 million units. The compromise value of 0.6 million is more appropriate, given that it is the variation in fixed costs that we are investigating.

Figure 12.3 shows the tornado diagram for the Littleton site. Note that the chart displays the lowest and highest possible values of each factor at the ends of the bars. Although the diagram does not provide as much information as Table 12.2, it conveys the same general message and clearly indicates where the best opportunities for uncertainty management are likely to be. For example, the variation in fixed costs is associated with a major variation in profit, and the same is true for open-market demand. In contrast, a relatively small variation in profit is associated with whether or not the contract is signed. Efforts to control variable costs also appear to be less crucial.

2. Repeat the above process for the next best option

This is only worth considering if the next best option has performed almost as well as that of the currently favored option in the initial risk analysis. If it has, or if the choice between the options is not clear, then this option may actually offer better opportunities if imaginative strategies can be designed to reduce risks and enhance returns. Figure 12.4 shows a tornado diagram for Callum Falls.

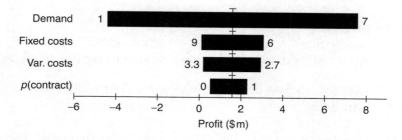

Figure 12.4 – Tornado diagram for Callum Falls

As expected, Callum Falls, with its much larger capacity but higher fixed costs, would only be worth considering if a strategy could be designed to make a high level of demand very likely, otherwise its profit will probably be below that which could be achieved at Littleton. At this stage it would probably be a good idea to keep Callum Falls 'in the frame' to see if a feasible 'high-demand' strategy can be designed.

Using brainstorming to create actions to improve the preferred policy

Creative thinking can be used by the management team to produce actions that will potentially reduce the risk and identify opportunities. Brainstorming is one technique that can enhance creativity. Other techniques for generating ideas include lateral thinking,[4] synectics, checklists and forced relationships.[5] Brainstorming was developed in the 1930s and is usually regarded as a method to be used with groups of people. Although it can be employed by individuals, the benefit of involving a group is that one person's ideas can help to stimulate even more ideas by other group members.

Underlying brainstorming is the idea that people's creativity is restricted because they tend to reject ideas at too early a stage. This may be because they impose imaginary constraints on a problem or make false assumptions. Alternatively, they may be unable to see a problem from multiple perspectives, or they stereotype problems and possible solutions and hence fail to see their wider potential. For example, negotiations with a customer may be seen as a financial issue. Viewing it as a marketing issue may enable non-financial incentives to be packaged with the product one is trying to sell.

Brainstorming has four basic rules:

(1) *Do not criticize ideas* – the solution to the problem may turn out to lie in an idea that, initially, may seem to be crazy.
(2) *Encourage participants to put forward any idea that they can think of* – particularly unconventional or outlandish ideas.
(3) *Aim to generate large quantities of ideas* – in that way there is a greater chance that one or more of the ideas will lead to a solution to the problem.
(4) *Encourage people to combine or modify ideas* that have already been put forward.

A brainstorming session can be run in several ways. However, ideally, in addition to the group members, it will involve a facilitator, whose role is to create a relaxed atmosphere, to encourage new ideas and to control the group's discussion, and a person to record the ideas put forward. At the start of the session the specific problem is defined (for example, how can we increase the probability of the major customer signing the contact?) and displayed on a board or screen. Then ideas are suggested one at a time and recorded. When the group appears to be unable to generate further ideas, the list is evaluated and the best ideas are chosen.

Table 12.3 – Ideas for risk management at the Two Valleys Company

Question	Ideas
How can we reduce fixed costs?	Try to renegotiate rent Run administrative tasks at company HQ rather than at local factory Contract out research and development Buy equipment that is easily upgraded if technology advances Contract out transport and delivery
How can we increase open-market demand?	Lower price Advertise in trade journals Increase number of sales representatives Attend more trade fairs Reduce percentage of defective components
How can we reduce variable costs per unit?	Reduce waste Increase frequency of service of manufacturing plant Reduce packaging Optimize inventory levels for finished goods Choose alternative supplier for materials Put product instructions on the Internet rather than supplying hard copy
How can we increase the chances of the contract being signed?	Offer a larger price discount Offer free delivery Offer extended warranty period Involve customer in ongoing design improvements Offer buy-back of old components in event of upgrade

Table 12.3 shows some typical ideas that might be generated through brainstorming for the Two Valleys Company. The best ideas will then need to be investigated to establish whether they are feasible and realistic, and they will also need to be costed. Recall that our analysis has revealed that answers to the first two questions are most likely to be of value. The simulation model can then be rerun with the revised inputs and the results assessed.

In this case, the following package of measures was investigated: (i) run administrative tasks at company HQ rather than at the local factory, (ii) contract out research and development, (iii) buy equipment that is easily upgraded if technology advances and (iv) put the product instructions on the Internet rather than supplying hard copy. All of the measures appeared to be feasible. The probability distributions for costs were re-estimated in the light of these changes, and the new model was simulated. Figure 12.5 shows the new and old cumulative probability distributions of annual

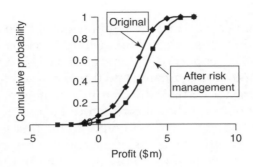

Figure 12.5 – The effectiveness of risk management measures

profit at Littleton. It can be seen that the effect of these measures is to push the bulk of the distribution to the right. This means that any given profit up to $7 million has a higher probability of being achieved, while the probability of a loss has been more than halved to 3%.

Summary

This chapter has shown that risks represented in decision models need not be regarded as immutable. The proactive manager who is unwilling to accept these risks passively can use the decision model to provide a structured approach to identifying where effort should be invested in creating strategies that reduce risks and improve payoffs. The use of creativity techniques like brainstorming can complement decision analysis by generating imaginative ideas for reducing risk and identifying opportunities from management teams. Once generated, these ideas can then be evaluated using the structure provided by decision analysis. The benefits of this structured approach to risk management can be significant, and the resulting courses of action can lead to much greater returns.

Exercise

(1) The AB Charity is planning its annual campaign to raise money. This year, three alternative methods are being considered: (i) street collections, (ii) a television advertising campaign and (iii) a direct-mail appeal. After using simulation to assess the risk associated with the alternatives, the charity's managers have opted for a direct-mail appeal.

The direct-mail appeal will involve sending out 343 000 letters to selected people. To encourage donations, these will include a free ballpoint pen displaying the charity's logo, and people not replying after 3 weeks will receive a reminder. While the fixed costs of the campaign and the cost of sending out each letter and reminder are known for certain, the charity's managers have had to estimate probability distributions for the following four factors:

(a) the percentage of people who will reply to the first letter in the North (N), Central (C) and South (S) regions of the country respectively;
(b) the average donation of those replying to the first letter in each of these regions;
(c) the percentage of people who will reply to the reminder in each of the three regions;
(d) the average donation of those replying to the reminder in each of the regions.

Probability distributions have been estimated for the different regions because their different economic conditions are likely to have a major effect on people's propensity to donate to the charity.

Figure 12.6 shows the cumulative probability distribution of net returns (i.e. the total value of donations *less* the cost of running the direct-mail appeal). It can be seen that there is approximately a 20% probability that the net returns will be negative, causing the charity to lose money. In the simulation, the possible losses extended to nearly $150 000.

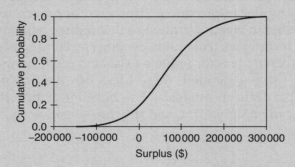

Figure 12.6 – Cumulative probability distribution for the AB Charity

The managers of the charity are keen to take action to reduce this risk, but are not sure where their actions should be directed? Figure 12.7 shows a tornado diagram for the appeal. The numbers at the ends of the bars show what are thought to be the highest and lowest possible values for each factor. For example, the possible average donation in the North is thought to range from $2 to $17.

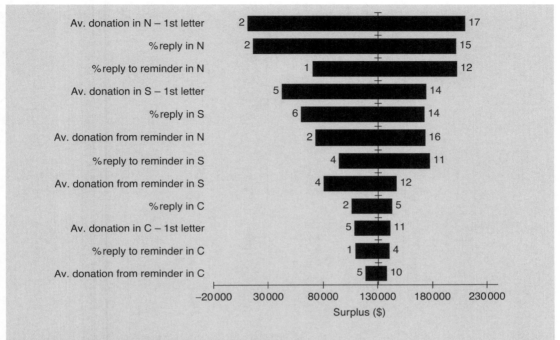

Av. donation in N – 1st letter	2		17
%reply in N	2		15
%reply to reminder in N	1		12
Av. donation in S – 1st letter	5		14
%reply in S	6		14
Av. donation from reminder in N	2		16
%reply to reminder in S	4		11
Av. donation from reminder in S	4		12
%reply in C	2		5
Av. donation in C – 1st letter	5		11
%reply to reminder in C	1		4
Av. donation from reminder in C	5		10

−20000   30000   80000   130000   180000   230000

Surplus ($)

Figure 12.7 – Tornado diagram for the AB Charity

(a) Identify the areas where risk management is likely to be most effective.

(b) Create a set of possible risk management strategies that might reduce the risk of the charity losing money and increase its expected return.

References

1. Chelst, K. and Bodily, S.E. (2000) Structured risk management: filling a gap in decision analysis education, *Journal of the Operational Research Society*, **51**, 1420–1432.
2. Rothkopf, M.H. (1996) Models as aids to thought, *Interfaces*, **26**, 64–67.
3. Chapman, C. and Ward, S. (2002) *Managing Project Risk and Uncertainty: A Constructively Simple Approach to Decision Making*, John Wiley & Sons, Ltd, Chichester, UK. This book contains many other practical ideas for exploring and managing uncertainty.
4. de Bono, E. (1990) *Lateral Thinking: A Textbook of Creativity*, Penguin, London, UK.
5. Evans, J.R. (1991) *Creative Thinking in the Decision and Management Sciences*, South-Western, Cincinnati, OH.

Decisions involving groups of individuals 13

Introduction

So far in this book we have focused on the individual decision-maker, but important decisions are often made by accountable managers working within small groups of people, most, or all, of whom have information that could be utilized in the decision-making process. Often, individuals may differ in their subjective probabilities of events, their utilities of outcomes or in their perception of the future courses of action that may become available as events unfold into the future.

If the opinions and values of individuals differ, how should the differences be resolved? Obviously, several individuals who are involved in decision-making bring together a larger fund of experience, knowledge and creative insights. It is intuitively reasonable that the chances of overlooking possible events and possible courses of action are diminished in group decision-making. Indeed, the synergy of individuals may make the overall quality of the group decision greater than the sum of the parts. The creation of juries, panels and cabinets as ways of reaching decisions can be seen to be based on this premise.

This chapter describes and evaluates ways of combining individual judgments to produce 'improved' judgments. There are essentially two approaches to the problem: mathematical and behavioral aggregation (although the approaches can be combined). *Mathematical aggregation*, which we will discuss first, involves techniques such as the calculation of a simple average of the judgments of the individual group members. In *behavioral aggregation* a group judgment is reached by members of the group communicating with each other either in open discussion or via a more structured communication process.

Two simple advantages arise from obtaining group judgments in decision analysis. First, more information about possible ranges of utilities and probabilities can be obtained, and it is then possible to perform sensitivity analysis on these ranges to see if the decision specified by the analysis is changed by these variations. Second, a group of people who are involved in such a decision process may become more committed to implementing the decision that is eventually made. As we shall see in the section on decision conferencing, this latter advantage can be a major one.

Mathematical aggregation

Ferrell[1] provides an excellent and comprehensive discussion of mathematical and other aggregation methods. Much of the following discussion is based on his review.

There are a number of advantages to be gained by using mathematical aggregation to combine the judgments of the individual members of a group. In particular, the methods involved are relatively straightforward. For example, we might ask each member of a group to estimate the probability that the sales of a product will exceed 10 000 units next year and then calculate a simple average of their estimates. This means that combined judgments can be obtained quickly. In addition, the group members do not have to meet. Their judgments can be elicited by telephone, post or computer, and therefore the influence of dominant group members is avoided. However, there can be serious problems with the mathematical approach, as the following, rather contrived, example shows.

Suppose that a production manager and an accountant have to make a joint decision between investing in a large- or small-volume processor. The payoff of the processor will depend upon the average level of sales that will be achieved during its useful life. Table 13.1 shows the production manager's subjective probabilities for the sales levels and his utilities for the different actions and outcomes. It can be seen that the expected utility of a high-volume processor is 0.4 (i.e. $0.4 \times 1 + 0.6 \times 0$), while for the low-volume processor it is 0.412 (i.e. $0.4 \times 0.1 + 0.6 \times 0.62$), so the production manager will just prefer the low-volume processor.

Table 13.2 shows the accountant's view of the problem. Her expected utilities are 0.5 for the high-volume processor and 0.51 for the low-volume processor, so she will also favor the low-volume processor. However, if we now take the average of the probabilities and utilities of the two individuals, we arrive at the figures in Table 13.3.

Table 13.1 – The production manager's utilities and probabilities

Action	Average sales levels		Expected utility
	High	Low	
Buy high-volume processor	1.0	0	0.4
Buy low-volume processor	0.1	0.62	0.412
Probabilities	0.4	0.6	

Table 13.2 – The accountant's utilities and probabilities

	Average sales levels		
Action	High	Low	Expected utility
Buy high-volume processor	1.0	0	0.5
Buy low-volume processor	0.52	0.5	0.51
Probabilities	0.5	0.5	

If these figures are used to make the decision, it can be seen that the 'preferred' group choice is the high-volume processor, in spite of the fact that both individuals prefer the low-volume one! We will discuss later whether it is valid or meaningful to average subjective probabilities or utilities, but first let us consider methods that can be used to aggregate judgments in general.

Aggregating judgments in general

Single-value estimates of factors such as costs, sales or times to complete a project are often used in decision analysis models when the use of a probability distribution for every unknown quantity would lead to a model that was too complex to be useful. Two methods of combining individual estimates of unknown quantities are considered below.

Taking a simple average of the individual judgments

First, we examine the situation where the individual group judgments can be regarded as being unbiased (i.e. there is no tendency to over- or underestimate), with each person's estimate being equal to the true value plus a random error that is independent of the errors of the other estimates. In these circumstances it can be shown that taking the simple average (or mean) of the individual estimates is the best way of aggregating

Table 13.3 – The average of the utilities and probabilities

	Average sales levels		
Action	High	Low	Expected utility
Buy high-volume processor	1.0	0	0.45
Buy low-volume processor	0.31	0.56	0.4475
Probabilities	0.45	0.55	

the judgments. The reliability of this group average will improve as the group size increases because the random error inherent in each judgment will be 'averaged out'. These group averages can be extremely reliable. For example, in 1906, Francis Galton[2] analyzed estimates made by 774 individuals in a competition held at a regional fair in England to guess the weight of an ox. Their average estimate was only one pound below the true weight of 1198 pounds. However, it can be shown that each additional member of the group will bring progressively smaller improvements in reliability, so that a point will be reached where it will not be worth the effort or cost of extending the group because a sufficiently reliable estimate can be achieved with the existing membership.

The situation described above is rarely encountered in practice. Generally, the members of the group will produce estimates that are positively correlated. For example, if one member has overestimated next year's sales, there will be a tendency for the other members to do likewise. This is likely to occur because group members often have similar areas of expertise or because they all work in the same environment where they are exposed to the same sources of information. If there is a high intercorrelation between the judgments of the group members, then little new information will be added by each additional member of the group, and there may be little point in averaging the judgments of more than a small group of individuals. For example, Ashton and Ashton[3] conducted a study in which a group of 13 advertising personnel at *Time* magazine were asked to produce forecasts of the number of advertising pages that would be sold by the magazine annually. When the simple average of individuals' forecasts was used, it was found that there was little to be gained in accuracy from averaging the forecasts of more than five individuals.

Taking a weighted average of the individual judgments

When some members of the group are considered to be better judges than others, it may be worth attaching a higher weight to their estimates and using a weighted average to represent the group judgment. For example, suppose that three individuals, Allen, Bailey and Crossman, make the following estimates of the cost of launching a new product: $5 million, $2.5 million and $3 million. We think that Allen is the best judge and Crossman the worst, and we therefore decide to attach weights of 0.6, 0.3 and 0.1 to their estimates (note that, if the weights do not sum to 1, then this can be achieved by normalizing them – see Chapter 3). The group estimates will therefore be

$$(0.6 \times \$5m) + (0.3 \times \$2.5m) + (0.1 \times \$3m) = \$4.05m$$

The main problem of using weighted averages is that the judgmental skills of the group's members need to be assessed in order to obtain the weights. Methods that have been proposed fall into three categories: self-rating, rating of each individual by the whole group (see, for example, de Groot[4]) and rating based on past performance. However, there can be difficulties in applying these methods. The first two approaches compound the individual's judgmental task by requiring not only judgments about the problem in hand but also judgments about the skill of individual group members. In some circumstances these problems can be avoided by using weights based on past performance, but as Lock[5] points out, even here there can be difficulties. The current judgmental task may not be the same as tasks in the past. For example, the quantity that an individual has to judge may be less familiar than quantities that have been estimated previously. Furthermore, past performance may be a poor guide where judges have improved their performance through learning.

Clearly, simple averaging avoids all these problems, so is it worth going to the trouble of assessing weights? Research in this area has consistently indicated that simple averages produce estimates that are either as good as or only slightly inferior to weighted averages (see, for example, Ashton and Ashton[3]). Ferrell[1] suggests a number of reasons for this. He argues that groups tend to be made up of individuals who have very similar levels of expertise and access to the same information. In the case of small groups, even if we are fortunate enough to identify the best individual estimate, its accuracy is unlikely to be much better than that of the simple average of the entire group's judgments. Ferrell argues that weighting is only likely to be worth considering where the group consists of 'a moderately large group of well-acquainted individuals that frequently works together and has a wide range of different types of expertise to bring to bear on questions that require an equally wide range of knowledge'. In the absence of these conditions, a simple average of individuals' judgments will probably suffice.

Aggregating probability judgments

When probabilities need to be aggregated, a number of problems emerge, as the following example shows. The managers of a construction company need to determine the probability that a civil engineering project will be held up by both geological problems and delays in the supply of equipment (the problems are considered to be independent). Two members of the management team are asked to estimate the probabilities, and the results are shown in Table 13.4. It can be seen that the 'group' assessment of the probability that both events will occur differs, depending on how the averaging was carried out. If we multiply each manager's probabilities together and then take an average, we arrive at a probability of 0.24. However, if we first average the managers' probabilities for the individual events and then multiply these averages together, we obtain a probability of 0.225.

Table 13.4 – Averaging probabilities

	p(geological problems)	p(equipment problems)	p(both)
Manager 1's estimates	0.2	0.6	$0.2 \times 0.6 = 0.12$
Manager 2's estimates	0.4	0.9	$0.4 \times 0.9 = 0.36$
			Average = 0.24 But:
Average of the estimates	0.3	0.75	$0.3 \times 0.75 = 0.225$

Because of these types of problem, a number of alternative procedures have been suggested for aggregating probabilities. One approach is to regard one group member's probability estimate as information that may cause another member to revise his or her estimate using Bayes' theorem. Some of the methods based on this approach (e.g. those of Morris[6] and Bordley[7]) also require an assessment to be made of each individual's expertise, and all are substantially more complicated than simple averaging.

Another approach is to take a weighted average of individual probabilities using one of the three methods of weighting that we referred to earlier. However, again there appears to be little evidence that weighting leads to an improvement in performance over simple averaging (see, for example, Winkler[8] and Seaver et al.,[9] as cited in Ferrell[1]).

What are the practical implications of this discussion? The most pragmatic approach to aggregating probabilities would appear to be the most straightforward, namely to take a simple average of individual probabilities. This method may not be ideal, as our example of the civil engineering project showed, but as von Winterfeldt and Edwards[10] put it: 'The odds seem excellent that, if you do anything more complex, you will simply be wasting your effort'.

Aggregating preference judgments

When a group of individuals has to choose between a number of alternative courses of action, how can we determine the option that the group prefers? Is it possible, or indeed meaningful, mathematically to aggregate their preferences to identify the preferred option? To try to answer these questions, we will first consider decision problems where the group members state their preferences for the alternatives in terms of simple orderings (e.g. 'I prefer A to B and B to C'). Then we will consider situations where a value or a utility function has been elicited from each individual.

Aggregating preference orderings

One obvious way of aggregating individual preferences is to use a simple voting system. However, this can result in paradoxical results, as the following example shows.

Three members of a committee, Messrs Edwards, Fletcher and Green, have to agree on the location of a new office. Three locations, A, B and C, are available, and the members' preference orderings are shown below (note that > means 'is preferred to'):

Member	Preference ordering
Edwards	A > B > C
Fletcher	B > C > A
Green	C > A > B

If we now ask the members to compare A and B, A will get two votes and B only one. This *implies* that A > B. If we then compare B and C, B will get two votes and C only one, which implies that B > C. Finally, if we were to compare A with C, C would get two votes and A only one, which implies that C > A. So not only do we have A > B > C but we also have C > A, which means that the preferences of the group are not transitive. This result is known as *Condorcet's paradox*.

When options are compared sequentially, this can lead to a number of problems. For example, the committee might compare A with B first, eliminate the inferior option and then compare the preferred option with C. Unfortunately, the order of comparison has a direct effect on the option that is chosen, as shown below.

If the group compared A with B first, then A would survive the first round. If A was then compared with C, C would be the location chosen. Alternatively, if the group compared B with C first, B would survive the first round. If B was then compared with A, then location A would be chosen.

Moreover, a clever group member could cheat by being dishonest about his preferences if the preferences of the other members were already known. Suppose that locations A and B are to be compared first. Edwards realizes that this will make C, his least preferred location, the final choice. He would prefer B to be selected, so he dishonestly states his preferences as B > A > C. This ensures that B, not A, will survive the first round and go on to 'defeat' C in the second.

These sorts of problems led Kenneth Arrow [11] to ask whether there is a satisfactory method for determining group preferences when the preferences of individual members are expressed as orderings. He identified four conditions that he considered a satisfactory procedure should meet:

(1) The method must produce a transitive group preference order for the options being considered.

(2) If every member of the group prefers one option to another, then so must the group.

(3) The group choice between two options, A and B, depends only upon the preferences of members between *these* options and not upon preferences for any other option. (If this is not the case, then, as we saw above, an individual can influence the group ordering by lying about his preferences.)

(4) There is no dictator. No individual is able to impose his or her preferences on the group.

In his well-known *impossibility theorem*, Arrow proved that, when more than two options are available, no aggregation procedure can guarantee to satisfy all four conditions. Not surprisingly, this significant and rather depressing result has attracted much attention over the years. It suggests that it is impossible to derive a truly democratic system for resolving differences of opinion. Any method that is tried will have some shortcoming.

Given that no method can be perfect, is it possible to devise an approach that is reasonably acceptable? Ferrell argues that *approval voting* is both simple and robust. In this system, individuals vote for all the options that they consider to be at least just acceptable. The group choice will then be the option that receives the most votes. Of course, this method ignores much of the available information about individual preferences. While you may consider alternatives A and B to be acceptable, you may have a preference for A. However, by ignoring this information, the method avoids the sort of paradoxical results that we have seen can occur with other methods.

Aggregating values and utilities

It is important to note that Arrow's impossibility theorem refers only to situations where individuals have stated the order of their preferences. A statement giving an individual's preference order does not tell you about that person's intensity of preference for the alternatives. For example, when considering three possible holiday destinations, you may list your preferences from the best to the worst, as follows:

> Rio de Janeiro
> San Francisco
> Toronto

However, your intensity of preference for Rio de Janeiro may be very much greater than that for San Francisco, while your preference for San Francisco may be only slightly greater than that for Toronto. As we saw in earlier chapters, an individual's intensity of preference for an alternative can be measured by determining either the value or, in the case of uncertainty, the utility of that course of action. The problem with aggregating the values or utilities of a group of individuals is that the intensities of preference of the individuals have to be compared. To illustrate this, let us suppose that a group of two people, A and B, have to choose between our three holiday destinations. For each person, values are elicited to measure their relative preference for the destinations. These values are shown below, with 100 representing the most preferred destination and 0 the least preferred:

Destination	Person A	Person B	Average
Rio de Janeiro	100	50	75
San Francisco	40	100	70
Toronto	0	0	0

If we take a simple average of values for each destination, it can be seen that Rio will be the group choice. However, our calculation assumes that a move from 0 to 100 on one person's value scale represents the same increase in preference as a move from 0 to 100 on the other person's scale. Suppose, for the moment, that we could actually measure and compare the strength of preference of the two people on a common scale. We might find that A is far less concerned about a move from his best to his worst location than B, so that, if we measure their value scales against our common strength of preference scale, we have a situation like that shown in Figure 13.1. The individuals' values measured on this common scale are shown below, and it can be seen that San Francisco would now be the group choice:

Destination	Person A	Person B	Average
Rio de Janeiro	40	50	45
San Francisco	16	100	58
Toronto	0	0	0

Is it possible to compare one individual's strength of preference with another's? French[12] examines a number of ways in which such comparisons could be made in theory, and shows that all the methods are likely to fail in practice. For example, the whole group might agree unanimously that person 1 prefers P to Q more than person 2 prefers X to Y. But what would happen in the likely event of this unanimity not being achieved? Alternatively, we might use money as the common yardstick for strength of preference. If person A is only prepared to pay \$100 to transfer from his worst to

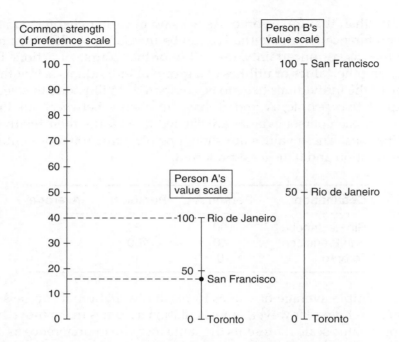

Figure 13.1 – Measuring individuals' strengths of preference against a common scale

his best holiday destination while person B is prepared to pay $1500, then can we say that B's strength of preference is greater than A's? If we answer yes to this question, then we must assume that $1 is equally valued by the two people, but what if A is a pauper and B a millionaire? Clearly, our 'objective' scale would lead us back to the problem of comparing individuals' strengths of preference!

In the absence of any obvious method for making interpersonal comparisons of intensity of preference, it seems that our search for a group value or utility function is futile. Nevertheless, the concepts of value and utility can still be useful in group decision-making. The derivation of individual values and utilities can help each group member to clarify his or her personal understanding of the problem, and also to achieve a greater appreciation of the views of other members. Moreover, a simple average of values and utilities may be useful in providing a rough initial model of the problem. Sensitivity analysis can then be used to test the effect of using individual values and utilities. This may reveal, for example, that certain options are to be preferred to others, irrespective of which individual's utility function is used. At the very least, the process should lead to a more informed discussion and debate.

This reference to group discussion and debate leads us to the next section, where behavioral aggregation methods are considered. We will begin by looking at the behavioral problems that can occur when a group of decision-makers meet to agree upon a course of action.

Unstructured group processes

One of the major conclusions of research work on descriptions of group decision-making is that of well-documented shortcomings. The presence of powerful individuals can inhibit the contribution of those who are lower down the hierarchy. Talkative or extrovert members may dominate the discussions. Indeed, even variations in seating arrangements can have the effect of encouraging or inhibiting individuals' contributions.

Janis[13] has documented a phenomenon that he has termed *groupthink* within group decision processes. Groupthink is essentially the suppression of ideas that are critical of the 'direction' in which a group is moving. It is reflected in a tendency to concur with the position or views that are perceived to be favored by the group. Of course, such forces may produce speedy judgments and commitment to action. However, such cohesive groups may develop rationalizations for the invulnerability of the group's decision and inhibit the expression of critical ideas. These pitfalls of groupthink are likely to result in an incomplete survey of alternative courses of action or choices. Such an incomplete search through the decision space may result in a failure to examine the risks of preferred decisions and a failure to work out contingency plans if the preferred course of action cannot be taken.

Overall, there have been very few laboratory tests of Janis's theory. One main reason is that laboratory researchers have found it difficult to achieve high levels of group cohesiveness, a primary antecedent of groupthink. Another approach to the verification of the theory has been the study of case histories.

One such study, by Esser and Lindoerfer,[14] analyzed the decision to launch the space shuttle *Challenger* on 28 January 1986. The outcome of that flight, the death of all seven crew members within minutes of launch, focused attention on the process leading to the decision to launch. The researchers carried out a 'content analysis' of the verbal transcripts of a Presidential Commission report on the disaster, and statements were coded as either positive or negative instances of the antecedents and consequences of groupthink. During the 24 hours prior to the launch of the *Challenger*, the ratio of positive to negative items increased significantly. During this time, the Level III NASA management was facing increased difficulties in maintaining their flight schedule, and this was expressed as direct pressure on the dissenters who wanted to delay the flight (the engineers) and 'mindguarding'. Mindguarding essentially refers to the removal of doubts and uncertainties in communications to others. In this instance, the Level III NASA management said to the engineers that they would report the engineers' concerns to the Level II NASA management, but they did not.

Janis argued that 'victims' of groupthink feel invulnerable in their decision-making and so fail to reappraise initially rejected alternative courses of action and do not search for information that could disconfirm the selected course of action. As such, they suffer from confirmation bias, which we discussed in Chapter 11.

The Delphi method

How can the potential power of groups be harnessed without encountering the serious problems that we have just discussed? One approach is to use *structured* group processes. These are designed to enhance group decision-making by removing or restricting the interaction between members of the group and controlling information flow. Delphi[15] is one such method that is particularly widely used. Essentially, Delphi consists of an iterative process for making *quantitative* judgments. Members of the group are referred to as panelists. The phases of Delphi are:

(1) Individual panelists provide opinions about the likelihood of future events, or when those events will occur, or what the impact of such event(s) will be. These opinions are often given as responses to questionnaires which are completed individually by members of the panel. The source of the opinion is made anonymous before the opinion is seen by other panelists.
(2) The results of this polling of panelists are then tallied, and *statistical* feedback of the whole panel's opinions (e.g. a range or the median of their estimates) is provided to individual panellists. Next, a repolling of individual opinions takes place. At this stage, anonymous discussion (often in written form) may occur so that dissenting opinion is aired.
(3) The process of obtaining individual judgments and feeding back statistical information on what the panel as a whole is thinking continues over a number of rounds until either a consensus emerges or the panelists are no longer changing their opinions.
(4) The output of the Delphi technique is a quantified group 'consensus', which is usually expressed as the median response of the group of panelists.

Note that simply using the median of a group's opinions at the end of the first round will provide more accuracy than that achieved by at least 50% of the individual panelists. To see this, consider Figure 13.2.

In Figure 13.2(a), where the true answer lies outside the range of estimates, the group median is more accurate than *one-half* of the group (the gray shaded area). In Figure 13.2(b), where the true answer lies inside the range of estimates, the group median is more accurate than the *majority* of panelists (the gray shaded areas).

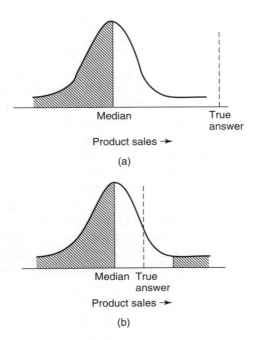

Figure 13.2 – The accuracy of the median estimate

With repolling and feedback, it is assumed that the median response of the group shifts nearer to the true value of the outcome to be predicted. Improvement is thought to result from (i) opinion change in 'swingers', who change their less firmly grounded opinions after receiving feedback about the opinions of other, anonymous, panelists, and (ii) opinion stability in 'holdouts', who are assumed to be more accurate than 'swingers'.

Delphi was designed to improve upon the traditional interacting group by adding structure to the process. Results generally suggest that Delphi groups are more accurate than traditional groups. In a review of research, Rowe and Wright[16] found that Delphi groups outperformed traditional groups by a score of five studies to one, with two ties, and with one study showing task-specific support for both techniques. Delphi has been compared with groups whose members were required to argue both for and against their judgments (the 'dialectic' procedure[17]). It has also been compared with groups whose judgments were derived from a single, group-selected individual (the 'dictator' or 'best member' strategy[17,18]) and groups that received rules on how to interact appropriately.[19] Based on this evidence, there appears to be no clear rationale for adopting any of these techniques in preference to Delphi.

Would it be better simply to average the forecasts of several individuals (a so-called 'statistical' group') rather than use Delphi? Researchers have compared the accuracy of such statistical groups with that of Delphi groups in two ways: through a straightforward comparison of the two approaches, and through a comparison of the quality of averaged estimates on the first and the final round in a Delphi procedure. The first, pre-interaction round is equivalent to a statistical group in every way except for the instructions given to individuals: Delphi panelists are led to expect further polling and feedback from others, which may lead panelists to consider the problem more deeply and possibly to make better 'statistical group' judgments on that first round than individuals who do not expect to have their estimates used as feedback for others. A first-round Delphi may, however, provide a better benchmark for comparison than a separate statistical group, because the panelists in the two 'conditions' are the same, thus reducing a potential source of great variance.

Rowe and Wright[16] reviewed the evidence for the relative values of statistical groups and Delphi groups and found that results generally support the advantage of Delphi groups over first-round or statistical groups by a tally of twelve studies to two. In five studies, the researchers reported significant increases in accuracy over Delphi rounds. Seven more studies produced qualified support for Delphi: in five cases, researchers found Delphi to be better than statistical or first-round groups more often than not, or to a degree that did not reach statistical significance. Two further studies found Delphi to be better under certain conditions but not others. Thus, the overall weight of empirical evidence suggests that Delphi groups should be used instead of statistical groups whenever feasible, because generally they lead to judgments that are more accurate.

Delphi has value in a number of situations. When experts are geographically dispersed and unable to meet in a face-to-face group, Delphi would seem an appropriate procedure. It enables members of different organizations to address industry-wide issues, or experts from different facilities within a single organization to consider a problem without traveling to a single location. Indeed, experts with diverse backgrounds are liable to have different perspectives, terminologies and frames of reference, which might easily hinder effective communication in a traditional group. The facilitator (or monitor team) can iron out such difficulties before the structured rounds of a Delphi.

Delphi might also be appropriate when disagreements between individuals are likely to be severe or politically unpalatable. Under such circumstances, the quality of judgments and decisions is likely to suffer from motive conflicts, personality clashes and power games. For example, people may be unwilling to change their mind, even when they realize that their current estimate is wrong, because of a fear of losing face. In Delphi, refereeing the group process and ensuring anonymity should therefore prove beneficial.

Rowe and Wright[16] summarize the following principles for using expert opinion in applications of Delphi:

- Use experts with appropriate domain knowledge.
- Use heterogeneous experts.

- Use 5–20 experts.
- For Delphi feedback, provide the mean or median estimate of the panel plus the rationales from all panelists for their estimates.
- Continue Delphi polling until the responses show stability. Generally, three structured rounds are enough.
- Obtain the final forecast by weighting all the experts' estimates equally and aggregating them.

Freeware for implementing Delphi is available on the Internet (www.forprin.com).

Prediction markets

Prediction markets offer an alternative method of obtaining estimates of probabilities and other quantities from a group of individuals. They involve people buying and selling contracts in the same way that shares are traded on a stock market. Typically, these contracts stipulate that their owner will receive a sum of money (say $1) if a particular event occurs and nothing otherwise. For example, a contract might state that, if candidate Smith wins the next Presidential election, you receive $1. Because they are traded on a market, the price of these contracts will vary. Suppose that the current price of a contract that will pay $1 if Smith wins the election is $0.25. If people consider that Smith has more than a 0.25 probability of winning, perhaps because a recent opinion poll suggests his campaign is going well, then they are likely to buy these contracts so that the price will rise. In contrast, owners of the contacts will probably be happy to sell them at $0.25 if they think Smith's chances are less than 0.25, so sending the price down. Thus, the current price of the contract can be interpreted as the market's view of the probability of the event occurring based on the latest information that is available to it. If the price rises to $0.60, then this is taken to imply that people now think that Smith has a 0.6 probability of being the election victor.

The same idea can be used to obtain estimates of quantities rather than probabilities. For example, a contract might pay out $1 for every percentage point in market share that a new product achieves by the end of its first year on the market. If the current price is $30 and you expect that it will achieve 50% market share, then you are likely to be prepared to buy the contract. If lots of other people buy, because they also think that a market share of more than 30% will be achieved, then the price will rise, and the new price is interpreted as the market's estimate of the expected market share.

It can be shown that certain theoretical conditions have to be met for the prediction market price to equate to the average belief among those trading on the market. In particular, they should produce accurate results where those trading are risk averse and where their beliefs are independently normally distributed around the true value.[20, 21] However, the reliability of markets may be robust to departures from these assumptions, and empirical studies of the performance of a wide range of markets suggest that they do yield accurate results, even where traders use play, rather than real, money.[22]

Some companies have used prediction markets to forecast the outcomes of research and development projects, successes of new products and regulatory outcomes.[21] For example, a market established within Hewlett-Packard led to more accurate sales forecasts than those obtained from the firm's individual sales experts.[23] Similarly, prediction markets have outperformed experts and other methods in forecasts of which films will be box-office successes and Oscar winners, outcomes of sports events and whether a software contract would be delivered on time.[21] Examples of prediction markets that are accessible on the Internet include the Iowa Electronic Market (www.biz.uiowa.edu/iem/), the Hollywood Stock Exchange (http://www.hsx.com/) and Bet2Give (https://bet2give.com).

A number of companies provide software for those who want to set up their own prediction markets (e.g. www.Inklingmarkets.com, www.Newsfutures.com http://www.newsfutures.com/ and www.Qmarkets.net). The person running the market will need to decide on initial prices for the contracts (typically, these will be set in the middle of the possible range of prices, e.g. at $0.50) and, if play money is being used, how much should be allocated to each trader at the start of trading (e.g. $500). The software is likely to contain a mathematical algorithm that determines how much the price changes following a purchase of a given number of contracts. It will also provide an interface allowing traders to make purchases or sell their contracts (when forecasting events, some interfaces helpfully explain that the price can be interpreted as a probability). Most software will also allow traders to access graphs showing how the price of contracts has changed over time.

What are the relative advantages and disadvantages of prediction markets compared with Delphi? Green et al.[24] provide a good summary of the pros and cons. Participants in prediction markets have a monetary incentive to reveal and think hard about their true beliefs, so the quality of judgments being aggregated is likely to be high. Second, unlike Delphi, or traditional meetings that elicit estimates at particular points in time, prediction markets run continuously, so they can instantly react to new information and build this into the current forecast.

However, to run a prediction market, it is necessary for the outcome of an event to be known at a defined period in the future and, if this time period is a long way off, then participants will have to be prepared to wait, possibly for years, to receive their potential payoff. These problems do not apply to Delphi and so it can be used in a wider range of estimation tasks. Also, for many people, making an estimate in Delphi is likely to be easier than translating their estimate into a market price, while in some cases it is difficult to formulate contracts in order to obtain predictions that are complex in nature. Another potential weakness of prediction markets is their vulnerability to manipulation by people who deliberately buy or sell large numbers of contracts in the hope of influencing the price. However, there is some evidence that such intervention usually only has a short-term effect.[21] A more serious danger is represented by 'cascades', where participants assume that a price movement is a response to some new information of which they are unaware, so they buy or sell accordingly, causing further price movements and further reactions. The result is an excessive change in the price. In addition, when anonymous reasons underlying judgments are exchanged in a Delphi process, people have an opportunity to learn and hence improve their estimates. In prediction markets, no such information is shared. Indeed, there is a replication of effort in that each participant has to seek out his or her own information independently. Finally, as we have seen, Delphi requires only 5–20 experts. In prediction markets there may be problems in obtaining accurate estimates from such a small number of traders.

In contrast to Delphi and prediction markets, decision conferencing, which we consider next, presents a socially interactive approach to decision-making in order to generate a shared *understanding* of a problem and to produce a commitment to action.

Decision conferencing

Decision conferencing was invented in the late 1970s by Cameron Peterson at a US-based consulting firm called Decision and Designs Incorporated. Essentially, decision conferencing brings together decision analysis, group processes and information technology over an intensive 2 or 3 day session attended by people who wish to resolve a complex issue or decision. In this context, a small group of people who have an input to a major decision are often seated on the perimeter of a round table and talk through their problem with a decision analyst, who acts to facilitate group interactions and knowledge sharing. In the background, another decision analyst uses interactive decision-aiding technology to model individual and group views on such issues as multi-attribute option evaluation and resource allocation. As we have seen in earlier chapters, the outputs of such modeling seldom agree with unaided holistic judgments. One major responsibility of the decision analyst is to explain the underlying logic of the modeling methods to the decision-makers. Only if the decision-makers can fully appreciate the methods are they likely to accept model-based choices over their own intuitive judgments. To quote Phillips:[25]

> As the results of the modeling become available to the participants, they compare these results to their holistic judgments. It is the inevitable discrepancies that arise, especially early in the modeling process, that drive the dialectic. By exploring these discrepancies,

understanding deepens and changes, and new perspectives are reflected back as changes to the model.

Eventually, participants are satisfied with the model and unable to derive any further insights from it . . .. The model has served its purpose.

Phillips is concerned not to impose an optimal solution by black-box methods:

If exploration of the discrepancy between holistic judgment and model results shows the model to be at fault, then the model is not requisite – it is not yet sufficient to solve the problem. The model can only be considered requisite when no new intuitions emerge about the problem . . .. Requisite models are not produced from people's heads, they are *generated* through the interaction of problem owners.

Therefore, the fundamental objective behind decision conferencing is to provide a synthesis of decision analysis techniques and the positive characteristics and dynamics of small-group decision-making. Shared understandings of problems are generated with the aid of decision-analytic techniques and social facilitation. Participants gain a sense of common purpose and a commitment to action. Sensitivity analysis allows participants to see if individual disagreements make a difference in the final preferred alternative or decision. Decision-analytic principles provide a *guide* to action, not a black box prescription for action.

We feel that it is intuitively reasonable that decisions that are conferenced to consensus are more likely to be implemented than the output prescriptions of complex black box decision analyses, which involve but a single decision-maker who may well have to justify his or her decision to others in the organization. In addition, decisions made by such groups are likely, because of the group commitment, to be 'made' to work.

However, a major question that still remains to be answered is: Are decisions that are conferenced to consensus more or less valid than unaided judgment or prescriptive solutions? For example, does the situational context of decision conferencing produce conditions for groupthink? Phillips[25] has argued that this is not so, as:

(1) Participants are not on home ground. Often decision conferences take place in hotels or in a specially designed room on the decision analyst's premises.
(2) The small group is carefully composed of people representing *all* perspectives on the issue to be resolved so that adversarial processes operate in the group to check bias and explore alternative framings of the decision problem.
(3) The decision analyst who acts to facilitate the conference is a neutral outsider who is sensitive to the unhelpful effects of groupthink and reflects this back to the group.

McCartt and Rohrbough[26] have addressed the problem of evaluating the effectiveness of decision conferencing. These investigators argued that attempts to link good decision outcomes to particular types of group decision support are extraordinarily difficult, as virtually all real-world applications of group decision support do not provide enough baselines of comparison (e.g. tests of alternative methods and techniques or alternative decisions) to satisfy laboratory-based experimental researchers.

For example, as noted above, with group commitment, poor decisions may be 'made' to produce good outcomes, otherwise the credibility of the senior executives who attended the decision conference would be in doubt. Good judgment and decision-making have been seen as one of the major characteristics of good managers! McCartt and Rohrbough conclude that any assessment of the effectiveness of a group decision process must be directed at the *process* itself and not at subsequent outcomes. In their study, these investigators followed up a cross-section of 14 decision conferences held by Decision Techtronics at the State University of New York at Albany. Using mailed questionnaires, they enquired about the perceived organizational benefits in the form of improved information management, planning, efficiency and morale. Those decision conferences that were rated as effective were found to be where participants perceived real benefit in the support of the decision analysis techniques and in the opportunity for open and extended discussion about the models that had been built. Ineffective decision conferences were characterized by executive teams convening to discuss a problem but feeling little pressure to reach consensus or construct a plan of action.

To date, thousands of decision conferences have been conducted in many countries worldwide.[27] The service is now offered by about 15 organizations and is an effective way of helping managers deal with complex issues facing their organizations.

Summary

In this chapter we described the advantages and disadvantages of mathematical and behavioral aggregation of opinion. Within mathematical aggregation techniques, simple and weighted averaging were contrasted. Unstructured and structured behavioral aggregation were described, and the processes involved in decision conferencing were outlined. Issues in the evaluation of the usefulness of decision conferencing were introduced.

Discussion questions

(1) A supermarket chain intends to open a new shop near Sheffield, in England, next year. Four possible locations have been identified: (i) Moortop (site A); (ii) Silver Hill (site B); (iii) Cheston Common (site C); (iv) the River Shopping Complex (site D). The decision on the location will be taken by four decision-makers who

have each used the simple multi-attribute rating technique (SMART) to help them to clarify their understanding of the decision problem (in the models, the monetary costs of the sites were treated as just another attribute). Details of the values that each decision-maker allocated to the sites are given below.

	Site			
Decision-maker	**A**	**B**	**C**	**D**
Brown	65	43	21	10
Jones	45	50	60	40
Smith	12	70	32	54
Thomson	23	45	50	70

Discuss the problems that are likely to be involved in obtaining a decision for the group and evaluate possible ways of tackling these problems.

(2) Because of recent increases in student numbers, East University has to decide whether to relocate from its existing campus at Byron Avenue to a new campus at Beach Park, a green-field site. The senior managers of the university have to agree on which course of action to recommend to the Governing Body. The main criteria to be used in the decision are the cost of developing the site, working conditions for staff and students, the public image of the university, scope for further expansion in the future, accessibility to public transport facilities and reduction in road congestion.

To provide a formal structure to the decision and a defensible rationale, SMART was used by each manager to determine his or her perception of the relative importance of the criteria listed above and how well the two options performed on these criteria. For each manager, this yielded a score for each course of action (for example, the University President's scores were 'Stay at Byron Avenue': 65.1, 'Move to Beach Park': 34.9). For each option, the scores for all the senior managers were averaged, and the results are shown below:

	Mean score
Stay at Byron Avenue	57.8
Move to Beach Park	42.2

These results were in complete contrast to the prevailing views expressed at the previous day's meeting of the senior managers, when there was apparent enthusiasm, particularly from the President, for the move to Beach Park. Discuss possible reasons for the discrepancy between the model's recommendation and the view of the senior managers that was apparent at the last meeting.

(3) A confectionery company has to decide whether to launch a new range of chocolate bars aimed at health-conscious professional people. You have been invited to observe all stages of the decision process and to attend meetings relating to the decision. What criteria would you use to judge the quality of the decision process?

(4) 'For decisions involving groups of people, decision conferencing is likely to be much more effective than the use of mathematical aggregation of individuals' judgments.' Discuss.

(5) You are invited to observe this month's meeting of the managers of a hospital, which will take place in the senior manager's office. The main item on the agenda relates to the issue of whether a particular ward should be temporarily closed because of funding problems. Before the meeting, the senior manager tells you that the hospital management prides itself on efficient decision-making. 'My staff and I work as a coherent team', he tells you. 'We are busy people, so at our meetings we don't waste time on endless discussion. There is usually little dissent and we make decisions quickly and with confidence that what we are doing is right. I think that you'll see that my colleagues will agree with me that the closure should go ahead.'

Draft a set of notes evaluating the senior manager's approach to decision-making and, if necessary, suggest ways in which the decision-making process at the hospital might be improved.

References

1. Ferrell, W.R. (1985) Combining individual judgments, in *Behavioral Decision Making*, ed. by Wright, G., Plenum Press, New York, NY, pp. 111–145.
2. Galton's original article is: Galton, F. (1907) VoxPopuli, *Nature*, **75**, 450–451. A recent account of his findings can be found in Surowiecki, J. (2004) *The Wisdom of Crowds*, Doubleday, New York, NY.
3. Ashton, A.H. and Ashton, R.H. (1985) Aggregating subjective forecasts: some empirical results, *Management Science*, **31**(12), 1499–1508.
4. de Groot, M.H. (1974) Reaching a consensus, *Journal of the American Statistical Association*, **69**, 118–121.
5. Lock, A. (1987) Integrating group judgments in subjective forecasts, in *Judgmental Forecasting*, Wright, G. and Ayton, P., John Wiley & Sons, Ltd, Chichester, UK.
6. Morris, P.A. (1983) An axiomatic approach to expert resolution, *Management Science*, **29**, 24–32.

7. Bordley, R.F. (1982) The combination of forecasts: a Bayesian approach, *Journal of the Operational Research Society*, **33**, 171–174.

8. Winkler, R.L. (1971) Probabilistic prediction: some experimental results, *Journal of the American Statistical Association*, **66**, 675–685.

9. Seaver, D.A., von Winterfeldt, D. and Edwards, W. (1978) Eliciting subjective probability distributions on continuous variables, *Organizational Behavior and Human Performance*, **21**, 379–391.

10. von Winterfeldt, D. and Edwards, W. (1986) *Decision Analysis and Behavioral Research*, Cambridge University Press, New York, NY.

11. Arrow, K.J. (1951) *Social Choice and Individual Values*, John Wiley & Sons, Inc., New York, NY.

12. French, S. (1988) *Decision Theory: An Introduction to the Mathematics of Rationality*, Ellis Horwood, Chichester, UK.

13. Janis, I.R. (1982) *Groupthink*, 2nd edition, Houghton Mifflin, Boston, MA.

14. Esser, J.K. and Lindoerfer, J.S. (1989) Groupthink and the Space Shuttle Challenger accident: towards a quantitative case analysis, *Journal of Behavioral Decision Making*, **2**, 167–177; see also Park, W.W. (1990) A review of research on Groupthink, *Journal of Behavioral Decision Making*, **3**, 229–245.

15. For reviews, see Parente, F.J. and Anderson-Parente, J.K. (1987) Delphi inquiry systems, in *Judgmental Forecasting*, ed. by Wright, G. and Ayton, P., John Wiley & Sons, Ltd, Chichester, UK; see also Rowe, G., Wright, G. and Bolger, F. (1991) Delphi: a re-evaluation of research and theory, *Technological Forecasting and Social Change*, **39**, 235–251; Rowe, G. and Wright, G. (1996) The impact of task characteristics on the performance of structured group forecasting techniques, *International Journal of Forecasting*, **12**, 73–90; Rowe, G. and Wright, G. (1999) The Delphi technique as a forecasting tool: issues and analysis, *International Journal of Forecasting*, **15**, 353–375.

16. Rowe, G. and Wright, G. (2001) Expert opinions in forecasting: role of the Delphi technique, in *Principles of Forecasting: A Handbook for Researchers and Practitioners*, ed. by Armstrong, J.S., Kluwer Academic Publishers, Norwell, MA.

17. Sniezek, J.A. (1989) An examination of group process in judgmental forecasting, *International Journal of Forecasting*, **5**, 171–178.

18. Sniezek, J.A. (1990) A comparison of techniques for judgmental forecasting by groups with common information, *Group and Organization Studies*, **15**, 5–19.

19. Erffmeyer, R.C. and Lane, I.M. (1984) Quality and acceptance of an evaluative task: the effects of four group decision-making formats, *Group and Organization Studies*, **9**, 509–529.

20. Grossman, S.J. (1976) On the efficiency of competitive stock markets where traders have diverse information, *The Journal of Finance*, **31**, 573–585.

21. Wolfers, J. and Zitzewitz, E. (2008) Prediction markets in theory and practice, in *The New Palgrave Dictionary of Economics*, 2nd edition, ed. by Durlauf, S.N. and Blume, L.E., Palgrave Macmillan, London, UK.

22. Pennock, D.M., Lawrence, S., Giles, C.L. and Nielsen, F.A. (2001) The real power of artificial markets, *Science*, **291**, 987–988.

23. Chen, K.-Y. and Plott, C. (2002) Information aggregation mechanisms: concept, design and implementation for a sales forecasting problem, Caltech Social Science Working Paper No. 1131.
24. Green, K., Armstrong, J.S. and Graefe, A. (2007) Methods to elicit forecasts from groups. Delphi and prediction markets compared, *Foresight: The International Journal of Applied Forecasting*, (8), 17–20.
25. Phillips, L.D. (1984) A theory of requisite decision models, *Acta Psychologica*, **56**, 29–48.
26. McCartt, A. and Rohrbough, J. (1989) Evaluating group decision support system effectiveness: a performance study of decision conferencing, *Decision Support Systems*, **5**, 243–253.
27. Phillips, L.D. (2006) Decision conferencing, Operational Research Group, Department of Management, London School of Economics, Working Paper LSEOR 06.85.

Resource allocation and negotiation problems 14

Introduction

In this chapter we will demonstrate how decision analysis models can be applied to two types of problem. Both of these usually involve groups of decision-makers. First, we will study problems where a limited resource has to be allocated between a number of alternative uses. For example, a group of product managers may have to decide on how next year's advertising budget should be divided between the products for which they are responsible. Similarly, a local police force might have to determine how its available personnel should be allocated between tasks such as crime prevention, traffic policing and the investigation of serious and petty crimes.

The central purpose of resource allocation models in decision analysis is to resolve what is known as the *commons dilemma*.[1-4] On the one hand, an organization can decentralize its decision-making, allowing each manager to make the best use of the resources that he or she is allocated. While this delegation of responsibility will probably motivate the managers, it is unlikely that the resulting set of independent decisions will lead to an allocation of resources that is best for the organization as a whole. The alternative is to centralize decision-making, but this may be demotivating, and the resulting allocation will not take into account the local knowledge of the individual managers. The dilemma can be resolved by the managers meeting as a group, possibly in a decision conference,[1] and examining the effect of trading off resources between their areas of responsibility. Of course, some managers may find that they lose resources as a result of this process, but these losses should be more than compensated for by the increased benefits of reallocating the resources elsewhere.

As we shall see, the number of combinations of options that are available in this sort of decision problem can be very large, so a computer is normally required to perform the appropriate calculations. One software product that has been designed specifically for this purpose is Equity (Catalyze Ltd). This package has been used to analyze the problem that we will consider in the first part of the chapter, and therefore much of the terminology that is associated with Equity has been adopted here. HiPriority (Krysalis Ltd) is an alternative product.

The second application relates to problems where two parties are involved in negotiations. Typically, these problems concern a number of issues. For example, in industrial relations disputes, negotiations may involve such issues as pay, holidays and length of the working day. As we shall see, in these circumstances, decision analysis can be used to help the parties to attain a mutually beneficial settlement.

Both of these applications rely on the concepts of multi-attribute value analysis, which were covered in Chapter 3, so it is worth making sure that you are familiar with these ideas before proceeding.

Modeling resource allocation problems

An illustrative problem

Consider the following problem, which relates to a hypothetical English furniture company. At the time of the analysis, the company was selling its products through 28 large showrooms which were situated on the edges of cities and towns throughout the country. Following a rapid expansion of sales in the mid-1980s, the company's market had been divided into four sales regions, North, West, East and South, and a manager had been made responsible for each. The North sales region, with nine outlets, had accounted for about 30% of national sales in the previous year, but the region had been economically depressed for some time, and the immediate prospects for an improvement in the position were bleak. The West region had only three outlets, and the company had been facing particularly stiff competition in this region from a rival firm. In the East region there was an even smaller operation, with only two outlets, but this was known to be a potential growth area, particularly in the light of the recent electrification of the main railway line to London. To date, the most successful sales area, accounting for 50% of national sales, had been the South. The company had a major operation here, with 14 showrooms, but, although the market in this region was buoyant, planning regulations meant that there had been a problem in finding suitable sites for the construction of new outlets.

The managers of the company were planning their strategy for the next 5 years, and the main problem they faced was that of deciding how the available resources should be allocated between the sales regions. For example, should they reduce the number of outlets in the North and reallocate the freed resources to the more promising East region? It was resolved that the key managers involved should meet as a group, with a facilitator available to structure a decision analysis model of the problem.

The main stages of the analysis

The decision analysis approach to resource allocation problems involves a number of stages, which are summarized below. Note, however, that the analysis rarely proceeds smoothly from one stage to the next. As a greater understanding of the problem emerges, it will often be found necessary to return to earlier stages in order to make revisions to the original model:

Stage 1: Identify the resources that are to be allocated, the areas to which they can be allocated and the various benefits that it is hoped this allocation will achieve.

Stage 2: Identify the possible strategies that are available for each area.

Stage 3: For each area, assess the costs and benefits of the different strategies.

Stage 4: Assess the within-criterion weights so that each benefit can be measured on a common scale.

Stage 5: Assess the across-criteria weights that will enable the values for the different benefits to be combined on an overall benefit scale.

Stage 6: Use a computer to calculate the costs and benefits for every package and identify the efficient frontier.

Stage 7: Propose a package that appears to achieve the desired objectives within the constraints of the resources available.

Stage 8: Use the computer to find if there are packages on the efficient frontier that offer higher benefits for the same cost as the proposed package (or the same benefits at a lower cost).

Stage 9: Perform a sensitivity analysis on the results to identify which other packages would be worth considering if more or less resources were available and to examine the effects of changes in the data used in the model.

Determining the areas, resources and benefits[5]

The first question the group faced was the determination of the *areas* involved in the problem. The term 'area', in this context, refers to an area to which resources might be directed. Typical areas might be different research and development projects, different functional areas of a business or different product lines.

In this problem, the group soon decided that the four sales regions were the areas, but in some problems the identification of the areas is not so easy. The key point to bear in mind is that, apart from the fact that they are competing for resources, the areas should be regarded as separate compartments, with a decision in one area having virtually no effect on a decision in another. Statements such as 'If department X chooses that option, then we ought to do this' may reveal a lack of independence.

Having identified the areas, the managers of the furniture company had to think about the nature of the resources that they would be allocating to the different sales regions. Again, this proved to be easy, as their main concern was the efficient use of the company's money. Of course, in some problems there may be several resources that are to be allocated, such as personnel, equipment and production facilities.

Next, the group was asked to identify the benefits that it hoped would result from the allocation of money between the regions. After some discussion, it was agreed that there were three main objectives:

 (i) to maximize the profitability of the company in the short term ('Profit');
 (ii) to maximize the company's *national* market share ('Market share');
(iii) to minimize the risk associated with any developments ('Risk'). (Note that we will be using values rather than utilities here, even though the decision involves risk – we discussed this issue in Chapter 3.)

Identifying the possible strategies for each region

The group of managers then considered the strategies that were available in each region, and these are summarized in Figure 14.1. For example, in the North, two strategies were identified. Either the operation there could be scaled down so that only three outlets would be retained (this might be sensible in view of the recent poor performance of the company in this region) or the status quo could be maintained.

Note that in Figure 14.1 the strategies for each region are organized in the order of the level of resources that would be required, with level 1 representing the lowest level of expenditure. The figure can also be used to identify the possible combinations of strategies that could be adopted. Each combination of strategies is referred to as a *package*, so that one example of a package would be: reduce the outlets operated in the North to three, expand the West's operation to six outlets and maintain the status quo in the other two regions. As one of the two strategies in the North could be combined with one of the three strategies in the West and one of the three strategies in the East, and so on, the number of packages that were available was $2 \times 3 \times 3 \times 3$, which equals 54. In many problems this number is much higher. For example, Phillips[6] refers to an application where there were over 100 000 possible packages.

Assessing the costs and benefits of each strategy

The next stage in the formulation of the model was the assessment of the costs and benefits that were associated with each strategy. Table 14.1 shows the figures that were elicited from the group after much discussion. Note that, with the exception of the

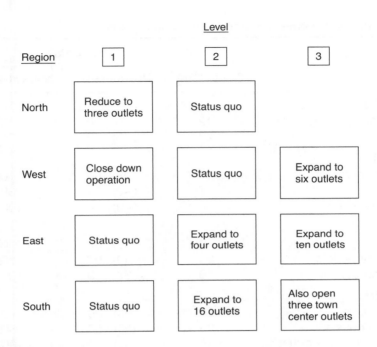

Figure 14.1 – Possible strategies identified by managers of the furniture company

monetary values, all the values in the analysis are measured on interval scales (see Chapter 3).

The first figures elicited from the group were the estimated costs over the next 5 years of carrying out each strategy. Closing down the operation in the West would be expected to save about $14 million.

Next, the performance of each of the strategies was assessed in relation to each benefit, starting with the North region. To do this, a value scale that ranged from 0 to 100 was used, with 0 representing the least desirable performance and 100 the most desirable. *This assessment was carried out separately by the group for each individual region*, so that in Table 14.1 the 100 in the 'Market share' column in the North region, for example, means that strategy 2 was thought to be the better of the two strategies available in the North for improving market share.

In the case of short-term profits, the group first estimated the profits that might result from the different strategies as monetary values (these figures are bracketed in the table), and these were then converted to values under the assumption that a linear value function was appropriate. Of course, in the case of 'Risk', a value of 100 denotes the strategy that was judged to be the least risky.

Table 14.1 – Values of the strategies in the individual regions

		Benefits		
Strategies	Costs ($m)	Profits ($m)	Market share	Risk
NORTH REGION				
(1) Reduce to three outlets	12	(6) 100	0	100
(2) Status quo	28	(−3) 0	100	0
WEST REGION				
(1) Close down operation	−14	(4) 100	0	100
(2) Status quo	7	(−2) 54	30	60
(3) Expand to six outlets	16	(−9) 0	100	0
EAST REGION				
(1) Status quo	2	(3) 100	0	100
(2) Expand to four outlets	25	(0) 91	25	70
(3) Expand to ten outlets	40	(−30) 0	100	0
SOUTH REGION				
(1) Status quo	20	(65) 100	0	100
(2) Expand to 16 outlets	25	(50) 50	80	40
(3) Add three town center outlets	45	(35) 0	100	0

Measuring each benefit on a common scale

Remember that the values were assessed separately for each region. This means that a movement from the worst performance (scoring 0) and the best performance (scoring 100) for a particular benefit in one region might be less preferable than the same movement in another region. For example (see Table 14.1), in the East, if the company expands to ten outlets rather than persisting with the status quo, the national market share score increases from 0 to 100. The same increase from 0 to 100 is obtained in the South if it adds three town center outlets rather than maintaining the status quo. However, when the group compared the actual improvements in national market share resulting from these changes, it found that the potential increases that could be achieved by investing in the South were only 60% as desirable as those that could be achieved by investing in the East. Indeed, it found that the potential market share improvement that could be gained by investing in the East was the greatest of all the regions.

This means that the group needed a common scale that would allow it directly to compare the '0 to 100' improvements in the different regions. To do this, it needed to assess *within-criterion weights*. Because the East offered the greatest improvement in

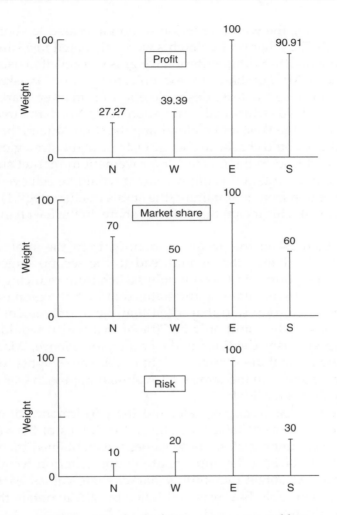

Figure 14.2 – The within-criterion weights for the furniture company problem

market share, it was allocated a within-criterion weight of 100 for this benefit, while the South was assigned a weight of 60. The within-criterion weights that were elicited for all the benefits are shown in Figure 14.2. We now give more details of how these were assessed.

For short-term profit, the weights were calculated directly from the group's original monetary estimates. Thus, the largest swing between the worst and best short-term profits offered by the different strategies was in the East (a difference of $33 million), and this swing was allocated a weight of 100. The swing between the worst and best level of profits in the North was only $9 million. As this was only 27.3% of the largest swing (i.e. $9/33 \times 100$), the within-criterion weight allocated to short-term profits in the North was 27.3. The other profit weights were calculated in a similar way.

For the other benefits, the within-criterion weights were elicited using a different approach. In the case of 'Market share', for example, the group was asked to imagine the package that would have the least desirable effect on market share. This would be the package that involved reducing the operation in the North to three outlets, closing down the operation in the West and maintaining the status quo in the other regions. It was then asked: if you could choose to change just one of the strategies in this package, which change would lead to the greatest improvement in market share? After some debate, the group thought that this improvement would be achieved if a switch was made in the East region from maintaining the status quo (strategy 1) to expanding to ten outlets (strategy 3). This meant that 'Market share' in the East region was assigned a weight of 100.

The facilitator then asked the group to identify, from the strategies available in the other regions, the change that would lead to the second largest improvement in market share. The group said that it would switch from reducing the operation in the North (strategy 1) to maintaining the status quo in that region (strategy 2). After further discussion, the group said that it felt that the improvement in market share resulting from this switch would only be 70% of that which would be achieved by the switch it had previously identified in the East region. Hence, 'Market share' in the North was allocated a within-criterion weight of 70. The weights for the South and West regions were assessed in the same way. A similar approach was used to elicit the within-criterion weights for 'Risk'.

Each benefit now has a common scale, and the performance of all the strategies can be assessed on this scale. Table 14.2 shows the values of the various strategies measured on these common scales. These values were obtained by multiplying each of the scores in Table 14.1 by the appropriate within-criterion weight and dividing by 100. For example, to obtain the South's market share values, each of the original values, 0, 80 and 100 in Table 14.1, was multiplied by 60% to obtain the new values of 0, 48 and 60 respectively.

Comparing the relative importance of the benefits

The managers next needed to assess the overall benefit of using a particular package by combining the values for the three benefits. This meant that they now had to determine a set of weights for these attributes. These weights are known as the *across-criteria weights*.

To derive the weights (which are shown in Figure 14.3), the facilitator looked for a region where a benefit had a within-criterion weight of 100, as this would show where there was the largest swing from the best to the worst position for that benefit. In fact,

Table 14.2 – Values of strategies with each benefit measured on a common scale

Strategies	Costs ($m)	Benefits Profits	Market share	Risk
NORTH REGION				
(1) Reduce to three outlets	12	27.27	0	10
(2) Status quo	28	0	70	0
WEST REGION				
(1) Close down operation	−14	39.39	0	20
(2) Status quo	7	21.27	15	12
(3) Expand to six outlets	16	0	50	0
EAST REGION				
(1) Status quo	2	100	0	100
(2) Expand to four outlets	25	91	25	70
(3) Expand to ten outlets	40	0	100	0
SOUTH REGION				
(1) Status quo	20	90.91	0	30
(2) Expand to 16 outlets	25	45.46	48	12
(3) Add three town center outlets	45	0	60	0

in this case all three benefits have their biggest swing in the East region (see Figure 14.2). He therefore asked the group of managers to consider this region, and asked them to imagine a strategy that offered the worst short-term profit (−$30 million), the poorest prospect for expanding market share and the highest (i.e. least desirable) level of risk. The managers were then asked: if you could change just one of these benefits to its best possible value, which would you choose? The group was unanimous that

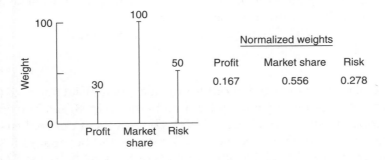

Figure 14.3 – The across-criteria weights for the furniture company problem

it would be most concerned to move to the best possible value for market share. This benefit was therefore given an across-criteria weight of 100.

The group's second choice was to move to the best possible position for risk. In fact, a move from the most risky to the least risky position was regarded as only 50% as important as the swing from the worst to the best market share position. 'Risk' was therefore allocated a weight of 50. A move from the lowest to the highest short-term profit (i.e. a move from −$30 million to $3 million) was the least preferred out of the possible swings, and, after some discussion, this benefit was assigned a weight of 30. The three across-criteria weights were then normalized (see Chapter 3), and these normalized weights are also shown in Figure 14.3.

Identifying the costs and benefits of the packages

It was now possible to identify the overall benefits and costs of any package. At this point the group was asked to propose a package that it felt would lead to the best use of the company's funds. (It was thought that around $70–80 million would be available to support the company's strategies in the four regions.) The package that the group suggested was a fairly cautious one. It simply involved maintaining the status quo in every region except the East, where an expansion of operations to four outlets would take place. From Table 14.2 it can be seen that this package would cost $80 million (i.e. $28 million + $7 million + $25 million + $20 million). It would result in profit benefits that would have a total value of 203.2 (i.e. 0 + 21.27 + 91 + 90.91), market share benefits of 110 and risk benefits of 112. Now that the across-criteria weights had been elicited, the overall benefits for this proposed package could be calculated by taking a weighted average of the individual benefits (using the normalized weights) as shown below:

$$\begin{aligned}
\text{Value of benefits} &= 0.167 \times (\text{value for profit}) + 0.556 \times (\text{value for market share}) \\
&\quad + 0.278 \times (\text{value for risk}) \\
&= (0.167 \times 203.2) + (0.556 \times 110) + (0.278 \times 112) \\
&= 126.2
\end{aligned}$$

If similar calculations were carried out for the least beneficial package (as identified by a computer), the value of benefits would be found to be 87.49. The corresponding figure for the most beneficial package is 159.9. The results of the analysis are easier to interpret if these values are rescaled, so that the worst and best packages have values of 0 and 100 respectively. As 126.2 is about 53.4% of the way between 87.49 and 159.9, the benefits of this package have a value of 53.4 on the 0–100 scale (i.e. this package

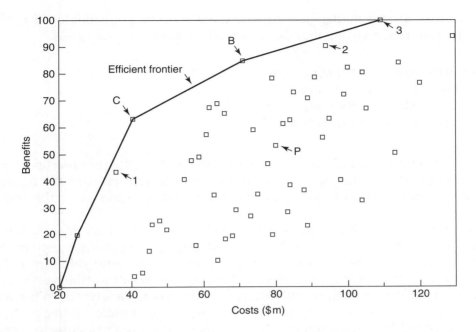

Figure 14.4 – Identifying the efficient frontier for the furniture company problem

would give 53.4% of the improvement in benefits that could be achieved by moving from the worst to the best package).

A computer can be used to perform similar calculations for all the other packages, and the results can be displayed on a graph such as Figure 14.4. On this graph, the efficient frontier links those packages that offer the highest value of benefits for a given cost (or the lowest costs for a given level of benefits).

Note, however, that the packages marked 1 and 2 on the graph do not appear on the efficient frontier, in spite of the fact that they offer the highest benefits for their respective costs. This is because the analysis assumes a constant rate of trade-off between costs and benefits (i.e. each additional point on the benefits scale is worth the same number of dollars). It can be shown that, if this is the case, then the efficient frontier will either be a continuous straight line or it will have the 'umbrella' shape shown in Figure 14.4, so that packages 1 and 2 will be excluded.

It can be seen from Figure 14.4 that the proposed package (represented by P) did not lie on the efficient frontier. When this is the case, the Equity package highlights two alternative packages. Package B is a package that will offer the 'best' level of benefits for a cost that is close to that of the proposed package, while package C is a package that will offer roughly the same level of benefits as the proposed package, but at the 'cheapest' level of costs.

Not surprisingly, the managers were interested in finding out about package B, and the Equity program revealed that this involved the following strategies:

In the North: Maintain the status quo
In the West: Expand to six outlets
In the East: Maintain the status quo
In the South: Expand to 16 outlets

This package would cost $71 million, which was less than the proposed package but would lead to benefits that had a value of 84.7, which was considerably higher. The group was surprised that the package did not involve any expansion in the promising East region.

The explanation for this was partly provided by the Equity program, which enabled the costs and benefits of each strategy to be compared for individual regions. Figure 14.5 shows the results for the West, East and South regions, with values of 100 and 0 representing the highest and lowest levels of benefits *for that region* (the North had only two available strategies, so the results for this region were not analyzed). When a graph has a shape like that shown in Figures 14.5(a) or (b), the 'middle' strategy will never be recommended by the computer. The reasons for this are analogous to those that led to the exclusion of packages 1 and 2 from the efficient frontier. This means that in the East the choice is between the status quo and a major expansion to ten outlets. The problem is that this major expansion would cost an extra $38 million, and the model suggests that this expenditure is not worthwhile given the limited funds that are available. It can also be seen that the opening of three town center sites in the South would actually lead to a loss of benefits, in spite of an extra expenditure of $20 million. (Note that these graphs do not take into account the within-criterion weights, so direct comparisons cannot be made between them.)

The group was now seriously considering the B package, but the facilitator suggested that it should first perform a sensitivity analysis before making a final decision.

Sensitivity analysis

The group's proposed package had been based on the assumption that funds of about $70–80 million would be available to finance the company's strategies. Because there was some uncertainty about how much money would actually be available, the group felt that it might be worth identifying the best packages if the company had more funds at its disposal. For example, it might be that an argument could be made for extra money if it could be shown that this would lead to a package with substantially increased benefits.

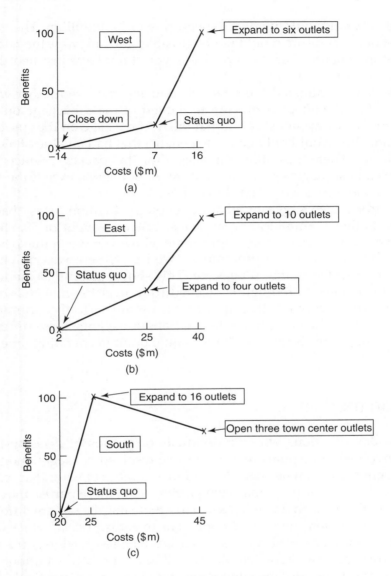

Figure 14.5 – Investigating the costs and benefits of strategies in the individual regions

The Equity software enables the user to explore the packages on the efficient frontier curve. Clearly, if more money is available, then this will involve a move along the curve to the right. Equity showed that the next package on the curve involved the same strategies as the B package, with the exception that in the East region an expansion to ten outlets would be recommended. This would lead to the maximum possible value of benefits of 100, but would involve expenditure of $109 million. The group agreed that this level of expenditure would not be feasible, and, anyway, the relatively small improvement in benefits over the B package would not have justified the increased costs, even if such funds were available.

The group also investigated the effect of reducing the money that was available to be invested (i.e. the effect of moving to the left of the B package on the efficient frontier curve). The computer showed that the next package on the curve would cost only $41 million, but would only generate benefits that had a value of 63 (in fact, this is the C package). There was little enthusiasm for this package, which would have involved the same strategies as the B package in all regions except the West, where the company's operations would be closed down completely.

One of the group then suggested that not enough attention to risk had been paid in the model. Rather than allocating an across-criteria weight of 50, she felt that a value of 70 would have been more appropriate. However, when this new value was entered into the computer, the program showed that there was no change in the strategies recommended by the B package. This shows again that models are often quite robust to changes in the figures elicited from decision-makers, so there is no need to be concerned about whether the assessments are perfectly accurate. Moreover, although members of the group may disagree about weights, these differences often do not matter, and, if this is the case, there is little point in spending time in debating them.

Negotiation models

We next consider situations where individuals or groups of decision-makers find themselves involved in disputes that need to be resolved by negotiation. As Raiffa[7] points out, negotiations can be characterized in a number of ways. For example, they may involve either two or more than two parties. Also, these parties may or may not be monolithic in the sense that within each party there may be several different interest groups. Some negotiations involve just one issue (e.g. the price at which a house is to be sold), while in other cases several issues need to be resolved (e.g. the weekly pay, holidays and training to which an employee will be entitled). In addition, factors such as whether or not there are time constraints, whether or not the final agreement is binding, the possibility (or otherwise) of third-party intervention and the behavior of the participants (e.g. are they honest, have they used threats?) will all vary from one negotiation problem to another.

Of course, some of the techniques we have met in earlier chapters might be useful when decision-makers are involved in negotiations. For example, decision trees can be used to represent the options open to a negotiator and the possible responses of his opponent. We focus here on an approach that can be helpful when a dispute involves just *two* negotiating parties who would like to reach agreement on *several* issues. As we shall see, it is possible to exploit the different levels of importance that the parties attach to each issue in order to achieve joint gains and so reach deals that are beneficial to both parties.

An illustrative problem

The managers of an engineering company were engaged in negotiations with a trade union. The union had put forward a package in which it demanded a 15% pay rise, an extra 3 days' holiday per year for all employees and the reinstatement of a group of workers who were fired after committing a breach of company regulations earlier in the year.

Figure 14.6(a) shows the management's value function over the range of possible pay awards (it was thought that an award of at least 3% would have to be conceded), together with their estimate of what the union's value function would look like. The managers attached the lowest value to an award of 15%, while this was the award that was most preferred by the union. Figures 14.6(b) and (c) show similar curves for the other two issues.

Weights were then elicited from the management team to reflect their view of the relative importance of swings from the worst to the best position on each issue, and these weights are also shown in Figure 14.6. Thus, for the management team, a swing from a 15% award to a 3% award was seen as the most important: a move from granting 3 days' holiday to no days was only 50% as important as this, and agreeing to the union's demand for worker reinstatement was only 10% as important. These weights, which were subsequently normalized, enabled the overall value to management of a particular deal to be measured. The management then made an assessment of the weights they thought the union would place on similar swings, and these are also shown in Figure 14.6.

The values to the management and union of any deal could now be calculated. After several meetings, the following tentative agreement had been reached: only a 3% pay award would be granted, but employees would receive an extra 3 days' holiday per year and the sacked workers would be reinstated. Table 14.3 shows how the value of this deal to the management and the union was calculated.

During the negotiations, one of the management team had used a computer to calculate the management and union values for all possible deals (assuming, for simplicity, that the percentage increase in pay would be a whole number). The results of these calculations are shown in Figure 14.7. On this graph the efficient frontier represents the set of agreements that are such that no party can improve its position without worsening the position of the other party (these agreements are said to be Pareto optimal). This means that, if an agreement does not lie on the efficient frontier,

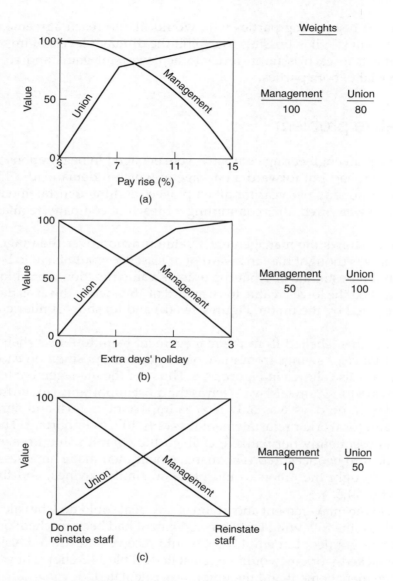

Figure 14.6 – Management and union value functions and weights

then other agreements are available that would either offer an improved position to both parties or allow one party to improve its position without doing so at the expense of the other.

It can be seen that the tentative deal (indicated by T on the graph) did not lie on the efficient frontier. All the agreements on the frontier between A and B were more

Table 14.3 – Calculation of values for the tentative management–union deal

	Value	Normalized weight	Value × weight
Management			
Pay rise of 3%	100	0.625	62.5
Three extra days' holiday	0	0.3125	0
Reinstatement of staff	0	0.0625	0
		Value of deal	62.5
Union			
Pay rise of 3%	0	0.348	0
Three extra days' holiday	100	0.435	43.5
Reinstatement of staff	100	0.217	21.7
		Value of deal	65.2

efficient, and it was therefore in the interests of both parties to try to improve on T by reaching one of these agreements. After much more bargaining, they eventually settled on deal X. This involved a 7% pay rise but only 1 day's extra holiday per year, although the staff who had been fired would still be reinstated. As the deal had a value

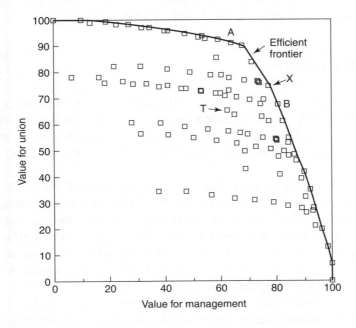

Figure 14.7 – Identifying the efficient frontier for the management–union negotiations

of 77.4 for the management and 74.9 for the union, it represented a clear improvement over the tentative deal for both parties.

It is obviously tempting to ask whether decision analysis can be used to determine an 'optimum' agreement from those available on the efficient frontier. The problem is that, in identifying such an agreement, we would have to compare the preference scales of the two parties. As we saw in the previous chapter when we considered interpersonal comparisons of preferences, such a comparison would require us to ask whether a swing from a value of 0 to 100 on the management's scale was greater or smaller than a similar swing on the union scale. For example, it may be that the management are far less concerned about a swing between these two values than the union, in which case perhaps an efficient deal should be selected that favors the union, but how can such comparisons be made?

In this problem we have assumed that management could make an assessment of the union's preferences and the trade-offs they were prepared to make. Of course, in the atmosphere of intense negotiations, with each party using bluff, pretence and what Raiffa[7] calls 'strategic misrepresentation' (i.e. 'exaggerating the importance of what one is giving up and minimizing the importance of what one gets in return'), such an assessment may be difficult to make. Nevertheless, in any negotiations it is necessary to form some idea of the other party's position, and analysis may lead to a sharper perception of this. In some situations, the parties in a dispute may be prepared to reveal their preferences to a third party, who will then guide them to (or, in some circumstances, impose upon them) an efficient deal.

Practical applications

Much of the early work in applying multi-attribute value analysis to negotiating problems was carried out by the consultants Decision and Designs Incorporated (DDI). This company helped US negotiators to formulate a negotiating strategy for the Panama Canal negotiations in 1974. Other applications can be found in Barclay and Peterson.[8]

The analytic approach was also adopted by a member of the US team in the 1978 negotiations between the United States and the Philippines over the status of the US bases on the islands. Raiffa[7] reports the experiences of the team member who argued that formal analysis led to a creative attitude to the negotiations. Rather than focusing purely on their own position and how it could be defended, the team were encouraged to look for ways of obtaining a better deal by trading off interests where their gain was not necessarily the other party's loss.

Phillips[6] reports the experiences of Cameron Peterson, a consultant with DDI. Peterson found that there were a number of advantages to be gained by bringing the decision analysis approach to bargaining problems. Negotiators could prepare in advance and anticipate the positions of other parties, and, by developing a clear understanding of the problem, they were able to be flexible and creative during the negotiations. There was also better communication within the negotiating team and between the team and their organization. However, the approach was found to be least effective where negotiators sought to preserve an air of mystery about their bargaining methods and skills. Rangaswamy and Shell[9] experimented with the use of a computerized negotiation support system and found that it led to better outcomes for both parties more frequently than negotiations that were carried out face to face or via emails.

Summary

In this chapter we first considered the application of decision analysis to problems where a group meets to decide how resources should be allocated between alternative uses. The problem was characterized by a small number of objectives but a very large number of possible courses of action, and a computer was therefore required to help in the comparison of the alternatives. The use of decision analysis facilitated group participation in the decision process, so that the conflict between centralization and local decision-making could be resolved. We then showed how decision analysis can help decision-makers who are involved in negotiations to identify improved deals that are in the interests of both parties.

Discussion questions

(1) What is the commons dilemma and how can decision analysis help to resolve it?
(2) Explain the distinction between within-criterion and across-criteria weights in resource allocation models.
(3) A group of executives have to allocate investment funds between six possible product lines. Their objectives are: (i) to maximize the *growth* of the company, (ii) to maximize *export* earnings, (iii) to maximize *profit* and (iv) to minimize *risk*. After much debate, the group decides to assign the following across-criteria weights: Growth 100; Exports 10; Profit 80; Risk 20. Discuss how these weights could have been derived and explain what they mean.
(4) Will the use of a decision analysis resource allocation model in a decision conference necessarily lead to an optimum allocation of resources?

(5) Explain why sensitivity analysis is important when using resource allocation models in a decision conference.
(6) What are the potential benefits of using decision analysis in negotiation problems?
(7) What is meant by an efficient deal in the context of negotiation problems?
(8) In what circumstances will the additive value model be inappropriate when modeling a negotiator's preferences?
(9) A retail chain would like to purchase a playing field from Bellton council and build a new supermarket on the site. The negotiations between the retailer and the council involve three key issues: (i) the price at which the council will sell the land, (ii) whether the supermarket will build a new community center to compensate the local people for the loss of the playing field and (iii) the extent to which the retailer will landscape the area around the supermarket when the construction is complete (there will either be no landscaping, 'partial landscaping' or 'complete landscaping').

Table 14.4 – Details of deals

Price of land	Community center	Landscaping	Value to retailer	Value to council
$2m	No	None	100.00	0.00
$2m	No	Partial	97.73	3.91
$2m	No	Complete	94.32	19.57
$2m	Yes	None	62.50	36.96
$2m	Yes	Partial	60.23	40.87
$2m	Yes	Complete	56.82	56.52
$3m	No	None	88.64	26.09
$3m	No	Partial	86.36	30.00
$3m	No	Complete	82.95	45.65
$3m	Yes	None	51.14	63.04
$3m	Yes	Partial	48.86	66.96
$3m	Yes	Complete	45.45	82.61
$4m	No	None	43.18	43.48
$4m	No	Partial	40.91	47.39
$4m	No	Complete	37.50	63.04
$4m	Yes	None	5.68	80.43
$4m	Yes	Partial	3.41	84.35
$4m	Yes	Complete	0.00	100.00

Given below are the values that the retailer and the council attach to possible land prices that might be agreed (0 = worst outcome, 100 = best):

Price of land	Retailer's value	Council's value
$2 million	100	0
$3 million	80	60
$4 million	0	100

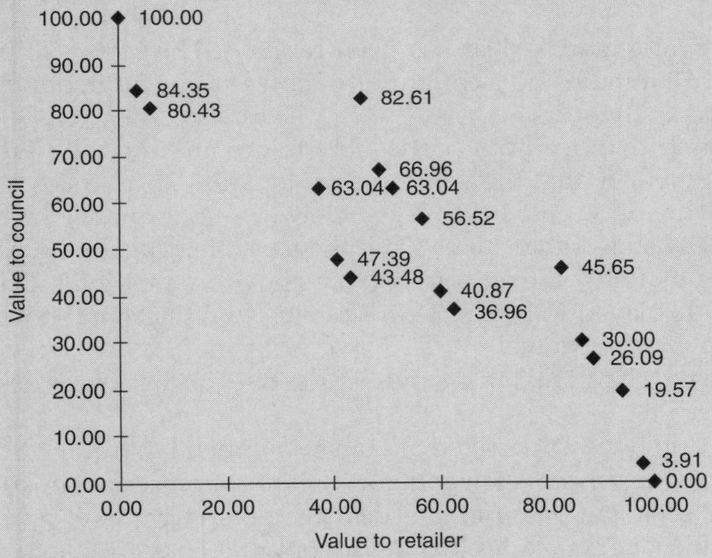

Figure 14.8 – Values of deals

The values attached to the possible levels of landscaping are shown below.

Landscaping	Retailer's value	Council's value
None	100	0
Partial	60	20
Complete	0	100

Details of the swing weights that the two parties attach to the three issues are shown below (100 = the most important swing):

Change in outcome	Retailer's weight	Council's weight
Land price increases from $2 million to $4 million	100	100
Community center not built to community center built	66	85
No landscaping to 'complete landscaping'	10	45

The following tentative deal has been reached. The land will be sold by the council for $2 million and a community center *will* be built, but there will be no landscaping of the site.

(a) Assuming that, for both parties, the issues are mutually preference independent, verify that the values of the tentative deal to the retailer and the council are 62.50 and 36.96 respectively (using normalized weights).

(b) Table 14.4 shows the values of all the possible deals to the two parties (assuming that only the outcomes given above are possible). This information is also displayed in Figure 14.8. The labels on the chart show the values of the deals to the council.

  (i) Use the chart and table to advise the two parties which deal they should agree on.

  (ii) Explain how you arrived at your recommendation.

(c) One of the supermarket negotiators favors your recommended deal because, having seen the value of the deal to the supermarket and the value to the council, he concludes that the supermarket has got a better deal than the council. Is his thinking correct? Explain your answer.

References

1. Phillips, L.D. (2007) Decision conferencing, in *Advances in Decision Analysis*, ed. by Edwards, W., Miles, R.F., Jr, and von Winterfeldt, D., Cambridge University Press, New York, NY.
2. Phillips, L. and Bana e Costa, C.A. (2007) Transparent prioritisation, budgeting, and resource allocation with multi-criteria decision analysis and decision conferencing, *Annals of Operational Research*, **154**, 51–68.
3. Hardin, G. (1968) The tragedy of the Commons, *Science*, **162**, 1243–1248.
4. Hardin, G. (1998) Extensions of 'The tragedy of the Commons', *Science*, **280**, 682–683.
5. Two case studies that illustrate processes for structuring the options, areas and benefits before using Equity are presented in: Montibeller, G., Franco, L.A., Lord, E. and

Iglesias, A. (2008) Structuring multi-criteria portfolio analysis models, Working Paper No. LSEOR 08.102, London School of Economics.

6. Phillips, L.D. (1989) Decision analysis in the 1990s, in *Tutorial Papers in Operational Research 1989*, ed. by Shahini, A. and Stainton, R., Operational Research Society.

7. Raiffa, H. (1982) *The Art and Science of Negotiation*, Harvard University Press, Cambridge, MA.

8. Barclay, S. and Peterson, C.R. (1976) Multiattribute utility models for negotiations, Technical Report DT/76-1, Decisions and Designs Inc., McLean, VA.

9. Rangaswamy, A. and Shell, G.R. (1997) Using computers to realize joint gains in negotiations: toward an 'electronic bargaining table', *Management Science*, **43**, 1147–1163.

Decision framing and cognitive inertia 15

Introduction

This chapter discusses the role of creativity in decision option generation. Are we able to recognize when tried-and-trusted ways of making decisions are out-moded, or do we, instead, tend to fall back on previously successful decisions and apply them in a habitual fashion? If the latter is the case, then we may be unable to recognize that rethinking a decision could be beneficial. The chapter analyses laboratory and real-world research on our ability creatively to improve our decision-making, and, finally, evaluates techniques that are designed to aid the creation of fresh decision options.

Creativity in problem solving

Imagine that you are given an 8 pint jug full of water, and a 5 pint jug and a 3 pint jug that are both empty. We will represent this as 8–8, 5–0 and 3–0, where the first figure indicates the size of the jug and the second figure indicates the amount of water in the jug. Your task is to pour the water from one jug into another until you end up with 6 pints in the 8 pint jug and 2 pints in the 3 pint jug (i.e. 8–6, 5–0 and 3–2).

What are the moves to change the initial state of the jugs and the goal state? Figure 15.1 gives the easiest series of moves. It is worthwhile working through this figure. First, jug 1 is used to fill jug 2. Then, jug 2 is used to fill jug 3. Next, the contents of jug 3 are poured into jug 1, and then, finally, the contents of jug 2 are poured into jug 3. Please check carefully that you understand this sequence before you read on.

Next, consider an 8 pint jug filled with water, an empty 5 pint jug and a 3 pint jug containing 1 pint of water (i.e. 8–8, 5–0 and 3–1). Figure 15.2 gives a series of moves to reach the goal state (8–6, 5–0 and 3–3). Let us again follow the logic of the moves.

	Jug 1	Jug 2	Jug 3
Initial state	8–8	5–0	3–0
Intermediate states	8–3	5–5	3–0
	8–3	5–2	3–3
	8–6	5–2	3–0
Goal state	8–6	5–0	3–2

Figure 15.1 – Moves to attain the goal state in the first water-jug problem

First, jug 1 is used to fill jug 2. Then, jug 2 is used to fill jug 3. Next, jug 3 is poured into jug 1, and then, finally, the contents of jug 2 are poured into jug 3. Do you follow the logic? In fact, *should* you follow the logic? If you feel that you should, then think again! A more efficient solution to the problem would be, simply, to pour the contents of jug 1 into jug 3. Luchins and Luchins[1] used problems similar to this with two groups of people. One group was given a series of problems that could *only* be solved by very similar sequences of moves. When this group was given a problem that *could* be solved by the familiar sequence *or* by a much simpler sequence, then the group applied the familiar, previously successful, sequence. In fact, the group members did not 'see' the simpler solution until it was pointed out to them. By contrast, the second group of people, who were immediately presented with the first group's final problem, saw the straightforward solution without difficulty. These studies demonstrate that thought can become *mechanized*, in that we tend automatically to follow a previously successful way of solving a problem without evaluating whether it is, indeed, best suited to the nature of the problem in hand.

Figure 15.3 presents another paper-and-pencil problem called the nine-dot problem.[2] Your task is to draw four continuous straight lines, connecting all the dots, without lifting your pencil from the paper. The correct solution is shown in the Appendix to this chapter. Try the problem first and then refer to the solution.

	Jug 1	Jug 2	Jug 3
Initial state	8–8	5–0	3–1
Intermediate states	8–3	5–5	3–1
	8–3	5–3	3–3
	8–6	5–3	3–0
Goal state	8–6	5–0	3–3

Figure 15.2 – Moves to attain the goal state in the second water-jug problem

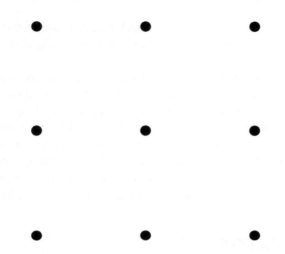

Figure 15.3 – The nine-dot problem

Consideration of our difficulties in solving the water jug and nine-dot problems indicates that the way in which a problem is 'framed' influences the type of solution that we see as appropriate.

How people frame decisions

The *decision frame* refers to how you view and structure a decision problem. It involves determining what must be decided, what the options are and which criteria will be used for choosing between the options. Consider a television station that has been experiencing a decline in its viewing figures over the past 2 years. There are several possible frames:

(1) The program-makers argue that a lack of funds to develop quality programs has led to the problem. To them, the courses of action that need to be considered include reducing administrative overheads to free resources for programs or increasing advertising rates to generate more funds.
(2) In contrast, the station's marketing managers blame a lack of investment in marketing. From their perspective, if they can obtain a larger budget, the key decision is: what is the best way to assign marketing funds to raise the profile of the station?
(3) Finally, a media consultant argues that the decline has occurred because the station has lost touch with its target audience – young viewers. Its programs have failed

to move with the times and now look staid and old fashioned. The key decision is how to change the character and mix of the programs and develop new ones.

Frames are bound to be simplifications of real problems, and each of them will only give a partial view of the decision problem. Difficulties can arise when a single frame is used unquestionably by managers, perhaps because of habit or professional specialism. This 'frame blindness' can lead to a failure to identify creative new solutions. It might also mean that a company continues to do business as it has always done – ignorant of the fact that its environment has fundamentally changed and that a complete rethink of its operations is required. We next discuss some problems that can arise because of decision frames, and then suggest ways of avoiding these problems.

Solving the wrong problem

From the 1940s to the 1970s, US car manufacturers used mathematical methods to determine the optimum length of production runs of particular car models. Changing from the production of one model to another took time while machinery was set up or reconfigured. This changeover time, which was taken to be between 6 and 8 hours, led to a loss of production, so frequent changes were undesirable. On the other hand, production runs that were too long led to high inventory levels and hence high inventory holding costs. The mathematical models were designed to identify the length of run that gave the best balance between the costs arising from lost production and the inventory costs.

Japanese manufacturers, particularly Toyota, framed the problem differently. They focused on reducing the changeover time (which US manufacturers assumed was fixed) and eventually got it down to 44 seconds. This saved thousands of dollars of production costs compared with their US rivals and almost led to the demise of the US car industry. The US managers had become stuck in a particular frame, which led them to invest considerable effort in solving the wrong problem.

Get hooked on complexity – overlooking simple options

It is often tempting to view decision problems through a 'technical frame' and to become so absorbed in the complexity of this approach that simple solutions go unnoticed. For example, there were a large number of complaints from passengers arriving at an airport terminal about the long waits they had to endure before their luggage appeared on the carousel. Much effort was expended in trying to improve the logistics and in investigating if the baggage handling system could be redesigned. In spite of this, the solution to the problem turned out to be simple.

Passengers alighting from aircraft had to follow a longer route before they got to the carousels, by which time their baggage was usually waiting for them. The number of complaints dropped to zero.[3]

Edward de Bono[4] reports a similar simple solution to a problem. The Red Telephone Company in Australia was losing money because telephone regulations meant that local calls cost the same amount, irrespective of the call's duration. As a result, people were often occupying its telephone kiosks for long periods, but generating only small amounts of cash for the company. The company needed a way to discourage long telephone calls, but financial disincentives were not permitted. The problem was solved simply by putting lead weights into telephone handsets so that people experienced discomfort if they made excessively long calls.

Imposing imaginary constraints and false assumptions on the range of options

Sometimes, decision-makers limit the range of options that they consider because they wrongly assume other options are infeasible. In the nine-dot problem that we looked at earlier, people usually make the false assumption that you cannot draw the lines outside the 'box' created by the dots. Beliefs like 'our customers would never accept this change to our product' or 'this development would be a technical impossibility' often go unchallenged. As we saw earlier, the US automobile industry assumed that the changeover time between car models could not be reduced below 6–8 hours, and they framed their decision accordingly. Similarly, many of Thomas Edison's inventions were thought to be infeasible by the scientific establishment of the day.

False assumptions can also rule out the consideration of courses of action that, in retrospect, would have been highly desirable. After the Polaroid camera was invented, Kodak assumed that customers who had purchased their films and cameras in the past would still be prepared to wait to have their photographs developed. They ruled out the option of moving into instant photography until it was too late and lost billions of dollars as a result. A similar mistake was made by manufacturers of Swiss watches, who assumed that their market for mechanical watches was unassailable when Japanese companies started making electronic quartz watches in the late 1960s. They did not respond to the challenge and sustained huge losses in market share and jobs.

Sensitivity to reference points

A study of satisfaction among Olympic medalists found that bronze medalists are often happier with their medal than silver medalists.[5] Similarly, studies of the levels of happiness of citizens in countries like the UK and USA have found that these have hardly changed over the past 40 years or so, in spite of increasing levels of wealth.[6]

What can account for these odd results? The answer lies in the fact that, when we evaluate outcomes or consequences, we examine how far these are from reference points. The bronze medalists compare their achievement to the reference point of not winning a medal at all and hence feel positive about the outcome. In contrast, the reference point for the silver medalist is a gold medal, and their achievement looks poor by comparison. Similarly, when evaluating your wealth, the reference points are likely to be the wealth you are accustomed to and the wealth of other people you are aware of. Thus, if everyone else has a similar increase in wealth to you, you probably will not feel any better off. So strong is this influence of reference points that a majority of Harvard students said they would prefer to live in the first of the two imaginary worlds below:[7]

World 1: You get $50 000 a year, while other people get, on average, $25 000.
World 2: You get $100 000 a year, while other people get, on average, $250 000.

This means that changing the reference point in a decision frame can lead to a totally different decision. Russo and Schoemaker[8] report on the case of a Texas manager who, in 1983, was facing a lot of opposition from his workforce over an average salary increase of 5%. The employees had as their reference points the recent 20% increase in the company's profits and the large wage increases that accompanied the high inflation of the 1970s. The manager then publicized the fact that a local competitor had only offered a 3% wage increase (and had threats of redundancies). A new reference point was created, and dissatisfaction quickly evaporated. The 'disease problem' referred to in Chapter 6 provides another example of how decisions can be reversed by changing the reference point.

Narrow bracketing of decisions

The way we mentally bracket groups of decisions together often influences how much risk we are prepared to take when making each decision. In companies, when projects are evaluated one at a time rather than part of an overall portfolio there is likely to be an extreme unwillingness to take risks. Taking a broader view by looking at all of the projects together can act as an antidote to this excessive risk aversion.

For example, Richard Thaler[9] was teaching a group of executives from one firm, each of whom was responsible for managing a separate division. He asked each whether he or she would be willing to undertake a project for the division if it had a 50% chance of generating a return of $2 million and a 50% chance of losing $1 million. Only three of the 25 executives accepted the gamble. However, when the company's CEO was asked whether he would like to undertake a portfolio of 25 of these investments, he nodded enthusiastically. From the CEO's perspective, losses on some of the projects would be more than compensated for by the gains on others.

Inertia in strategic decision-making

Real-world studies

In the strategic decision-making literature, frame blindness is closely linked to what has been termed 'cognitive inertia'. Many writers on strategic management have argued that, for survival, an organization must retain or improve its alignment with the external world. However, often companies can find themselves continuing to use a frame that becomes outdated as the world outside the company changes. These companies exhibit strategic inertia as the current frame becomes more and more deeply embedded in the organization and commitment to an inappropriate strategy increases. The UK and US auto industries again provide a good example of this. As we have seen, up to the late 1970s they adopted a production-oriented frame. This focus on production was characterized by a desire for optimum manufacturing efficiency, long product runs and few models. Henry Ford famously said, 'We'll give the consumer whatever color he wants, as long as it is black.' In contrast, other countries' frames were more customer oriented – responsiveness to changes in customer demand was the focus. In the UK and the US, the high level of commitment to a – previously successful – production-oriented strategy was slow to adapt to a world where changes in customer preferences meant that past demand was no longer predictive of the future demand.

Managers' mental models of the world, exemplified by the use of a single frame, are analogous to single visual perspectives on a scene. One viewpoint through a window *frame* may mean that only part of the external world is in view while another observer, looking through a different window frame, may see more (or less) of the external environment. Additionally, the *past experience* of the observer shapes (mis)interpretation of events that occur. Hodgkinson and Johnson[10] studied the variability between individual managers' mental models of competitive structures in the UK grocery retailing industry. They found considerable variation in the nature and complexity of industry views from managers both within and between companies. The nature of this diversity was associated with the functional roles that individual managers held.

Barr et al.[11] argue that inappropriate mental models may 'prevent managers from sensing problems, delay changes in strategy and lead to action that is ineffective in a new environment'. For example, Porac et al.[12] studied competitive models of senior managers in the Scottish knitwear industry. Although the Scottish knitwear producers account for less than 5% of world production, when the managers were asked to define their competitors, the serious competitors were almost exclusively nominated as Scottish. In our perceptual analogy, this is equivalent to a single familiar viewpoint giving a restricted view of the world. In addition, if the observer has little experience beyond that gained through the familiar viewpoint, then newly emerging events in the world can only be interpreted from within this perspective. Barr et al. argue that munificent environments may confirm outdated mental models, in that organizational weaknesses, even if perceived, may go unaddressed if firms enjoy profitability.

Johnson[13] used a single longitudinal case study of the UK retail clothing industry to study decision-making processes. His focus was on the (mis)match between changes in the firm's strategy as it sought to succeed in a changing environment. He sought to identify whether incremental (i.e. small, step-by-step) changes in strategy were beneficial or harmful to overall survival and success. He concluded that market signals of a failing strategy were not interpreted as such, and that managers, in a previously successful business, sought to reduce the perceived importance of such dissonant information – such that the prevailing strategy did not keep pace with environmental change. He concluded that the sensing of external signals is muted because the signals are not meaningful in themselves but take on relevance from the viewpoint of the managers' model. Political pressures within the organization acted to quell dissonant or 'deviant' opinion that recognized the true importance of the information.

In summary, the literature on cognitive inertia argues that, as the external world changes, then mental models that managers use to interpret events also change. But changes in mental models are likely to be incremental and thus not well matched *if* the environmental change is discontinuous. Additionally, if individual members of management teams do express dissenting opinion about the (in)appropriateness of current strategy, then such dissent is likely to be stifled by the majority favoring incremental change. Recognition of any mismatch between strategy and environment is thus likely to be belated rather than timely.

The empirical work on cognitive inertia has tended to be in-depth analysis of case histories rather than systematic study of the generality of the phenomena illustrated (often very persuasively) in the case studies.[14] However, in the psychological laboratory, similar behavior has been intensively studied, and the question of the validity of judgment has been a major research focus. It is to this research that we now turn. Our focus will be on drawing inferences from the pattern of the laboratory findings on the quality of human cognition for understanding failures in strategic cognition. In Chapter 10, we provided a catalogue of the results of research in the psychological laboratory and discussed possible implications of these for probability assessment. In this chapter, our focus is somewhat different: we exemplify those psychological processes that, in our view, underpin cognitive inertia.

Studies in the psychological laboratory

As we saw in Chapter 10, research within what became known as the 'heuristics and biases' paradigm focused on the rules of thumb that decision-makers can use in making judgments. The overall conclusion of this research was that the heuristic principles used could lead to bias. Some authors went as far as to coin the phrase 'cognitive cripple' to describe man's performance on laboratory paper-and-pencil tasks.[15] Several aspects of this research link directly to the phenomenon of strategic inertia as we have described it. In a number of investigations, Edwards and his colleagues[16] found that unaided revision of opinion was often *less* than Bayes' theorem (a normative theory of opinion revision, see Chapter 9) would prescribe. This result was termed *conservatism*. Most of the laboratories' research has used the 'book-bag-and-poker-chip' paradigm. The basic paradigm was as follows. The experimenter holds three opaque book bags. Each contains 100 poker chips in different, but stated, proportions of red and blue. The experimenter chooses one bag at random, shuffles the poker chips inside and successively draws a single poker chip from the bag. After each draw, the poker chip is replaced and all the poker chips are shuffled before the next draw.

The subject's task is to say how confident (in probability terms) he or she is that the chosen bag is bag 1, bag 2 or bag 3. The data from a large number of laboratory studies, using tasks very similar to the one described, show that the amount of opinion revision is often less than the theorem would prescribe. *However*, the *amount* of conservatism shown in a particular task is highly situation specific. Pitz *et al.*[17] documented an 'inertia effect' where people tended *not* to revise their probabilities downward once the *initial* part of a sequence of data had favored one of the hypotheses (bags) under consideration. In other words, people seem unwilling to reduce their probabilities on favored hypotheses following disconfirming evidence. Highly diagnostic data are not recognized as such. Winkler and Murphy[18] argued that this is because, in the real world, data are *often* unreliable and all data may be (inappropriately) treated as such. Ayton and Wright[19] review the evidence for the pervasiveness of conservatism in the revision of opinion. One conclusion is that individuals are able to match their opinion revision to a slow-changing environment, but, if environmental change is fast (i.e. information received is highly diagnostic), then opinion change lags behind. Such a lag typifies descriptions of strategic inertia in business situations. Additionally, as we demonstrated in Chapter 10, Tversky and Kahneman[20] identified a heuristic called *anchoring and adjustment* where people made insufficient adjustments from initial estimates, or anchors, even when this anchor was implausible. Bolger and Harvey[21] found strong evidence for the generality of the anchor-and-adjust heuristic in judgmental forecasting. Forecasts made by people tended to be too close to the most recent observation, so that they underestimated underlying changes in the series they were forecasting.

Evans[22] reviewed another bias in judgment, which is termed the *confirmation bias* (we introduced this in Chapter 11). This refers to people's tendency to test a hypothesis in a manner that is more likely to minimize rather than maximize the chances of falsification. For example, the four-card selection task illustrates this.[23] In this procedure, an individual is told a rule such as 'if a card has a D on one side, then it has a 4 on the other side'. He/she is then shown four cards lying on a table, which display on their facing sides the following symbols:

D R 4 6

The individual is then asked to decide which cards need to be turned over in order to find out whether the rule is true or false, i.e. seek out evidence to investigate the truth of the rule. Most individuals say that only the D must be turned, or else the D and the 4. But turning the 4 is irrelevant, as the rule would allow any letter to be on the back. Most individuals do not choose the card 6 – which could well demonstrate the falsity of the rule.

In another related study, individuals are told that the experimenter has a rule in mind that classifies sets of three integers, which we will call triples. The individual is then told that an example of a triple that conforms to the experimenter's rule is 2 4 6. The individual is then instructed to try to discover the rule by generating triples for testing. The experimenter provides feedback, telling the individual in each case whether the triple conforms or not. Individuals are instructed not to announce the rule until they are quite sure that they know it. The experimenter's rule is, in fact, simply 'any ascending sequence', but most people formulate hypotheses such as 'ascending in equal intervals' and test triples such as 4 8 12 or 20 40 60, etc. Eventually, they announce their rule and are convinced of its correctness. In other words, individuals formulate positive tests that can never be falsified.[24]

In the real world of strategic decision-making, such clear-cut falsifying evidence will be very rare and, perhaps, is therefore even less likely to be sought out and/or be recognized as significant for the falsification of a currently followed strategy. Taken together, the laboratory results of conservatism in opinion revision, anchoring and insufficient adjustment and the confirmation bias are analogies of inertia and instrumentalism in strategic decision-making. Additionally, generalization of these laboratory results suggests that inertia and incrementalism may well be pervasive in strategic thinking.

Non-rational escalation of commitment

Another approach in behavioral decision-making has focused on the unwillingness of individuals (and groups of individuals) to reverse a series of decisions if they feel high personal responsibility for poor outcomes occurring early in the sequence. *'Non-rational escalation of commitment'* refers to the tendency of individuals to escalate commitment to a previously selected course of action to a point beyond that which a rational model of decision-making would prescribe. In many studies, individuals who hold themselves responsible for a poor initial decision throw good money after bad and fail to recognize that time and/or expenses already invested are sunk costs. The decision-maker, in face of negative feedback about the consequences of his earlier decision, feels the need to affirm the wisdom of it by further commitment of resources so as to 'justify' the initial decision or provide further opportunities for it to be proven correct. Negative feedback is rationalized away as ephemeral rather than carrying an important message about the quality of the prior decision. Staw and Ross[25] showed that the tendency to escalate commitment by high-responsibility individuals was particularly pronounced where there was some way to develop an explanation for the initial failure such that the failure was viewed as unpredictable and unrelated to the decision-maker's action (e.g. the economy suffered a severe setback and this caused ...). Bazerman *et al.*[26] showed that groups who made an initial collective decision that proved unsuccessful allocated significantly more funds to escalating their commitment to the decision than did groups who 'inherited' the initial decision.[27]

Clearly, the social processes causing escalation of commitment will tend to magnify any inherent inertia towards a currently followed strategy. Here are two well-known examples of non-rational escalation of commitment:

(1) *The Tennessee–Tombigbee water project*. This huge construction project involved building a set of locks designed to connect the Tennessee and Tombigbee rivers so that the US state of Tennessee would be opened up to the Gulf of Mexico. By 1981, the costs incurred had already amounted to over $1 billion. However, new estimates revealed that the cost of completing the project from that point forward would be greater than the potential benefits. The US senators involved with the project argued that 'To terminate a project in which $1.1 billion has been invested represents an unconscionable mishandling of taxpayers' dollars' and 'Completing [the project] is not a waste of taxpayers' dollars. Terminating a project at this stage of development would, however, represent a serious waste of funds already invested.' The project was completed in 1985, but will never pay back the costs incurred in its construction.

(2) *Concorde*. The supersonic aircraft was developed in the late 1960s and early 1970s by France and Britain. However, before the project's completion it was clear that it was unlikely to be an economic success because few orders had been placed for it and costs were escalating. As a result the British and French governments considered abandoning the project. One of the main arguments against abandonment was the money that had already been spent, and the project was allowed to continue with further resources being invested in it. Although it was a technological marvel, the plane eventually cost around $1 billion to develop. Only 20 planes were built, and these were virtually given away to the two countries' national airlines. The project has never made a profit and the huge cost has largely been borne by French and British taxpayers.

Overall, the results of research on escalation of commitment indicate that, once a great deal of time, effort and resources have been invested in a selected course of action *and* the outcomes are not as good as expected, the 'responsible' decision-maker will tend to feel that there is 'too much invested to quit now'. But resources *already invested* are non-recoverable *sunk costs* and, logically, should not be considered in the decision of whether or not to continue or discontinue commitment to a course of action.

How people react to a threat

Janis and Mann's *conflict theory*[28] describes a number of basic patterns of coping with a challenge (threat or opportunity). Intense conflicts, Janis and Mann argue, are likely to arise whenever a person has to make an important decision. Such conflicts become acute if the decision-maker becomes aware of the risk of suffering serious losses from whatever course of action is selected – including pursuing further the current course of action. Decisional conflicts refer to simultaneous opposing tendencies within the individual to accept or reject a given course of action. The most prominent symptoms of such conflicts are hesitation, vacillation, feelings of uncertainty and signs of acute emotional stress whenever the decision comes within the focus of attention. According to Janis and Mann, several types of decisional behavior called 'coping patterns' are a direct result of the conflict. *Defensive avoidance* can take three forms: *procrastination* involves postponing the decision; *buck passing* involves shifting the responsibility of the decision to someone else; *bolstering* includes exaggerating the favorable consequences of a course of action and minimizing the unfavorable consequences.

Defensive avoidance is preceded by high stress, as the risks attached to the current option(s) are seen as serious, but the coping patterns act to reduce the stress to acceptable levels. Clearly, once having made a stressful high-consequence decision – without the option of buck passing the responsibility elsewhere – an individual's coping pattern of bolstering the decision involves components of the escalation process described earlier.[29]

Additionally, a small, highly cohesive management *team* faced with a decision dilemma is likely to become so concerned about group solidarity that individual deficiencies in information processing and decision-making will be magnified. Structural faults in the organization (such as insulation of the management team from individuals or groups of individuals who might challenge their decision-making, homogeneity of the management team's social background and lack of methodical, even-handed procedures for dealing with controversial issues) will tend to produce '*groupthink*'[30] in such high-consequence situations. As we saw in Chapter 13, groupthink is essentially the suppression of ideas that are critical of the 'direction' in which a group is moving. It is reflected in a tendency to concur with the position and views that are perceived as favored by the group. Such a cohesive group may develop rationalizations for the invulnerability of the group's decision or strategy and inhibit the expression of critical ideas by dissenting members of the management team. These pitfalls of groupthink are likely to magnify individual failure to evaluate carefully alternative courses of action or choices. Such incomplete appraisal of a decision may result in a failure to examine the risks of preferred decisions and a failure to work out contingency plans if the preferred course of action fails. A high level of group cohesiveness *and* a high external source of threat or stress are primary antecedents of groupthink. Overall, the consequences of groupthink will tend to magnify the inertia processes.

Overcoming inertia?

How can the biasing elements of the results from the psychological laboratory be reduced? Ideally, Russo and Schoemaker[8] argue, problems should be examined through more than one frame of reference. Organizational interventions that enable the manager to view the external world through multiple frames will facilitate strategic thinking. But how can multiple perspectives on a decision problem be facilitated such that new, creative decision options are recognized? Several of the decision researchers have addressed these issues, but the prescriptions have often been general calls to 'be alert' rather than clear-cut guidance for overcoming bias or generating new decision options. For example, Rubin[31] recommends that, in situations that could lead to escalation, as a decision-maker you should 'set limits on your involvement and commitment in advance' and 'remind yourself of the costs involved'. Russo and Schoemaker argue that managers should take an 'experimenting' approach to decisions and be willing to change decisions if they do not produce results. Further, they advocate that organizations should evaluate their managers on the basis of good decision processes rather than good outcomes because many decisions are risky and learning from failures is useful! Irving Janis,[30] in discussing ways of overcoming groupthink, recommends that the leader should: withhold his or her ideas at first; encourage new ideas and criticisms; make sure that the group listens to minority views; and use processes designed to delay consensus.

Russo and Schoemaker,[8] in discussing framing, argue that you should 'challenge the actions that you normally take on an issue', 'seek a devil's advocate viewpoint – welcome diverse opinions' and 'be creative'. One tool that they advocate to achieve 'frame awareness' is their 'frame analysis worksheet', which, essentially, asks decision-makers 'what aspects of the situation are left out of consideration?', 'what does the frame emphasize?' and 'how do other people think about this question differently from the way you do?' For example, in considering a car purchase decision, questions in the worksheet might elicit the response that used or foreign cars are not considered and neither is leasing. Further, the decision-maker's major emphasis (i.e. frame) might be on getting the cheapest car that will satisfy the need to carry a family of five at the lowest total operating costs per mile. Additionally, the decision-maker might respond that other people emphasize (i.e. frame) the decision in terms of lifestyle image (e.g. rugged 4 × 4s) or performance and handling (e.g. sports car similarities). Figure 15.4 details possible responses by the owner of the fast print and photocopy business that we discussed in Chapter 3 to Russo and Schoemaker's frame analysis questions.

Notice that the *reference point* of the owner is 'the good profitability of my business in its current location'. Psychologically, the owner will tend to judge alternative office relocation possibilities for his enforced move against this reference point on the profitability yardstick. If his current office's profitability is well above average, then

FRAME ANALYSIS WORKSHEET

The issue or issues the frame addresses (in a few words):

• where to relocate a fast print and photocopying business

What boundaries do I (we) (they) put on the question? In other words, what aspects of the situation do I (we) (they) leave out of consideration?

• the relocation is to be within 8 miles of the town center
• buying not considered
• won't consider another town/country

What yardsticks do I (we) (they) use to measure success?

• profitability and good working conditions

What reference points do I (we) (they) use to measure success?

• the profitability of my business in its current location

What metaphors – if any – do I (we) (they) use in thinking about this issue?

• Better the devil you know than the devil you don't

What does the frame emphasize?

• attracting new small customers
• continuing as before
• keeping costs low

What does it minimize?

• change of business/market segment

Do other people in the fast print and photocopy industry (fill in your own field) think about this question differently from the way I (we) (they) do?

• some would try and get a space in a big department store
• some would focus on building relationships with largish organizations such that the exact location of the business itself was immaterial to high turnover

Can I (we) (they) summarize my (our) (their) frame in a slogan?

• I am being forced to relocate and want to carry on my business in the same town

Figure 15.4 – An example of a response to Russo and Schoemaker's frame analysis questions

the potential profitability of alternative locations will tend to be seen as losses *relative* to his current position – even if the alternatives are well located and potentially *fairly* profitable. As we discussed earlier in this chapter, choices involving losses tend to lead to risk-seeking behavior. Alternatively, if it happened that the owner's choice of alternative office locations was between several offices that offered *greater* potential for profitability than his current office, then the alternatives would tend to be seen as gains *relative* to his current position. In such circumstances, his choice would tend to be risk averse.

Overall, skillful use of Russo and Schoemaker's frame analysis worksheet *may* prompt 'multiple frame awareness', which can be used to challenge whether the decision-maker's current or usual frame is, in fact, the most appropriate. However, evaluations of the worksheet's effectiveness have not yet been conducted. It is perhaps too early to say whether it can truly promote creative decision-making and overcome mechanization and inertia in decision-making.

Studies in the psychological laboratory and cognitive inertia: a synthesis

Altogether, conservatism in opinion revision, anchoring and insufficient adjustment, little weight placed upon disconfirming information, escalation of commitment and groupthink are likely to result in *overconfidence* in the perceived degree of alignment between strategy and environment. Such overconfidence is, we believe, likely to be relatively untouched by interventions such as calls to 'be alert'. As such, previously successful ways of making decisions will be adhered to. As we saw in Chapter 10, over-confidence in judgment is a systematic and pervasive finding of behavioral decision research.

Figure 15.5 presents our view of a systemic relationship between the results of behavioral decision research that we have detailed in this chapter. In this diagram, we attempt to integrate the results of the laboratory-based research with current knowledge of inertia in strategic decision-making.

In the diagram, the resting state of the system is that of a low perceived level of environmental threat leading to low stress level, which leads to strategic inertia.

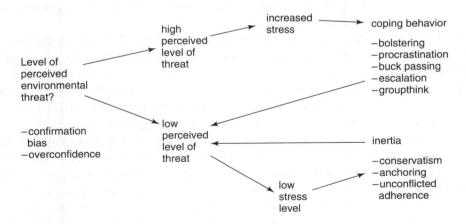

Figure 15.5 – The relationship between the perceived business environment and the strategic decision process

Conservatism, anchoring and unconflicted adherence to the currently followed strategy characterize this resting state. Nevertheless, the environment is monitored for environmental threats, but this monitoring is attenuated by confirmation bias and overconfidence. If the environmental threat is so severe that it *is* perceived as threatening unconflicted adherence to the current strategy, then the stress level rises and, soon afterwards, coping patterns such as bolstering, procrastination and buck passing are evidenced. Bolstering is characterized by escalation of commitment to the current strategy, and, in general, groupthink processes lead to perceived invulnerability and the suppression of critical ideas. Such coping patterns lower the perceived level of environmental threat, which results in a lowered stress level and so to inertia in strategic decision-making. Overall, our model proposes that we are, generally, routine thinkers rather than creative thinkers. The systemic processes in the model encourage the replication of previously successful ways of making decisions.

Summary

In conclusion, we feel that creativity in decision option generation is, in general, likely to be rare. Mechanization of thought processes or frame blindness seem, intuitively, to be widespread. Our model of inertia in strategic decision-making suggests that, especially in stressful, high-consequence situations, the degree of adherence to a previously successful strategy will increase rather than decrease. Russo and Schoemaker's frame analysis worksheet has the components to prompt awareness of alternative framings of a decision problem, but its efficacy in business decision-making is, as yet, unproven. Clearly, techniques to promote creativity in the generation of decision options – beyond the familiar – are not well developed.

However, the practice of scenario planning, which we will detail in the next chapter, *can*, we believe, act as a means of overcoming strategic inertia, as it implicitly accepts that managers' 'best guesses' about the course of future events and about the appropriateness of strategic choice may be mistaken. Essentially, scenario planning interventions in organizations construct multiple frames of the future states of the external world, only some of which may be well aligned with current strategy. This construction process is systematic and structured and, as such, complements other techniques such as the frame analysis worksheet. Advocates of scenario planning also argue that its process methodology can counter groupthink by allowing minority opinions about the future to have 'airtime' relative to majority opinion. Essentially, the process of scenario planning provides conditions under which the appropriateness of the continuation or escalation of a particular strategy can be falsified, as the degree of alignment between a strategy and a range of plausible futures is the focus of attention.

Discussion questions

(1) Does following a previously successful way of solving a problem have advantages as well as disadvantages?
(2) What business situations are likely to enhance any organizational tendency towards strategic inertia?
(3) Does your own organization suffer from any form of frame blindness or strategic inertia? If so, why are others in your organization unable to recognize and deal with this? What methods would you recommend using to overcome such limited perceptions?
(4) Apply the questions in the frame analysis worksheet to a major decision that you, or your organization, are currently facing. To what extent are new decision options created, or previously ignored options given renewed attention?

Appendix

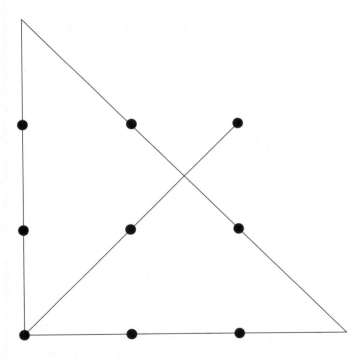

Figure 15.6 – Solution to the nine-dot problem (Figure 15.3)

References

1. Luchins, A.S. and Luchins, E.G. (1959) *Rigidity of Behavior*, University of Oregon Press, Eugene, OR.
2. Scheerer, M. (1963) Problem solving, *Scientific American*, **208**, 118–128.
3. Evans, J.R. (1991) *Creative Thinking in the Decision and Management Sciences*, South-Western, Cincinnati, OH.
4. de Bono, E. (1992) *Serious Creativity*, HarperCollins, London, UK.
5. Medvec, V., Madey, S. and Gilovich, T. (1995) When less is more: counterfactual thinking and satisfaction among olympic medalists, *Journal of Personality and Social Psychology*, **69**, 603–610.
6. Layard, R. (2005) *Happiness. Lessons from a New Science*, Penguin, New York, NY.
7. Solnick, S. and Hemenway, D. (1998) Is more always better? A survey on positional concerns, *Journal of Economic Behaviour and Organisation*, **37**, 373–383.
8. Russo, J.E. and Schoemaker, P.J.H. (1989) *Decision Traps*, Doubleday, New York, NY.
9. Thaler, R.H. (1999) Mental accounting matters, *Journal of Behavioral Decision Making*, **12**, 183–206.
10. Hodgkinson, G.P. and Johnson, G. (1994) Exploring the mental models of competitive strategists: the case for a processual approach, *Journal of Management Studies*, **31**, 525–551.
11. Barr, P.S., Stimpert, J.L. and Huff, A.S. (1992) Cognitive change, strategic action and organizational renewal, *Strategic Management Journal*, **13**, 15–36.
12. Porac, J.F., Thomas, H. and Baden-Fuller, C. (1989) Competitive groups as cognitive communities: the case of Scottish knitwear manufacturers, *Journal of Management Studies*, **26**, 397–416.
13. Johnson, G. (1988) Rethinking incrementalism, *Strategic Management Journal*, **9**, 75–91.
14. For a review, see Hodgkinson, G.P. (1997) The cognitive analysis of competitive structures: a review and critique, *Human Relations*, **50**, 625–654.
15. Slovic, P. (1972) From Shakespeare to Simon: speculations – and some evidence – about man's ability to process information, *Oregon Research Institute Bulletin*, **12**, 10–23.
16. For example, Phillips, L.D., Hayes, W.L. and Edwards, W. (1966) Conservatism in complex probabilistic inference, *IEEE Transactions in Human Factor in Electronics*, **7**, 7–18.
17. Pitz, G.F., Downing, L. and Reinhold, H. (1967) Sequential effects in the revision of subjective probabilities, *Canadian Journal of Psychology*, **21**, 381–393.
18. Winkler, R.L. and Murphy, A.M. (1973) Experiments in the laboratory and the real world, *Organizational Behavior and Human Performance*, **10**, 252–270.
19. Ayton, P. and Wright, G. (1994) Subjective probability: what should we believe? In *Subjective Probability*, ed. by Wright, G. and Ayton, P., John Wiley & Sons, Ltd, Chichester, UK.
20. Tversky, A. and Kahneman, D. (1974) Judgment under uncertainty: heuristics and biases, *Science*, **185**, 1124–1131.
21. Bolger, F. and Harvey, N. (1993) Context sensitive heuristics in statistical reasoning, *Quarterly Journal of Experimental Psychology*, **46A**, 779–811.
22. Evans, J.St.B.T. (1987) Beliefs and expectations as causes of judgmental bias, in *Judgmental Forecasting*, ed. by Wright, G. and Ayton, P., John Wiley & Sons, Chichester, UK.

23. From Wason, P.C. (1966) Reasoning, in *New Horizons in Psychology I*, ed. by Foss, B.M., Penguin, Harmondsworth, UK.
24. For a review, see Klayman, J. and Ha, U.-W. (1987) Confirmation, disconfirmation, and information in hypothesis testing, *Psychological Review*, **94**, 211–228.
25. Staw, B.M. and Ross, J. (1978) Commitment to a policy decision: a multi-theoretical perspective, *Administrative Science Quarterly*, **23**, 40–64.
26. Bazerman, M.H., Giuliano, T. and Appelman, A. (1974) Escalation in individual and group decision making, *Organizational Behavior and Human Decision Processes*, **33**, 141–152.
27. For a review and linkages to organizational decision-making, see Drummond, H. (1994) Escalation in organizational decision making: a case of recruiting an incompetent employee, *Journal of Behavioral Decision Making*, **7**, 43–56.
28. Janis, I.L. and Mann, L. (1979) *Decision Making*, Free Press, New York, NY.
29. For a review of conflict theory, see Mann, L., Barnett, P., Radford, M. and Ford, S. (1997) The Melbourne decision making questionnaire: an instrument for measuring patterns for coping with decisional conflict, *Journal of Behavioral Decision Making*, **10**, 1–19.
30. Janis, I.L. (1972) *Victims of Groupthink*, Houghton Mifflin, Boston, MA. For a recent review of groupthink, see Park, W.-W. (1990) A review of research on groupthink, *Journal of Behavioral Decision Making*, **3**, 229–245.
31. Rubin, J.Z. (1980) Experimental research on third party intervention in conflict: toward some generalizations, *Psychological Bulletin*, **87**, 379–391.

Scenario planning: an alternative way of dealing with uncertainty

Introduction

Scenario planning is an alternative way of dealing with uncertainty to that encapsulated in decision analysis. This chapter outlines the conceptual approach, provides a step-by-step guide to scenario construction and shows how decisions can be evaluated against scenarios of plausible futures. Finally, we show how scenario planning can be combined with the SMART approach to decision-making with multiple objectives, which we detailed in Chapter 3.

First, consider the following quotation from an article in the magazine *Newsweek* that was published on 28 January 1991. The article was written by a journalist who was analyzing the reasons for US unpreparedness for Saddam Hussein's invasion of Kuwait:

In the days leading up to the invasion, the intelligence agencies sent President Bush a list of predictions. The list was arranged in order of probability. 'None had as their first choice the prediction that Saddam Hussein would attack', says one intelligence operative who saw the reports. Prediction No 1 was that Saddam was bluffing. Prediction No 2 was that he might seize part of the Rumaila oilfield that straddles Iraq and Kuwait and possibly Warba and Bubiyan islands, two mudflats blocking Iraq's access to the Persian Gulf. It was assumed that he would pull back from Kuwait once the islands were secured. 'The line we kept hearing around here was that he has just massed there along the Kuwait border to drive up the price of oil', recalls one senior Pentagon officer. 'If people were saying he is for real and he is going to invade, it was not briefed to us as definite'.

Several sounder voices did predict an invasion but they went unheard. One midlevel Mideast analyst at the CIA got it right, but his warning 'got lost' in the momentum of the opposing consensus. Marine Corps Officers, scanning satellite photos that showed Iraqi air-defence units, tanks and artillery deployed forward at the Kuwait border, surmised that this could only mean an invasion, but they kept their silence because of bureaucratic pressures. The Defence Intelligence Agency's top analyst for the Middle East was convinced that

Saddam would invade and warned the Senate Intelligence Committee that the dictator might not be bluffing. His own shop did not buy it. The DIA went along with the pack.

While the Iraqis and the Kuwaitis gathered in Jeda for a final haggle over oil and borders, the House Foreign Affairs Committee summoned John Kelly, the assistant secretary of state covering the Mideast, to explain what was going on. 'If Iraq for example charged into Kuwait for whatever reason, what would our position be with regard to the use of US forces?' chairman Lee Hamilton inquired. 'That, Mr Chairman, is a hypothetical or a contingency question, the kind which I cannot get into', Kelly replied.

Source: D. Waller, T. M. Defrani, A. McDaniel, M. Garrard, R. Wilkinson, C. Dickey, J. Bartholet and D. Pedersen, The Path to War, *Newsweek* 28 January 1991 – http://www.newsweek.com/id/121588/page/4

From this journalistic analysis, three major points emerge. The first is that consideration was only devoted to those events seen as most likely. The second is that a process akin to 'groupthink' (see Chapter 13) took place, in that, once the group of decision-makers had made up its mind what was going to happen, even *conclusive* information that the prediction (decision) was poor did not change the prediction. Those individuals who expressed dissenting opinion soon quelled their dissent and 'went along with the pack'. Given such (inappropriate) confidence in the prediction of Saddam Hussein's intent, contingency planning for events seen as of low probability was minimal or zero.

How could the invasion have been predicted? Would knowledge that subjective probabilities are often overconfident (cf. Chapter 10) have helped? Would an understanding and appreciation of the nature of the heuristics that can lead to biased estimates of subjective probability be helpful in producing more valid assessments? Perhaps, perhaps not. Consider Figure 16.1, which presents two straight lines of equal length. Next, consider the same two lines but with 'arrowheads' attached. The original lines (i.e. the shafts of the 'arrows') now *seem* of unequal length. Your knowledge of their equality of length does *not* reduce the effect of the *visual* illusion. Indeed, the heuristics and resultant biases that we documented in Chapter 10 were originally

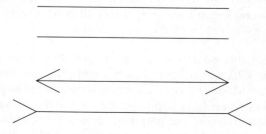

Figure 16.1 – The Müller–Lyer illusion

characterized by Kahneman and Tversky as 'cognitive illusions'. If *cognitive* illusions share the same nature as visual illusions, then knowledge of the cause of an illusion may not, by itself, reduce or remove the illusory effect.

The practice of scenario planning implicitly accepts that managers are *not* able to make valid assessments of the likelihood of unique future events and that 'best guesses' of what the future may hold may be wrong. This view is in harmony with Gerd Gigerenzer's argument that probability theory does not apply to single events (see Chapter 10). Advocates of scenario planning also argue that it can counter groupthink by allowing minority opinions about the future to have 'airtime' relative to majority opinion.

How do scenarios achieve this? The first point to note is that a scenario is not a forecast of the future. Multiple scenarios are pen-pictures of a range of *plausible* futures. Each individual scenario has an infinitesimal probability of actual occurrence, but the *range* of a *set* of individual scenarios can be constructed in such a way as to *bound* the uncertainties that are seen to be inherent in the future – like the edges on the boundaries surrounding a multidimensional space.

Scenarios focus on key uncertainties *and* on certainties about the future, and they use this information to construct pen-pictures in an information-rich way in order to provide vivid descriptions of future worlds. By contrast, subjective probabilities entered into a decision tree provide numerical values that can be used in an expected utility calculation. The judgment process that produced such numbers is often not verbalized or recorded. When individuals disagree about their subjective probabilities for a critical event, then decision analysis practice is often to take an average, or weighted average, rather than to explore, in detail, the reasoning processes underlying individuals' assessments. Inherent in such analysis is the assumption that it is useful and possible to attempt to predict the future, whereas scenario planning assumes that the best that can be done is to identify critical future uncertainties and plan for the range of futures that could, plausibly, unfold. Essentially, scenarios highlight the reasoning underlying judgments about the future and give explicit attention to sources of uncertainty *without* trying to turn an uncertainty into a probability. A major focus is *how* the future can evolve from today's point in time to the future that has unfolded in the horizon year of the scenario – say 10 years hence. The relationship between the *critical* uncertainties (as they resolve themselves – one way or the other), important predetermined trends (such as demographics, e.g. the proportion of the US population who are in various age bands in, say, 10 years' time) and the behavior of actors who have a stake in the particular future (and who will tend to act to preserve and enhance their own interests within that future) is thought through in the *process* of scenario planning such that the resultant pen-pictures are, in fact, seen as plausible to those who have constructed the scenarios.

In the next section of this chapter we provide a concrete example of one quick way to construct extreme scenarios. In a subsequent section we introduce a second, more sophisticated, method of scenario construction that produces less extreme and, arguably, more plausible scenarios.

1. Identify the issue of concern and the horizon year that will be captured in the scenarios.

2. Identify predetermined trends that have some degree of impact on the issue of concern.

3. Identify critical uncertainties, that when resolved (one way or the other), have some degree of impact on the issue of concern.

4. Identify the degree to which the trends and resolved uncertainties have a negative or positive impact on the issue of concern.

5. Create extreme worlds by putting all positively resolved uncertainties in one scenario and all negatively resolved uncertainties in another scenario.

6. Add the predetermined trends to both scenarios.

7. Check for internal coherence. Could the trends and resolved uncertainties coexist in a *plausible* future scenario?

8. Add in the actions of individuals and/or organizations who will be impacted by the future described in a scenario. What actions would they take/have they taken to satisfy their own interests?

Figure 16.2 – Steps in scenario construction: the extreme-world method

Scenario construction: the extreme-world method

Figure 16.2 gives the eight major steps in the construction of scenarios.

The first step is to identify an issue of concern, around which the scenarios will be constructed. Key issues often concern the survival and viability of an organization, or one of its divisions, in an environment that is known to be changing and that might change in a way that is inhospitable to that organization with its current competencies and core capabilities.

In the example we will develop now, the key issue of concern is the survival and profitability of a European-based semiconductor manufacturing company.[1] The predetermined elements and trends, as seen by the company's key personnel, are listed in Figure 16.3. The impacts of these trends on the survival and profitability of the

		Impact
T1	Increased product complexity	+ve
T2	Shortening product life cycles	+ve
T3	Increasing demand for cheaper packaging	−ve
T4	Customers prefer to buy from European suppliers	+ve
T5	Increasing demand for shorter supply lead time	+ve
T6	Increasing overall demand for integrated circuits	+ve
T7	Far East production costs remain lower	−ve
T8	Low level of local competition	+ve

Figure 16.3 – Predetermined trends

				Impact
U1	EU import duty requirements	u11	Higher	++ve
		u12	As is	+ve
		u13	Lower	−ve
U2	Demand for ceramic device types	u21	Higher	++ve
	(replaced by plastics)	u22	As is	+ve
		u23	Lower	−ve
		u24	V. low	−−ve
U3	Success of new technology	u31	Fast	+ve
		u32	Slow	−ve
U4	Reaction of local competition	u41	Strong	−ve
		u42	Weak	+ve
U5	Internal corporate volumes	u51	High	+ve
		u52	Low	−ve
U6	Internal manufacturing policy	u61	Make	+ve
		u62	Buy	−ve

Figure 16.4 – Key uncertainties

semiconductor manufacturing company are also given. Figure 16.4 gives the key un-certainties, the ways in which these uncertainties can resolve themselves and their impact on the issue of concern.

Next, the positive impact uncertainties and all the predetermined elements are clustered together, and a 'storyline' is developed that interlinks as many of these elements as possible. The focus is on developing a plausible chain of events that is, to some degree, causally related and that shows how the future will unfold to result in the *end-state* captured within the horizon year of the particular scenario. The same process is then repeated for a negative scenario.

Figure 16.5 gives two illustrative short scenarios that are based on the trends and uncertainties listed in Figures 16.3 and 16.4. The third scenario detailed in Figure 16.5 is an extrapolation of the present and is often called the 'status quo' scenario.

Notice that uncertainty u11 and uncertainty u42 in Figure 16.4 are to some degree internally incoherent, i.e. incompatible, with one another. For example, if EU import duties were high, then reaction of *local* competition (i.e. from within the EU) would *not* be weak. Therefore, this particular combination of resolved uncertainties is not described in the scenarios because it is implausible.

The example scenarios in Figure 16.5 are not fully developed because the reaction of the Far East producers of plastic packing to the 'technology boom' scenario has

Positive Scenario: Technology Boom

New packaging technologies are developed rapidly and are widely adopted at the expense of the traditional packing methods of plastic and ceramics. Ceramic packaging all but disappears. The overall market demand increases significantly on the back of the improved capabilities of the new technology.

The manufacturing expertise for the new technology resides with only a few key companies worldwide. The new market entry costs are high. EU import duties are maintained at high levels to protect local manufacturing of the new technologies. Vendor choice is dependent on technology advantage rather than price.

The corporation is able to exploit this trend by leveraging its established skill base. All new products are manufactured internally with the scope to convert existing products and bring their manufacture back in-house.

Negative Scenario: Plastics Dominate

Plastic packaging technology has resolved power dissipation and high pincount difficulties. Virtually all packaging applications are now in plastic. The overall market volume expands rapidly.Ceramic packaging all but disappears. New technologies such as multichip modules and chip on board are slow to realize their potential.

The manufacturing expertise and infrastructure to manufacture the new plastic packages reside only in the Far East. EU regulations abolish import duties on packaged semiconductor devices. Customers would prefer to buy in Europe but can't; virtually all subcontract assembly is carried out in the Far East.

Faced with an erosion of the competitive advantage of its ceramic manufacturing expertise, the Corporation has no choice but to switch to plastic packaging for all products. All package manufacturing is subcontracted out to Far East operators. The internal skill base and manufacturing infrastructure disappear.

Status Quo Scenario: Business as Usual

The overall demand for semiconductor devices continues to increase at the current rate. The demand for ceramic packages remains at the current levels with moderate increases in the higher pincount package styles. The remainder of the market is dominated by plastic packages, especially small outline products. Opportunities for new packaging technologies such as (MCM) and Chip on Board (COB) remain limited.

There is no significant change in EU import duty regulations and therefore little change in the cost differential between manufacturing in Europe and the Far East. European subcontractors are used for prototyping and low-volume work with the larger production volumes being sent to the Far East. Entry barriers for new competitors remain high. The Corporation continues to manufacture its complex, leading edge products internally. The remainder is assembled either internally or externally, dependent on cost. Overall volumes are maintained at current levels.

Figure 16.5 – Three scenarios

not been thought through and incorporated. Given more fully developed scenarios – we will detail a fully developed scenario later in this chapter – the next stage after the construction of the scenarios is complete is to utilize them in a decision-making process.

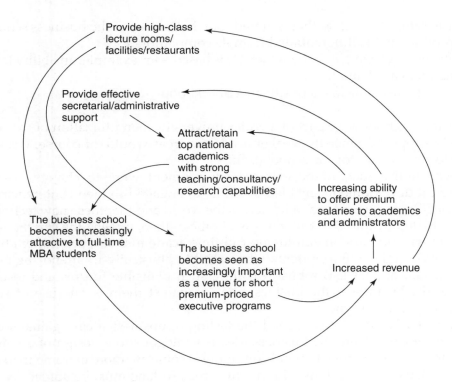

Figure 16.6 – An illustrative business idea for a business school

Using scenarios in decision-making

There are two ways in which scenarios can be used in decision-making. The first is to test the viability of a current 'business idea' against the plausible futures represented in the scenarios. In the abstract analytical sense, a business can be thought of as a business idea. A business idea is the *systemic* linking of the business's competencies and strengths. For example, a possible business idea for a business school is illustrated in Figure 16.6.

Here, the *strengths* that the business school possesses are summarized in short statements. The impact of the deployment of these strengths produces revenue, and the reinvestment of the revenue obtained produces a self-reinforcing cycle or positive feedback loop that would, in a stable environment, be a *robust* business idea that would become less and less replicable by competitors – without serious investment from a competitor school – over a period of time.

Overall, a business idea should specify three major elements of a business's attempt to be successful:

(1) The *competitive advantage* that is aimed for – in the case of the business school, this is a product that is differentiated from its competitors.
(2) The *distinctive competencies* on which (1) is based – for example, an ability to attract top national academics.
(3) The *growth* mechanism – a positive feedback loop.

If the business school were part of a wider university, then utilization of the school's revenue to support financially weaker academic areas would, of course, weaken the positive feedback loop for the school itself.

However, notice that, if the external environment were to change – say that technological developments enabled students to engage in video conferencing with *internationally* recognized academics across the world and that these new technologies were easy to deploy into the students' own homes – then, *perhaps*, the *current* business idea – with its emphasis on employing full-time academics and providing attractive learning environments for students who are able physically to attend the business school – would appear less robust. Creating such plausible futures and testing the essence of the business – the business idea – against them is one use of scenario planning in a decision process.

Kees van der Heijden[2] has likened the testing of business ideas against scenarios to 'wind tunneling'. Here the business idea is analogous to a design of an airplane. The scenarios are analogous to wind conditions – some are more extreme than others, but all are plausible conditions within which the airplane must be able to fly. Under some wind conditions the airplane may be harder to keep airborne, but, essentially, its airframe (i.e. business idea) must be robust.

The second way to utilize the scenarios in a decision process is to evaluate lower level strategies or decisions. In the business school example, this might be an evaluation of a decision option to focus R&D investment in producing CD ROM versions of course materials. In the semiconductor manufacturing company example, it might be the decision option of maintaining or increasing investment in new ceramic packaging production technology. Essentially, a current strategy, a contemplated strategy or a range of alternative strategies can be evaluated for robustness against constructed scenarios. Figure 16.7 gives a matrix representation of this evaluation process.

Often, no one strategy performs well against the whole range of constructed scenarios. If you consider strategies 1, 2 and 3, it can be seen that strategy 1 maximizes the minimum payoff (cf. the maximin criterion which we discussed in Chapter 6). Given a simple choice between strategies 1, 2 and 3, strategy 1 would seem the most robust choice *if* we felt it was not possible to say that one scenario was more likely than another – recall that this is an explicit assumption underpinning scenario planning as a technique for dealing with uncertainty (we will discuss a more formal approach to evaluating strategies at the end of the chapter). Note, however, that there is an additional row in Figure 16.7, entitled 'new strategy', which the very act of scenario

	SCENARIO 1	SCENARIO 2	SCENARIO 3
STRATEGY 1	✓✓✓	✓	✗
STRATEGY 2	✗✗	✓	✓
STRATEGY 3	✓✓	✗✗	✓✓✓
NEW STRATEGY	✓✓✓	✓✓✓	✓✓✓

Figure 16.7 – Testing the robustness of strategies against scenarios

planning may incubate in the mind of the decision-maker as he or she ponders the set of plausible futures encapsulated in the scenarios.

This ability of scenario planning to stimulate creative thinking is perhaps best illustrated by a 'real' scenario contained in Figure 16.8. This scenario was one of several constructed for a corporation that was involved in moving raw materials and finished goods around the globe.[3] The company was concerned with the (re)location of its major depots, so that they would be at the hub of future trading networks. It follows that the scenarios were constructed to represent plausible future trading patterns in the EU and the rest of the world. The corporation tested the robustness of choice of alternative countries and cities against the scenarios. Several cities that were not in the choice set *prior* to the scenario construction became favorites in the *subsequent* decision process, as they were found to be robust against a range of plausible future world trading patterns. These trading patterns were encapsulated and bounded by the scenarios that were constructed to capture the range of plausible futures.

So far we have described one method to bound these futures – a simplified method that uses an extreme positive scenario, an extreme negative scenario and a more neutral, status quo or 'business as usual' scenario. Some practitioners of scenario planning caution against presenting the decision-maker with such extreme worlds, as

'PLENTY FOR ALL'

I. Global Perspective

World economic growth picked up appreciably–driven by the success in bilateral trade talks, a surge in US exports, a strengthening employment situation in Europe and lowering real cost of oil.

The signs of economic recovery were reflected in a rapid growth in global trade. The trade among developed economies continues to dominate, but an increasing proportion of the expanding markets involve developing countries. Institutions, frustrated by low interest rates in the developed countries and encouraged by opportunities in the less developed countries, invest many billions of dollars of their managed funds in the newly created financial institutions and ventures around the world. Latin America and central Europe (increasingly integrated with the EU) are the major beneficiaries.

Japan's new-found market liberalism and détente with the USA reinforce general optimism about the future. Japan's proximity to the potentially massive consumer markets in Russia and China led the Japanese government to sanction heavy investment in these countries and to build up the commercial infrastructure around Maizuru, facing the expanding container port of Vostochny on Russia's east coast.

Western Europe's high direct production costs continue to reduce its competitiveness in the world. Lower direct costs in central and eastern Europe offer a competitive lifeline for western European manufacturers, a lifeline they take with some alacrity. Foreign direct investment increases significantly in terms of increased joint ventures and wholly owned subsidiaries. Pressure is successfully applied to speed up the process of integration of Poland, Hungary and the Czech Republic. Western exports to Russia of consumer goods also increase rapidly. Belarus and the Baltic states benefit from their geographic siting in attracting infrastructure investment and aid from the West.

Hungary continues to attract the majority of investment from the USA, but its partners in the Vise–Grad–Triangle rapidly close the gap opened up in the first half of the decade.

The EU and US axis (which successfully argued concessions in addition to GATT from their G7 partners) resolves to further reduce market access barriers. G7 initiated gilt-edged guarantees to the developing countries, and attractive non-reciprocal trade arrangements persuade many of the less developed countries to reduce their own trade barriers. This has mutual benefits, but more importantly promotes an atmosphere of trust and the first real moves toward comprehensive credit union agreement.

II. Regional Perspective

As the necessary constitutional and legislative reforms have been carried out in the first half of the decade, the more advanced developing countries in central and eastern Europe achieve acceptable political stability and continue to maintain tight fiscal policies under guidelines set by the IMF. The situation continues to improve in the second half of the decade. There is a general commitment of the governments of the countries to liberalization policies, and the move to democracy continues, thus speeding up the accomplishment of the privatization process. This results in expansion of the private sector into the majority of services and industries before the turn of the century.

Although aid provided by the industrialized countries remains weak owing to their own internal problems during the recession, EC aid increases from the second half of the decade. Germany, in particular, provides aid for Hungary and the Czech Republic.

Institutional investment and foreign direct investment also pick up considerably in the second half of the decade as the emerging financial system and markets of the Vise–Grad–Triangle countries, Belarus and Russia become more attractive to the investors as compared with the traditional markets in developed countries. The EU brings forward negotiations for a free trade agreement with the Vise–Grad–Triangle and Russia as it is willing to open up its market to exports from these countries. This increases their ability to pay for their imports and restructuring.

In central Europe, consumer confidence grows rapidly as clear indications are seen of increased prosperity in the region. In the East, Russia recovers its economic balance and growth in GDP and again begins to grow in importance to the countries in eastern Europe, particularly in terms of consumer markets.

Figure 16.8 – A 'real' scenario of future trading patterns

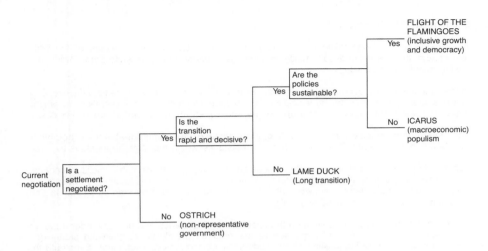

Figure 16.9 – An output of a 'driving forces' scenario structuring methodology

their very extremeness may cause doubts among their clients – the business managers – about their plausibility. Another way to construct scenarios that has found favor among practitioners is described next.

Scenario construction: the driving forces method

This method shares much in common with the first method that we introduced, in that the critical elements in the decomposition process are predetermined elements and uncertainties. However, in the driving forces method, *degrees* of predictability and uncertainty are allowable, and the outputs of the scenario construction process are not, usually, extreme scenarios. Nevertheless, the output scenarios from this method also bound the perceived uncertainties in a similar way to the scenarios produced in the extreme-world scenario construction method that we discussed earlier.

Figure 16.9 gives an example structure of four scenarios for the (then) future of South Africa that are *driven* by the *forces* whether or not there is a negotiated settlement, whether or not the transition to majority rule is rapid and whether or not the economic policies of a majority government are short or long term. Figure 16.10 details the scenarios that were constructed by a team led by Adam Kahane in mid-1991. The horizon year of the scenarios is 2002. These scenarios of the social and political environment in South Africa would be useful to an international company that was considering three decision options: whether to maintain, reduce or increase its investments and overall presence in South Africa.[4] Figure 16.11 gives the key steps in the driving forces method.

Scenario 1: Ostrich

As a result of the steps taken by the De Klerk Government and the outcome of the white referendum, the international community becomes more tolerant towards white South Africa, and the National Party in particular.

In the light of this, the government hardens its negotiation position. At the same time the liberation movements are perceived to be too radical and lose support internationally. The liberation movements maintain their bottom line. A stand-off results and constitutional negotiations break down.

The government decides to form a new 'moderate alliance' government that is unacceptable to the liberation movements. This results in mass resistance which the state suppresses by force.

Although large-scale sanctions are not reimposed, the economy remains in the doldrums because of massive resistance to the new constitution. This resistance leads to escalating repression and violence, and the business climate worsens. This in turn leads to economic stagnation and decline, accompanied by a flight of capital and skills.

The government also fails to deliver on the social front. Resistance and unrest render effective social spending impossible and large outlays are required merely to maintain the status quo. Because society's major inequalities are not addressed, the vicious cycle continues. Eventually the various parties are forced back to the negotiation table, but under worse social, political and economic conditions than before.

Scenario 2: Lame Duck

Various forces and considerations drive the major parties towards a negotiated settlement. The present government, for example, recognizes the necessity or inevitability of extending full political rights to the disenfranchised but fears irresponsible government. This fear is shared by some of the major international actors.

On the other hand, the liberation movements fear the return to repressive minority rule if they do not make significant compromises. Such considerations lead to a transitional arrangement with a variety of sunset clauses, slowly phasing out elements of the present system, as well as minority vetoes and other checks and balances aimed at preventing 'irresponsible' government.

Such a long transition of enforced coalition incapacitates the government because of lowest common denominator decision-making, which results in indecisive policies. It purports to respond to all, but satisfies none. In consequence, the social and economic crises are inadequately addressed.

Although the transitional government succeeds in being goal directed and effective, it is incapacitated because of the logic of a long transition. Uncertainty grows on the nature of the government that will emerge after the transition.

Regardless of how moderate the declarations of the majority parties in the coalition may be, fears of radical economic policies after the period of a long transition remain. Investors hold back, and there is insufficient growth and development.

Scenario 3: Icarus

In this scenario, a popularly elected democratic government tries to achieve too much too quickly. It had noble origins and good intentions but pays insufficient attention to economic forces.

The government embarks on a massive spending spree to meet all the backlogs inherited from the past. It implements food subsidies, price and exchange controls and institutes other 'quick fix' policies.

The initial results are spectacular growth, increased living standards, improved social conditions, little or no increase in inflation and increased political support.

Figure 16.10 – Adam Kahane's four South African scenarios

But after a year or two the program runs into budgetary, monetary and balance of payments constraints. The budget deficit well exceeds 10%. Depreciations, inflation, economic uncertainty and collapse follow. The country experiences an economic crisis of hitherto unknown proportions which results in social collapse and political chaos.

At this point, the government either does a 180 degree about-turn (while appealing to the International Monetary Fund and the World Bank for assistance) or it is removed from office. The result is a return to authoritarianism and an abandonment of the noble intentions that originally prevailed.

Scenario 4: Flight of the Flamingoes

Flamingoes characteristically take off slowly, fly high and fly together.

A decisive political settlement, followed by good government, creates conditions in which an initially slow but sustainable economic and social take-off become possible. The key to the government's success is its ability to combine strategies that lead to significant improvements in social delivery with policies that create confidence in the economy.

Access to world markets and relative regional stability are gained, but South Africa does not receive massive overseas investments or aid on the scale of a Marshall Plan.

The government adopts sound social and economic policies and observes macroeconomic constraints. It succeeds in curbing corruption in government and raises efficiency levels.

It makes well-targeted social investments that lead to a decrease in violence and give people confidence that many of the social needs will be met in the longer term.

Once business is convinced that policies will remain consistent in the years ahead, investment grows and employment increases. Initially, this growth is slow, because confidence does not return overnight, but over the years higher rates of growth are attained, and an average rate of growth of close to 5% is realized over the period.

The overall income of the upper-income groups grows between 1 and 3% a year.

Figure 16.10 – (*Continued*)

Within the 12 steps shown in Figure 16.11, note that step 1 is analogous to step 1 in the extreme-world methodology that we described earlier in Figure 16.2. At step 2 in the driving forces scenario structuring method, a multitude of elements will emerge from a group 'brainstorm' about the issue of concern. Many of the elements that emerge will address the *external* environment, in that the predetermined elements and uncertainties are *not* under the control of the individual, group or organization that they will affect. These are the elements that it may be appropriate to incorporate in the scenarios, and these elements should be carried forward to step 3. Other elements will have to do with areas where the individual/group/organization *has* control, i.e. they are decision or strategy options. As decisions and strategies are to be evaluated *against* the scenarios at the final step, these decision options should be *removed* at step 2 and reconsidered in the final step of the scenario planning process – when such options are evaluated for robustness against the range of constructed futures.

1. Identify the issue of concern and the horizon year that will be captured in the scenarios.
2. List anything that seems related to the issue of concern. Write each element on a 'post-it'.
3. Place each 'post-it' on the scenario structuring space, below, in relation to its perceived predictability/unpredictability and low impact/high impact on the issue of concern.

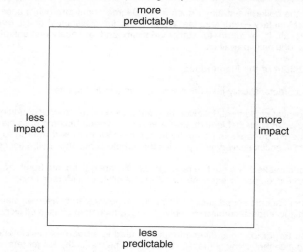

4. Focus on the 'post-its' in the bottom right-hand corner, i.e. high impact/low predictability events. Try to cluster these 'post-its' into groups of *interrelated* events such that the 'post-its' in one grouping are interrelated among themselves but unrelated to the 'post-its' in other groupings.
5. From these clusters, try to identify a smaller number of underlying 'driving forces' that link these uncertainties/events at a deeper level.
6. Of the driving forces identified, which two or three really would make a difference to the decision maker and his/her business?
7. For each driving force try to capture the range of outcomes by two extremes.
8. Experiment by thinking of combinations of the extremes of one of the driving forces with the extremes of each of the other driving forces. From these 'thought experiments', develop the skeletons of three or four scenarios. Select short 'catchy' names that encapsulate the essence of the scenarios.
9. Inspect 'post-its' in the three other quadrants of the scenario structuring space. Place these elements into one or more of the skeleton scenarios created in step 8, in order to 'flesh' them out. Check that elements contained in the top left quadrant could, in principle, appear in any of the skeleton scenarios. If not, reconsider the coherence of the elements of each scenario.
10. Begin to develop each scenario 'storyline'. One way to start this process is to place all the elements within a scenario along a 'timeline' that starts at today's point in time and ends at the point in time captured in the scenario horizon year. Look for causality between elements. Storylines are more plausible when (some) elements are causally related. Time precedence is often a good cue to *potential* causality.
11. Review the scenarios in light of their utilization of the original elements in the bottom right-hand quadrant of the scenario structuring space. Are all the high impact/low predictability elements *bounded* by the range of scenarios that have been constructed?. If not, consider creating more scenarios to capture and structure the remaining elements in the quadrant.
12. Evaluate the business idea *or* strategic options against the futures represented in the scenarios.

Figure 16.11 – Steps in scenario construction: the driving force method

In our *first* method for constructing scenarios (see Figure 16.2) we described, in step 8, a method of including those individuals/organizations who would be impacted by the futures described in the scenarios and would therefore act in their own interests as particular futures started to unfold. Another way of capturing *degrees* of such 'stakeholder' involvement and intervention is to construct a matrix such as that shown in Figure 16.12.

One of the outputs of step 2 of the driving forces method will be the names of stakeholders. Those elements can be placed on the 'stakeholder structuring space' of Figure 16.12 and consulted again after step 9.

As we saw in Figure 16.7, the outcome of the decision process in scenario planning is *not* the selection of the option with the highest expected value or utility but the selection of the most 'robust' decision in the face of an unpredictable future. This is also the focus of step 12 in the driving forces method of scenario construction. An additional focus is on the generation of more robust decision options. Generation of such robust options reduces uncertainty, which, as we saw in Chapter 15, is psychologically important for decision-makers who tend to prefer certainty to choice between risky options.

However, even if a fundamentally robust option cannot be developed, scenario thinking also provides other benefits. World views can be communicated easily in an organization via the medium of the scenario 'stories'. Additionally, once a story has been read, and the reasoning underlying its unfolding understood, a future has been 'rehearsed'. Thus, once the early events in a scenario occur, the decision-maker will be able to anticipate how the future will unfold. These 'trigger events' will be seen as *information* among the stream of *data* that impacts upon the decision-maker.

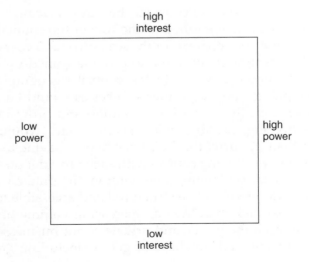

Figure 16.12 – Stakeholder structuring space

Just as the new purchaser of a particular make of car becomes very sensitive to the number of models of that make on the road and the differences in levels of equipment, etc., the scenario thinker becomes sensitive to a scenario starting to unfold and becoming reality. Such sensitivity can lead to *early* contingency action towards an unfavorable future.

Alternatively, new business opportunities can be quickly grasped as soon as favorable scenarios begin to unfold. Such early recognition and reaction to an emerging future is seen, by some practitioners, as more useful than the creation of robust strategic options.

Typical outcomes of the scenario planning process include:

(i) confirmation that the business idea is sound or that new strengths need to be added to create more robustness;

(ii) confirmation that lower level business choices are sound or that alternative new options are more robust;

(iii) recognition that none of the business options is robust, and therefore contingency planning against unfavorable futures is necessary;

(iv) sensitivity to the 'early warning' elements, which are precursors of desirable and unfavorable futures.

The next case study illustrates the impact that a scenario intervention can have upon an organization – showing that scenario thinking can invoke early contingency action towards avoiding unfavorable futures.

Case study of a scenario intervention in the public sector[5]

In this case study, we were asked to consider the futures facing a local council in the UK. The issue of concern was identified as the role of the council in the developing 'information age', and the horizon year for the scenario was 5 years hence. The council was being directed by central government to provide 'joined-up services' such that, for example, when a family moved into the council's geographical area, both the council's (and their public agency partner's) services would be configured around that life event. This meant that service information and provision in areas such as refuse collection, schooling, health service, taxation, etc., would be provided in a tailored way, rather than, as currently, the citizen herself having to achieve the joining up of service provision by initiating contact with each provider on an individual basis.

At the time of the scenario planning intervention, the public was increasingly expecting information and services to be structured and accessible to suit them, *not* the service providers. In parallel, there was an increasing volume of electronic transactions taking place between the public and private sector businesses, such as Internet banking and Internet-facilitated purchase of goods (including groceries) from local and distant vendors.

In this context, the council was considering introducing call centers to cope with the influx of telephone calls. A general idea was to provide the 'joining up via knowledge of the telephone operators', but this course of action was in the early stages of consideration – driven, in the main, by approaches from a national telecoms company that had expertise in the provision of call centers.

During the scenario intervention, five clusters of high-impact/low-predictability events were identified. These were as follows:

(i) *Partner agendas* – whether partner organizations share the values of the council, the commitment to involvement, willingness to share resources, etc.

(ii) *Information mapping and understanding the basics of the business* – how do current systems relate to knowledge management? Can duplicate systems be integrated/eliminated, etc.?

(iii) *Public ownership* – is the commitment to involvement a solution or an ideology? Will the public be with the council? How does it relate to cultures of youth and the underclasses? Will participation be hijacked by pressure groups, etc.?

(iv) *Central agencies as help or hindrance* – what is the real agenda of central government? Does system centralization conflict with democracy, etc.?

(v) *Opportunities and constraints offered by new technologies* – what *resource implications* are there for the change process? What will be the *macroeconomic factors* of relevance? How will change be managed and what will be the new *organizational design* required to implement joined-up government in the future?

Prior to the scenario workshop, further input to the participants' expanding frame of thinking was gained by the invitation of a small number of external experts – remarkable people – to present views on the limits of the future of information and communication technology (ICT), its application to public sector management and the nature of governance and society. Input here from a telecommunications designer put technological capability forecasts into the wider context of the telecommunications industry's then current financial commitments, the global economic situation, etc., while the application capabilities of ICT were demonstrated by 'virtual visits' to leading-edge developments in Australia. The scenario workshop was structured around our facilitation of the participants' initial identification of the widest possible range of driving forces that could produce change over the next 5 years. This was an open-ended process, in that no time limit was placed upon it, and it was conducted initially in round-robin format, such that all 25 members provided input in turn until each ran out of ideas. Over a period of some 90 minutes, over 120 driving forces were identified by individuals and clarified by the group in terms of the plausible polar outcomes within the council's context of operations. The driving forces and polar outcomes were recorded separately and related by number coding (driving force 1 produced polar outcomes 1A and 1B, 2 produced 2A and 2B, etc.) on magnetic hexagons on large wall-mounted boards, so that the entire group could share the content and the process of manipulation of ideas without intervention by us, or without any individual member of the group constraining the thinking according to their own agenda. The driving forces were then clustered by the participants as a group – through a process of manipulation of the hexagons, accompanied by open discussion, argument, negotiation and compromise, again with the aims of investigating perceived casual relationships and surfacing a manageable number of higher level concepts without reduction. The participants themselves defined these higher level concepts by agreeing encapsulating titles for each cluster. These higher level concepts were then ranked by the participants, first according to the relative impact they were considered likely to have on the business, and second by the perceived relative degree of unpredictability as to what the outcomes of this impact might be over the next 5 years.

In accordance with the adopted scenario approach, the scenario dimensions were derived from the two higher level concepts that, while not directly driving each other, were considered to have the combination of greatest impact, with highest degree of unpredictability as to the outcomes. These scenario dimensions related to the fields of:

(i) *the democratic process* – primarily concerned with the balance between central and local government and the effect of the balance struck between these upon delivery of services at the local level by the council;
(ii) *value creation* – concerned with the speed of development of new technologies, the capacity for individuals and organizations to internalize these and their use to become more productive.

In relation to the democratic process, the participants saw unpredictability as to whether decision-making would rest with individuals and with businesses, with minimum intervention from government and the public sector agencies, or whether society would move towards a collectivism in which community issues would come into force. In relation to value creation from new technologies, there was unpredictability as to whether technology would be adapted to human needs, unleashing a new productivity through unimpeded uptake, or whether technology uptake would be subject to institutional constraints. The latter situation would see the development of a division between those who have access to and skills to use technologies and those who have either not got access to or cannot use them. In both cases, the impact of the outcomes was considered to have a major impact upon the council.

Through the processes of discussion, negotiation and argument, a combination of the two polar extremes for each of the two identified driving forces enabled the participants to build up four rich and internally consistent pictures of each of the possible futures. These four separable and yet plausible futures were recognized by participants as their own creations – rather than descriptions of futures that were favored by the external consultancy team. After the full group had completed this stage, four subgroups then each worked with one member of the facilitation team in order to develop the storyline over time for one of the scenarios. These smaller groups considered the relationship between different factors in terms of perceived cause and effect and chronology. They considered the starting point of the story in relation to aspects of the present, the key events – decisions, developments, exercises of power by key stakeholders, etc. – that would determine and describe its unfolding and the end state that would define it. These short histories of the future were designed, constructed, named and made sense of by the participants themselves, not by us, and were therefore the wholly owned intellectual property of the council and its partners. They were not represented as 'good' or 'bad' worlds, nor was any presented as more or less likely than any other. All four were seen as entirely plausible developments that were worthy of consideration in planning the way forward towards modernizing and joining up government through the adoption of new technologies. However, each presented different challenges and different opportunities to the council.

The scenario titles and key identifiers are as follows:

Forward to the past

In this future, centralization dominates over dispersed and local governance, and central government runs the show. There are real barriers to change, with restricted funding for local government, mismatches in the geographical boundaries of councils in relation to areas of wealth and employment and a reluctance to share accountability across councils and agencies. The adoption of new technologies and the resultant productivity improvement in the public sector have come at the expense of local councils, with a drive towards centralization at government level and to centralization or privatization of services at the local level. This future may mark the beginning of the end for local government.

Free enterprise

Here, there is emancipation of the public and a drive away from the paternalism of the old-style bureaucratic governance. The 'customer rules' and market forces are delivering – but only for some. For those with access to, and the capability of using, new technologies, there is a public free spirit, with '24 × 7' access to the 'new public sector trade'. While there are drives towards achieving economies of scale, there is a challenge to the concept of 'one size fits all', with a demand for premium services from those who can afford to pay extra for them. There is, however, serious polarization in society, with exclusion from the new society of the underclass who can either ill-afford or who are ill-equipped to use the emerging technologies.

People's kailyard[6]

In this scenario, there is increasing interest in the democratic process, but primarily at a superficial level rather than with the fundamentals. As such, there is a tendency towards seeking the 'quick fix' to immediate problems, with fear of adverse publicity and media reaction to any perceived failure. New technologies open up new channels of communication from citizenry, and there is greater social inclusion at the superficial level with public consultation processes, but a resultant move towards concentration upon dealing with complaints rather than with serving needs and improving services. As such, there is reinforcement of top-down and fragmented government, lack of real public accountability and an ever-increasing gap between the reality and potential for service effectiveness.

Technology serves

Here, there is a combination of technology facilitating increased access by the citizenry and development of a proactive form of civic governance that is based upon meaningful dialogue between citizens and government. Elected members or their officers are enabled to act at the local level for all members of society, including the 'invisibles' and the 'excluded'. National government settles the subsidiarity debate in favor of local democracy and supports trailblazing projects that demonstrate the competence of civic governance, for example in the field of social housing. Here, the new technologies facilitate a new form of joined-up government from the bottom up.

Each of the subgroups presented its scenario outline to the full participant group, with the key differences between each clearly differentiating the possibilities for a range of plausible futures. In 'Forward to the past', there is seen a downward spiral, a vicious circle towards greater centralization and limited or no local government in the future. In 'Free enterprise', local government is unencumbered by bureaucracy, but there is delivery of 'premium services' for those who can/will pay, but with increased polarization, disenfranchisement and fallout in society. In the 'People's kailyard', there is mediocrity and, surrounded by legislation, cross-organizational boundaries, non-standard protocols, etc.; there is much talk of change, but a continuous finding of new problems to talk about, so no change. 'In Technology serves', there is a future in which the group's common aspirations, visions and desires for change are seen to be enabled.

Through discussion of the underlying trends and major driving forces that underpinned each of the scenarios, the council themselves derived an initial set of key implications that were seen to be fundamental to their immediate thinking/acting, if they were to be effective in exerting whatever influence they might reasonably have over the reality of the future that will unfold over the next 5 years. These were as follows:

(1) Northshire Council must lead from the front, with bold steps in developing an integrated and inclusive approach to technological innovation. The dangers of the small-step and short-term approach were highlighted in the kailyard scenario – where central government stepped in to take control from local government.

(2) The council must promote democracy in action, by making the new technologies serve the people and by using technology to develop 'civic governance'. They must bring local government closer to the community level, developing high levels of ability to listen and respond to citizen wants and needs. They must develop transparency and accountability in their deeds and actions, with policies that are meaningful to the public.

(3) New technologies must be used to demonstrate the competence of local government, achieving public confidence and support through the provision of responsive, community-oriented services and more customized services, while at the same time applying the technologies to support inclusion and to reduce inequalities.

(4) Northshire Council must use the new technologies in order to promote itself as the 'home for sustainable value creation'.

(5) The council must proactively promote and lobby for settlement of the subsidiarity debate in favor of governance at the local level.

(6) Finally, in developing short-term solutions to immediate problems, the council must watch out that long-term aspirations remain the guiding light.

Following the outcomes of the scenario project and the resultant debate within Northshire Council on the above implications, there have been strategic decisions taken in support of fostering the concept of joined-up government and seeking to foster the relationship with central government, of whatever political persuasion, while promoting the case of Northshire in the widest political and business arenas. In addition to these strategic decisions, there has been operational action in seeking to establish a Web-based knowledge and transaction system that will promote a citizen and business-focused interface between new integrated service demand and provision by the council and its partners.

Benefits from the scenario interventions were seen to be:

(i) shared insights for participants in the process;
(ii) alternative ways forward tested against scenarios;
(iii) motivation for action from these insights;
(iv) agreement on a well-defined way forward;
(v) agreement on technology choice to support the way forward.

As such, the pre-intervention concerns with call center provision had been replaced by a focus on developing Internet and intranet capabilities to provide information and services to citizens – in the form of both (i) single service transactions and (ii) integrated transactions involving multiple service delivery.

In short, the scenario workshop invoked an 'organizational jolt' to routine 'business-as-usual' thinking. The major insight was that continuing with business-as-usual was a fragile strategy against the constructed futures.

The scenario approach to decision-making in the face of uncertainty contrasts with decision-analytic approaches, as participants in the scenario project were able to consider plausible future scenarios *prior* to evaluating strategic options. In decision analysis, options for action are determined first, and outcomes are predicated upon the selected options – 'if we do this, what might happen?'. Our case example illustrates that the scenario approach opened up the participants' thinking to alternative framings of the nature of the future, and they were able to reconsider and redesign strategies in response to these futures.

Scenario thinking can be contrasted with alternative future methodologies such as Delphi. As we saw in Chapter 13, in Delphi applications the focus is, by contrast, on determining the collective opinion of a group of experts on a well-defined issue that is to be *forecast*. Four necessary features characterize a Delphi procedure, namely anonymity, iteration, controlled feedback of the panelists' judgments and statistical aggregation of group members' responses. Anonymity is achieved using self-administered questionnaires (on either paper or computer). By allowing the group members to express their opinions and judgments privately, one may be able to diminish the effects of social pressure from dominant or dogmatic individuals, or from a majority. Ideally, this should allow the individuals to consider each idea based on merit alone, rather than based on potentially invalid criteria (such as the status of an idea's proponent). Furthermore, by iterating the questionnaire over a number of rounds, one gives panelists the opportunity to change their opinions and judgments without fear of losing face in the eyes of the (anonymous) others in the group. By contrast, the participants in scenario workshops interact socially, but the interaction is structured by facilitators – individuals who have expertise in the scenario process.

Our comparative views on scenario planning, decision analysis and Delphi are given in Table 16.1.

In summary, our case example supports the use of scenario planning as an organizational intervention that enhances individual and team views about the nature of the future. This enhanced understanding is, as we have demonstrated, likely to invoke an action-oriented response from decision-makers in the organization.

Combining scenario planning and decision analysis

In spite of the advantages of scenario planning, we saw in Figure 16.7 that the evaluation of strategies against objectives was relatively informal. When a number of

Table 16.1 – The components of the methodologies

	Scenario planning	**Decision analysis**	**Delphi**
Future orientation	Multiple frames of the future are constructed during the process	Decision analysis is conventionally undertaken within a singular general frame of the future	Delphi is usually focused on forecasting the occurrence of a single event or quantity
Structure of judgment inputs	Qualitative decomposition into critical uncertainties and trends. An emphasis on understanding causality	Quantitative decomposition into probabilities, payoffs and decision trees	Structuring is achieved by the controlled exchange of information between anonymous panelists over a number of rounds (iterations)
Information orientation	Scenario team members exchange existing opinions on issues of concern, and 'remarkable people' systematically provide insight into issues of critical uncertainty	Fresh information may be sought if the analysis indicates that a decision is sensitive to small changes in judgmental inputs	Expert panelists exchange their existing estimates. Individual experts can hold, or change, their estimates on the basis of feedback on the estimates of other panelists
Process orientation	All those with dissenting opinions are given 'airtime'. Thus, individual expressions of opinions are initially of focal interest before they are combined with the opinions of others	Focus on combining divergent opinions by averaging and reduction	The statistical average of the estimates on the final Delphi round is taken as the group judgment
Action orientation	The result is shared understanding, within the management team, of causally determined futures that can galvanize managerial action to avoid unfavorable futures or facilitate the occurrence of favorable ones	The result of the analysis is a single recommended decision for subsequent implementation	None

objectives are involved, there are clear dangers in this approach. We saw in Chapter 2 that unaided decision-makers often respond to complex decision problems by using simplifying mental heuristics, such as lexicographic ranking, when evaluating options against multiple objectives. The result may be that the evaluation of strategies will be incomplete or distorted because undue attention is paid to particular objectives, at the expense of others.

Because of this, we believe that decision analysis techniques based on methods like SMART and SMARTER (see Chapters 3 and 4) can usefully complement scenario planning by formalizing the process of evaluating strategies. We believe that the use of these techniques can bring considerable advantages to scenario planning. The decomposition of objectives should sensitize planners to the substantive issues involved in the evaluation of strategies. This may yield deeper insights and possibly enhance the ability of planners to create and design strategies. Moreover, decision analysis provides a common language of communication between different stakeholders, and hence allows the communication of minority views.[7] It allows for specialist inputs into the planning process when problems are multifaceted, so that there are no overall experts.[8] The result should be a common understanding of problems,[9] or at least a common set of terms to discuss a problem,[8] and possibly a resolution of conflicts.

The objective of the approach we outline below is to inform and structure debate and to increase awareness of key issues, rather than to prescribe an 'optimal solution'. The intention is to identify strategies that perform well, or at least acceptably, over the range of plausible scenarios. Consistent with scenario planning, there is no attempt to assess probabilities for the scenarios or to maximize expected values.

The main stages of the approach are shown below:

Stage 1: Formulate scenarios.

Stage 2: Formulate objectives.

Stage 3: Design alternative strategies.

Stage 4: Check strategies for feasibility; remove infeasible strategies.

Stage 5: For each objective:
- (a) rank all the strategy/scenario combinations from best to worst;
- (b) allocate a score of 100 to the best strategy/scenario combination and 0 to the worst;
- (c) allocate scores between 0 and 100 for intermediate strategy scenario combinations.

Stage 6: Remove strategies whose performance on any objective is such that the strategy is unacceptable.

Stage 7: (a) Consider 0 to 100 swings in strategy/scenario combinations and rank these swings in order of importance.
- (b) Attach a weight of 100 to the most important swing and measure the importance of other swings on this scale. Normalize the weights so that they sum to 1.

Stage 8: For each strategy/scenario combination, use the attribute scores and weights to determine a weighted aggregate score.

Stage 9: Use the matrix of strategy/scenario aggregate scores to assess and compare the strategies' performance, paying particular attention to the robustness of performance over the range of scenarios.

Stage 10: Perform sensitivity analysis.

While the approach is very similar to SMART (see Chapter 3), a crucial difference is the ordering of the stages of the analysis. The alternative strategies are not considered until the plausible scenarios have been formulated *and* the objectives determined. This latter deviation from SMART reflects Keeney's concern[10] that objectives should be identified before alternatives because this is more likely to facilitate the design of imaginative options and identification of new opportunities. We next use a simplified case study to demonstrate the approach. Note that, in practice, switching backwards and forwards between the stages is likely as an increased understanding of the problem develops.

Illustrative case study

This case study concerns a newly privatized national mail company that needs to formulate strategies with a 10-year planning horizon. To date, the company has been protected by legislation that allows it to operate as a monopoly on letter deliveries. This protection has engendered a culture of muddling through (i.e. minor adjustments to policies in reaction to events, with no clear sense of overall direction). However, the environment within which the company may operate in the future is likely to change fundamentally. For example, there is a possibility that it will lose its monopoly position, while technological developments pose long-term threats to the volume of letter mail.

Stage 1: Formulate scenarios

For simplicity, only two 'extreme-world' scenarios will be used here:

Scenario 1: (DOG FIGHT)   The company loses its monopoly. Rival companies take several years to develop their own delivery systems, but within 5 years there is keen competition on price, delivery times and reliability. Growth in the usage of electronic communications, particularly by direct marketing organizations, leads to a large reduction in the total volume of paper mail that needs to be delivered. This reduction is exacerbated by poor economic conditions.

Scenario 2: (MAIL MOUNTAIN)   The company retains its monopoly on letter delivery. In spite of increases in the use of electronic communications, taxes levied on e-mail messages mean that paper mail remains popular. Buoyant economic conditions lead to increases in the volume of mail generated by direct marketing organizations. Increased 'home working' also leads to increases in the number of paper documents that need to be delivered by mail.

Stage 2: Formulate objectives

Value trees (see Chapter 3) can be useful here. The five objectives identified are to maximize (i) short-term profit, (ii) long-term profit, (iii) market share, (iv) growth and (v) the flexibility of any strategy. Flexibility refers here to the extent to which a strategy can be adapted to the different conditions that might prevail *within* a given scenario (e.g. to counter the changing tactics of rival companies).

Stage 3: Design alternative strategies

Alternative strategies are given below:

A Continue with the current strategy of specializing in letter delivery, still taking advantage of increased mechanization where appropriate, by buying the technology from foreign suppliers (STATUS QUO).
B Continue specializing in letter delivery, but allocate very large amounts of investment to R&D with the objective of becoming a world leader in letter-sorting technology (R&D).
C As A, but also diversify into electronic communications by becoming an Internet service provider and by seeking to merge with a telecommunications company (DIVERSIFY).

Stage 4: Check strategies for feasibility

Strategies need to be screened to check that they are feasible (e.g. capable of being funded or capable of being supported logistically and technologically). In this case it is assumed that all three strategies are feasible.

Stage 5: For each lower-level objective in the objectives hierarchy

(a) *Rank all of the strategy–scenario combinations from best (1) to worst (6) in terms of performance against that objective. Examples of ranks for two of the objectives are given below.*

Objective: maximize long-term profit

	Scenario	
Strategy	**DOG FIGHT**	**MAIL MOUNTAIN**
STATUS QUO	6	2
R&D	5	1
DIVERSIFY	4	3

Thus, the R&D strategy under the MAIL MOUNTAIN scenario would, it is thought, lead to the best long-term profit, while the STATUS QUO strategy under the DOG FIGHT scenario would yield the worst.

Objective: maximize share of letter market

	Scenario	
Strategy	**DOG FIGHT**	**MAIL MOUNTAIN**
STATUS QUO	5 =	1 =
R&D	4	1 =
DIVERSIFY	5 =	1 =

(b) *Allocate a score of 100 to the best strategy–scenario combination and 0 to the worst.*
(c) *Allocate scores between 0 and 100 to represent the performance of intermediate strategy–scenario combinations against the objective.*

These scores do not need to be exact. The process of determining them and the focused thinking that this engenders are likely to be at least as valuable as the quantitative result that is obtained at the end of the analysis. For our two example objectives, the scores are shown below:

Objective: Maximize long-term profit

	Scenario	
Strategy	**DOG FIGHT**	**MAIL MOUNTAIN**
STATUS QUO	0	80
R&D	30	100
DIVERSIFY	50	60

Objective: maximize share of letter market

	Scenario	
Strategy	**DOG FIGHT**	**MAIL MOUNTAIN**
STATUS QUO	0	100
R&D	80	100
DIVERSIFY	0	100

Stage 6: Remove strategies whose performance on any objective, in any scenario, renders the strategy to be unacceptable

This is an important stage in the analysis. It should serve to alert decision-makers to the dangers of pursuing particular strategies. It may also, of course, enable strategies to be modified to avoid such dangers. (Note that removal of a strategy will necessitate a reallocation of scores where that strategy was the only one to score either 0 or 100 against a given objective.) In this case it is assumed that all strategies are acceptable.

Stage 7: (a) Compare 0 to 100 swings in strategy–scenario combinations for the objectives. Rank these swings in order of importance

In Chapter 3 we argued that swing weights should be used to compare the 'importance' of objectives. Here, this will involve ranking the importance of the *range* (or 'swing') between the worst and best performances on the different objectives. Comparing these '0 to 100' swings in scores for the objectives of the national mail company leads to the following ranks:

Swing	Rank (1 = most important swing)
Worst long-term profit to best	1
Least market share to highest	2
Least flexibility to most	3
Least growth to highest	4
Worst short-term profit to best	5

(b) *Attach a weight of 100 to the most important swing and compare it with the importance of the other swings on a 0–100 scale*

The weights assessed for the mail company are given below. For ease of calculation it is conventional to normalize the weights so that they sum to 100. This is achieved by simply dividing each weight by the sum of the weights and multiplying by 100:

Swing	Weight	Normalized weights
Worst long-term profit to best	100	50
Least market share to highest	40	20
Least flexibility to most	30	15
Least growth to highest	20	10
Worst short-term profit to best	10	5
Sum	200	100

Stage 8: Obtain an aggregate score for each strategy–scenario combination

For each scenario, an aggregate score can now be obtained to measure the performance of a given strategy over all the objectives. This is calculated by multiplying the score for each objective by the normalized weight for that objective, summing the resulting products and dividing by 100. For example, the performance of the STATUS QUO strategy in the MAIL MOUNTAIN scenario is calculated as follows:

Objective	Weight	Score	Weight × score
Short-term profit	5	100	500
Long-term profit	50	80	4000
Market share	20	100	2000
Growth	10	70	700
Flexibility	15	10	150
			Total 7350

Aggregate score $= 7350/100 = 73.5$.

By repeating this process for all of the other strategy–scenario combinations, the following matrix is obtained:

Aggregate scores

	Scenario	
Strategy	**DOG FIGHT**	**MAIL MOUNTAIN**
STATUS QUO	4.5	73.5
R&D	41.5	87.5
DIVERSIFY	42.3	76.0

Stage 9: Use the matrix to compare the strategies' performance

The scores show that the STATUS QUO is dominated by both the R&D and DIVERSIFY strategies. It performs worst under both scenarios and therefore does not appear to be a strategy that is worth considering. While there is little to choose between the R&D and DIVERSIFY strategies in the DOG FIGHT scenario, the R&D strategy is clearly superior in the MAIL MOUNTAIN scenario. Provisionally, the R&D strategy appears to be the most attractive. Of course, it is possible that, by fostering new insights into the problem, the decision analysis process will enable new and more robust strategies to be designed.

Stage 10: Perform sensitivity analysis

The scores and weights used in the analysis were based on rough-and-ready judgments. Also, in a group of decision-makers there are likely to be different opinions, or minority views, on which scores and weights are appropriate. For these reasons it can be useful to investigate the effect of changes in these values on the aggregate scores of the strategy–scenario combinations. Often, the relative performance of strategies is robust to changes in these judgmental inputs. This can sometimes lead to the resolution of disputes between members of a planning team, who, for example, may see that the same strategy is always superior whichever pair of competing weights is attached to an objective.

Note that the approach we have just outlined makes the strong assumption that decision-makers' priorities for the different objectives will be the same under the different scenarios. In some circumstances it may be appropriate to apply different weights for different scenarios. Montibeller *et al.*[11] have therefore suggested extending the approach to incorporate this by developing separate multiattribute models for each scenario. They have demonstrated their method by applying it to a decision involving a warehouse development in Italy.

Issues and limitations in scenario planning

In this section we describe two issues relating to the application of scenario planning. The first issue has to do with the organizational context for a scenario planning intervention – we show that some contexts are non-receptive. The second issue and limitation have to do with the range of scenarios that are generated in a scenario intervention – is the range of generated scenarios broad enough to cope with a full range of extreme, but still plausible, futures?

Organizational context and scenario planning

At the end of Chapter 15 we argued that a high level of perceived threat in the business environment will initiate coping behavior in the minds of an organization's managers – such as (i) bolstering a currently followed, but failing, strategy, (ii) postponing the decision over what course of action to take to recover the situation and (iii) trying to pass the responsibility for the decision to others. The most appropriate point for a scenario planning intervention in an organization is, theoretically, after there is recognition that the environmental threat to the organization's current strategy is high, but before these psychological processes are activated. As yet, however, little is known about whether or not there is a time delay, and, if so, how long, between management's recognition of a serious environmental threat to current strategy and the activation of coping patterns. Janis and Mann's model[12] proposes that the engagement and deployment of coping patterns are automatic and subconscious, such that individual managers will not recognize their deployment. Once the coping patterns have been deployed, recognition of the need for, and the value of, scenario planning may be lost.

Next, we summarize the results of a failed scenario planning intervention and link this to the operation of these coping patterns.

Case study of an unsuccessful scenario planning intervention

Hodgkinson and Wright[13] interviewed nine individuals comprising the senior management team of a major corporation (Beta Co.) that was facing a crucial decision dilemma. The interviews were conducted prior to a scenario planning exercise in which all of the interviewees were subsequently active participants. There was clear evidence that the organization's current strategic direction was failing and the management team was experiencing difficulty in developing acceptable, alternative strategies. Although it was apparent that the Beta Co. organization had strong competencies underpinning its existing business idea, it was equally apparent that there was no longer alignment between this success formula and the requirements of a changing environment. Quotations from the management team interview data were categorized under Janis and Mann's headings.

The following exemplar quotations illustrate that the management team perceived the risks to be serious if the organization failed to change its current strategy:

- *The business needs more income streams . . . therefore, diversification is crucial now to build other significant income streams* (participant 1).
- *A key danger is that there is too much emphasis on our core business activity – new technology could result in the death of [Beta Co.'s main offering] by 2005, 2010, 2015. Who knows when? We need to move to new areas that will result in new revenue streams . . . . The failure of [Beta Co.] to develop alternative revenue streams would be another bad scenario* (participant 2).
- *If we go on as we are, in 10 years from now we won't be here* (participant 3).
- *There is a perception around here that [Beta Co.] has very much got all its eggs together in one basket. If one of [Beta Co.'s major customers] pulled out . . . . At a personal level, I am very much concerned that we have job security* (participant 5).

At the same time, the risks were also perceived to be serious if the organization did change its strategy, as is illustrated by the following quotations:

- *We are a group of talented amateurs rather than experienced in areas of potential diversification* (participant 4).
- *[Beta's latest experimental venture] has been a protracted and salutary experience. There are very few short-term gains to be made* (participant 6).
- *We are naive on the business side. [Beta Co.'s latest experiment venture] is necessary for our future, but we have had a slightly unrealistic view of how easy or difficult it would be to break into an existing market in which potential customers have settled relationships and [Beta Co.] has no track record* (participant 7).

It was also clear, as evidenced from the quotations below, that the senior management team was also attempting to shift responsibility (i.e. 'pass the buck') to the board of directors of the company for adhering to a strategy that was obviously failing:

- *Our main board director is on the record as having said that [Beta Co.] should make an attempt to adapt to changing market conditions* (participant 1).
- *The board faces a key decision, not us. They need to take a keen interest in terms of what shape [Beta Co.] should take in the future* (participant 3).
- *We have to try and resolve the diversification issue one way or the other, but I am not sure that this is a decision we can take* (participant 7).

Equally, there was also compelling evidence of delay and procrastination among the management team, as demonstrated by the following quotations:

- *The failure to diversify would probably mean the business would still be OK in 10 years from now, but after 15 years it would be starting to decline* (participant 1).
- *There is still mileage in [Beta Co.'s offering] for the next 10 years* (participant 5).
- *Things will be slower than most people think . . .. We are 20 years away from complete change, i.e. our business will still be serviceable in 20 years' time* (participant 6).
- *There is no real rush to adapt . . . 5–10 years away there will still be a healthy market for [Beta Co.'s main offering]* (participant 7).

Finally, there was evidence of bolstering the current failing strategy:

- *The slow part of change in our industry is of benefit to us . . .. If [Beta Co.] becomes the only [provider of its current main offering] there will be less pressure on us to develop other products . . .. [Beta Co.'s] current performance and historic record are its key strength* (participant 2).
- *One of the problems we face in respect of new product is customer inertia . . .. Customers are generally conservative because they don't want the hassle of changing [suppliers]. These same forces are potentially prolonging the life of [Beta Co.'s current main offering] . . . within the next 2–3 years* (participant 2).
- *Ultimately, I was brought in [to Beta Co.] to play a key role in enabling the organization to diversify and/or add to its core business, though diversification may not be needed if [Beta Co.] becomes [the major player within the market of its current main offering] within the next 2–3 years* (participant 2).

To summarize to this point: the company's strategy was failing and the management team were having difficulty developing a new strategy; they were aware that failure to change the strategy, i.e. 'do nothing', was a high-risk option but equally perceived risks in making changes; and evidence of all three defensive avoidance behaviours (buck passing, procrastination and bolstering) were present. At the same time, the following quotations indicate that, in addition to the above, there was a clear deficiency in terms of information search and contingency planning:

- *I believe you can always buy the skill you need. You may have to pay a bit more or wait a bit* (participant 1).
- *We don't know enough about the real strategic aims of [Beta Co.'s main customers]* (participant 4).
- *We lack understanding of real customer requirements . . .. We know even less about potential customers* (participant 4).

- *There is a learning process we need to go through, but I am sure we can do it and beat the competition* (participant 5).
- *Another key requirement is for investment in R&D to secure the organization's future through the creation of new revenue streams, but how should this be done?* (participant 2).
- *I guess we ought to be doing other things to protect ourselves* (participant 5).

Hodgkinson and Wright concluded that the subsequent scenario planning exercise put the nature of the future into sharp focus for Beta Co. It revealed that several technological changes, regarded by the participants as predetermined factors rather than critical uncertainties, would eventually replace the company's main offering. Unfortunately, none of the strategic alternatives devised by the participants was robust against the range of futures constructed in the scenarios, and essentially the company could only continue with its current, failing, strategy. As an appropriate alternative strategy could not be devised, the scenario process served only to 'rub salt into a wound' that had been superficially healed by the earlier enactment of psychological coping processes.

Dealing with low predictability

Consider the following events that have occurred in the last 25 years: 9/11, the rise of SMS text messaging, the predominance of Google, the collapse of share prices on 19 October 1987, Black Monday and the global financial meltdown of 2008. Would these major changes in the business environment have been captured in any scenario planning process? The answer to this is that we don't know. These high-impact events had a low level of predictability beforehand. For example, causes of the 9/11 attack were analysed in detail by journalists and commentators with post-event hindsight. But coverage of likely terrorist attacks within the US continent was mute, pre-event. Recall that the driving forces method of scenario development utilizes participants' perceptions of high impact/low predictability/event clusters to drive scenario construction. However, even so, it may be that major changes that do, in fact, occur in the environment will remain outside the scenario storylines that are developed.[14]

Given that some high-impact events may not be included in the scenario storylines, it follows that the decision-maker should be alert to the degree to which a strategic option is: (i) *flexible* – i.e. investment can be upscaled or downscaled at any point in the future; (ii) *diversified* – i.e. following the option that diversifies the firm's current major offering(s) by providing either a different technology base, a different production base or a different customer base; (iii) *insurable* – i.e. allowing the possibility of insuring against extreme downside risk. This prescription can be implemented as a necessary checklist that must be completed in any option evaluation or as part of a more formalized multi-attribute evaluation of options against scenarios – much like the process that we described in our illustrative case study of the newly privatized national mail company earlier in this chapter.

If aspects of the future are seen as being inherently unpredictable, then the value of having the option to defer a decision will have value. As such, a company can pay for an asset later and earn interest on the money in the meantime. If conditions for an investment improve, then the organization will not lose out, and if conditions worsen, then the organization can decide not to acquire an asset. Options thinking can enable risks to be managed – flexibility is an asset in itself. For example, in 1997, Merck signed an agreement with Biogen to develop an asthma drug. The agreement involved potential 'stage payments' over several years, during which the success of the development, the drug market, safety rules, and so on, could all change. Merck paid Biogen to retain the option, at each stage, to either 'scale up' or 'abandon'. Thus, Merck's upside was unlimited and its downside was capped by the payment made, in advance, to Biogen.

Conclusion

Scenario thinking can be used as a way of evaluating decision options, as we have described above. As we have seen, used in this way, scenario thinking avoids any need to think probabilistically and allows a variety of viewpoints about the future to be reflected.

However, scenario planning is a practitioner-derived approach to dealing with uncertainty in decision-making. It is not based on an axiom system – as is decision analysis – and so different practitioners tend to promote different methodologies to construct scenarios. We have described just two here – the extreme-world method and the driving forces method. As we have seen, scenario thinking emphasizes the construction of causal 'storylines' that describe how the future will unfold. Willem Wagenaar,[15] in a study of how judges reach decisions in courtrooms, has found, analogously, that judges and juries do not weigh probabilities that a defendant is guilty 'beyond reasonable doubt'. Instead, such decision-makers evaluate scenarios that describe *why* and *how* the accused committed the crime. One such scenario is, in principle, contained in the prosecution's indictment. The prosecution tells the story of what happened and the court decides whether that is a true story or not. 'Good' stories provide a context that gives an easy and natural explanation of why the 'actors' behaved in the way they did. So, storytelling via scenario planning may be a natural way of making sense of the world. Kees van der Heijden[16] argues that, because of its focus on causality, scenario planning is intuitively more attractive to managers than approaches such as decision trees, which are essentially ways of choosing between gambles with different expected values (or utilities). Additionally, van der Heijden argues, decision-tree analysis requires a rigorous, yet *static*, definition of a decision problem. By contrast, decision-makers experience and acknowledge the continuing fluidity of an emerging decision context and feel, he argues, uncomfortable with any further loss of flexibility introduced by decision analysis. Scenario planning does not evaluate options against uncertainties in a single process of analysis. Instead, once the range of plausible futures has been defined, these futures can be utilized over an extended time period as and when new decision options are developed and subsequently tested in the 'wind tunnel' conditions.[17]

In spite of these advantages, we have also argued that some decision analysis methods can usefully complement scenario planning. The use of methods based on multi-attribute value analysis is likely to reduce the complexities of evaluating strategies against multiple objectives in multiple scenarios. A more insightful approach to strategic decision-making should be the result. Finally, we discussed two issues and limitations with scenario planning – sometimes the organizational climate may be unreceptive to thinking about the future, and sometimes it may be worth planning for low predictability by keeping one's options open.

Discussion questions

(1) Decision trees, scenario planning and keeping one's options open are three ways of dealing with uncertainty in the business environment. What are the advantages and disadvantages of each approach?

(2) To what extent does the scenario planning process contain components that are likely to prompt the recognition and resolution of the problems of frame blindness and strategic inertia?

(3) Some commentators argue that scenario planning is best suited to the long-term future and major strategic decisions but decision analysis focuses on short-term operational decisions. Do you agree? In what other ways do the domains of applicability of scenario planning and decision analysis differ?

(4) Consider your organization. What major trends (predetermined elements) and uncertainties will have a significant impact, either positive or negative, on its viability in the next 15 years? Create a range of scenarios, using either the extreme-world or driving forces methods, to incorporate these elements. Next, consider your organization's defining strategy (or business idea). Does it perform robustly against the scenarios? If it does not, what aspects of the strategy should be changed?

References

1. Adapted from Irvine, I.W. (1992) *Change Management: How a Manufacturer is Learning to Compete in New Markets*, Strathclyde Graduate Business School MBA Dissertation.
2. Van der Heijden, K. (1996) *Scenarios: the Art of Strategic Conversation*, John Wiley & Sons, Ltd, Chichester, UK.
3. Adapted from Ng, S.M.W. and McConnell, D. (1993) *Development of a Coherent European Strategy as Part of a Global Strategy for a Multi-national Corporation in Liner Industry*, Strathclyde Graduate Business School MBA Dissertation.
4. Adapted from Kahane, A. (1992) The Mont Fleur scenarios, *Weeky Mail* and *Guardian Weekly*, Bellville, South Africa.
5. Cairns, G., Wright, G., Bradfield, R., Van der Heijden, K. and Burt, G. (2004) The application of scenario planning to internally-generated e-government futures. *Technological Forecasting and Social Change*, **71**, 217–238.
6. 'Kailyard' is an old Scots term for 'cabbage patch' and was selected by participants in the subgroup to describe a level of minimum subsistence for members of society – in spite of vast amounts of energy expended on tending the 'cabbage patch'.
7. von Winterfeldt, D. and Edwards, W. (1986) *Decision Analysis and Behavioral Research*, Cambridge University Press, Cambridge, UK.
8. Keeney, R.L. (1982) Decision analysis: an overview, *Operations Research*, **30**, 803–838.
9. Phillips, L.D. (1984) A theory of requisite decision models, *Acta Psychologica*, **56**, 29–48.
10. Keeney, R.L. (1992) *Value Focused Thinking*, Harvard University Press, Cambridge, MA.
11. Montibeller, G., Gummer, H. and Tumidei, D. (2006) Combining scenario planning and multi-criteria decision analysis in practice, *Journal of Multi-Criteria Decision Analysis*, **14**, 5–20.
12. Janis, I.L. and Mann, L. (1979) *Decision Making*, Free Press, New York, NY.
13. Hodgkinson, G.P. and Wright, G. (2002) Confronting strategic inertia in a top management team: learning from failure, *Organization Studies*, **23**, 949–977; Hodgkinson, G.P. and Wright, G. (2006) Neither completing the practice turn, nor enriching the process tradition: secondary misinterpretations of a case analysis reconsidered, *Organization Studies*, **27**, 1895–1190; see also Wright, G., van der Heijden, K., Bradfield, R., Burt, G. and Cairns, G. (2004) The psychology of why organizations can be slow to adapt and change: and what can be done about it, *Journal of General Management*, **29**, 21–36; Wright, G., van der Heijden, K., Burt, G., Bradfield, R. and Cairns, G. (2008) Scenario planning interventions in organizations: an analysis of the causes of success and failure, *Futures*, **40**, 218–236.
14. For more discussion, see Wright, G. and Goodwin, P. (2009) Decision making and planning under low levels of predictability, *International Journal of Forecasting* (in press).
15. Wagenaar, W.A. (1994) The subjective probability of guilt, in *Subjective Probability*, ed. by Wright, G. and Ayton, P., John Wiley & Sons, Chichester, UK.
16. Van der Heijden, K. (1994) Probabilistic planning and scenario planning, in *Subjective Probability*, ed. by Wright, G. and Ayton, P., John Wiley & Sons, Chichester, UK.
17. For further reading on scenario planning, see Wack, P. (1985) Scenarios: uncharted waters ahead, *Harvard Business Review*, Sept.–Oct., 73–90; Wack, P. (1985) Scenarios: shooting the

rapids, *Harvard Business Review*, Nov.–Dec., 131–142; Schoemaker, P.J.H. (1995) Scenario planning: a tool for strategic thinking, *Sloan Management Review*, Winter, 25–40; Bradfield, R., Wright, G., Burt, G., Cairns. G. and van der Heijden, K. (2005) The origins and evolution of scenario techniques in long range business planning, *Futures*, **37**, 395–812; Wright, G., Cairns, G. and Goodwin, P. (2009) Teaching scenario planning: lessons from practice in academia and business, *European Journal of Operational Research*, **194**, 323–335.

Alternative decision-support systems and conclusions 17

Introduction

In this chapter we present an overview of two further ways of aiding decision-making: linear modeling and expert systems. *Linear modeling* involves building a statistical model of a person's judgments or predictions and subsequently utilizing the model instead of the person. *Expert systems* relate to building a model of the decision processes of an expert decision-maker. In a similar way to linear modeling, the expert system representation of the decision-maker is subsequently used instead of the person.

From the above short overviews it is clear that these decision-aiding technologies – as well as all the other decision-aiding approaches that we have discussed in earlier chapters – require the elicitation and representation of human judgment. As we shall see, linear modeling and expert systems place different emphasis on the assumed quality of the judgmental input. In this chapter we will first introduce the decision-aiding technologies and then compare and contrast them, both with each other and then with both decision analysis and scenario planning. Our focus will be on the domains of applicability of the different approaches and on the validity of the resulting decisions.

At the end of the chapter, we consider whether intuition-based snap judgments should have any role in management decision-making. We conclude by offering some final words of advice on how to apply decision analysis.

Expert systems

What is an expert system?

Expert systems are one offshoot of research into artificial intelligence (AI). The aim of AI is to represent the totality of human intelligence and thought within a computer system. Within AI research are such fields of study as:

(1) *Voice/image recognition.* The aim here is to produce systems that can recognize verbal visual inputs and respond appropriately to them. Until recently, systems could only recognize a few score of spoken words which were given as short commands by an individual whose voice patterns had previously been learnt by the computer. But now, computer systems have been developed that can recognize handwriting and perform voice and image recognition functions similar to those of a human being. Until a few years ago, such systems were not thought achievable.

(2) *Robotics.* While applications are now increasingly common in manufacturing, for example, the ultimate objective of robotics is to produce machines that 'think' and 'act' like humans. If producing voice and image recognition systems such as the ones mentioned above is now conceivable, then robotic research to produce machines with the flexibility of people presents more complex problems to the AI researcher.

Early research on expert systems was also focused on relatively complex problems such as diagnosing the disease from which a person is suffering. The aim was for the system to perform the diagnosis in the same way as an expert physician. However, general diagnosis turned out to be a difficult problem and, even now, after many person-years of effort, none of these general-purpose systems is in routine use. One reason for this is that the systems were developed by academics who were more interested in producing academic papers to further their careers. Relatively simple practical problems that can be solved easily hold no challenges (or publications) and so tend to be avoided by university-based researchers. More recently, *commercial* advantage has been seen in picking the 'low-hanging fruit', and it is these expert systems, built in person-months rather than person-years, that form the focus of this section. As we shall see, they are often targeted on a particular area of expertise.

Several definitions of an expert system have been proffered, but the Expert Systems group of the British Computer Society provides a generally agreed and workable definition that it *is the modeling, within a computer, of expert knowledge in a given domain, such that the resulting system can offer intelligent advice or take intelligent decisions.* One important addition to this definition is that the system should be able to *justify* the logic and reasoning underlying its advice or decision-making – we shall return to this point later when we discuss the uptake of advice-giving systems.

It follows that expert systems act as *decision aids or decision-support systems* by giving *advice* to a (non-expert) human decision-maker. Expert systems can also act as *decision-makers* without any human–computer dialogue or interaction. Finally, expert systems can act as *trainers* by instructing human novices to become experts in a particular area of expertise.

Three brief sketches will give the essence of these distinctions:

(1) A fisherman goes into a tackle shop. He wants to catch a certain type of fish in the particular river conditions where he fishes. The expert system questions him

about the fish, river conditions and weather, etc., and *advises* him to use a certain type of fly or bait.

(2) In a factory, the sensors within a machine indicate an imminent component failure. The expert system *decides* to close the machine down and alert a particular fitter to attend the problem. At the same time, the expert system orders the required spare part from the storeroom and dispatches it to the fitter.

(3) A school student works through mathematical problems with an expert system. After the student has worked through a series of problems, the system diagnoses the underlying cause of the observed errors, gives the student some extra problems to confirm the diagnosis and then proceeds to give *tuition* in the required mathematical skills.

What is expert knowledge?

The nature of human knowledge is an area of much debate and controversy. However, it assumes a more concrete form in the practice of *knowledge engineering*. For expert systems, this is the skill of obtaining and manipulating human knowledge so that it can be built into a computer model that in some ways behaves like an expert. Gaining the knowledge from the expert, an initial focus of knowledge engineering, is termed *knowledge elicitation*, and this is usually concerned with obtaining knowledge from *people* rather than documents. In fact, the knowledge of experts goes far beyond that contained in textbooks. For example, Wilkins *et al.*[1] cite the case of medical expertise where, in spite of years of textbook study, students are unable to show *diagnostic expertise*. This is achieved from an 'apprenticeship period' where they *observe* experts in real diagnoses and attempt to duplicate the skill by practicing themselves. Indeed, expert knowledge consists of many *unwritten* 'rules of thumb':

> [it is] . . . largely heuristic knowledge, experimental, uncertain – mostly 'good guesses' and 'good practice', in lieu of facts and figures. Experience has also taught us that much of this knowledge is private to the expert, not because he is unwilling to share publicly how he performs, but because he is unable to.

> He knows more than he is aware of knowing . . .. What masters really know is not written in the textbooks of the masters. But we have learned that this private knowledge can be uncovered by the careful, painstaking analysis of a second party, or sometimes by the expert himself, operating in the context of a large number of highly specific performance problems.

Sometimes in order to understand one expert's actions, the expertise of another is required. For example, in organized human/machine chess matches, a high-ranking player is often present in order to explain the likely reason for each player's moves.

Similarly, in eliciting medical expertise, a doctor can be employed to observe a patient–doctor interview and infer the reasons for questions asked of the patient.

Given the 'hidden' nature of expert knowledge, it is not surprising to find research in the area of knowledge engineering pointing to the difficulties of elicitation. Hayes-Roth et al.[2] have described it as a 'bottleneck in the construction of expert systems'. For example, communication problems arise because not only is the knowledge engineer relatively unfamiliar with the expert's area or 'domain' but also the expert's vocabulary is often inadequate for transferring expertise into a program. The 'engineer' thus plays an intermediary role with the expert in extending and refining terms. Similarly, Duda and Shortcliffe[3] conclude that:

> The identification and encoding of knowledge is one of the most complex and arduous tasks encountered in the construction of an expert system . . .. Thus the process of building a knowledge base has usually required an AI researcher. While an experienced team can put together a small prototype in one or two man-months, the effort required to produce a system that is ready for serious evaluation (well before contemplation of actual use) is more often measured in man-years.

Wilkins et al.[1] reinforce this view and note that attempts to automate the 'tedious' and 'time-consuming' process of knowledge acquisition between expert and 'engineer' have so far proved unsuccessful. It is clear that knowledge elicitation for expert system development shares many characteristics with knowledge elicitation for decision analysis, discussed in Chapter 7.

How is expert knowledge represented in expert systems?

Having completed the difficult process of elicitation, the knowledge must be represented in a form that can be implemented in a computer language. This is most commonly achieved in the form of *production rules*. For example:

IF a car is a VW Beetle, THEN the car has no water cooling system.

More formally

IF (condition in database), THEN (action to update the database).

Production rules can have multiple conditions and multiple actions. The action of a production rule may be required to ask a question of the user of the system or interact with a physical device in addition to updating the database. Production-rule-based expert systems often use many hundreds of rules, and so control of their action becomes a serious problem for the knowledge engineer.

The *control structure* determines what rule is to be tried next. The control structure is often called the rule interpreter or *inference engine*. In response to information gained from the user in interaction with the expert system, the inference engine selects and tests individual rules in the rule base in its search for an appropriate decision or advice. It usually does this by *forward chaining*, which means following pathways through from known facts to resulting conclusions. *Backward chaining* involves choosing hypothetical conclusions and testing to see if the necessary rules underlying the conclusions hold true. As an added complication, we note that the rules elicited from experts often contain a degree of uncertainty. For example:

> IF a car won't start, THEN the cause is *likely* to be a flat battery but it *could be* lack of fuel and *might be* . . .

Most expert systems that can tolerate uncertainty employ some kind of probability – like a measure to weigh and balance conflicting evidence. It is important to recognize the significance of the user–system interface in systems design. Expert systems are often used by non-experts. Successful systems must be able to interface effectively with their users in order to:

(1) gain the information needed to test the rules;
(2) give understandable advice in plain English and justify the logic and reasoning underpinning the advice given or decision made.

Psychologists, rather than computer programmers, have the sort of skills necessary to build appropriate interfaces. Consequently, successful knowledge engineers integrate both computing and psychological skills.

Wright and Ayton[4] have differentiated two key indicators of whether an expert system can be built within a reasonable timeframe. These are:

(1) That the subject domain has been formalized. One measure of formalization is that manuals exist. Of course, the expert may have devised short cuts through a manual and/or internalized it.
(2) That the subject domain is amenable to verbal expression. One measure of this is that the expert should feel confident that he/she could communicate his/her expertise to a novice over a telephone link.

If these two key indicators are satisfied, then both the process of eliciting the knowledge from the expert and subsequent programming of this knowledge, as rules, are relatively straightforward. Overall, expert systems are often developed to reproduce experts' decision-making processes in relatively narrow speciality areas. In the next sections, we focus on commercial applications in marketing and financial services.

Marketing applications

A well-documented, and successful, set of expert system developments in marketing relate to utilization of scanning data at checkouts in supermarkets and other stores. As Brown and Goslar[5] note, consumer purchase data can now be automatically collected at point-of-sale through scanner systems. Scanning systems allow analysis of purchase time, place, amounts, outlet type, price and promotional discount. Mitchell *et al.*[6] focus on the use of expert systems to analyze such scanner data. As they note, the increased availability of these data has severely tested the ability of marketing management to analyze them. The change from bimonthly store audit data to weekly store-level scanner data results in a 10 000-fold increase in the *available* data.[7] How should these data be analyzed? One suggestion[8] is that human modes of analysis can be replicated on an expert system. The focus is on the automation of the more repetitive and mechanical aspects of the data analyst's task (such as noting differences and trends) in order to ensure consistency in decision-making and decreased analysis time.

As Mitchell *et al.* report, humans skilled in the analysis of scanner data have several advantages, mainly in their ability to recognize change points in time series data and construct a causal explanation of these changes.[6] They do not advocate that expert systems should be developed to provide complete automation of the analysis, but rather they assist the planner by providing a 'first-cut' analysis of the data, relieving the market professional of simpler, more structured, routine data analysis tasks. For example, one scanner-based expert system is based on the concept that market share is inversely related to price.[9] This system is sensitive to time periods in which the share has gone up (or down) or the price has gone down (or up). Such relationships are summarized and reported to the marketer.

Eisenhart[10] provides a description of what we believe is best practice in expert system deployment, in that a business case can be quantified for the application. Here, Texas Instruments' own expert systems group designed an expert system (called ES^2) that runs on a PC and that evaluates whether potential sales prospects really would benefit from Texas Instruments' expert systems products/customized applications. To use the system, potential customers answer questions that explore whether expert systems would solve their problem, while at the same time educating them about the basis of the technology. Finally, the system makes an overall recommendation on whether the prospect needs an expert system. ES^2 has had immediate *measurable* payback to the small expert system division at Texas Instruments, in that 80% of the 'potential' leads are eliminated. As 'an initial in-person qualification trip currently costs $1000 and takes from 1 to 2 days', the savings to Texas Instruments are substantial. (Texas Instruments' field analysts previously had to accompany salespeople to answer technical queries; ES^2 can thus be categorized as an advice-giving system.)

Financial services applications

Of those applications that have attracted the greatest interest from insurers, *life under-writing* has proved the most prominent. Life underwriting is, essentially, the process of evaluating risk associated with insuring an individual, and matching the individual to the actuarial (a definition that applies to the underwriting of all types of risk and policy). More specifically, life underwriters assess the information that they receive from a standard application form, in combination with any additional information that may have been requested (such as medical reports from the applicants' doctors or medical examinations taken for the purpose of the application). The task of the un-derwriter is then to match the applicant to the particular mortality table that correctly predicts the statistical probability of the individual succumbing to death over the term of the policy.

On the basis of the comparison of the applicant to the statistical norm, the under-writer decides whether the application is accepted, declined or accepted but with additional premiums or waivers of coverage for certain conditions. The skill of under-writers appears to be in the internalization of key heuristics about risk, which enables them rapidly to scan application forms for important phrases or indicators, only then referring to the manuals or mortality tables that they have available – in contrast to inexperienced underwriters who need to do this referencing in most cases.

A number of expert systems have been built to perform the life underwriting tasks, although these vary somewhat according to their objectives. One system, built in collaboration with a leading UK life insurance company,[11] was designed ostensibly as an underwriter trainer, but with the potential for upgrading to an automated system.

This system modeled the decision processes of a senior underwriter whose thought processes matched, to a degree, the decision-making processes documented in life insurance manuals. It also allowed junior underwriters to be trained to the level of the modeled expert, by requesting information from the junior underwriters on how clients had answered the questions on their application forms, and then by justifying its own underwriting decision through help screens.

Figure 17.1 gives the underwriting options. The system was built in six modules: occupation, geography, lifestyle/AIDS, financial, hobbies and medical. Each module contained the rules that the senior underwriter used to assess risk. Figure 17.2 presents a small example of the rule base of the geographical module.

Note the similarity between decision tree representations in decision analysis and the representation of the sequence of rule testing in the expert system.

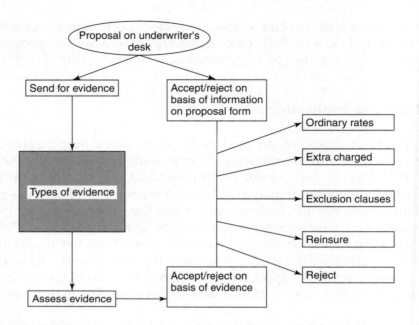

Figure 17.1 – Underwriting options

The knowledge elicitation was performed between two knowledge engineers and one 'expert'. Knowledge elicitation techniques included interviews, *card sorting* and *context focusing*.[4] Card sorting consisted of the knowledge engineer writing down on cards the names of, say, countries. In one version of the card-sorting technique, the expert chose three countries at random (the cards were face down) and then had to sort them into two groups so that the countries named on two of the cards were more similar to each other in some respect than to the third country. In this way, the knowledge engineer was able to explore the way in which an underwriter views countries in terms of risk dimensions. Context focusing consisted of the knowledge engineer playing the role of a novice underwriter who had in front of him a completed life-proposal form. The senior underwriters' task was to help the novice come to an underwriting decision by means of telephone communication. The sequence of rule testing engaged by the expert was recorded by the knowledge engineer and provided one means of identifying the priority of rules.

One set of rule testing with high priority is given below:

Has every question on the proposal form been answered?
IF yes, THEN ask:
Is the current proposal sum insured within no evidence limits?
IF yes, THEN ask:

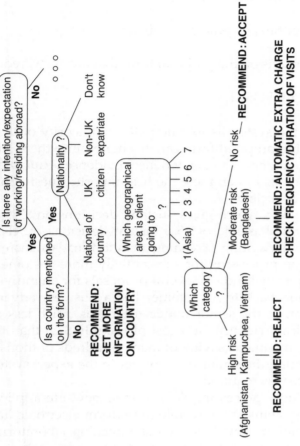

IF applicant intends/expects to
work/reside abroad
THEN check if his or her destination is
indicated on the proposal form
ELSE check for some other geographical
details . . .

IF the country applicant intends to visit is
indicated on proposal form
THEN look for indicators of the
applicant's nationality on the form
ELSE get information from the applicant
about the country s/he is destined for
(exit module)

Following branch for a UK citizen
destined for Asia only:

IF the country indicated is Afghanistan,
Kampuchea or Vietnam ('high risk')
THEN the recommendation is to reject the
proposal (exit module)

IF the country indicated is Bangladesh
('moderate risk')
THEN the recommendation is to charge
extra depending on the
frequency/duration of visits (exit module)
ELSE any other Asian country
recommendation is to accept the
proposal with no geographical extra charge
(exit module)

Figure 17.2 – The rule base of the geographical module

Are there any previous sums assured in force?
IF no, THEN ask:
Are height and weight within acceptable parameters?
IF yes, THEN ask:
Are there any other questions on the proposal form that are answered
'yes'?
IF no, THEN ACCEPT PROPOSAL.

One development of the system is to automate the majority of the underwriting process. Details from a life proposal form can be entered into the system at a branch office by a clerk with no underwriting experience. Evidence is automatically sent for where required, with details of complete medical reports, questionnaires, etc., also entered into the system by a clerk.

The automated processing, which gives 'instant' decisions on 85% of applications (as opposed to a previous baseline of 65% instant decisions by clerical staff who consulted a simplified underwriting 'screening' manual), leads to increased speed and consistency of application processing for substantially more customers. In addition, as insurance brokers typically send off several proposals for an individual customer, the first positive decision back to a customer has a business advantage. Another calculation revealed that, as the senior underwriter was much less comprehensive in this request for medical evidence (at a cost of roughly $75) than the deliberately conservative 'screening' manual, a saving of many hundreds of thousands of dollars could be achieved by letting the senior underwriter in the expert system *decide* when further medical evidence was required.

Some companies are now processing 90% of their new life applications through expert systems. Extant systems are now able to perform electronic data interchange with third-party information providers such as screening laboratories. The biggest benefit is seen to be time saving in the turnaround of life proposals.

However, another argument is that expert systems that enhance speed of turnaround time should not be deployed without careful consideration, because customer relationships need to be built for long-term retention. Such relationships have, at least in the past, been built on face-to-face meetings of field agents and potential customers – where policy alternatives are discussed and confidence in subsequent recommendations is established.[12]

The expert systems built by Nippon Life[13] and by the Swiss Reinsurance Co.,[14] among others, have attempted to produce *fully* automated systems. In these cases, the system builders have attempted to automate the entire life underwriting procedure by encoding their extensive underwriting manuals into knowledge bases.

The extent to which this has proved feasible is still an open question, for the law of diminishing returns applies at a certain stage, where it becomes less and less economic to encode the rules required to deal with the last few per cent of all cases (which was left, in one system,[11] for expert underwriters to deal with). However, none of the systems described above represents *complete* replacements for underwriters, who are seen as invaluable because they are still required to deal with the most difficult of cases and to handle *changes* in risk assessment circumstances, with which the systems themselves are unable to deal. For example, updates are required to the rule bases when formerly peaceable countries that a proposed insured plans to visit become war zones.

Of prime interest here, however, is the nature of the underwriting domain, which has made it amenable for the implementation of viable expert systems.

If one considers the nature of this task more closely, then it is apparent that it:

(i) involves repetitive components;
(ii) is a clearly structured logical process;
(iii) is a high-volume task;
(iv) involves the utilization of knowledge that is fairly static (otherwise the system would require vast amounts of updating and reprogramming);
(v) involves variation in human performance which could (beneficially) be made more consistent.

Furthermore, and importantly, the underwriting domain complies with the two criteria set out by Wright and Ayton[4] for commercial viability, namely that most of the rules for underwriting tend to be formalized in manuals (in the case of life underwriting, these are produced by underwriters in collaboration with actuaries and chief medical officers), and that the domain is also verbally communicable in a step-by-step fashion to novices. Indeed, before the expert system was developed, this is how novices were trained. These factors ensure that the knowledge elicitation and engineering aspects of devising the expert system are achievable – aspects whose difficulty and pertinence to eventual system success are often underestimated. Indeed, one survey[15] found that expert systems in use in the UK were not designed to cross functional and organizational boundaries but were instead utilized to automate relatively simple problem domains.

Where next?

In our view, expert systems exist as a technology with unquestionable potential for providing financial benefits and savings through improvement in service. The important issue, however, concerns the identification of the most appropriate domains for such system implementation.

Next, as examples, we detail two application areas that have strong potential in financial services: (i) back-office detection of fraud and (ii) point-of-sale advice-giving for personal financing planning. In both cases, the benefits of expert system technology can be applied for competitive edge.

Back-office fraud detection systems

In the back office at Chemical Bank[16] in New York, an expert system automatically flags unauthorized and suspected fraudulent transactions in the bank's $1 billion-a-day foreign exchange business. The rule base modeled in the expert system was elicited from one-to-one questioning of Chemical Bank's auditors whose job it was to identify trades that broke the law or showed poor judgment.

Chemical Bank will not reveal the actual rules in their system, but they involve monitoring the dollar volume for certain types of trade, deviation from historical norms and other 'disruptions' of historically prevalent trading patterns.

At American Express,[17] expert systems are also in place. Prior to implementation of the expert systems, American Express's previous computerized authorization system handled 85% of their credit card purchase authorizations. The remaining 15% (questionable transactions) were forwarded to human authorizers. At the time, American Express employed approximately 300 authorizers to handle over a million transactions per month. This task of handling questionable transactions required numerous activities which usually included: consulting an individual's credit record (which had to be called out of as many as 13 databases) and conducting a conversation with the customer or merchant. This gathered information would be applied to a body of knowledge and policy rules that were derived from all the past experience, history and statistical analysis that American Express had accumulated over the years. These rules were listed in the authorizer's training manual (which consisted of several hundred pages). Each authorizer was usually required to process approximately 26 transactions per hour; about 150 transactions per day. Decisions on whether or not to approve these questionable transactions had to be made quickly and carefully.

By the early 1990s, American Express faced forecasts predicting an increasing need for authorizing staff owing to an increasing volume of transactions. Now in place is an expert system that processes almost all of the 15% of questionable transactions previously handled manually. The system provides the operator with a recommended decision along with the relevant reasons as to why that decision was made. The expert system is not only an adviser to the authorizers, it also authorizes millions of dollars of credit without human involvement.

The expert system draws on data from 10–12 databases, applies complex 'expert reasoning' and, if necessary, engages in a dialogue with the telephone operator, gathering any extra information required to approve or deny the authorization.

Survey results[18] indicate that the major use of expert systems in the UK is in processing loan and credit applications, such as those now handled by expert systems at American Express. In the USA, mortgage lenders use expert systems to review loan applications for compliance with federal and state laws. The rules that comprise the expert systems are reviewed and approved by legal experts to ensure compliance.[19] Subjective, qualitative assessments of loan applicants, such as the perceived character of the borrower, play an important part in evaluation of applicants for agricultural loans, and these perceptions are elicited from system users to be utilized in an expert system's decision-making process.[20]

Point-of-sale advice-giving systems

The use of expert systems to provide customers with financial planning and advice would give financial institutions *both* a product that the public would like *and* the means of gathering information that could be used to create cross-selling opportunities. Notably, financial planning is a formalized and structured process where the knowledge domain is, to all intents and purposes, relatively complete. The person operating the system does not need to have specialist expertise, but can, with the aid of a suitable system, still offer expert advice. As Pickup[21] documents, research has shown that many people would be prepared to pay up to $150 to have a comprehensive personal plan, aimed at maximizing his/her existing resources and setting out how to achieve his/her financial goals. Once an individual goes through the planning process (providing details of his/her financial situation, personal and family details, pension arrangements and retirement aims), the institution producing the plan will almost certainly have obtained more useful information on that individual than the other financial institutions with which the individual has dealings.

In addition, the need to train staff (perhaps in the high street branch of a building society) to a high level and regularly update their knowledge and expertise is greatly reduced. Expert system technology helps to facilitate placing more people in the front office where sales are made.

Brown *et al.*[22] provide a further discussion of the issues in personal financial planning and document eight systems in use in the USA. Several of the systems provide 40–50 page reports that give recommendations for asset management, investment strategies, tax-saving strategies, life insurance needs, etc. These researchers note that the pace of new financial product introductions and the frequency of modifications to the Internal Revenue code underpin the need for periodic updates to an expert system's knowledge base. However, such updates are easily and reliably achieved.

Overall, such expert systems:

(i) improve company image through more efficient service;
(ii) improve the quality and consistency of decision-making;

(iii) provide better communication of knowledge across an organization;
(iv) provide an accessible reference source for crucial knowledge.

Further, an indirect benefit is that the sales staff also broaden their own skill and knowledge by observing and studying the relationship between the expert system's advice and the customer's characteristics. In addition, less time is spent on the process of preparing a client's report, leaving more time for direct client contact.

Conclusion

In this section we have argued that formalization and completeness of the knowledge base are key benchmarks for subsequent operationalization of that knowledge as an expert system, and that systems that automate a part of the business process that was previously judgmental are beneficial. A strong business case can be made for automating an expert underwriter's decision-making processes and utilizing the resulting expert system at an early phase of back-office transaction processing.[23] Advice-giving systems at front-office point-of-sale can enhance the sales capabilities of front-office financial services staff. Such advice-giving systems also enable the collection of detailed customer profiles.

One recent study reviewed these two roles of expert systems – either replacing or supporting the decision-maker – and concluded that expert systems that replace decision-makers do improve the efficiency of decision-making, but that expert systems utilized in advisory roles do not save users' time.[24] Another study found that novice users of expert systems tend to accept systems' recommendations, while more-expert users have a stronger interest in examining the explanations that the systems generate for particular recommendations.[25] As such, expert users are interested in comparing the recommendations of the systems with their own judgment. In fact, this focus on evaluation and verification may be a precondition for acceptance of systems by more-expert users. We shall return to this issue of intuition versus advice after we have introduced and examined the use of statistical models in prediction, which we review next.

Statistical models of judgment

Most statistical models of judgment involve the use of a formula that is designed to represent, as closely as possible, the way that experts arrive at their judgments. It is then possible to replace the experts with the model, in the hope that this will yield improved estimates or decisions.

For example, the following formula might represent how a sales forecaster makes a judgmental estimate of next month's sales for a product:

Forecasters prediction of number of units that will be sold next month
= 2100 + 0.8 × TV advertising expenditure next month
+ 0.4 × newspaper advertising expenditure next month
− 425 × price to be charged next month

If the company is spending \$50 000 on TV advertising next month, \$6000 on newspaper advertising and charging a price of \$20 for each unit of the product, we would therefore expect our forecaster to make a prediction of 2100 + 0.8(50 000) + 0.4(6000) − 425(20) = 36 000 units. In this model, the three variables that we assume the sales forecaster is using to make her predictions (TV advertising expenditure, newspaper advertising expenditure and price) are often referred to as cues. The values of 0.8, 0.4 and −425 are estimates of the weights that the forecaster places on each piece of information when making a forecast.

Our model is an example of a *linear* model because it assumes that, each time one of the cues is increased by a certain amount, it will result in the same change in the forecaster's prediction. For example, it assumes that each \$1000 increase in TV advertising expenditure will lead to an 800 unit increase in the sales that the forecaster will predict, irrespective of how much has already been spent on advertising. In practice, if we go on increasing advertising expenditure by \$1000 amounts, then our forecaster might expect the effectiveness of each extra amount of advertising to diminish. If this were the case, our model would not be a true representation of how she arrives at her judgments. In spite of this, linear models often provide reasonable approximations to real-life situations.

How can we obtain our model of how the forecaster makes her predictions? One method is to collect a large set of data on her past predictions of sales. For each prediction we would also record the values of each of the cues used by the forecaster when the prediction is made. Statistical methods like multiple regression analysis[26] can then be used to find the model that gives the best fit to these data. This means that we obtain a model that should give the best approximation to the judgmental strategy employed by the forecaster to make her forecasts. This model is sometimes called a policy-capturing or a 'bootstrapping' model.

Having obtained our model, an obvious question is: which will lead to the most accurate sales forecasts – the forecaster continuing to make her intuitive forecasts each month (as she always has) or our statistical model of her judgmental strategy? The model will have the advantage that it will average out the forecaster's inconsistencies. Give her the same information on two different occasions and, as a human being, she is likely to make different forecasts. For example, on some days her attention may be elsewhere when the forecast is required. But the model will always provide a reliable forecast based on the value of the cues. However, the model will not be able to capture the forecaster's ability to use the cues in a non-linear way. For example, as we have argued, she, rather than the model, has the ability to take into account the possibility that increasing advertising expenditure is subject to the law of diminishing returns. She might also know, or believe, that TV and newspaper advertising reinforce each other, so that their overall effect is greater than the sum of their separate effects. Our linear model of her will not reflect such insights. [27]

In spite of these caveats, research overwhelmingly suggests that in most areas of application – including forecasting and diagnosis – a linear model of a person's judgmental strategy will usually outperform the judge on whom the model is based. This is thought to be because the benefits of eliminating the judge's inconsistencies far outweigh his or her ability to use the cues in a non-linear way. For example, one study investigated a group of venture capitalists who were considered expert in identifying high-potential new ventures. [28] Venture-capitalist-backed ventures survive at a much higher rate than those ventures backed by other sources. Nevertheless, 20% of venture-capitalist-backed firms still fail within 5 years. The study found that bootstrap models of the venture capitalists outperformed all but one participant who achieved the same accuracy rate as the bootstrap model. Dawes [29] noted:

> I know of no studies in which human judges have been able to improve upon optimal statistical prediction . . .. A mathematical model by its very nature is an abstraction of the process it models; hence if the decision-maker's behavior involves following valid principles but following them poorly these valid principles will be abstracted by the model.

However, researchers investigating the effectiveness of using linear models have reached more surprising conclusions. In one classic study, Dawes and Corrigan [30] found that linear models that involved giving all the cues *equal* weights made more accurate predictions or diagnoses than models that contained differential weights for the cues (it should be noted that the variables in these equal-weighted models were first 'standardized' so that they all had the same amount of variation – using the same weights for cues measured in single units and cues measured in thousands of units would not make sense). This result suggests that the key role of the forecaster or diagnostician should be limited to the specification of which cues should be included in the linear model rather than on the differential weighting of those cues. Thus, using one's knowledge of 'what to look for' in making a judgment may be the natural province of the human expert. For example, in a study by Einhorn, [31] expert doctors coded biopsies of patients with Hodgkin's disease and then made an overall rating of severity. These overall ratings were very poor predictors of survival time, but the variables the doctors coded made excellent predictions when used in a linear model. A recent (2006) special issue of the *Journal of Behavioral Decision Making* reviewed the status of linear models as replacements for expert judgment. [32] The conclusion confirmed the finding of 50 years earlier: judgment is best used to devise predictive models, but the final act of combining the predictive variables is best done mechanically by a linear additive model.[33]

Are there any circumstances where we might expect a person's judgment systematically to outperform a linear model? We might expect this when the judge has access to extra information that was not available to the model. But, as Dawes *et al.*[34] have pointed out, the small number of studies that have provided decision-makers with access to preferred sources of information have generally shown the superiority of the statistical model. Human judgment can also theoretically improve on statistical modeling by recognizing unexpected events that are not included in the model's formula and whose occurrence will countervail the actuarial conclusion. Dawes *et al.* argue that such events are rare, but this may be the exact situation where it is best to make a judgmental intervention. Meehl[35] used the term 'broken leg cue' when he referred to the fact that the knowledge that a certain person had just broken his or her leg would invalidate any predictions of a person's movements (e.g. to the theater, particular restaurants, etc.) based on historic statistical data. Some studies[36,37] provide evidence of the higher quality of human judgment compared with statistical models when 'broken leg' cues are part of the information available for decision-making.

In summary, this research suggests that experts may have the ability to recognize the significance of extramodel information and use it appropriately. Such characteristics of experts can, potentially, be captured in expert system representations of knowledge. For example, in the life underwriting system that we described earlier[11] there is underlying statistical information on whether those applicants for life insurance who hold a private pilot's license pose an additional risk – they do not. There is also statistical information on whether farmers are at increased risk than members of other occupations – they are not. Plus, people who live in Australia are also not any more at risk than those who live in, say, the EU. However, the senior underwriter knew that the combination of these three factors in one application for life insurance would indicate more risk than the additive sum – because such a combination could identify a farmer with a huge farm who frequently flies by small airplane to remote parts of the farming estate, a large life insurance risk. This non-additive insight was one of many captured in the rule base of the life underwriting system. However, research on the formal combination of bootstrapping models with expert insights such as this is, as yet, relatively undeveloped.[38]

If linear models are so effective, why aren't they more prevalent in practice?

In the USA, a quarter of a million people are admitted unnecessarily to hospital each year with suspected heart failure. Yet, using seven predictive indicators (four were based on quantifications of a patient's medical history and three were summary measures of electrocardiogram tests), a linear model was developed that was correct 85% of the time.[39] Because of its predictive success, use of this decision aid was made mandatory for physicians in one major hospital. However, after some time, its use was made a voluntary choice. From then on, the linear model was used to aid diagnosis of only 3% of patients with suspected heart failure. Why did this very effective decision aid not get consulted more often? It seems that decision-makers feel strongly that the key to predictive success is to discern patterns in cues, and the simple linear combination captured in the statistical modeling is seen as too simplistic.

For example, in the end-of-chapter exercises in Chapter 10, we invited you to discuss the assessment of the likelihood that a named 17-year-old male car driver would be involved in a road traffic accident in the course of the next year. Imagine that you predicted that the named driver wouldn't be in involved in an accident and were successful in this prediction. You would probably come to believe that your ability to discern safe drivers from less-safe ones was well honed. Of course, the percentage of drivers in the category who have accidents is relatively small, and so an accurate prediction would not be surprising. Nevertheless, in such an instance, you would probably feel that the quality of your intuitive judgment was good – by recalling this easily available successful prediction and also the cues about the young driver's character that enabled you to assess his driving style and ability. One study of decision aid neglect found that decision-makers who had access to the statistical equation underpinning an effective decision aid often didn't bother to examine the workings of the method.[39] The tendency was for the decision-makers to rely on their own judgment and, later, report that they performed better on the prediction task than the advice offered by the decision aid – although the fact was that the decision aid outperformed their intuitive judgments. One participant in the study commented: '... the statistical equation gave me more confidence if it was similar to my original guess. If it was different, I went along with my gut instinct rather than use the equation. If I had absolutely no idea, I went with what the equation gave me.'[40]

In fact, people are much more likely to follow a recommendation that comes from an expert, for example a physician, rather than one that comes from a statistical model.[41, 42] We place trust in experts, and following a physician's recommendation reduces the feeling of one's own responsibility for a decision compared with choosing to follow the recommendations of a computer. Much research has focused on the evaluation of advice and has shown that we assume the most confident individuals are also the most likely to be correct. Also, when we pay for advice, we are more likely to follow it than when we receive it for no cost. When advisors differ in their advice, then we tend to follow the advice that is held in common by several advisors, and we tend to give outlying opinions little weight. All this means that advice from linear models will tend to be discounted in favor of either (i) our own intuitive judgment or (ii) (if we are unsure of our own judgment) advice from confident human beings – especially if the human advisors are in agreement with one another. Expert systems that provide the user with explanations of the advice given are more likely to be heeded than the unexplained, although accurate, predictions of linear models.

Comparisons of decision–aiding techniques

Essentially, *decision analysis* using *decision trees* is utilized for unique or one-off decisions under uncertainty. The decision-maker provides the decision analyst with the temporal sequencing of possible acts and events (the decision tree), his or her opinion about the likelihood of events (subjective probabilities) and his or her subjective valuation (utilities) of the consequences of particular act and event combinations or outcomes. The whole approach is predicated on the notion that decomposition and subsequent recomposition of a decision problem will improve decision-making. As we have seen, the implicit theory is that we humans have limited information-processing capacity, and that the expected utility computations are best left to the analyst's computer. Nevertheless, decision analysis still makes the assumption that the decision-maker's prime inputs of subjective probability and utility have validity. Recall that the practice of sensitivity analysis focuses elicitation methodologies on 'critical' assessments. In a similar manner, the *bootstrapping* approach involves the assumption that decision-makers are able to identify the key predictor variables to be entered into the prediction equation. Optimal weighting of the predictor variables' impact on the prediction equation is best left to the statistical modeling techniques. In contrast to decision analysis, bootstrapping models are best deployed in repetitive decision-making situations where only scores on the predictor variables vary from one prediction to another.

In more dynamic environments, where fresh predictor variables may be expected to be added to the cue variable set or where the possibility of 'broken leg' cues occurring is pronounced, bootstrapping systems will be less successful and may be best overridden by holistic judgment.

By contrast with decision analysis, *scenario planning* makes the assumption that subjective probability assessments for unique, one-off events are of poor quality. The focus of scenario planning is the construction of a range of plausible futures and the subsequent evaluation of strategic choices against these futures. Here, the focus is on creating a robust strategic decision that performs well across the range of futures. In many ways, choice using scenario planning is analogous to the maximin decision principle. However, the process of scenario planning also creates conditions for the creation and evaluation of new decision options. Additionally, even if robust decisions cannot be identified or created, scenario planning's process of 'rehearsing the future' serves to sensitize the decision-maker to the occurrence of the early events entailed in the unfolding of particular scenarios. Such early warnings are likely to prompt swift deployment of contingency action.

Overall, the process of scenario planning is, we believe, likely to promote multiple *framings* of the future. Such reframing is, we feel, likely to provide suitable conditions that will prompt recognition of inertia in strategic decision-making, or mechanization of thought. By contrast, decision analysis contains no process methodology to aid such reframing. For this reason, our view is that scenario planning is a useful non-quantitative precursor to a quantitative decision tree analysis. Additionally, we detailed a method that combines scenario planning with *multi-attribute value theory*. This combination provides an approach to decision-making that is fully complementary to decision tree analysis but places little reliance on the decision-maker's ability to provide inputs of subjective probabilities for unique events. As we have argued, subjective probability assessment for such events can only be achieved by the use of heuristic principles which may produce bias. Nevertheless, both decision tree analysis and scenario planning are predicated on the notion that the decomposition and subsequent recomposition of judgment are thought to produce an improvement over unaided holistic decision-making.

Expert systems, in contrast, are predicated on the assumption that expert, informed, *holistic* decision-making is valid. Conventional approaches to assessing the adequacy of a system focus on the convergence between the system's decision/diagnosis/advice and those of the expert who is modeled in the system. Although expert decision-making is conventionally decomposed into if/then production rules, no normative theory or statistical technique oversees the aggregation or selection of these rules into an optimal set or sequence for execution when the system is used.

In common with bootstrapping models, expert systems are most useful in repetitive decision or advice-giving situations. The reason for this is simple: if the conditions that lead to a decision or piece of advice are rarely encountered, then the knowledge engineering time needed to model that 'leg' of the decision tree may not be cost effective. In many commercial applications it is far better if the need for extrasystem human expertise is recognized by the system and a complex problem is handed over to an expert for resolution. For example, in the life underwriting system outlined above, infrequent combinations of medical conditions and medical treatments that *could*, potentially, indicate that a proposal concerns a poor life risk are dealt with by the chief underwriter.

Overall, there are several differences in the domain of applicability of decision analysis, scenario planning, bootstrapping models and expert systems. One commonality to all is the primacy of human judgment. As we saw in Chapter 10, human judgment is likely to be good when practice and useful feedback provide conditions for the quality of judgment to be evaluated. In decision analysis practice, the decision analyst working on (what is usually) a unique decision can only check the *reliability* of the decision-maker's inputs of probability and utility. Questions to do with the validity (e.g. calibration) of the assessments are much more difficult to evaluate for one-off assessments given by non-practiced assessors. Fortunately, sensitivity analysis provides a fallback that at least allows identification of critical inputs. Decision conferencing techniques allow further analysis and discussion of these inputs. Clearly, in the absence of 'the truth', an achievable alternative of a group consensus or, at least, knowledge of the variability in the groups' estimates is useful knowledge.

We have argued previously that decisions, once made, are often 'made' to work. For this reason, questions to do with the validity of decision analyses are often raised but seldom answered. Most often, the question of validity is sidestepped and questions concerning the 'valuation' of decision analysis are raised instead, as we saw in Chapter 13 when considering decision conferencing. Questions on the validity of linear modeling are more easily answered, as the method is most useful under conditions of repetitive decision-making. As we have seen, this method has shown evidence of incremental validity over the holistic judgments/predictions of the judge on whom the model is based.

Questions relating to the validity of expert systems have often not been asked. Most often, expert system researchers have been concerned with problems of redundancy, conflicts, circularity (e.g. self-referencing chains of inference) and incompleteness in rule sets. When the validity issue is analyzed, the level of analysis is usually a comparison of the expert's and the completed expert system's decisions or advice when both are presented with example cases. The resulting error rate, i.e. the proportion of 'incorrect' decisions or advice given by the system, is often summarized by a simple percentage count. However, as we have seen in our discussion of linear models, human judgment contains a random error component. The benefit of linear modeling is elimination of this error by averaging techniques. Hence, the incremental validity of the model of the judge over the judge's holistic decisions/predictions. Methods of validating expert systems have not, to date, been able systematically to identify and extract the random error component in human judgment. The only method at the knowledge engineer's disposal by which to identify such a component within the expert system representation of the expert's knowledge is to ask the expert to introspect on the rule set.

Snap decisions and decision analysis: why not trust our initial intuitions?

Several recent management-focused books and articles have expounded the quality of initial intuitions about a decision problem. For example, Sadler-Smith and Shefy (p. 87)[43] have argued that:

> ... expertise ... resides at a level below consciousness, arises cognitively, affectively, and somatically, and is manifested as a 'hunch' or 'gut feel' ... an abstract feeling of certitude about the rightness or wrongness of a course of action. When used intelligently, intuition has the potential to enhance executive judgment and decision-making ... intuition is pervasive,

automatic, and involuntary; therefore executives have much to gain from being able to accept it and manage it.

In a book entitled *Gut Feelings: Short Cuts to Better Decision Making*, Gerd Gigerenzer[44] discusses examples of accurate unthinking performance. One example is that of a sports player catching a fly ball in either a basketball or cricket game. If you ask a professional player, then, likely, he would not be able to verbalize his technique. Neither could a dog who catches a flying Frisbee. Do players and dogs calculate parabolic trajectories and factor in their own velocity towards the flying ball? One study[45] identified a 'gaze heuristic' that can account for the strong intuitive catching performance of man and beast. Here, the running mammal fixates its gaze on the moving ball and adjusts its own speed so that the angle of gaze (onto the ball) remains constant. In this way, the ball is caught by a technique that is largely unconscious and requires little in the way of information – it is, in Gigerenzer's words, a fast and frugal heuristic.

In another example of the power of quick-acting intuition, Gigerenzer[44] describes how expert golfers perform better under time pressure Here, for the experts, taking time to analyze the pros and cons of the best shot to take in a particular situation did not result in a better choice of shot, whereas the reverse held true for novice golfers. Similarly, expert chess players choose their moves well under time pressure, while less experienced players do not. An ability to generate the best option first is characteristic of experience. For experienced firefighters and pilots, the best option also 'pops up first', whereas novices benefit from reflection.[46] For experts, more information is not necessarily a good thing, and neither is having more time to think and analyze options. Spontaneous intuitive choice can select the best option for us. We may not need consciously to consider alternative options.

But what are the psychological mechanisms that extract the salient cues to the best option from a complex environment like that in a firefighting context? Gary Klein[46] argues that long-term experience in a particular decision-making context is the key to recognizing both an emergent situation and an appropriate option. For example, an experienced fire-chief may see both a particular color of smoke and a particular force of the smoke billowing and recognize, or suspect, that toxic chemicals are burning and so issue special breathing apparatus to his firefighters. Thus, experts are able to take appropriate actions without comparing and analyzing options when faced with a problem or situation that they recognize from experience. Conscious evaluation of options is not part of this recognition-and-linked-action process. In his book, Gigerenzer describes one study where participants were shown 10 000 pictures for 5 seconds each. Remarkably, 2 days later the same participants, on average, correctly identified 8300 of these pictures from a much wider selection. In short, the recognition heuristic may enable us to match a single action or option to a particular problem. With correct recognition, choice between options is not necessary, as the single option that is generated first is likely to be the most appropriate. Recall the power of the recognition heuristic that we discussed in Chapter 2.

But are initial impulses or intuitions always correct? In a book entitled *Blink: The Power of Thinking Without Thinking*,[47] Malcolm Gladwell set out to illustrate the general appropriateness of 'snap' judgments and decisions, but also to separate when we should be wary of initial intuitions. As Gladwell points out, snap decisions can be wrong. One example he describes is when police officers make a snap judgment that a suspect is reaching for a gun. Moments later, the dead suspect's fingers are found to be clutching a wallet. An incisive review of Gladwell's book argued that the author failed to distinguish situations where initial intuition can be appropriate and where it can be faulty. In their own analysis of Gladwell's case examples, Hogarth and Schoemaker[48] find that snap judgment is likely to be accurate when decision-makers have extensive experience in similar situations. Here, feedback on the appropriateness of past judgments and decisions is likely to be good, much like that of the weather forecasters that we discussed in Chapter 10. To our mind, such situations – where the decision-maker is experienced and in a familiar context – are likely to be those where operation of the recognition heuristic is best placed to prompt a single appropriate response: either a judgment or action.

Our conclusion from this discussion is that when you have to make a choice you should monitor and record your initial intuition or impulse about which is the best option. You should then generate alternative options, and next – using the range of techniques in this book – challenge your initial intuition with the results of a decision analysis. In this way, your initial intuition will either be confirmed or changed. As we discussed in Chapter 3, any conflict between holistic and intuitive preferences should be examined in order to provide a deeper understanding of a decision problem. As such conflicts are explored, both initial intuition and initial modeling will, likely, be revised and changed, and the discrepancy between the analytical results and intuitive judgment will be reduced. In our experience, the essential value of decision analysis is in this challenge to initial gut feeling and the changed intuition that is a common outcome of the challenge.

Designing decisions so that people make the 'best' choice

The focus of this book has been on enabling individuals and groups to improve their decision-making by identifying the biases that are associated with unaided decision-making and by presenting methods that are designed to increase understanding of decision problems. Suppose that decision analysis has helped identify the best course of action in a given circumstance. Is it possible to encourage others, who may not have participated in the decision process, to make the same decision? Without the benefit of decision analysis, these individuals may be subject to the many decision biases that we have identified in earlier chapters. They may be unrealistically optimistic, take unwarranted risks, be excessively cautious or overweight short-term advantages at the expense of better long-run gains. For example, typically, people neglect to contribute to pension schemes in spite of this being in their long-term interests. They may also behave in ways that are likely to be injurious to their long-term health – by excessive smoking or excessive eating of junk food. Individuals may choose to act to maximize their own interests to the detriment of society as a whole – for example, by excessive consumption of mineral-based energy sources.

Recently, Richard Thaler and Carl Sunstein[49] published a highly influential book called *Nudge. Improving Decisions about Health, Wealth and Happiness*, which discusses how a 'choice architecture' can be used to design decisions in such a way that the decision-maker is encouraged in a subtle way to make the 'right' decision. We can alter people's behavior in predictable ways without forbidding options or significantly changing incentives and disincentives. Putting fruit at eye level in a supermarket counts as a nudge, and so does not displaying cigarette packets in supermarket newspaper kiosks. Knowing how people think, we can design choices that make it easier for people to choose what is best for themselves, their families and society. For example, people can be asked to opt out rather than to opt in to a pension scheme, so that the default position is that they become members of the scheme. The same system can be used for organ donation. In Denmark, Germany, the UK and the USA, where organ donation is an opt-in decision, the proportion of potential organ donors is 4%, 12%, 17% and 28% respectively. In countries where organ donation is the default decision (Poland, Portugal, France, Hungary and Austria), the proportion of organ donors is 99.9%.[50] Goldstein *et al.*[51] discuss how well-designed defaults can be employed by companies to benefit both themselves and their customers. They describe how AT&T initially set the mailing of a printed itemized bill – which listed all data transmissions – as the default option for Apple iPhone customers. Some bills turned out to be 300 pages long, and so the default position proved costly for the company and caused an environmentally focused outcry from dismayed customers. By simply making the issue of a summary bill the default option, costs were reduced and customers were happier. But perhaps a better default option would be electronic billing.

Some final words of advice

If you have a decision problem – one that is difficult and important so that you are planning to use decision analysis to give you guidance and insights – then how should you approach the problem? Could you be solving the wrong problem? How much effort should you devote to the analysis? In this final section, we give advice on the way to use decision-aiding techniques to approach decision problems.

It is all too easy to rush into making a decision. Difficult unresolved decisions can be uncomfortable to live with, so that there is often a desire for speedy action. Indeed, in some organizations the person who makes speedy decisions may be regarded as strong and decisive, while more cautious colleagues may be seen as weak and vacillating. Even if there is no time pressure on the decision-maker, old habits, narrow vision, preconceptions and overconfidence may lead to the decision being made without spending time to step back and take a broad view of the problem.

The use of one or other of the decision-aiding techniques we have described in this book might reduce these dangers, but it will not necessarily remove them. For example, an elegant decision analysis model does not guarantee that the right problem has been solved, or that effort has been devoted to the appropriate parts of the problem or that the right people have been involved in the decision. Indeed, the model might do harm. By lending an impression of rigor to the decision, and by causing the decision-maker to focus on the detail rather than the wider view, the false belief that the chosen course of action is the right one may be heightened. Before applying decision analysis to a problem it is therefore a good idea to step back and consider the following questions.

Are my assumptions about the business environment and the future valid?

We saw in Chapter 15 that managers can make decisions on the basis of false or overly narrow views of the environment within which they operate. The effects of changes in the world, such as technological developments or competitor behavior, may therefore not be addressed. There may be a misplaced confidence that the future will be the same as the past, so that uncertainty and potential threats may be underestimated or ignored. For major strategic decisions we therefore recommend the use of scenario planning (Chapter 16) before carrying out any decision analysis. By directly addressing key uncertainties and trends and their interrelationship with the behavior of key actors, and by bringing together the perspectives of different people, a broader and more enlightened view of the problem is likely to emerge.

Who should I involve in the decision?

There are a number of reasons why you might want to bring other people into the decision process. Specialists can bring their expert knowledge to appropriate parts of the problem. Different individuals can come to the problem from different perspectives, so that a broader view of the problem is generated. A commitment to action is more likely to result when those responsible for implementing the decision have been involved in the process and have developed a shared understanding of the problem. As we saw in Chapters 13 and 15, there are many dangers associated with decisions involving groups, and so the decision process should be carefully planned, with methods like decision conferencing being considered. Several of the cases cited in Chapter 1 show that decision analysis can be an extremely effective way of bringing together groups of individuals involved in the decision. It provides a common language of communication between different specialists and may help to resolve conflicts that may otherwise prevent the successful implementation of the decision.

Have I made an adequate search for alternative courses of action?

The insights yielded by decision analysis may lead to the development of new alternatives, but there is no guarantee of this if the problem analyzed is seen as a choice between a fixed set of alternatives. Additionally, as we have argued, decision-making is, in general, likely to be mechanistic and show cognitive inertia. However, techniques to aid the development of new options are relatively underemphasized in decision analysis. Intuitively, it would seem sensible to spend time looking for alternative courses of action *before* using decision analysis to evaluate them. Both the frame analysis worksheet and scenario planning are useful here. The focus within the frame analysis worksheet is on providing alternative framing of decision options, while in scenario planning the focus is on generating alternative frames of plausible futures. Within these futures, alternative courses of action may be more or less robust.

How much effort is the decision worth? Which aspects of the problem require the most effort?

Obviously, some of the decision-aiding techniques that we have described in this book are more costly in terms of time and effort than others. For example, the application of SMARTER to a problem is likely to involve far less effort than multi-attribute utility. Similarly, decision conferencing will usually be more expensive to conduct than allowing the decision to be taken by a single individual. It is therefore advisable to make an assessment of the importance and nature of the problem before proceeding with the analysis.

Major decisions, such as the siting of nuclear power stations, will merit more effort and more detailed models than the problem of choosing a new PC for the accountant's office. Remember that the main purpose of decision analysis is to produce insights and understanding. This begs the question, what parts of the decision problem need to be illuminated? Is it the entire problem or just certain aspects? Do some parts require more effort than others? For example, in one decision the key issue may be determining the structure of the problem, in another it may be assessing the risk of alternative courses of action, while in a third it may be determining the key attributes. Sometimes a partial analysis is sufficient: a decision tree without payoffs or probabilities may be sufficient to clarify the structure of the decision; a value tree used without further analysis may be sufficient to clarify objectives. Similarly, a first-cut attempt at building one or two scenarios may be sufficient to overcome strategic inertia and prompt the search for more robust strategies. More specifically, in a SMART application there is little point in devoting most of the decision-making effort to fine-tuning the attribute weights while neglecting the key problem of identifying and agreeing what the attributes are in the first place.

Overall, the *degree* of analysis of a decision problem is, in itself, a matter of judgment. Initial attempts at structuring and analyzing a decision may bring early benefits, whereas an analysis that attempts to embrace all the details of a problem may produce little additional benefit. In general, we support Larry Phillips' view that the role of the range of decision-aiding techniques is to produce *additional* insight into the solution of decision problems with the result that *new* intuitions and *higher* level perspectives are generated. As such, the key benefit of decision analysis is in its ability to challenge and change initial intuition.

Which method(s) are likely to help with my decision problem?

Table 17.1 gives a list of the techniques that we have covered in this book and matches them to the type of decision problems that they are designed to address.

Summary

In this chapter we introduced two additional ways of aiding decision-making: expert systems and linear models. In common with decision analysis and scenario planning, these decision-aiding technologies involve a substantial component of judgmental modeling, but they are applied in different circumstances and place differing emphases on the nature and assumed validity of the judgmental components. We then compared intuitive snap decisions with those based on analysis and also showed how the setting of default decisions can be used to encourage people to make better choices. Finally, we gave some general advice on the application of decision-aiding methods and summarized the techniques that have been covered in this book.

Table 17.1 – Summary of the techniques covered in the book

Problem	Method/concept	Chapter
Clarifying objectives	Value trees	3
	AHP hierarchies	4
Comparing alternatives over several objectives	SMART	3
	SMARTER	4
	Even Swaps	4
	AHP	4
	MACBETH	4
	Multi-attribute utility theory	6
Structuring the options and outcomes	Decision trees	6, 7
	Influence diagrams	7
Assessing and managing risks	Risk analysis	8
	Probability wheels	11
	Event trees	11
	Fault trees	11
	Log-odds scales	11
	Uncertainty management	12
	Scenario planning	16
Comparing options under conditions of uncertainty	Expected values	5, 6
	Maximin criterion	6
	Utility	6
	Decision trees	6, 7
	Influence diagrams	7
	Stochastic dominance	8
	Mean–standard deviation approach	8
	Scenario planning	16
	AHP	4
Automated repeated decisions	Bootstrapping	17
	Expert systems	17
Group decision-making	Delphi	13
	Prediction markets	13
	Decision conferencing	13
	Mathematical aggregation	13
	EQUITY models	14
Negotiation	Negotiation models	14

References

1. Wilkins, D.C. Buchanan, B.G. and Clancey, W.J. (1984) Inferring an expert's reasoning by watching, *Proceedings of the 1984 Conference on Intelligent Systems and Machines*, Oakland, MI.
2. Hayes-Roth, R. Waterman, D.A. and Lenat D. (1983) *Building Expert Systems*, Addison-Wesley, Reading, MA.
3. Duda, R.O. and Shortcliffe, E.H. (1983) Expert systems research, *Science*, **220**, 261–268.
4. Wright, G. and Ayton, P. (1987) Eliciting and modelling expert knowledge, *Decision Support Systems*, **3**, 13–26.
5. Brown, S.W. and Goslar, M.D. (1988) New information systems for marketing decision making, *Business*, July/September, 18–24.
6. Mitchell, A., Russo, J.E. and Wittink, D.R. (1991) Issues in the development and use of expert systems for marketing decisions, *International Journal of Research in Marketing*, **8**, 41–50.
7. McCann, J.M. and Gallagher, J.P. (1990) *Expert Systems for Scanner Data Environments*, Kluwer, Dordrecht, Netherlands.
8. Bayer, J. and Hunter, R. (1991) Miner, manager and researcher: three modes of analysis of scanner data, *International Journal of Research Marketing*, **8**, 17–29.
9. Alpar, P. (1991) Knowledge-based modelling of marketing managers' problem-solving behaviour, *International Journal of Research in Marketing*, **8**, 17–29.
10. Eisenhart, J. (1988) Computer-aided marketing, *Business Marketing*, May, 49–55.
11. Bolger, F., Wright, G., Rowe, G., Gammack, J. and Wood, B. (1989) Lust for life: developing expert systems for life assurance underwriting, in *Research and Development in Expert Systems*, ed. by Shadbolt, N., Cambridge University Press, Cambridge, UK.
12. West, D. (1996) Expert systems undergo a renaissance, *National Underwriter*, 29 July, **31**(2).
13. Shirouzou, T. (1989) Computerised underwriting in Nippon Life Insurance, *Journal of Insurance Medicine*, **21**, 243–245.
14. Friedman, J.Y., Otis, B.W. and Franchick, E. (1990) Decision insurance for an insurance insurer, *Information Strategy: The Executive Journal*, **6**, 33–39.
15. Coakes, E., Merchant, K. and Lehaney, B. (1997) The use of expert systems in business transformation, *Management Decision*, **35**, 53–58.
16. Laplant, A. (1993) Bank's expert system acts as a fraud watchdog in currency exchange, *Infoworld*, **15**(4), 54.
17. Bridge, T. and Lin, Y.L. (1992) Expert systems in banking, *Canadian Banker*, **99**(4), 20.
18. Coakes, E. and Merchant, K. (1996) Expert systems: a survey of their uses in UK business, *Information Management*, **30**(5), 223–231.
19. Tech News (2005) *Mortgage Banking*, November, 111.
20. Bryant, K. (2001) ALEES: an agricultural loan evaluation expert system, *Expert Systems with Applications*, **21**, 75–85.
21. Pickup, M. (1989) Using expert systems for personal financial planning, *The World of Banking*, March–April, 21–23.
22. Brown, C.E., Nielson, N.L. and Phillips, M.E. (1990) Expert systems for personal financial planning, *Journal of Financial Planning*, July, 137–143.
23. Technology and Underwriting (1998) Insurance and Technology, February, 51.

24. Edwards, J.S., Duan, Y. and Robins, P.C. (2000) An analysis of expert systems for business decision making at different levels and in different roles, *European Journal of Information Systems*, **9**, 36–46.

25. Arnold, V., Clark, N., Collier, P.A., Leech, S.A. and Sutton, S.G. (2006) The differential use and effect of knowledge-based system explanations in novice and expert judgment decisions, *MIS Quarterly*, **30**, 79–97.

26. Montgomery, D.C, Peck, E.A. and Vining, G.G. (2006) *Introduction to Linear Regression Analysis*, 4th edition, John Wiley & Sons, Inc., New York, NY.

27. Note that our model is being used to represent how a judgmental forecaster makes sales forecasts, but we could use a similar approach to represent how a person makes decisions. For example, a loan officer might decide either to grant a loan or not to grant a loan. In this case, special techniques like logistic regression or discriminant analysis can be used to obtain the model and hence predict the decision that the person would have made.

28. Zacharakis, A.L. and Meyer, G.D. (2000) The potential of actuarial decision models: can they improve the venture capital investment decision? *Journal of Business Venturing*, **15**, 323–346.

29. Dawes, R.M. (1975) Graduate admission variables and future success, *Science*, **187**, 721–743.

30. Dawes, R.M. and Corrigan, B. (1974) Linear models in decision-making, *Psychological Bulletin*, **81**, 95–106.

31. Einhorn, H.J. (1972) Expert measurement and mechanical combination, *Organizational Behavior and Human Performance*, **7**, 86–106.

32. Morerea, O.F. and Dawes, R.M. (2006) Clinical and statistical prediction after 50 years: a dedication to Paul Meehl, *Journal of Behavioral Decision Making*, **19**(5).

33. For further discussion, see Bishop, M.A. and Tront, J.D. (2002) 50 years of successful predictive modeling should be enough: lessons for philosophy of science, *Philosophy of Science*, **69**, S197–S208; Ganzach, Y., Kluger, A.N. and Klayman, N. (2000) Making decisions from an interview: expert measurement and mechanical combination, *Personnel Psychology*, **53**, 1–20; Bell, T.B., Bedard, J.C., Johnstone, K.M. and Smith, E.F. (2002) @RISK: a computerized decision aid for client acceptance and continuation risk assessments, *Auditing – A Journal of Practice and Theory*, **21**, 97–113.

34. Dawes, R.M., Faust, D. and Meehl, P. (1989) Clinical versus actuarial judgement, *Science*, **243**, 1668–1673.

35. Meehl, P.E. (1957) When shall we use our heads instead of the formula?, *Journal of Counselling Psychology*, **4**, 268–273.

36. Johnson, E.J. (1988) Expertise and decision under uncertainty: performance and process, in *The Nature of Expertise*, ed. by Chi, M.T.H., Glaser, R. and Farr, M.J., Erlbaum, Hillsdale, NJ.

37. Blattberg, R.C. and Hoch, S.J. (1990) Database models and managerial institution: 50% model and 50% manager, *Management Science*, **36**, 887–899.

38. Bunn, D. and Wright, G. (1991) Analysis of the interaction of judgmental and statistical forecasting models, *Management Science*, **37**, 510–518.

39. Corey, G.A. and Merenstein, J.H. (1987) Applying the ischemic heart disease predictive instrument, *The Journal of Family Practice*, **25**, 127–133.

40. Seick, W.R. and Arkes, H.R. (2005) The recalcitrance of overconfidence and its contribution to decision aid neglect, *Journal of Behavioral Decision Making*, **18**, 29–53.
41. Promberger, M. and Baron, J. (2006) Do patients trust computers? *Journal of Behavioral Decision Making*, **19**, 455–468.
42. Önkal, D., Goodwin, P., Thomson, M., Gönül, M.S. and Pollock, A. (2009) The relative influence of advice from human experts and statistical methods on forecast adjustments. *Journal of Behavioral Decision Making* (in press).
43. Sadler-Smith, E. and Shefy, E. (2004) The intuitive executive: understanding and applying 'gut-feel' in decision-making, *Academy of Management Executive*, **18**, 76–91.
44. Gigerenzer, G. (2007) *Gut Feelings: Short Cuts to Better Decision Making*, Penguin, London, UK.
45. McBeath, M.K., Shaffer, D.M. and Kaiser, M.K. (1995) How baseball and out-fielders determine where to run to catch a fly ball. *Science*, **268**, 569–573.
46. Klein, G. (2003) *The Power of Intuition: How to use Your Gut Feelings to Make Better Decisions at Work*, Doubleday, New York, NY.
47. Gladwell, M. (2005) *Blink. The Power of Thinking without Thinking*, Little, Brown & Company, New York, NY.
48. Hogarth, R.M. and Schoemaker, P.J.H. (2005) Book review: Beyond Blink: A Challenge to Behavioral Decision Making, *Journal of Behavioral Decision Making*, **18**, 305–309.
49. Thaler, R.H. and Sunstein, C.R. (2008) *Nudge. Improving Decisions about Health, Wealth and Happiness*, Yale University Press, New Haven, CT.
50. Johnson, E.J. and Goldstein, D.G. (2004) Defaults and donation decisions, *Transplantation*, **78**, 1713–1716.
51. Goldstein, D.G., Johnson, E.J., Herrmann, A. and Heitmann, M. (2008) Nudge your customers toward better choices, *Harvard Business Review*, **86**(12).

Suggested answers to selected questions

Chapter 2

(3) She would choose Barbados. Several of the later options are cheaper, have a longer duration and are closer to the beach.

Chapter 3

(2) (a) Ultraword, Easywrite and Super Quill are on the efficient frontier.
  (b) Easywrite has the highest aggregate value of 82.5 (this value is obtained after normalizing the weights).
  (c) This implies that the two attributes are not mutually preference independent, so the additive model may not reflect your preferences accurately.
(3) (a) Design A will offer the highest aggregate value for benefits as long as the weight for environmental impact is below about 11. If the weight is higher than this, then design C offers the highest-valued benefits.
  (b) Designs A, C and D are on the efficient frontier.
  (c) The manager is prepared to pay $4000 for each extra benefit point (i.e. $120 000/30). A switch from design D to design A would cost only $731.7 for each extra benefit point (i.e. $30 000/41) and would therefore be worth making. However, a switch from A to C would cost $4705.8 per extra benefit point (i.e. $80 000/17) and would therefore not be worth making. Therefore, choose design A.
(4) (a) Rail/ferry has the highest value for aggregate benefits, i.e. 81.
  (b) Rail/ferry and road/ferry lie on the efficient frontier.
  (c) The manager is prepared to pay $1167 for each extra benefit point (i.e. $70 000/60). A switch from road/ferry to rail/ferry would cost $567 for each extra benefit point (i.e. $30 000/53) and is therefore worth making. Therefore, choose rail/ferry.

(5) (c) Values: Inston, 56; Jones Wood, 66; Peterton, 36.8; Red Beach, 46.4; Treehome Valley, 43.6.
   (d) Jones Wood and Red Beach lie on the efficient frontier.
   (e) Jones Wood has the highest aggregate benefits whatever weight is assigned to visual impact.
(6) (a) The attributes may not be mutually preference independent. Preferences for candidates with better ideas may depend upon their commitment to translate these ideas into action.
   (d) Candidates B, C and D are on the efficient frontier.
   (e) A switch from B to C would cost $45.4 per extra benefit point; a switch from C to D would cost $1200 per point. The personnel manager is prepared to pay $8000/23 = $347.8 per point, so C should be selected.

Chapter 4

(1) (c) Direct and Royal are on the efficient frontier.
(3) (b) If the approximation method is used, the scores for the cars are as follows. The Arrow scores 0.247, the Bestmobile 0.533 and the Commuter 0.220, so the Bestmobile should be chosen.
   (c) For 'Cost' the inconsistency ratio $= 0$, showing that the judgments are perfectly consistent. For 'Style', using the approximation method, the inconsistency ratio $= 0.07$, which is below 0.1, so there should be no concerns about inconsistency.

Chapter 5

(1) (a) Assuming that the classical approach is valid: 120/350.
   (b) Assuming that the relative frequency approach is valid: 8/400.
   (c) 0.5 using the classical approach, although the relative frequency approach suggests about 0.515 in some Western industrialized countries.
   (d) Assuming that the relative frequency approach is valid: 21/60.
   (e) This will be a subjective probability.
(2) (a) 0.25; (b) 0.6; (c) 0.95.
(3) (a) 64/120; (b) 79/120; (c) 67/120; (d) 85/120; (e) 74/120.
(4) (a) (i) 41/120; (ii) 18/64; (iii) 23/56; (iv) 53/120; (v) 32/64.
(5) (a) (i) 40/100; (ii) 30/100; (iii) 45/100; (iv) 25/30; (v) 25/40.
(6) (a) 0.001; (b) $0.9 \times 0.95 \times 0.8 = 0.684$.
(7) (a) 0.192.
(8) 0.48.
(9) 0.00008.

(10) 0.6.
(11) (a) 2.76 requests; (b) discrete.
(12) $94 000.

Chapter 6

(1) Option 2 has the highest expected profit of $24 000.
(2) The speculator should purchase the commodity (expected profit = $96 000).
(3) Carry one spare (expected cost = $5400).
(5) (a) Bid $150 000 (expected payment = $90 000); (b) bid $100 000 (expected
utility = 0.705, assuming a 0–1 utility scale).
(7) The Zeta machine (expected utility 0.7677).
(8) (b) Choose the metal design (expected utility 0.7908, assuming a 0–1 utility scale).

Chapter 7

(1) (b) Invest in the development and, if it is successful, go for large-scale production
(expected returns = $1.65 million).
(c) Do not invest in the development if the probability of success is less than about
0.387.
(d) Not investing in the development now has the highest expected utility
(0.6 as against 0.5625 if the development goes ahead). This is true as long
as the probability of a successful development is less than 0.64.
(2) The engineer should attempt to repair the machine himself and, if necessary, make
a second attempt. (Note, however, that the decision is very close: the expected cost
of attempting the repair himself is $30 780, as opposed to $30 880 if the specialist
local company is called in immediately. Sensitivity analysis is therefore advisable.)
(3) (b) Westward should *not* bring the launch forward (expected profit = $3.005 mil-
lion, as opposed to $2.68 million for bringing the launch forward and $0 for
not launching at all), and, if the rival launches first, they should increase their
level of advertising.
(c) The policy is totally insensitive to changes in these probabilities, i.e. not bringing the launch forward is the best option whatever estimates are used for the
probabilities of beating the rival.
(4) (b) The Authority should erect a cheap temporary barrier, but if the barrier is
damaged they should *not* repair it (the expected cost of this policy is $1.275
million, as opposed to $1.48 million for doing nothing and $1.716 million for
erecting an expensive barrier).
(5) (a) The 20-person team gives the lowest expected costs of $11 600.

   (b) The manager should now use a 15-person team and hire the equipment only if the overhaul is behind schedule on the Saturday evening. (Note that the two expected costs are very close, $11 400 for the 15-person team and $11 600 for the 20-person team, which suggests that sensitivity analysis should be carried out.)

(6) They should initially choose to develop zylogen. If the development has not been completed after 3 years, they should modify the zylogen approach. If, after a further 2 years, development is still not complete, they should switch to the alternative HMP acid approach. The expected development time of this policy is 5.27 years, as opposed to 6.2 years if HMP acid is developed at the outset.

Chapter 8

(1) (a) The profit probability distribution is $0: 0.08; $100: 0.20; $200: 0.24; $300: 0.30; $400: 0.18.

   (c) The probability distribution estimated from simulation is $0: 0; $100: 0.20; $200: 0.30; $300: 0.30; $400: 0.20.

(3) (b) Assuming that the mean–standard deviation screening procedure is valid, only designs 1, 2 and 6 lie on the efficient frontier. Design 6 offers higher returns but also has a higher level of risk than designs 1 and 2.

(5) (a) The option of replacing the plant with new equipment exhibits first-degree stochastic dominance over the option of extending the existing plant.

   (b) Replacing the plant with new equipment also exhibits second-degree stochastic dominance over the option of moving the company's operations.

Chapter 9

(1) (i) p(high sales) $= 0.7$; p(low sales) $= 0.3$.

   (ii) Posterior probabilities: p(high sales) $= 0.4375$; p(low sales) $= 0.5625$.

(2) p(sales exceed 1 million units) $= 0.4615$.

(3) p(machine accidentally overfilled) $= 0.2963$.

(4) p(minerals in commercial quantities) $= 0.8182$.

(5) (a) (i) Build new plant (expected NPV $= $450 000$); (ii) EVPI $= $85 000$.

   (b) The company should now expand existing plant (expected NPV $= $390 750$).

(6) (a) (i) Plan for medium sales (expected profit $= $164 000$); (ii) EVPI $= $64 000$.

   (b) The company should still plan for medium sales (expected profit $= $152 190$).

(7) Expected value of test $= 399 (subject to rounding).

(8) (a) (i) The product should be launched (expected NPV = $18 million); (ii) EVPI = $12 million.
   (b) EVIl = $5.11 million, therefore it is worth test marketing the product.

Chapter 11

(4) (b) The manager's average Brier score is 499.8/600 = 0.833.
   (c) His Brier score would always have been 0.75.

Chapter 14

(9) The chart shows that the deal with a value to the council of 45.65 is efficient in that it would offer gains over the tentative deal to *both parties*. The table shows that this deal is: land price $3 million, no community center, complete landscaping.

Index